# The Armed Forces
# in Contemporary Asian Societies

## About the Book and Editors

This book integrates current knowledge about the military, political, economic, and cultural roles of the armed forces in sixteen Asian countries, examining the interplay of these factors and their bearing on each society's civil-military relations. The authors explore the history, current status, and potential future course of each country. Analyzing all key Asian armed forces, they provide a comprehensive view of the military's domestic role—a crucial factor in assessing the foreign and defense policy options facing Asia as a whole.

**Edward A. Olsen** is associate professor of national security affairs and coordinator of Asian-Pacific Studies at the U.S. Naval Postgraduate School. **Stephen Jurika, Jr.**, is adjunct professor of national security affairs at the school.

# The Armed Forces in Contemporary Asian Societies

edited by Edward A. Olsen
and Stephen Jurika, Jr.

Westview Press / Boulder and London

*Westview Special Studies in Military Affairs*

The views expressed in this book are solely those of the authors and do not represent the positions or policies of any agency or department of the United States Government.

All rights reserved. No part of this publication may be reproduced or transmitted in any form or by any means, electronic or mechanical, including photocopy, recording, or any information storage and retrieval system, without permission in writing from the publisher.

Copyright © 1986 by Westview Press, Inc., except for Chapters 11 and 12, which are in the public domain.

Published in 1986 in the United States of America by Westview Press, Inc.; Frederick A. Praeger, Publisher; 5500 Central Avenue, Boulder, Colorado 80301

Library of Congress Cataloging in Publication Data
Main entry under title:
The Armed forces in contemporary Asian societies.
  (Westview special studies in military affairs)
  Bibliography: p.
  1. Asia—Armed Forces—History—20th century—Addresses, essays, lectures. 2. Sociology, Military—Asia—History—20th century—Addresses, essays, lectures. 3. Civil-military relations—Asia—History—20th century—Addresses, essays, lectures. 4. Asia—Armed Forces—Military activity—Addresses, essays, lectures.
  I. Olsen, Edward A. II. Jurika, Stephen. III. Series.
  UA830.A764  1986      306'.27'095      85-688
  ISBN 0-8133-0160-2

This book was produced without formal editing by the publisher.

Printed and bound in the United States of America

∞ The paper used in this publication meets the requirements of the American National Standard for Permanence of Paper for Printed Library Materials Z39.48-1984.

# Contents

Introduction, *Edward A. Olsen and Stephen Jurika, Jr.* ............ 1

## PART ONE
## EAST ASIA

1 The Role of the Armed Forces in Contemporary China,
  *June Teufel Dreyer* ......................................... 25

2 Taiwan's Armed Forces, *Edward W. Ross*................... 55

3 Japan's Self-Defense Forces, *James H. Buck* ............... 70

4 The Societal Role of the ROK Armed Forces,
  *Edward A. Olsen* ........................................... 87

5 North Korea: A Garrison State, *Gregory F. T. Winn* ....... 104

## PART TWO
## SOUTHEAST ASIA

6 The People's Army of Vietnam, *Douglas Pike* ............. 123

7 The Political Dynamics of Military Power in Thailand,
  *David Morell*............................................... 138

8 The Role of the Armed Forces and Police in Malaysia,
  *Robert L. Rau* ............................................. 153

9 The Role of the Military in Singapore,
  *Patrick M. Mayerchak*....................................... 170

10 The Role of the Indonesian Armed Forces,
   *Harold W. Maynard*......................................... 186

11 The Changing Role of the Philippine Military During
   Martial Law and the Implications for the Future,
   *William E. Berry, Jr.*..................................... 215

12  The Vanguard Army: The *Tatmadaw* and Politics in
    Revolutionary Burma, *Jon A. Wiant* ...................... 241

PART THREE
SOUTH ASIA

13  Civil-Military Relations in Post-Colonial India,
    *Glynn L. Wood* .......................................... 271

14  The Role of the Military in Contemporary Pakistan,
    *Stephen Philip Cohen* ................................... 285

15  The Armed Forces in Bangladesh Society, *Jeffrey
    Lunstead* ................................................ 309

16  The Military and Politics in Afghanistan: Before and
    After the Revolution, *Ralph H. Magnus* .................. 325

PART FOUR
CROSS-REGIONAL ANALYSIS

17  Regional Threat Environments in Asia: Problems of
    Aggregation, *Sheldon W. Simon* .......................... 347

About the Contributors ....................................... 367

# Introduction

*Edward A. Olsen*
*Stephen Jurika, Jr.*

There are many published studies of Asian security affairs available. As Asia's strategic importance becomes more evident to Westerners due to its population, economic prowess, and power, such studies are certain to proliferate. The present study does not focus on the international political, economic, or military affairs of Asia but on the domestic role of Asian armed forces in contemporary Asian societies. Discrete studies of this type have been done previously, but never have studies of *all* the key Asian armed forces—from Northeast to South Asia—been brought between two covers. This volume is an effort to fill that void and expand our understanding of this vital subject. Comprehending the dynamics of Asian armed forces' domestic roles is crucially important if we are to assess correctly the foreign and defense policy options on Asia's horizons. In this sense, the chapters in this volume provide collectively the basis for further research into contemporary Asian strategic affairs as well as insights into the military's role in the domestic affairs of individual countries.

All of the chapters are revisions of papers presented originally at a conference on "The Role of the Armed Forces in Contemporary Asia" held at the Naval Postgraduate School, Monterey, California in August 1982.[1] The participants were chosen for their expertise in the political-military affairs of an Asian country. The countries addressed represent three sub-regions of Asia: East Asia (China, Taiwan, Japan, South Korea, and North Korea), Southeast Asia (Vietnam-Laos-Cambodia, Thailand, Burma, Indonesia, Malaysia, the Philippines, and Singapore), and South Asia (India, Pakistan, Bangladesh, and Afghanistan). Southwestern Asia,

---

[1]The conference was part of a research project sponsored by the Naval Research Foundation. Subsequent assistance for preparing the papers for publication was provided by the Earhart Foundation. The editors and authors express their appreciation for this assistance, but the views remain solely those of the authors and not their employers or any of the sponsors.

with the partial exception of Afghanistan, which falls into two categories, was excluded because—as the "Near East"—it is not popularly considered "Asia" in the context of the issues raised here. Central Asia, dominated by the Soviet Union with its essentially European military leadership, also was excluded on a similar basis.

Despite these exceptions, this volume represents an unusually comprehensive cross section of studies on Asia's armed forces. "Asian studies" frequently is a self-segregating field with little cross fertilization between, for example, East Asia and South Asia. Such academic barriers, though unfortunate, reflect the reality of contemporary Asian international affairs where longstanding cultural divisions remain between the Sinic and Indic realms. Bringing together specialists on somewhat disparate countries at once helps to underline the similarities and differences throughout Asia's experiences with its armed forces.

The contributors to this volume were provided a set of core questions for guidance and were asked to answer them for "their country." Not all questions applied to all the countries and no two authors responded in precisely the same way. Furthermore, the many idiosyncracies in this number of country studies precludes uniformity of narrative presentation. Despite this predisposition to diversity, there is a purposeful thread of unity connecting these chapters which gives the subject matter a set of common themes and identifies the commonalities in the societal roles of Asia's armed forces. We shall examine these themes to provide an integrated conceptual schema for the reader and a useful background for the separate chapters.

All of the chapters address the origins of the armed forces' status in their host society. This basically requires a two-fold approach. First, the armed forces' histories are surveyed to discern the importance of their colonial-era origins, the roles they played in the parent society's independence movement or search for nationalism, and the extent to which an armed anti-imperialism was metamorphosed into some variant of militarism. Second, the contemporary military roles of the armed forces are assessed in meeting the real strategic needs of the host society. This requires analysis of the external and internal threat perceptions which inform the society's elites and an examination of the offensive and defensive capabilities of the armed forces against country X's requirements, or the "guns versus butter" approach. In short, we attempt to clarify why the armed forces do or do not have political power and the societal clout that accrues from its possession.

Having described the degree to which the armed forces enjoy power, the authors next assess what the military is doing with that power. How successful are the armed forces as societal modernizers in country X? This role is evaluated historically, in contemporary terms, and with an eye on the future. It requires analysis of the political, economic, technological, and intellectual activities of the armed forces. Central to the evaluation is an examination of military influence (direct or indirect) versus militarism. The strength of civil-military relations, the levels of intra-military factionalism, and the prospects for civilian political rule are all crucial foci of analysis.

Explicitly to make the noted connections for the reader, we shall (1) delineate the similarities and differences between the origins of the armed forces in each country; (2) compare and contrast each army's military use of power; and (3) discuss how countries with differing degrees of authoritarianism are alike and different. This should assist in making connections while reading each article and provide a base for further inquiry into the possible reasons for the similarities and differences highlighted.

## East Asian Armed Forces

While long on military tradition, Japan's experience with national military forces is proportionately quite short. Two distinct processes of development shaped the armed forces; the first the Imperial Japanese Army and the Imperial Japanese Navy from 1870 to 1945, and the second the evolution of the National Police Reserve (1950) to the tri-service, Ground-Maritime-Air Self-Defense Forces (1954), which constitute Japan's armed forces today.

The Imperial military forces were manned through conscription, national compulsory education was introduced, and by the 1890s the Imperial forces were ready to support national goals. They performed effectively in wars against China and Russia, in World War I, and in the 1920s and 1930s in major invasions on the Asian mainland.

Japan's modern forces emerged after its defeat in World War II and Occupation by the victorious Allied Powers. Fearing the resurgence of militarism and the reappearance of swaggering aggression, the Allies literally dismantled the Japanese military machine and replaced it with a National Police Reserve capable of maintaining internal security. Under the observant eyes of its erstwhile enemies Japan has gradually fashioned its Self-Defense Forces to provide a minor capability for defense against external attack.

The origins of China's armed forces are lost in antiquity but by 1901 three main types of military organizations existed. The Manchu banner forces, the regional armies commanded by civil officials, and the Self-Strengthening Army at Nanking amounted to warlord bandit forces. It was not until 1927 that the Chinese Communist Party established a military arm, known as the Red Army. Renamed the People's Liberation

Army (PLA), it evolved into a well disciplined force which provided support for the party's expansion in, and eventual control of, the Chinese mainland.

Korean history records some military campaigns, and rival kingdoms carried on struggles for domination, yet the use of military means to achieve political ends was largely alien to Koreans. The modern military forces of North Korea derive from the Japanese occupation of Manchuria in 1931, when many Koreans served with Chinese Communist forces in Manchuria or under Soviet military command in Siberia. From these came the cadres of North Korea's post-1945 army and partisan and tradition which has become official military legend. In 1946 North Korea activated public security units to maintain domestic order and security.

Formation of a conventional military force appears to have begun covertly about 1946, shortly after the public security forces were formed. Formal establishment of the Korean People's Army was announced by public decree in 1948, even before the fruition of the Democratic People's Republic. The North Korean armed forces had been equipped and trained by the Soviet Union.

When U.S. forces occupied the Korean peninsula in 1945 there were no appreciable indigenous armed forces, and little military experience among Koreans. Russian intentions in North Korea and the ominous developments there slowly became apparent to officials in Washington and Seoul. Even less clear to them was an appropriate response. While fostering the newborn Republic of Korea, U.S. policy was essentially a holding action, assisting in the creation of governmental and societal institutions a sovereign state should possess. None were overwhelmingly successful, least of all the novice ROK armed forces. When the Korean War erupted in 1950, the U.S., drawing on Koreans with Japanese military and police experience, embarked on a crash program to create truly viable and powerful armed forces in the Republic of Korea. They succeeded, perhaps too well.

The Nationalist Chinese Army's presence on Taiwan preceded its defeat by the Chinese Communists in 1949. Since then the remnants of the Nationalist forces sought refuge on Taiwan, reestablished the Government of the Republic of China and, with major U.S. assistance in equipment and training, forged a modernized army to repel an expected invasion by the Communists. The Korean War renewed Taiwan's access to U.S. military supplies, equipment and advisors, permitting it to embark on a program of force development and a more aggressive deployment of its forces.

East Asia was ambivalent in that Japan had a military tradition and embarked on ventures which resulted in the subjugation of Korea and

Taiwan, and aggressive onslaughts against China from 1894 to 1945; while the more civilian Confucian traditions of China, Korea and Taiwan preferred scholars to soldiers and suffered the ensuing consequences.

## Southeast Asian Armed Forces

The first elements of the People's Army of Vietnam were a collection of assorted self-defense forces used to protect Indochinese Communist Party officials from French wrath in the early 1930s. World War II provided the opportunity for Vietnamese Communists to form a united front organization called the Viet Minh, which organized guerrilla bands loosely referred to as the Viet Minh Army. Concurrently, the Vietnamese Communists were developing a separate but parallel military establishment. From 1942 to late 1944 they tested their creation, the Armed Propaganda Team. On December 22, 1944 the first Team was formed, marking the formal founding of PAVN whose first regular unit appeared in 1950. In 1951 the first PAVN infantry division (formed in China) was launched against the French and a year later PAVN heavy artillery appeared often on the battlefields. The PAVN victory over the French at Dien Bien Phu in 1954 wrote finis to French Colonialism in Southeast Asia and spawned the basic structure of PAVN as a national armed force for North Vietnam.

Military power has traditionally been very important in the Thai political system. The Sukothai and Ayudhya kingdoms underwent early militarization and engaged in countless wars, enhancing the importance of military leaders. The Thai army, once the instrument of power for absolute monarchs, since the early 1930s has become highly politicized and owing allegiance to factional military statesmen-politicians. The modern Thai Army is U.S. equipped and trained, better led and more effective than ever before but no less factionalized and politicized. Thailand, above all, is dominated by the military and is a classic example of civilian ineffectiveness.

Like the Thai model, the Indonesian armed forces also traced their origins to conscripts of the small indigenous kingdoms, until Dutch colonial rule was established. The Dutch experimented with small auxiliary infantry and cavalry units of Indonesians. Between the two World Wars the Dutch had organized Indonesians into a 3,000 man police Army (KNIL), in the hands of Dutch officers. In 1943 the Japanese created two large organizations to provide manpower for the war effort, Heiho and Peta. The latter, more important for the future Indonesian army, was designed to assist Japanese troops to defend Java from Allied attack, and grew to about 38,000 men. The Japanese appointed Indonesian battalion commanders but denied communication between Peta units, so there was no central indigenous leadership.

The Indonesian Armed Forces (ABRI) were formed during the 1945–1949 struggle for independence from Holland. ABRI sprang from the Indonesian masses; it was not created by civilian politicians, nor by the Dutch or the Japanese. During the 1950s and 1960s the military leadership concentrated on eliminating warlords, suppressing rebellions and combating attempts to transform Indonesia into an Islamic state. By mid-1965 Army leaders stood firm against the Communist Party's alliance with the President. By 1978 events prompted a major revitalization of the Indonesian Armed Forces, with emphasis on updating the equipment inventory, especially in infantry weapons, combat aircraft and naval vessels. ABRI today is a highly professional and competent force.

Perhaps because of its strategic location and small size, Singapore is unique among Southeast Asian states in creating a citizen-soldier military establishment, consisting of a regular corps assisted by a conscript reserve. Prior to independence, British colonial forces provided for the defense of Singapore. During World War II the Volunteer forces suffered heavy casualties and were reformed only in 1949. In 1954 the colonial government attempted to conscript a defense force but gave up after one year. After Singapore separated from Malaysia and became independent on August 9, 1965, the Singapore Volunteer Corps (SVC) was renamed the People's Defense Force. Singapore's armed forces (SAF) are based on the Israeli model, with males serving thirty months and reserves serving forty days each year up to age forty. Over a decade, Singapore has built up a substantial reserve force of well trained personnel.

Not unlike Singapore, and also a former British colonial possession, Malaysia formed police units under British control, some of which were used in paramilitary roles. In 1913 the British considered fielding a Malay defense corps but not until 1932 was permission granted by London. Development of the armed services was slow prior to independence, since British, Australian and New Zealand units were responsible for the external defense and internal security of Malaya.

Infantry units were slowly added to the Malay Regiment in 1947 and the early fifties. The Naval service became the Royal Malayan Navy in 1952, and the Royal Malayan Air Force was formed in June 1958. Since 1964 the armed forces and police have expanded in manpower as well as quantity and quality of weapons, aircraft and ships. Cooperation with Singapore in the joint defense of the area is a singular achievement.

Other than police, no Philippine armed forces existed before the establishment of the Republic of the Philippines on November 15, 1935. The National Defense Act of 1935 provided the legal base for the creation of the Army of the Philippines, which comprised all developing land, sea, air and national police forces. The Philippine Constabulary, established by the U.S. shortly after taking over the Philippines after the Spanish-American War, was abolished and furnished the cadres for the new army. The Constabulary's air component became the Philippine Air Force and a small naval unit, the Off-Shore Patrol, was organized in 1939.

In 1941 the Philippine Army and its air and naval elements were inducted into the U.S. Army, Far East, and so served until after World War II when they were detached from U.S. control and became national forces again. In 1947 they were renamed the Armed Forces of the Philippines, although the Army comprised the only major component of those forces.

A military assistance agreement with the U.S. enabled the Philippines in 1947 to reequip, train and provide logistic support so badly needed by the Philippine forces. In the same year a Bases Agreement with the U.S. provided for several operational air and naval bases in the islands and, in 1951, a bilateral Mutual Defense Treaty became effective, underscoring the shared strategic and defense interests of the two nations.

In Burma the British colonial Army enlisted primarily Indian soldiers and troops recruited from Burma's multi-ethnic minorities, yet in 1942 scarcely ten per cent of the Army was Burman. Its retreat in the face of the Japanese discredited it both as a military force and as an organization for Burmese nationalism. The Japanese retained a small Burman force, reorganized the Burma National Army under the effective control of Japanese officers, and began a military training program for 800 Burman officers, of whom about a third were sent to Japan for advanced training. In 1943, Japan granted Burma's independence and Ne Win assumed command of the independent *Bama Tatmadaw*, or Burma Army.

Although Burma accepted a British military mission and British material as part of the 1948 Independence agreement, this was terminated in 1953, and a similar U.S. offer in a proposed security agreement was also rejected. The *Tatmadaw* developed a force suited for counterinsurgency, its principal security task. Unfortunately, the leaders of the nationalist army came out of a political tradition rather than a military one, and the pattern of civil-military relations emphasizing the separateness of the military from politics never had a chance to develop. The Army has never been far from the heart of politics since.

A quick recapitulation of the Southeast Asian realm highlights the British colonial legacy in Singapore, Malaysia and Burma, the French colonial experience in Indochina, and the Dutch colonial paternalism in Indonesia. Only Thailand, a buffer between the British and the French, escaped colonial status yet is among the most closely controlled by the military. Each colonial power established its own-officered security forces from whose ranks emerged the leaders of nationalist movements.

## South Asian Armed Forces

Initially, the Indian military was not a revolutionary army that had overthrown the colonial oppressor but a military establishment created to sustain British rule. This establishment was passed along to the independent nations of India and Pakistan as a part of their colonial legacy. While the Indian military inherited the pivot position of the British Indian Army between Europe and the Far East, and a tradition of policing everything "east of Suez," that changed with the Sino-Indian war of 1962 and, while the Indian military has not recaptured the strategic position held by its colonial antecedent, it has established clear-cut dominance in South Asia.

The Indian Army is the fourth largest in the world and is deployed to fight a two-front war, assuming hostile action from Pakistan and China. The Army and Air Force have an integrated plan for India's defense, while the Navy, which received the least attention in defense policy discussions and even less budgetary support, appears to rely on its Royal Navy traditions and a newly won sense of importance in the defense triad.

The Pakistan military remains hostage to its British colonial origins. It inherited much of the British view of civil-military relations and this view is passed on to succeeding generations at the Pakistan Military Academy, the Staff College, and in informal discussions in the messes. An element peeled from the colonial British Indian army, the Pakistan military's sphere of influence was recruitment, training, discipline, and strategic planning; the actual use of the military, from the most minor "aid to the civil" operation to the strategic deployment of the Indian Army in the Persian Gulf, Southeast Asia, and elsewhere was a political— and hence a civilian—decision.

Some of Pakistan's earliest political leaders were aware of the army's proconsulate tradition, and made some effort to ensure that it would not re-emerge in an independent Pakistan. The Royal Pakistan Navy and the Royal Pakistan Air Force have shed the "Royal" in their titles but remain relatively unimportant adjuncts of the main military force, the Pakistan army. Civilian attempts to control the military ended in failure and by the early 1980s an Army General was simultaneously President of Pakistan, Chief Martial Law Administrator and Chief of the Army Staff. He also held positions of authority within the military, the martial law system that governs Pakistan, and the government itself.

Bangladesh had two births, both traumatic. It was first born in 1947 as East Pakistan, and reborn in 1971 when it seceded from Pakistan to form the independent nation of Bangladesh.

The pre-1947 British Indian Army contained almost no Bengalis, whom the British did not consider one of the martial races. The Bangladesh army was a derivative of the Pakistan military forces, making up in 1948 about five percent of those forces. Pakistan also formed a para-military force, the East Pakistan Rifles, essentially a border patrol force. When the Pakistan Army cracked down in March 1971 the East Pakistani units rebelled and deserted, and soon formed the nucleus of the *mukti bahini*—theoretically a unified force but in reality an aggregation of numerous bands owing allegiance to particular leaders. The poorly trained and badly armed *mukti bahini* enjoyed little success against the Pakistan Army, and idependence was achieved only through the intervention of India.

The three services were re-formed as the armed forces in April 1972, grossly deficient in equipment. Major military aid was provided by the USSR and Yugoslavia but the Army lacked heavy weapons and the Navy could not perform even the most routine patrol. Beset with major problems from disaffection, rivalries, factionalism and smuggling, the armed forces intervened in Bangladesh politics, mutinied, then finally assumed complete control, as martial law was imposed and the government dismissed on March 24, 1981.

The status and tradition of the military in Afghan society and history represent the paradox of a highly warlike society almost totally lacking in organized military forces. The Afghans are steeped in an heroic military tradition: they maintained their freedom against the Moghul Empire, ended the dynasty of the Safavids, and overthrew the Hindu Mahrattas before enjoying relative success against the British at the height of their expansionist glory from 1838 to 1919. Of all Islamic nations only the Afghans had never submitted to occupation or subservience—until the Russians invaded their nation in December 1979.

In 1953 Sardar Khan, a professional general and provincial governor, saw that the only way to modernize Afghanistan was to start with the army—but to do this effectively required massive foreign aid. Political considerations made him turn to the Soviet Union, which responded the following year with a $25 million military aid package. Training in the USSR was provided for about a fourth of the officer corps, many of whom became Soviet agents and sympathizers. The new model army could scarcely be called a modern force. After serious coups in 1973 and 1978, which showed the Afghan military clearly lacking in truly national focus or ideology, the bulk of the officer corps was lost, physically by desertion or joining the anti-regime fighters, or morally as they attempted to hold their positions while doing as little as possible. The failure of the officer corps hastened the disintegration of the military as a whole. Within a year the army had been reduced to less than half its nominal strength, and it was rapidly losing its war against the Afghan people.

The Soviet invasion to prop up a Communist regime removed the last pretense that the regime was a truly national one. This transformed a civil war into a war of national liberation against the foreigner, something clearly understood by all Afghans.

In sum, South Asia has the benefits and hindrances of a British colonial legacy; its states are hampered by multi-ethnic rivalries, diverse languages and unharmonious religious beliefs; economic development is in its infancy, yet India and Pakistan have strong armed forces and antipodal goals while Afghanistan labors under the provocations of Soviet occupation.

### Military Use of Power: East Asia

The outstanding characteristic of pre-WWII civil-military relations in Japan was the ability of the military, especially the IJA General Staff, to monopolize military affairs by a variety of administrative and constitutional devices, and to exclude civil officials, permitting the military to interfere in, and often control, broad areas of domestic and international policy. The military employed the power thus gained to expand by aggression the Imperial domain, control foreign policy and develop the industrial complex to support its war machine.

Since its defeat in WWII, the Japanese armed forces were shorn of their powers, deprived of unlimited budgets, relegated to a subordinate position in ministerial representation, and controlled totally by elected civilian officials.

China's Red Army on the other hand was unequivocally subordinate to the Chinese Communist Party (CCP), accepted the primacy of political over military goals, employed its forces to build and maintain the national economy, and ultimately became a model for Chinese society. Since civilian control of the military was a firmly held value in traditional Chinese society, the Army worked at raising the position of the soldier from the bottom of the traditional social hierarchy.

The Chinese military were used in the Korean War when China felt threatened, and suffered serious losses after early victories. Since then the armed forces have been deployed along the Sino-Soviet border, maintaining public order, and in forays into Vietnam. There is heavy military representation in party and government organizations, and frequently a PLA man holds concurrently the top party, government, and military positions in a province.

In North Korea, the Military Commission of the Party's Central Committee has ultimate political control over the military structure, a parallel to China's control system. Normal operational control, however rests with the Ministry of the People's Armed Forces, a non-Party governmental structure. Military officers play a prominent role in the upper echelons of the DPRK government and KWP.

North Korean society is highly militarized, and a large percentage of the citizenry is directly involved in some form of military activity through regular or auxiliary units.

The role of the ROK armed forces in South Korea is very important. Since 1961 the government has been controlled by the military, more specifically the Army. The Republic of Korea is under a military regime; and it is worthwhile to note that the major role of the armed forces is not in harmony with Korean traditions, and may well prove a passing phenomenon.

The Park coup ushered in the direct and indirect military rule which persists today. The ROK military elite behaves according to a largely un-American code. The rigid hierarchies and the blatant perquisites accorded rank are quite un-American. The ROK army is the last organized enclave of the Japanese Bushido spirit, in sharp contradistinction to U.S. forces and the ROK military is a key actor in South Korean politics. The indirect influence of the military is pervasive but more difficult to evaluate. Their presence on the strategic, political, economic and social fronts is so overwhelming that they appear to gain influence by sheer numbers and position.

The Republic of China (Taiwan) is another former Japanese colony in which the armed forces play a dominant role in three significant spheres. They are a visible symbol and an extension of KMT legitimacy and authority. Senior military officers have considerable power and influence in the domestic political balance of power and the national decisionmaking process. And, at yet another level, the military contributes substantially to the economic and social development of Taiwan.

Another example of the military's power is its role in internal security. Permanent martial law on Taiwan gives the military the right to arrest and detain civilians without formal charges, or without trial, for long periods. Finally, associations of certain military leaders with their U.S. counterparts enhanced their positions by being identified with weapons procurement and technology acquisitions. Such associations have been a valued power base.

Perhaps the military role could be summed up by noting that the armed forces have been transformed from an occupying army to the defenders of Taiwan's value system.

## Military Use of Power: Southeast Asia

Quite unlike the PRC, the two Koreas and Taiwan, Malaysia's civilian control of the government has been established and unbroken since independence in 1957. Further, the civil service plays a major role in the direction and control of the armed forces and the police.

Neither the police nor the military has ever attempted to play a political role or sought political power. The leadership of the armed forces, police, the political world and civil service is all Malay, from the same language stream and social strata of Malay society, and they share similar values and views. Both the army and the police have made major social and economic contributions in the rural areas.

The armed forces of Singapore (SAF) have not played a critical role in nation building, nor, in general, have they played a significant part in the contemporary politics of Singapore. The military provides internal security in the multi-ethnic state but cannot hope to defend the island nation against a determined aggressor.

Unlike military establishments in neighboring political systems, there have been no military strong men to challenge civilian political authority, and there has been no appreciable inter-service rivalry. The Armed forces' major contribution to the economic development process is producing trained personnel who, on leaving the services, are prepared to assume productive employment.

Vietnam's million-man PAVN, and the half dozen paramilitary elements which total an additional million, began an armed struggle in South Vietnam. Eighteen PAVN divisions occupied the South and established a military government to deal with resistance there, while many soldiers in uniform performed economic duties in the north. They were assigned agricultural tasks, and such duties as building roads, bridges, and housing.

PAVN's first post-Vietnam War test occurred in 1978 with the invasion of Kampuchea, fanning out and occupying the country in a matter of days. When Chinese assistance to the opposition was increased, PAVN operations bogged down. Then the PAVN found a new enemy, a Chinese limited invasion of Vietnam in February 1979. The Chinese moved through the mountains north of Hanoi, stopped just short of debouching onto the plain leading to Hanoi, then withdrew. Since then there has developed a systematic military arrangement between the USSR and Vietnam, an alliance in all but name.

## Introduction

The most recent combat experience for Indonesia's ABRI has been in Timor where Fretelin, a radical group, declared independence from Portugal in 1975. Occasional combat operations are still necessary, and a military team administers the province of East Timor, instead of the Ministry of the Interior.

Indonesia showed increasing interest in damping the threat from the north: the Vietnamese invasion of Kampuchea, China's border clashes with Vietnam, China's support of the Khmer resistance forces, and increased Soviet aid to Vietnam. The government commenced patrolling its northern waters and reacting to incursions into its territorial seas. It is also concerned with the archipelago regime and is mustering forces to defend it.

Indonesia's Navy is acquiring the capability of patrolling the 200-mile economic zone, and contesting sea control in the South China Sea where Vietnam has laid claim to the Natuna Islands oil and gas deposits.

Meanwhile, in the Philippines, President Marcos used the military as a primary means to exercise his political power by maintaining martial law. The Army has been employed in attempts to control two major insurgent organizations: the New People's Army (NPA) and the Moro National Liberation Front (MNLF). Despite intensive efforts by both the Army and the Constabulary after 1972 to destroy the NPA it is stronger than ever and has spread its operations to adjoining islands. The MNLF presents a more serious challenge; it is extremely costly in terms of casualties, forces deployed and resources. There is no end in sight to the struggle caused largely by Christian Filipinos displacing Muslims on the farmlands of Mindanao and Sulu.

In a countryside exposed to Vietnamese military power along the Kampuchean and Laotian borders, where thousands of refugees from the carnage in Indochina have flocked, the Thai Army has been curiously disengaged except for sporadic drives against communist dissidents and the political involvement of its senior leaders. The phenomenal split within the Thai Army is clear, the consensus of the recent past quite unlikely in the future, the indecision—and search for legitimacy—of military factions continues, and military rule in Thailand is far more difficult than in the past.

The leaders of Burma's nationalist army came from a political tradition rather than a military one. No pattern of civil-military relations emphasizing the separateness of the military from politics ever really developed. The *Tatmadaw* gained the upper hand over the insurgencies and minority uprisings by 1953 and has become a homogeneous institution. It had spent the twelve years since Independence fighting to preserve the Union. The military saw itself as a national security force and developed a small unit tradition well suited to the internal security problems.

## Military Use of Power: South Asia

In Bangladesh, the military, while unstable, was still the most powerful institution in a society noted for the instability of its institutions. On March 24, 1981 the military assumed complete control, martial law was imposed and the government dismissed. The Bangladesh military's principal role lies in combating insurgent movements, a seemingly unending task.

India has an Army prepared to fight on two fronts. From its humiliation by the Chinese PLA in 1962, to the stalemate with Pakistan in 1965, to the Bangladesh campaign of 1971, the Indian military has been near center stage in the national decisionmaking councils. The military has done quite well in maintaining a relatively stable pattern of growth and functions.

Since the communist coup of 1978 in Afghanistan and the arrival of increasing numbers of Soviet military advisers, a growing guerrilla war against "counter-revolutionary bandits" has consumed the limited resources of the Afghan military. As military organization and authority disintegrated, the army was under the great strain of fighting against its own people. Ordinary soldiers deserted in droves, the feeling of nationalism was shattered and the old rivalries of ethnic identities, tribe, village, family and religion assumed overweening importance.

The Soviets assumed that their massive invasion would awe the *mujahidin*, reunite the communist party and establish a more conciliatory policy acceptable to the people and the non-communist political leaders. The Soviet invasion had exactly the reverse effect, and the nation became a battleground.

There are armies that guard their nation's borders, there are armies concerned with protecting their own position in society, and there are armies which defend a cause or an idea. The Pakistan Army does all three. Since Independence in 1947 it has been active in maintaining internal order and in protecting Pakistan's permeable and often ill-defined borders. It has used its power and special position to ensure that it received adequate weapons, resources, and manpower. It has always regarded itself as the visible affirmation of the idea of Pakistan, and many officers have argued for an activist role in reforming or correcting the society where it has fallen below the standard of excellence set by the military.

Unfortunately, the military has succumbed to the incompetence and lack of leadership exhibited by the civilian political leadership, and become a massive bureaucracy constrained by its own past.

### Authoritarianism

There is an oft-forgotten truism that through their endeavors to strengthen internal stability and international status, ruling elites create modern military forces, then fall prey to their own creation. Nowhere is this more true than in Asia, where coups, counter-coups, and assassinations vie with almost continuous intrigue for attention.

The Japanese Imperial Precepts of 1882 encouraged loyalty, propriety, valor, fidelity, and simplicity for all military men and the Emperor promised never to relinquish his command prerogative to his ministers. Until the New Japan emerged in 1952 authoritarianism was firmly entrenched in the governmental system and the society. Contemporary Japan is governed (since 1955) by the Liberal Democratic Party which has almost total control over the nation's military.

Across the East China Sea, the People's Republic of China adopted a state constitution in 1982 which diluted the role of the PLA in domestic politics, and control of the military is in the hands of the Party Central Committee's Military Commission. Authoritarianism is inculcated in Chinese culture, however, and inertia is massive. Certainly, the government of the PRC is authoritarian, with power of life and death, exile, punishment, transfer, and movement over its billion people.

Abutting China's northeastern border, North Korea is an overwhelmingly authoritarian garrison state. Kim Il Sung and the coterie of officers personally loyal to him secured dominance over the armed forces and the subsequent political development of North Korea. Kim is President, Commander-in-Chief of the Armed Forces, and the General Secretary of the Korean Workers Party. The Military Commission of the Party's Central Committee, headed of course by Kim, has ultimate authority over the military. Like the PRC, North Korea is organized, led, indoctrinated, and controlled as a revolutionary society, and everyday life in North Korea assumes the aspects of military life in the armed forces of other nations.

The Republic of Korea (ROK) is also a highly authoritarian state, since the government is run by a military regime whose influence permeates every facet of life in the country. The involvement of the ROK armed forces in a variety of political actions has roused the greatest controversy surrounding their activities, and is the clearest example of actions which emulate their prewar Japanese model rather than their contemporary U.S. mentors.

Not unexpectedly, the Republic of China's (Taiwan) military forces are a visible symbol and an extension of KMT legitimacy and authority. Then, too, senior military officers wield considerable influence and power in the domestic political balance of power and the national decisionmaking process. At yet another level, the military makes a substantial contribution to the economic and social development of Taiwan. Accordingly, the KMT-led mainland minority dominates the political life of the island whose population is 85 per cent Taiwanese. A state of martial law was declared in 1949 and continues to this day. Authoritarianism is the key to power and is omnipresent.

Just south of the PRC and across the South China Sea from Taiwan, the People's Democratic Republic of Vietnam is still another prime example of authoritarianism rampant, since political control within the Vietnamese political system is reserved exclusively for the Communist Party. The Party monopolizes power and any political activity in which an ordinary Vietnamese engages is merely participatory. Day to day political activity at the top, within the upper reaches of the Party, consists of struggles within factions, and *bung di,* or "faction bashing," is the chief mode of political conduct.

Ever since the military's intervention in 1932 brought to an end several centuries of absolute monarchy, the armed forces — especially the army—have exercised dominant political power in Thailand. Thai political dynamics have revolved around the army; its infantry and tank battalions, its generals and colonels, its dominance over and yet cooptation of the civil bureaucracy, the business community, political parties, and even nascent labor, farmer, and student organizations. Compared to other nations, Thailand ranks high in the frequency of military intervention.

The Thai military has also been successful in coopting civilian specialists to implement and manage the national development effort. The bureaucracy has been controlled by the assignment of military officers to crucial positions of authority over civilians and by the continual process of coopting bureaucrats to work amiably for the military regime. The many cabinet and bureaucratic positions held by senior military officers give them access to budgets, personnel, and the other sinews of power. But military rule in Thailand in the 1980s is far more difficult than in the past.

Totally unlike Thailand, Malaysia's control of the government has been established and unbroken since independence in 1957, and the civil service plays a major role in the direction and control of the armed forces and police. Malaysia seeks to combat internal challenges and instability as well as possible external threats by promoting economic and social development for its people in order to guarantee political stability. It enjoys substantial success as an authoritarian democratic system, with an excellent record of internal defense against an insurgency of thirty-four years' duration.

Next door in Singapore, as in Malaysia, the military plays no significant role in politics. While Singapore possesses one of the smaller military forces in Asia, its citizen army and professional air force and navy constitute one of the best conceived military establishments in the region. Singapore's political system—of a relatively open nature by Asian standards—and dynamic leadership of the region provide the attractive climate for investment and economic development by its neighbors and overseas entrepreneurs.

Quite unlike the relative calm and solid British colonial tradition of Malaysia and Singapore, the Republic of the Philippines has been under martial law, dejure or defacto, since September 1972. President Marcos has increased the powers he wields by using the military as a primary means to exercise his political power and, as a result, the military has become a dominant actor in domestic politics.

Considering its tutelage under U.S. adminstration from the turn of the century to 1946, and the trappings of participatory democracy demonstrated through a Commonwealth stewardship, the Philippines has lain supine since martial law and submitted to corruption, incompetence, and subversion of the democratic process. President Marcos prorogued the legislature, censored the free press, established military tribunals to try civilians, and imprisoned political opponents, arrogating to himself (and the army) authoritarian political power. Though martial law was lifted in 1981 the substance remains. The armed forces were involved in the assassination of Marcos' main opponent, Benigno Aquino.

The February 7, 1986 election pits an experienced, crafty, and ailing President Marcos against Benigno Aquino Jr.'s widow Corazon, whose political naivete is surpassed only by the adroit manipulative skills of running mate Salvador H. (Doy) Laurel. Marcos and his cronies, in both the Armed Forces Philippines (AFP) and the New Society elite, control the media, the corruptive bureaucracy, and significantly—the "logistics"—a Filipino euphemism for money. We expect the president to close the schools, forbid participation by U.S. and international observers in closely monitoring the election, and overwhelm his opposition by closing the Philippine banks perhaps a few days before February 7th—as he did in the elections of 1969.

Unfortunately, whoever wins, the massive and brutal assaults on Philippine resources will continue, only with new faces grubbing at the same old trough. A new oligarchy will supplant the old and the Republic of the Philippines will pay dearly. The AFP is expected to support

Philippine constitutional processes during the instability which will surely follow the elections.

Only ninety miles to the southwest of the Philippines is the sprawling, vast archipelago of Indonesia, where political power is in the hands of the armed forces, and the military appears to be the only group capable of governing the nation effectively.

Military leaders created the modern state of Indonesia and have fought repeatedly to secure it from both internal and external threats. The military elite has created Golkar, a federation of functional groups that effectively serves as the government's political party, dominated of course by the military. Senior military officers clearly dominate the centers of political power in Indonesia, and active and retired military personnel occupy roughly half the top positions in the country's central bureaucracy. One would expect that the authoritarian exercise of power is pervasive, at every level of society and in the national economy as well.

Adjoining Thailand is another authoritarian state where, on March 2, 1962, the Burma *Tatmadaw* staged a bloodless coup, overthrowing the government and ending Burma's fitful post-Independence flirtation with parliamentary socialism. The coup brought to power a group of officers who, once they had consolidated their power within the Revolutionary Council, were committed to revolution in Burma. Although its politicized leadership exchanged battledress for mufti in 1972, the *Tatmadaw* remains the focus of power, and decisions involving Burma's future will involve the military centrally in plotting new options.

Economic and political turmoil accelerated in the first three years after Bangladesh independence, strongly affecting the armed forces. The government showed little ability to run the nation and Mujib's rule became even more autocratic. By 1975 he modified the constitution and appointed himself president with dictatorial powers. All opposition parties were banned. Naturally, there followed coups and attempted coups, enlisted men mutinied, and the nation was in turmoil until General Zia became president and martial law was instituted.

It is clear that the Bangladesh military is the predominant institution in Bangladeshi society, and has the power to enforce its will upon the political system—or even to create the political system. Authoritarianism appears entrenched in Bangladesh.

India, next door to Bangladesh, received the British legacy of a competent civil service, good rail and road communications, and a tradition of parliamentary democracy based on adult suffrage. It has demonstrated a stable political system despite the trauma of partition in 1947, displacement of millions of refugees, four wars, insurgencies and several forms of civil violence.

In 1975 Prime Minister Indira Ghandi demonstrated that the parliamentary system could be displaced by a Prime Minister with a two-thirds majority in parliament, and any analysis of India's political system must list that possibility against the greater possibility that parliamentary democracy will be sustained. Her assassination put India's democracy under additional strains.

In Pakistan the army, like any massive bureaucracy, is constrained by its past. It knows that intervention may be necessary but that it must be limited in scope and time. Yet the diversity in Pakistani society and the slow growth of what the military would regard as a community of responsible politicians make it difficult for them to relinquish power.

President Zia and his close advisers have launched Pakistan on a new political course, combining both their religion and their military sub-tradition of order, discipline, and building organizational structures from below. The government is authoritarian, using Islam and systematic attempts to unearth and destroy all traces of independent centers of political power, including censorship of the press, the judiciary, and Pakistan's already enfeebled intellectual class.

In Afghanistan, the communist Karmal regime is totally dependent upon Soviet support and military control of the country. After more than a century of effort by the government to unify the Afghan nation, largely by military means, the disintegration of the military and the involvement of Afghans in a vast, popular and disorganized guerrilla war of national liberation may ultimately give birth to a genuine Afghan nation—but at an incalculable price.

Nearly all the chapters address the sensitive topic of authoritarianism in the military way of doing things, and how this tendency restricts freedom and democracy. Common to many of the states' military regimes is a perceived lack of legitimacy. A government which lacks that legitimacy can no longer presume to be the arbiter of morality, and the police and army—who perform tasks on the margins of moral behavior—rapidly find themselves in an untenable position.

Whether a country is influenced by a left-of-center or conservative style of armed forces establishment, the extent of authoritarian spread is a touchy subject. Popular support for the armed forces is problematical throughout much of Asia, depending greatly on the political acumen of the military's leadership. In some instances the level of popular support is a matter of great controversy. The authors try to hew to non-partisan objectivity in presenting their views.

## External Factors

Last, all the chapters assess the character of external relations vis-a-vis country X's armed forces. This requires an assessment of the impact of foreign aid and training and the role of major foreign powers. As Americans writing primarily for an American/Western readership, considerable emphasis is placed on the importance of Asian developments to the United States.

There is no formal chapter of "conclusions," for it is impossible to generalize in a meaningful way about situations as disparate as Japan, North Korea, and Burma. Instead, a final chapter is offered by an Asian regional affairs specialist which aggregates the specific conditions in the various Asian countries by assessing prospects for regional cooperation versus regional conflict.

Since there will be no formal "conclusion" to this volume, we consider it important to offer some generalizations about the commonalities which appear throughout these pages. In contrast to much that appears in the press emphasizing the negative aspects of military influence in various countries' societal development, a thread of evenhandedness runs through the chapters, acknowledging the good as well as the bad. Though none of the studies constitute an apologistic appraisal, many of them display considerable understanding of and sympathy for the utilitarian value of the military as an institution which can foster societal progress under certain circumstances. To some, this may seem excessively conservative. However, it reflects the objective reality of Asia today. Along with the warts, the authors also try to show the positive side of military influence over civilian society. Like it or not, ham-handed ogres and sophisticated technocrats exist in the armed forces of many of the countries under review. Their co-existence is one of the most glaring commonalities in these pages.

Another commonality among a surprising proportion of the countries being studied is the greater success the armed forces enjoy in non-military endeavors than in military endeavors. Except for those countries where an external threat is manifest and ever-present, the military proficiency of most Asian armed forces is open to doubt. However, in nearly all the countries the armed forces constitute a valuable source of often rare skills, experience, and leadership which benefit the civilian society when they are transferred to civilian managerial, production, or entrepreneurial endeavors. This means that many Asian countries' "military" leaders are more military in name than in fact. The politicized "non-military" military may well be criticized for questionable combat effectiveness, but when it comes to providing a dose of discipline for societies in flux they tend to do a respectable job.

Still another commonality is the questionable origin of authoritarianism in those Asian countries where an authoritarian military establishment exercises great influence. There is little doubt the armed forces reinforce authoritarian tendencies, but there is ample reason to view the military/authoritarianism relationship as a chicken-and-egg situation. This symbiotic causality is very important to bear in mind as one assesses responsibility for the successes and failures of Asia's military and civilian leaders.

The widest commonality is the pervasive and accepted corruption, found in many of Asia's armed forces. A concomitant of power, personal networks and elitism, such corruption is endemic and largely ineradicable.

Lastly, there is one cautionary note that appears as a commonality between the lines of all the chapters: beware of cultural relativism and racism when evaluating the standards of other societies. Westerners have every right to evaluate and judge other societies' practices as they affect Western interests, and they can legitimately praise or criticize the societal roles of Asia's armed forces. However, this does not translate into a right to tell Asians what is good for them on their own terms. Consequently, as readers ponder the analyses offered here, they should recall the perspectives of the authors and realize the inherent limitations of outsiders to effect permanent change in any of these cultures.

# PART ONE
# East Asia

# 1

# The Role of the Armed Forces in Contemporary China

*June Teufel Dreyer*

### Historical Development

*Evolution of the Maoist Model*

The Chinese Communist Party (CCP) formally established a military arm on August 1, 1972. Then known as the Red Army, its members included idealistic but untrained communists, deserters from warlord armies, peasant militia, and bandits. Mao Zedong believed that the last category was the most numerous. His complaints about officers mistreating their troops, lack of discipline, and "the roving insurgency mentality"—i.e. banditry—indicate the difficulties of welding this disparate group into a fighting force in support of communist goals. Communist leaders were concerned that the Red Army would degenerate into the warlord bandit force that formed an important part of its origins.

Despite this inauspicious start, the CCP was able to wrest power from its Guomindang (GMD) rivals, and founded the People's Republic of China in 1949. During the intervening two decades the Red Army, renamed the People's Liberation Army (PLA), had evolved into a well-disciplined force which provided effective support for the party's expansion in, and eventual control of, the Chinese mainland. In the process, it had developed certain standards referred to collectively as the Maoist model. However, it is important to remember that the model evolved gradually, and that leaders other than Mao played important parts in its development. Major elements of the model include:

1. *The military as an instrument for the achievement of political goals.* As such, the military must be unequivocally subordinate to the CCP. This is the origin of Mao's frequently quoted statement that "political power grows out of the barrel of a gun. The party must always control the gun; the gun must never control the party." After the founding of the PRC, soldiers were expected to assume responsibilities for organizing the masses and helping them to establish political power. Within the army, party control was exercised through an elaborate

hierarchy of party committees headed by commissars, paralleling the military chain of command at all levels.

2. *The relative importance of acquiring correct political views over the acquisition of advanced technology as a technique of army building.* A corollary of the primacy of political over military goals, this tenet is similar to biblical beliefs such as "if our hearts are pure we will fight with the strength of ten thousand men." Sustained attention to military training or weaponry was criticized as "a purely military viewpoint," as opposed to correct views which emphasized the importance of people—i.e. people with politically correct ideology—over weapons.

3. *Close relations between the army and the people.* Mao maintained that, without the support of the masses, the successful pursuit of war, like any other political action, is impossible. Comparing the masses to water and the army to fish, he noted that an army that fails to maintain rapport with the people will be opposed by them. Such an army, by its actions, dries up the water that supports it. A creed called "the three main rules and eight points for attention" was devised to train soldiers to treat the masses with honesty and respect. The three rules are (1) obey orders at all times, (2) do not take a single needle or piece of thread from the masses, (3) turn in everything captured. The eight points are: (1) speak politely, (2) pay a fair price for what you buy, (3) return everything you borrow, (4) pay for everything you damage, (5) do not hit people or swear at them, (6) do not damage crops, (7) do not take liberties with women and (8) do not ill-treat captives. Those who failed to live up to its standards were severely punished. In addition, military units were expected to give aid to civilians in time of emergency.

4. *The strategy of people's war.* The army, supported by paramilitary forces and a sympathetic populace, would lure the enemy deep into its territory until the invading force was overextended and dispersed. Communist troops would avoid the defense of fixed points, preferring highly mobile guerrilla-type tactics to isolate enemy units from one another. The element of surprise was considered crucial. When superior force could be concentrated against the dispersed units, communist troops were to surround and destroy them. When this could not be done, they withdrew and practiced harrassment. After a protracted period, the exhausted, demoralized enemy would surrender.

5. *A high degree of democracy within the military.* From the earliest days of the Chinese Communist army, Mao insisted that officers must not mistreat soldiers and that officers should eat, work, study, and sleep alongside their men, "sharing weal and woe" with them. Nonetheless, Mao drew a distinction between democracy, of which he approved, and absolute egalitarianism, which he emphatically opposed. For example, he commented caustically on the folly of soldiers invoking the principles

of democracy to prevent officers from riding horses in the performance of their duties.

6. *Economic functions of the army.* To minimize the costs of the military to society, the army was to strive for maximum self-sufficiency. Insofar as possible, units were to raise their food, mend their clothing, and construct and service their barracks. In addition to its military duties, the army was to help build and maintain the civilian economy. During the early years of the PRC, military units played important roles in the agrarian reform movement, and in establishing irrigation projects and industrial enterprises.

7. *The army as a model for society.* In addition to being of the people and for the people, the army was to serve as a model for mass behavior. China's leaders likened their efforts to solve the country's economic and social problems to a battle, and enjoined citizens to emulate the army's energy, organization, discipline, and devotion to duty while launching a concerted attack on the evils of the old society. The slogan "[let] everyone [be] a soldier" referred to civilian personnel engaged in economic and social reforms. Conversely, PLA members were expected to exemplify the virtues of socialist society and be models of collective behavior and self-reliance for the masses. The PLA was also expected to indoctrinate its soldiers with socialist norms.

8. *Lack of clear distinctions between military and civilian leadership.* A high percentage of the early leaders of the PLA had little or no formal military education. Moreover, before the communist takeover of China, political and military power were nearly indistinguishable. The close connection between military and civilian administration continued for several years after the communist party came to power. The new government divided China into regions headed by Military and Administrative Committees, which exercised both civil and military functions. When the regions were abolished, many military leaders assumed administrative duties. Subsequently, some who had received formal military training, and others who had not, assumed positions in the military, or in the party and government organizations supervising it. While such career patterns of exit from and re-entry into the military are far from the majority, they have occurred often enough, and at a high enough level, to mute the distinctions between the military and civilian leadership. For example, Wei Guoqing, a military academy graduate, held several important military positions during the revolutionary war and for several years after it. In 1958, he became First Party Secretary of the newly founded Guangxi Zhuang Autonomous Region, and was one of a handful of First Party Secretaries to survive the Cultural Revolution. In 1977, he returned to the military as head of the PLA's General Political Department, serving until late 1982.

## Assessing the Maoist Model

Mao's followers claimed that his concept of the military and its relationship to society are revolutionary and a startling break with the past. These claims are often premised on a fallacious comparison: contrasting Mao's ideals with the reality of the badly degenerated civil-military relationships that characterized early twentieth-century China. A more valid comparison would be between Maoist ideals and the ideals of the classical Chinese tradition. Here one finds striking similarities between the Maoist model and concepts prevalent in China for millenia. As a case in point, the phrase "the army is the fish and the people the water" is first found in the works of Mencius, a disciple of Confucius who wrote in the third century B.C. Other "revolutionary" concepts derive from Sun Zi, the great military theorist who predated Mencius by several centuries. And the principle of isolating and surrounding an enemy to destroy him is basic to *weiqi*, or Chinese chess.

Civilian control of the military was also a firmly held value in traditional Chinese society. Much of the credit for putting down the rebellions that plagued nineteenth century China belongs to scholar-statesmen who assumed command of armies without benefit of prior military training. They too believed that correct ideology (in their case, Confucianism) is more important than advanced technology. Traditional China also favored the idea that an army should be self-sufficient, insofar as possible. Chinese armies in outlying areas were expected to raise their own food and provide for most of their other needs since at least the sixth century.

The Maoist military model is not simply a restatement of traditional Chinese attitudes toward the military but represents the selective choice of certain elements from the past and the disavowal of others. One notion unequivocally rejected was the position of the soldier at the bottom of the traditional social hierarchy, in which scholars occupied the top position, followed by peasants and merchants. The elements of classical Chinese military tradition Mao borrowed were combined in a blend which, although falling short of ingenious creativity, was innovative and well suited to the situation the party found itself in prior to 1949.

## "One divides Into Two:" The Divergence Between Theory and Practice

Although the CCP now portrays its military activities during the pre-1949 period as a series of heroic encounters against numerically and technologically superior Japanese and Guomindang forces, the Red Army actually devoted very little effort to fighting the Japanese and won an easy victory against badly mismanaged and demoralized GMD forces. Up to this point, therefore, the chief formative influence on the military had been internal to the Chinese Communist community. In Samuel Huntington's terminology, the societal imperative, that which arises from the preeminent social forces, ideologies, and institutions of the community, had been the dominant force shaping the formation of the Red Army.

Following the founding of the PRC, the military, now renamed the People's Liberation Army, played an important domestic role. Soldiers contributed to the rehabilitation of China's battle-scarred economy. They also assisted in the land redistribution process, set up state farms, and supported the collectivization of industry and agriculture. In addition to its economic functions, the army played an active political role. PLA work teams brought the party's message to areas that had little exposure to communism, and helped to establish communist organs of political power. The army kept vigilance against the sabotage activities of anticommunist remnant groups, thus aiding the party to consolidate power.

However, the PRC's entry into the Korean War in late 1950 gave increased emphasis to external determinants in shaping the PLA: what Huntington has termed a functional imperative, stemming from the threats to a society's security. Certainly, external military threats to the newly founded socialist regime had always concerned the party's leadership. But when Chinese communist soldiers, fighting beyond their country's borders for the first time, confronted the United Nations forces, these concerns became increasingly salient.

Committing their best units, under the command of Marshal Lin Biao, to battle, the Chinese leadership apparently anticipated a relatively quick and easy victory, feeling that their superior military doctrine could defeat the better-equipped foe. After two months of initial successes, weaknesses in firepower, air support, logistics, and communications became painfully evident. PLA weapons and tactics were ineffective against the enemy's superior technology and mechanization, and the Chinese Communist forces suffered heavy casualties. Morale plummeted. Lin Biao was replaced by Marshal Peng Dehuai, and the Chinese armies fell back to defensive positions. Additional troops reinforced them, the Soviet Union increased its aid to the Chinese military, and eventually the Korean War was stalemated.[1]

This experience convinced many PRC leaders, both within and outside the military, that a reassessment of the PLA's organizations, strategy, and tactics was needed. Clear differences of opinion emerged among them. Some leaders, generally characterized as left-wing or radical, preferred closer adherence to the principles of the Maoist model, and others, generally termed moderates, wished to include more emphasis on technological modernization, specialization in training and functions, and a higher degree of military professionalization in general. The reasonably close synthesis between theory and practice achieved in the pre-1949 years had given rise to a contradiction. In Mao's terminology, one had divided into two. The army's role within society as an exemplar of ideology and a force for economic development had come athwart its role as defender of that society from outside attack. The two roles created two different sets of needs, in some respects opposed to one another. The tensions between them or, to continue the Maoist metaphor, the contradiction between thesis and antithesis became associated with the names of the two Korean War commanders: Lin Biao, undoubtedly backed to some degree by Mao, favored closer adherence to the principles of the past, while Peng Dehuai advocated more modifications thereof.

While the internal politics of these debates are unknown, it is clear that significant changes in the direction of specialization and professionalization took place within the Chinese military during the mid-1950s. In 1954, the PRC adopted its first constitution, and Peng Dehuai was named the new government's first Minister of Defense. It was under his aegis that many of these changes occurred:[2]

1. *The modernization of weaponry.* The Soviet Union sent substantial quantities of tanks, planes, artillery, and ordnance to China to aid the PRC during the last phase of the Korean War and for several years thereafter. Much of this equipment was obsolescent and supplied in smaller quantities than the Chinese leadership wished. Nonetheless, the equipment significantly upgraded the PLA's arsenal. With this materiel came several thousand Soviet military advisers to instruct the Chinese in its use and to aid the PRC in establishing its own defense industry. This transfer of equipment and personnel led to a strong Soviet influence on the development of the PLA.

2. *Training and discipline.* The introduction of more advanced weaponry called for higher education for soldiers and also required longer periods and more specialized kinds of training. Military personnel spent more time in these pursuits and less on economic development projects, whether on behalf of the society as a whole or for the benefit of the PLA itself. Increasing specialization also created a need for the careful coordination of the many different specialties, which called for tighter discipline. Training methods reflected the experience of Soviet advisers and placed greater attention on concepts which had not been a part of the Chinese experience, and at times were even antithetical to Chinese concepts.

3. *Rank system.* In early 1955, a rank system established fourteen categories ranging from second lieutenant to supreme marshal. Officers were also classified into categories based on fields of specialization. Educational qualifications were established for entry into the various ranks, and a more formal system for entry into

military schools was set up as well. Officers were required to wear the epaulettes and insignia of their rank, and a system of military honors was introduced. The establishment of ranks was accompanied by changes in the method of remuneration. The old system of providing military personnel with food and a small allowance to cover incidental expenses was replaced by one of cash payments based on rank. In 1960, the ratio between the pay of a marshal and that of a private was 160 to one.[3]

4. *Conscription.* A conscription law was devised and passed in mid-1955 regularizing the recruitment of military personnel. The law enabled whatever number of recruits had been decided upon to be selected from an already-established pool of those who were eligible, rather than relying on volunteers as had been the practice.

These reforms improved the efficiency of operation and overall combat capabilities of the PLA. However, increasingly audible voices within the leadership and from the population at large complained that these advances in the PLA's ability to cope with external threat had come at the expense of ideological principles and were detrimental to domestic social progress. The external and interal determinants influencing the development of the PLA were in conflict again.

Critics charged that the cherished socialist values of democracy and egalitarianism were being destroyed, arguing that conscription had sharpened distinctions between amateur and professional soldiers, and that the rank system had encouraged status distinctions and arrogant behavior among the officers. Establishing educational qualifications for officers meant that an increasing number of them were drawn from the bourgeois classes, to whom education had been available. Not having risen from the ranks diminished their ability to understand the problems of the rank-and-file. Officers who no longer ate with their troops were less motivated to deal with complaints of poor quality food, and, while stricter discipline might increase efficiency in a battlefield situation, it also made officers less likely to ask for the opinions of their subordinates. In a clear violation of PLA tradition, some officers meted out physical punishment to their troops. As officers gave less attention to their subordinates, they gave more to weapons procurement and maintenance, negating the principle of the primacy of people over weapons.

Relationships between the military and the civilian population had also become strained. Civilian homes and land had been requisitioned by the PLA for barracks and training grounds; peasants' crops sometimes fell victim to army maneuvers. Civilians resented displays of conspicuous consumption by more affluent military families, and some PLA members supplemented their income through black market activities. Others infuriated civilians by taking liberties with local women.

Increasing specialization of functions led to a sharper distinction between military and political work within the PLA. Commissars complained that commanders made decisions without consulting them, with officers arguing that since commissars did not trouble themselves with military matters, their opinions were of little value. The number of party members in the armed forces declined during the late 1950s, and some units did away with commissars completely. This undermined the principle of party control over the military. Many, feeling that the Soviet model was inappropriate in the Chinese context, held it responsible for distorting the PLA's principles.

Efforts to rectify these perceived distortions during the anti-rightist campaign of 1957 were escalated the following year as part of a massive economic, social, and political experiment known as the Great Leap Forward. Officers were required to attend prolonged political study sessions and an "Officers to the Ranks" program called for commanders to spend one month each year eating, sleeping, working, and passing their leisure time with soldiers. The performance of such tasks as digging ditches, growing vegetables, and cleaning spitoons was expected to lessen officers' arrogance and give them a better understanding of their troops. PLA members were reminded of the importance of good relations with civilians, and the army worked on behalf of economic development on an unprecedented scale. The PLA reportedly contributed fifty-nine million days to economic development in 1958 alone. Although statistics during the Great Leap Forward were grossly distorted, the PLA was undoubtedly heavily involved in non-military activities, leaving little time for training. Simultaneously, the militia was raised to virtual parity with the PLA. The "everyone a soldier" movement of 1958 claimed to have enrolled over two hundred million ordinary citizens in the militia. Maoist radicals envisioned that allocating an important role to the militia would make the country better able to fight a true "People's War," while simultaneously debunking the PLA's mythical claims of expertise. The disparity between military and civilian living standards was redressed through such measures as lowering officers' pay and reducing the quality of the army's food and uniforms.

The Great Leap Forward was a tremendous failure. Shortages of food and other basic necessities left hundreds of millions of people hungry, cold, and disaffected with their government. At the party's Lushan Plenum of August 1959, Defense Minister Peng Dehuai reportedly took Mao to task for the sufferings the Great Leap had caused the people, and was summarily dismissed from his position. He was replaced by Lin Biao. Since Peng had been considered the champion of military professionalism, and Lin the exemplar of more radical Maoist conceptions of the military, one might be tempted to interpret Peng's dismissal as simply a triumph of the Maoist model over that of military professionalism. The reality is more complex. Although Peng almost certainly resisted radical policies that he felt weakened PLA morale and combat capabilities, the proximate cause for his dismissal appears to have been his criticisms of the economic and social policies of the Great Leap Forward—something a purely professional soldier would be tempted to avoid public comment on. And it fell to Lin to regularize and reorganize the PLA into a force capable of ensuring the country's defense—a task which required some degree of professionalization. Secret Chinese military documents published domestically in 1961, which came into US hands, describe the sorry state into which the PLA had fallen.[4] Widespread malnutrition and poor sanitary conditions had sapped the army's strength. Weapons maintenance had deteriorated and accidents due to faulty equipment had risen, particularly in the air force where equipment was expensive and hard to replace. Repudiation of the Soviet model had exacerbated strains in Sino-Soviet relations to the point where the Soviet Union had withdrawn its technicians and aid. This further compounded the problems of equipment replacement. PLA morale was dangerously low.

By October 1962, the PLA had improved to the extent that it gained a decisive victory over Indian forces during a confrontation in the Himalayas. The Chinese triumph was made easier by India's poor planning and mismanagement. Nonetheless, the PLA successfully coped with long supply lines through difficult terrain inhabited by a hostile population of Tibetans, who had revolted against Chinese rule in 1959. Whatever the Indian shortcomings, China's performance was impressive.

Lin refurbished the military through a variety of measures, some consonant with Maoist ideas and some with those of moderate professionals.

Radicals were pleased by Lin's vigorous efforts to reassert the party's control over the military, including strengthening the Military Affairs Commission (MAC) of the Party's Central Committee. Commission directives revitalized the system of party committees within the military and restored commissars to a position of parity with commanders. The MAC also initiated an intensive campaign to instill a sense of political loyalty in the rank-and-file soldier. A "5 Good" movement admonished soldiers to excel in political thinking, military training, work style, fulfillment of tasks, and physical education; prizes were awarded to outstanding units and individuals. This was followed by a campaign to learn from Lei Feng, a young soldier who had died in the line of duty. Excerpts from what was alleged to have been Lei's diary were published to inspire soldiers to emulate his many noble virtues.

Moderates were pleased when the number of work days in the PLA devoted to economic development was drastically reduced, leaving more time for training. The "Officers to the Ranks" program continued, but on a smaller scale and with a different purpose. Rather than lessening the distinctions between officers and common soldiers, the program now facilitated the transmission of directives from the top echelons to the bottom and enabled officers to exercise better control. The militia was also reorganized so as to appeal to advocates of military professionalism: it was reduced in size and salience, directed more toward economic development than military activities, and subordinated to joint party-PLA control, as opposed to its previous virtual parity with the PLA.[5]

Both radicals and moderates could take comfort from Lin's pronouncements on the issues of people versus weapons and of democracy within the military. In the former, the original statement of "people over weapons" gave unqualified preference to people. While reiterating the slogan, Lin added that cadres "should on the one hand oppose the purely technical viewpoint which departs from reality, and on the other oppose the empty-minded politician who disregards techniques and professional operations." Lin applied the same sort of subtle modification to the concept of military democracy. Although Mao himself had carefully qualified the limits of democracy, persons acting in his name during the Great Leap Forward had not been quite so careful. Lin, while strongly supporting the concept of military democracy, defined it so as to include the need for discipline and exclude equalitarianism and anarchism, thus encompassing both radical and professional views.

In 1964, the Chinese leadership indicated its approval of the military by launching a mass campaign to "learn from the PLA." Citizens were enjoined to apply the army's skill at being both ideologically correct and technically proficient (both "red" and "expert," to use the slogan then current) to their daily lives, and to the work of party and government organizations. Lin Biao had, it appeared, achieved a successful synthesis of the PLA's different roles.

During the next year, it became obvious that the synthesis was more apparent than real. Mao decided that the "learn from the PLA" campaign had not been a success, and that the army was insufficiently radical. In May 1965, in a move that was clearly pro-radical and anti-professional, the PLA's rank system was abolished. In the same year the army newspaper, the *Liberation Army Daily* (LAD) began an attack on "bourgeois" writers and journalists that led to the Cultural Revolution. Significantly, the opening shot of this attack was the denunciation of a play set in the Ming dynasty, but whose hero bore a curious resemblance to Peng Dehuai, Lin's predecessor as Secretary of Defense. The piece was authored by a young Shanghai radical, one of a group whose cause would later be opposed by professionals in the army. In August 1966, the party's Central Committee met and reorganized to strengthen the power of radical elements within the PLA, and specifically of Lin Biao. To further radicalize China, Mao called on the young people of China to "bombard the headquarters" of established authority and "drag out the bourgeois elements." Chaos ensued, as party, government, and educational institutions ceased to function, and leading figures in all fields were attacked and obliged to defend themselves. Factional fighting disrupted economic processes, and all expertise, including military expertise, came under attack as bourgeois and anti-Maoist. The PLA was not immune from these disruptions and many of its leaders became targets of attack, but the military suffered less than most other institutions due to concern about external attack. Relations with the Soviet Union had deteriorated, and the United States maintained a large and potentially troublesome force in Vietnam, near China's southern border. Internal factors also tended to bolster the army's position: the chaos of the Cultural Revolution occasionally reached the point that the army had to be called upon to restore domestic order. Although the PLA was enjoined to "support the left," its peacekeeping mission put the army on the side of the moderates. Radicals were critical of the PLA's conduct in such instances.[6]

Although some military officers such as Lin Biao were sympathetic to leftist views, these interventions on behalf of domestic order convinced leading radicals that the army as a whole could not be relied on to support them. In that year, the Shanghai radical group began to organize the militia as a counterweight to the PLA. These activities were scarcely noticeable at the time, however. The army emerged from the Cultural Revolution with greatly increased powers. Mao had ordered the PLA to back worker-peasant teams entering the universities during the summer of 1968 to quell student violence. The PLA ran study classes to "re-educate" Red Guards and became a fixture on university campuses and in industrial enterprises. There was heavy military representation on the party and government organizations that emerged from the Cultural Revolution, and frequently a PLA man held concurrently the top party, government, and military positions in a province. In April 1969, the CCP's Ninth Party Congress adopted a new constitution which named Lin Biao as Mao's successor.

Although Lin was an avowed radical and apparently had an even more radical constituency, any further moves away from military professionalism were inhibited by deteriorating Sino-Soviet relations. Serious skirmishing on the eastern border began in March 1969, and spread to the western border in the summer. The PLA's military training increased as did emphasis on the care and maintenance of weapons. Lin Biao's death under mysterious circumstances in the fall of 1971 was followed by a purge of officers loyal to him, and presumably also radical in their views.

Official propaganda alleges, rather unconvincingly, that Lin died while attempting to flee the country after his plot to kill Mao Zedong was discovered. It is also possible that Lin was murdered by more moderately oriented fellow officers who resented the enormous increase in the power of Lin and those military men associated with him. This theory is consonant with the Shanghai radicals' renewed efforts in 1973 to make the militia a counterweight to the PLA: when Lin and the radical officers associated with him were removed from power, the power of the Shanghai group was correspondingly reduced, and they sought to expand their influence through the militia instead.[7] The theory also fits Mao's rotation of eight of the eleven military region commanders in December 1973.[8] Although the commanders assumed leading military positions in different regions, they lost the positions they had had in provincial party and government, and were not given new ones. The transfers thus reasserted the party's control over the gun, which must have seemed particularly necessary in view of the loss of power by left-wing officers.

The radical-inspired reorganization of the militia had the same aim: many of the People's Armed Forces Departments (PAFDs), through which the PLA exercised control over the militia, were abolished, and the militia put under a new organization, the military headquarters, which was subordinate to the party. The reorganized militia incorporated public security and firefighting functions. The militia was further strengthened by diverting to it substantial weaponry, much of which was produced by factories in Shanghai, the radicals' base of power. The new militia was urban-based, to take advantage of pro-radical sympathies in cities vis-à-vis the conservative attitudes in rural areas, which had typically been the mainstay of the militia.[9] In 1975, a new Chinese constitution gave the militia equal status with the PLA.[10]

These moves did not go unnoticed by moderates. Deng Xiaoping, purged from his post as party Secretary-General during the Cultural Revolution and rehabilitated only in 1973, became the symbol of resistance to radicals and the champion of military professionalism. In January 1975, Deng was named PLA Chief of Staff, and appointed to the party's Military Affairs Commission (MAC). Deng bluntly characterized the army as in a "mess" created by its "support the left" work during the Cultural Revolution. He pledged that the PLA would be prepared to fight future wars in terms of "iron and steel." Deng also opposed the new-style militia, even sending the PLA to disband unruly militia elements in Hangzhou during the summer of 1975.[11] Radicals interpreted these actions as negating the primacy of politics over the gun and of people over weapons. At this time both Mao Zedong and Premier Zhou Enlai were elderly and ailing, and the radicals' opposition to Deng and his policies was intensified by fears that he might assume their positions. They were able to oust Deng from power as a result of the Tienanmen Incident in April 1976, in which the militia played a highly publicized role.[12] But when Mao died, in September

1976, radicals' attempts to stage a militia-led uprising to put themselves in power failed dismally. Only in Shanghai did it assume major proportions. The PLA aborted the uprising with apparent ease, simultaneously destroying the power of radical leaders. Hua Guofeng, a compromise candidate, succeeded Mao Zedong and, a few weeks after his funeral, jailed the radical leaders, including Mao's widow. Deng, apparently backed by moderate professionals in the military, was rehabilitated during the summer of 1977. Almost immediately he assumed his old position as Chief of the General Staff of the PLA, and also became a vice-chair of the MAC, which was renamed the Military Commission (MC). In February 1980, Deng resigned as Chief of Staff in favor of Yang Dezhi. Yang is regarded as his protege. Hua Guofeng, in addition to heading the party and the state, chaired the MC. Subsequently, Deng assumed the position of MC chair and removed Hua from his positions as head of the party and state, in favor of two Deng proteges, Hu Yaobang and Zhao Ziyang.

The pendulum again swung in the direction of professionalism. Deng, his views clearly unchanged by his past disgrace, instituted sweeping reforms designed to change virtually every aspect of Chinese society. As these concerned the PLA, the reforms involved

- the technological modernization of the military
- a reworking of strategic doctrine
- restriction of the PLA to an essentially military role
- reduction of the military role of the militia, while retaining the institution to help in economic development and provide reserves for the PLA
- reorganization of the PLA so that it became smaller, younger, better educated, and more rigorously trained than in the past
- reassertion of party and government control over the military

## The Chinese Military in Contemporary Chinese Society

Much ambiguity exists over the PLA's position in China, both in terms of its functional imperative to defend the country and in the societal imperative of relationships to domestic institutions and values. This ambiguity can be traced to the historical causes outlined earlier, and notably to the conflict between radical revolutionary and moderate professional ideologies. Deng Xiaoping's reforms have produced strains throughout the society. While the long-term effects of these reforms on the military and its relationship to Chinese society remain to be seen, their impact during the past several years should provide insights into the probable course of events.

*Domestic Political System and Decisionmaking Processes*

The closed nature of the Chinese system with its controlled press, and the blurred distinctions between civil and military roles in the PRC complicate the problem of assessing the exact degree of PLA influence over the domestic political system and its decisionmaking processes. For example, was Marshal Peng Dehuai's August 1959 attack on the policies of the Great Leap Forward made in his capacity as a military commander or as a civilian leader? There is little information available, and much of that must be viewed with skepticism.[13] Moreover, it is probable that neither Peng nor his adversaries viewed the civil-military distinction as relevant. Our inability to give a clear-cut answer underscores the difficulty of measuring the PLA's influence over China's decisionmaking processes.

In recent years the opposition of segments of the PLA to certain of Deng Xiaoping's reforms (Deng himself had been a military leader) resulted in the modification or postponement of several reforms. On others, PLA resistance had little or no effect. Radical sentiment within the PLA has thus far successfully blocked the reinstitution of military ranks, a measure strongly favored by Deng and professionally oriented elements of the military. In the summer of 1981 the official Xinhua news agency issued a Chinese-language transmission of a speech by Yang Dezhi, chief of the PLA's general staff. Yang was quoted as saying that "in order to strengthen the modernization program in the army, we are planning to reinstitute a system of military ranks." Four hours later, Xinhua rebroadcast Yang's speech in both English and Chinese.[14] The transmissions were identical to the earlier broadcast, save that the sentence on reinstituting ranks was omitted. A new military service law passed in May 1984 called for the reinstitution of ranks,[15] but as of early 1985, it had not yet been done.

Radical revolutionary elements in the military were also influential in mitigating Deng's de-Maoification campaign. A long-delayed public statement on the legacy of the late chairman was released in April 1981. The statement appeared first in LAD, the army newspaper, as a speech by a prestigious commander, Huang Kecheng, who was simultaneously a ranking member of the Party's Central Discipline Inspection Commission. Praising Mao's early contributions to the revolution, Huang admitted that the Chairman had made mistakes in his later years, from some of which he, Huang, had personally sufffered. However, this did not negate the value of Mao's earlier good deeds. In fact, Huang speculated, Mao's errors may have stemmed from his overexertions on behalf of the revolution, which had "overtaxed" his brain. In repudiating Mao, the party might suffer the "crisis of belief" that troubles many other countries. Therefore, in the interests of the party, the state, and the one billion citizens of China, the positive features of Maoism should be reaffirmed. In a passage clearly aimed at the PRC's current leadership, Huang blamed Mao's "imprudence" on "little direct contact with day-to-day life and the masses. [His] democratic style became poor . . . the whole party ought to draw lessons from this."[16]

Other attempts to mollify leftist elements within the PLA included the publication of an article entitled "Mao Zedong's Military Science Will Forever Be a Treasure of the Chinese People" by the party's leading theoretical journal, *Red Flag*,[17] and a resumption of Mao study within the PLA.

PLA opposition also influenced a modification of Deng Xiaoping's liberalization in the literary sphere. In April 1981, when Huang Kecheng's speech on Mao was published, LAD attacked a play written by an army cultural worker.[18] Entitled *Bitter Love*, its plot is a thinly disguised allegory on unrequited patriotism, with the protagonist's loyalty to his country being rewarded by its persecution of him and his eventual death. LAD's charges that the play was anti-socialist and counterrevolutionary initially received little attention outside the army. The play won a literary award in June 1981 and was made into a movie, but the army pressed its case, and a few months later the campaign against *Bitter Love* was renewed, this time with broad media support. Its author made a public self-criticism, and the government introduced more stringent guidelines for literary creations.[19] However, when LAD renewed its attack on the liberalization of literature and art on the eve of the 12th Party Congress, Deng struck back. The paper was forced to make a self-criticism, and Wei Guoqing, the head of the PLA's General Political Department, was removed from office.[20] Despite losing his job, Wei appears to have won his point: the emphasis on heroism and spiritual purity in military literature continues.

On other matters, the army has been less influential. It delayed the appointment of Geng Biao, Deng Xiaoping's nominee for defense minister for nine months but, to weaken resistance to the appointment, Deng removed the commanders of eight of China's eleven military regions, replacing them with persons more amenable to his programs.[21] However, Geng's failure to win the support of the military led to his being replaced in November 1982 by Zhang Aiping. This was accompanied by further transfers of military region commanders.

Rumblings of PLA discontent with the military budget have not appreciably bettered the army's allocations. A 20 percent increase in the military budget for 1979, to cover the costs of the Sino-Vietnamese war, was followed by sharp cuts in 1980 and 1981, bringing the 1981 total to almost precisely that of 1978. The 1982 figure showed a 6 percent increase over 1981, generally considered a concession to the military in return for its support. However, the Chinese budget is calculated in terms of current rather than constant *yuan,* and there was considerable inflation in the PRC from 1979 through 1981. In constant *yuan,* the PLA's budget for 1982 is somewhat less than that of 1978. The 1982 military budget increase may nonetheless have been important in a symbolic sense. The PLA's allocation remained unchanged in the 1983 and 1984 budgets.[22]

In other areas, the army's efforts have been still less successful. Army opposition to Deng's curtailment of military dependents perquisites resulted in only token gestures to improve their lot. PLA resistance to having five elderly former military leaders tried, along with the much-excoriated Gang of Four did not prevent the trial from taking place as scheduled. And the clearly expressed opposition of both veteran leaders and the PLA rank-and-file to Deng's agricultural policies has resulted in no discernible changes in those policies—which are popular with the peasants, who constitute four-fifths of the country's population.

The state constitution adopted in December 1982 contains provisions which seem intended to further mute the role of the PLA in domestic politics. The document establishes a new institution, the Central Military Council, to direct the armed forces. Its head is responsible to the National People's Congress. Apparently there has already been controversy over the position: the draft constitution circulated in April 1982 limited the CMC chairperson to two consecutive five-year terms, whereas the constitution presented for ratification in December contained no such restriction.[23] Additionally, it is unclear whether the state CMC will supersede, complement, or perform an adversary role with regard to the Party Central Committee's Military Commission. As of early-1985 Deng Xiaoping chairs both organizations.

*Civil-Military Relations*

Civil-military relations in China have deteriorated over the past fifteen years, a fact frankly acknowledged by the leadership since 1980. The PRC's problems are no more serious, and in many cases are a good deal less troublesome, than those of other developing countries, but they are embarrassing in a society that has prided itself on maintaining a relationship between army and people comparable to that between fish and water. At issue are civilian perceptions of the excessive privileges garnered by the military and their dependents, and civilian resentment of highhanded treatment by the military.

It is scarcely surprising that the military, for many years portrayed by official media as an elite organization and a model for civilians to emulate, should have accrued certain privileges consonant with its exalted status. The growth of professionalism, which set the army still further apart from the rest of society, also encouraged this accretion of status and privilege. To reduce these disparities, the abolition of ranks in 1965 was accompanied by a change to plain uniforms not very different in shape or material from those worn by most civilians.

However, neither this nor the Cultural Revolution succeeded in erasing army-civilian differences, for despite its attack on privilege, the Cultural Revolution enhanced the power of the PLA. The PLA, the only force capable of maintaining order, emerged from the Cultural Revolution stronger than before. Leftist attempts to build the militia into a counterforce to the PLA collapsed in 1976, and a coalition of military leaders was instrumental in bringing Deng Xiaoping to power in 1977.

Deng's liberalization movement, which flowered in 1978 and 1979, encouraged people to air their grievances, to which they responded quickly and enthusiastically. In Beijing, thousands of university students shouting anti-militarist slogans staged a protest march and sit-in at Party headquarters, demanding the removal of an army artillery unit from their campus. The army refused to depart, arguing that since it planned to expand its personnel, it needed more space. The unit entered the campus on Mao's orders in 1968, and continued to occupy the premises even when it was no longer needed.[24] In Guangzhou, the army was persuaded to vacate eighteen houses it had occupied since the Cultural Revolution,[25] but at the close of that year, one delegate to the National People's Congress complained that at least ten PLA units remained quartered in the Imperial Palace in Beijing, to the detriment of the national treasures therein.[26] The PLA apparently also occupies many apartment buildings and other residential complexes. Since China has an acute housing shortage, and alternative quarters are rarely available, the army's reluctance to move is understandable, as is civilian resentment when they do not do so.

Other issues have caused civil-military friction. When public security forces proved inadequate to deal with civil unrest and rising crime rates resulting from Deng's liberalization policies of 1978-1979, army units were ordered to patrol the streets of major cities. This caused considerable civilian resentment when the almost inevitable excesses of PLA authority occurred.[27] Poor civil-military relations fed by particular local grievances were responsible for brief army revolts in Xinjiang during 1981, and in Shanxi in 1982. The Xinjiang incident was regarded as quite serious, since it involved a traditionally anti-Han Chinese Turkic minority with kinfolk living across the nearby border with the Soviet Union. Top leaders, including Deng Xiaoping, toured the area to investigate and plead for calm.[28]

The military is not solely to blame for the deterioration of civil-military relations. According to a Chinese press report, one civilian power company actually attempted extortion against the PLA: it cut off electricity to a military area during a surgical operation, and refused to turn the power back on until given sixty military coats.[29] However, the military is most often criticized by the media and, interestingly, the most far-reaching criticism of military treatment of civilians has been that of PLA member, Ye Wenfu (see below, Cultural/Ethnic Patterns).

The government has encouraged civil-military forums to discuss grievances,[30] extracted apologies where it believes apologies are due, and ordered the PLA to perform services for the civilian population, including such unpleasant tasks as garbage collection and spitoon cleaning, to induce humility. Certain military dependent privileges have been curtailed, as has the use of chauffeured cars for higher-ranking officers. How long these restrictions will last depends upon the government's determination. In China, as elsewhere, rescinded privileges have a tendency to gradually reappear. But the army has been somewhat humbled. It must be galling for an institution that was once held up as the model for all China to be told, as the PLA was in December 1981, to learn from the PRC's women's volleyball team.[31]

## Intra-Military Political Dynamics

There is little evidence of inter-service rivalries in the PLA. Some competition over budgetary allocations may be assumed to exist. But, in contrast to many countries, the navy and air force do not seem to hold particular service points of view which would cause them to wish to develop in ways different from those desired by the army. One reason may be the comparative youth of the navy and air force, which were founded only after liberation. There has also been some transfer of officers between the services, thus inhibiting the development of inter-service rivalries. The overwhelming size of the army (3,600,000) relative to the navy (360,000) and air force (490,000) may also be a factor.

Attempts to analyze the intra-military political dynamics of China have included such issues as power struggles, generational politics, field army loyalties, and conflicts between military professionalists and adherents of Maoist concepts of revolutionary warfare. All suffer from insufficient evidence. The last-mentioned factor, however, although often oversimplified, appears to be the most convincing explanation of Chinese military politics.

It is often assumed that this conflict will die, as younger, more technology-oriented professionals replace the elderly devotees of standards developed during the Yenan period. This author believes such prognoses to be simplistic. PLA opposition to the abandonment of Maoist agricultural and military policies in favor of Deng's reforms spanned the entire command structure and range of ages.[32] Moreover, while it is unlikely that many PLA commanders feel that Mao's military tactics should be applied exactly as they were in the 1930s and 1940s, they can make a strong argument for the continued validity of most of his principles. Maoist technological simplicity, mobile warfare, guerrilla tactics, and a flattened command structure are well-suited to the sort of defensive war on its own soil that the PRC is likely to face in the foreseeable future. In addition, budgetary constraints will not permit the purchase, or the indigenous development and production, of large quantities of sophisticated weaponry. Even were they to suddenly become available, the PLA lacks the skilled personnel to use and maintain them. Thus, the principles of People's War, in modified form, seem a realistic alternative to the acquisition of sophisticated weaponry. To laud its superiorities is to make a virtue of necessity.

Advocates of Maoist principles are opposed by a more professionally-minded group who favor the acquisition of more modern technology, increased attention to positional warfare, and the reimposition of military ranks. They point out that China may not always be able to fight on its own soil, where the principles of People's War are most applicable, and that the PLA's performance in Vietnam in 1979 showed inadequacies that can be corrected only by substantial reforms. While professionals and revolutionaries subscribe to the slogan "People's War under modern conditions," there is no consensus on its content. What modifications should be made, and under what conditions these might be applied, continue to be debated.

Apart from the controversy over modernization, the main issues dividing the PLA in recent years have centered on Deng Xiaoping's reforms and their relationship to the military. Principally these include

- the extent of the deMaoification process
- liberalization in art and literature
- the introduction of free market agricultural policies
- regularization of the PLA.

Deng was rehabilitated with the help of elements within the army. Chief among them are believed to be Ye Jianying, Wei Guoqing and Xu Shiyou, old soldiers of considerable repute. Given Deng's outspoken comments on military professionalism before he was purged, it must be assumed that those who helped in his rehabilitation were sympathetic to his views, Yet within a few years of his rehabilitation, Deng's policies brought him into conflict with all of them, and their public words and actions since then have made them appear more leftist than professional.

Deng Xiaoping's chief supporters in the army may be assumed to include Yang Dezhi, whom Deng chose as chief of the PLA's general staff, Qin Qiwei, commanding the Beijing Military Units, and Zhang Tingfa, the chief of the PLA's air force. All have spoken out against "leftism in the army,"[33] and Zhang has in addition urged the military to "avoid endless quibbling over matters of the past . . . and look forward into the future."[34]

Ye Jianying recently announced his retirement "from the first line" of duty,[35] Xu Shiyou has been removed as commander of the Guangzhou Military Region, and Wei Guoqing was dismissed as head of the General Political Department. Yet all remain personally powerful, and can be presumed to command the loyalties of substantial segments of the military. Both Ye and Wei retain their seats on the Party Central Committee's Politburo, and Ye is a member of the Politburo's Standing Committee as well.

Some of the followers of these men and their views will probably be removed by Deng's early 1980s campaign to scale down the PLA. While publicized as a move to streamline the PLA by weeding out the overaged, unskilled, uneducated, and corrupt, the unannounced targets of the campaign are leftists in the army. However, since an estimated two-fifths of the PLA are believed to harbor leftist views,[36] it will be difficult to remove all of them without further damaging troop morale.

A former State Department analyst noted that the military's "ideological debates of the past two years have produced no clear winner or prevailing line."[37] The professional, pro-Deng, group within the military has increased its power but needs the support of others and will make concessions, though not necessarily permanent ones, to gain this support.[38] Meanwhile, debate is likely to continue.

*Economic Development*

The use of the PLA for domestic economic construction, which characterized the late 1950s in an exaggerated form, continues to receive modest attention in the Chinese media. Since use of the military in civilian agricultural and industrial work is favored by leftists, while professionals advocate increased attention to training activities, and since Deng Xiaoping is committed to the professionalization of the military, one would expect a good deal of attention to be paid to training activities and to discussions of strategy and tactics. To a certain extent this is indeed the case. However, the PLA remains an important force in economic construction, and has even taken on new commitments. Apart from a desire to placate leftists, possible reasons include

- the present difficulties of the Chinese economy
- the leadership's desire to raise living standards by providing more consumer goods
- an attempt to better civil-military relations by providing PLA aid to civilian projects

- the need to utilize major portions of the defense industry which had been idled by cuts in the military budget.

The most salient feature of the PLA's involvement in economic development during the past several years has been the redirection of large parts of the defense industry to the production of consumer goods. Civilian products were expected to make up 30% of the total output value of all China's military industrial enterprises in 1980, and to increase rapidly the following years. Several hundred products, ranging from washing machines to socks, are manufactured.

The PLA's Capital Construction Corps[39] contracted to construct buildings for civilian use, and the army was involved in a major afforestation project during spring 1982. The army is expected to help in flood and drought prevention work, and in emergencies such as earthquakes and floods. The air force has reequipped a number of its planes for crop-dusting and other activities in support of agricultural and animal husbandry, a mission which is expected to be of twenty years' duration. The military is not always enthusiastic about undertaking economic construction activities, and occasionally substantial government pressure is needed to induce the PLA to complete its projects on schedule.

It is difficult to estimate the impact of these economic activities on the Chinese economy as a whole. The percentage of the PRC's defense industry now devoted to civilian production is estimated at between thirty and forty percent. This will surely increase the amount of consumer goods available, and may result in lower quantities of defense-related items. The impact of the PLA's other activities is probably less. The number of personnel involved in economic construction activities appears to be small relative to the Chinese economy as a whole, although the projects tend to be highly publicized and visible. Moreover, the PLA is a very large force, so that the diversion of a portion of its labor to economic construction probably does not seriously affect its fighting capabilities. Such activities as tree planting and disaster prevention and relief tend to involve large numbers of troops, but are sporadic and typically do not consume long periods of time. The shortages of fuel and ammunition caused by tight budgets probably impact more heavily on training than does the PLA's economic construction activities.[40]

## Foreign and Defense Policy Objectives

There is little evidence indicating the PLA's influence over foreign or defense policy objectives. The PLA is unhappy with budgetary restrictions, and would like to purchase or develop more modern weaponry. A debate on how much to rely on foreign technology and how much on indigenous development is rarely spoken of directly, but is presented in the form of historical allegory. There is also a debate on the priority of defense for China's sparsely populated northwestern province of Xinjiang.[41] The decision to invade Vietnam in February 1979 seems to have been Deng's, and he was criticized by several members of the Politburo when the army's performance there left something to be desired.[42] Whether these critics included Ye Jianying, or what the opinions of Wei Guoqing and Xu Shiyou were, are unknown.

*Ethical/Spiritual Standards*

A perceived deterioration in the PLA's ethical and spiritual standards has concerned the Chinese leadership. Some instances of corruption, abuse of power, and low troop morale were discussed freely in the press. Others, when published, resulted in severe criticism of the author, and still others are open secrets, spoken of by Chinese in widely separated geographical areas, but do not appear in the press.

Several of Deng Xiaoping's reforms have reduced the attractiveness of joining the PLA, with consequent effects on troop morale. New, free market agricultural policies allow peasants to increase their incomes as they increase crop yields, and families want to keep able-bodied youth at home, where they can contribute to the household's prosperity. To lose a child to the army is to suffer a financial loss. This is particularly so since the allowances once given to military dependents have been suspended, and the families of some PLA members have suffered hardships as a result.

While Deng's agricultural reforms have made life in the countryside more attractive, other reforms have made it difficult to leave. Previously, one could change one's registration permit from the countryside to the city at the time of demobilization from the army. Ex-soldiers also received preference in obtaining sought-after factory jobs. Under the new system, demobilized soldiers' registration permits are transferred to their place of recruitment. Thus, the PLA no longer serves as a conduit for those who wish to leave the countryside. With reduced career prospects and low pay, PLA members have difficulty finding marriage partners.[43]

The net effect of these reforms has been to reduce the attractiveness of military service for rural youth, heretofore the mainstay of the PLA. Nor are urban youth regarded as adequate substitutes. While typically better educated than their rural counterparts, they are fewer in numbers, generally unwilling to join the army, and regarded by their officers as ill-disciplined and unsuited to military life.

Some of these recruitment problems might be mitigated by Deng Xiaoping's plans to reduce the size of the army by approximately one million, but this has not happened. Deng's plans call for elimination of personnel at the higher levels, demobilizing those who had planned to make the military a career. They find themselves unwillingly severed from the PLA, and obliged to seek civilian employment at mid- or late career, and in a tight job makret. There have been reports of public disturbances by unemployed soldiers. One, on Hainan Island, involved a confrontation between public security forces and a thousand disgruntled veterans.[44] In another, the so-called "Disillusioned Army" mustered half of its claimed 6,000 members to terrorize a county in western Guangdong. The group allegedly planned an escalation of activities, eventually leading to the formation of an independent base area in the nearby mountainous border with Guangxi province.[45] The symbolism of the Disillusioned Army adopting the same course of action pursued by the young Mao Zedong in his struggle against the Guomindang could not have been pleasing to the government.

Austere defense budgets have exacerbated existing discontent with military life, and it is not surprising that many soldiers have turned to corruption. While part of the reason may lie in the straitened financial circumstances of PLA members, this does not explain why corruption is most lucratively practiced at the highest levels. Marshal Ye Jianying, working through one of his children who lives in Hong Kong, has purchased a luxury apartment building in one of the world's most expensive real estate areas, and is believed to have other, extensive financial investments as well. The alleged misdeeds of Ye and other PLA leaders are common gossip throughout China. It is unlikely that all the stories are true, but the fact that they are believed is important in itself.

At lower levels also, PLA members have used their increased access to vehicles, ability to travel, and proximity to border areas to take bribes and smuggle goods. All services are involved. In Tibet army men were discovered to have set up a lucrative operation to smuggle local treasures into Nepal[46] for sale on the antique market there. Cadres of the South China Sea Fleet were charged with taking bribes involving the sale of fuel at speculative prices,[47] and air force planes have been used to smuggle gold, liquor, and high quality cigarettes to Beijing and Guangzhou.[48]

The government has directed public security units to crack down on smuggling and illegal transactions by the PLA. It has also tried to alleviate the problems caused by demobilization. Army officers who retire are to be paid their full salaries plus a bonus of one yuan (about US$ .55) per month for each year of PLA service. They are also entitled to a considerable sum to cover the cost of building a home, said to be sufficient to construct "a beautiful Western-style house complete with a garden."[49] The rank-and-file are helped to find employment.[50] However, few jobs are available, there is civilian competition for them, and the difficulties in civil-military relations will not be helped by showing favoritism to veterans. Others, who are described as "afraid of hardships and fatigue" are urged to be more enthusiastic about military training, and regard discomforts as a sacred task on behalf of the revolution.[51] A nationwide campaign was begun to learn from Lei Feng, with his sense of devotion to duty. Officers have been told to patrol the streets to correct instances of sloppy bearing and appearance on the part of the soldiers, and to deal strictly with military indiscipline.[52] While it is too early to judge the results of these efforts, it is at least certain that the campaign to learn from Lei Feng has been received with stunning indifference.

*Cultural/Ethnic Patterns*

1. *Cultural.* The military has a considerable impact on cultural patterns in China. A cultural affairs division subordinate to the PLA's GPD is of substantial, though undisclosed, size, and contains authors, theatrical workers, and musicians. As exemplified by the play and movie *Bitter Love*, there is a wide domestic audience for the products of PLA cultural workers. A much larger proportion of the PRC's movies seem to have war themes than those of Western countries, with the PLA typically portrayed at its most courageous and heroic.

PLA leaders have not been pleased with the trend of military cultural work. Soldiers have been found singing and listening to love songs and looking at pornographic videocassettes smuggled in from Hong Kong.[53] This "bourgeois poison" has begun to infect indigenously created products as well. A Beijing newspaper, noting a trend toward war films with love themes, expressed doubt that there could be much time for romance on the battlefield. Drawing from a recently-produced film on the Sino-Vietnamese War, the article's author pointed out:

> There is not much space inside a tank, and not everyone can operate one. However, in the film entitled "Tank 008" for the sake of love, a nurse was inappropriately squeezed into the tank. Moreover, she acts as an ammunition loader. . . . Films with a military theme should attach even more importance to facts and seriousness.[54]

Still more troublesome to the leadership than an overemphasis on romance has been a trend toward explicit literary criticism of military leaders. The most celebrated examples of these, the poetry of PLA member Ye Wenfu, are biting attacks on corruption and abuse of power at the highest level. One of his best-known works is a scathing indictment of a military leader who uses public funds to install a bathtub in his basement.[55] Other literary works have depicted military leaders as rapists and smugglers.

The authors of unacceptably critical works have been persuaded to make public self-criticisms. Group song fests have been scheduled for soldiers, featuring revolutionary songs. All tapes and videotapes used by the military must be registered with the authorities, and be available for inspection. Inspirational plays on military themes were produced, and in March 1982 *Kunlun*, a new periodical "devoted mainly to publishing literary works based on military themes" made its debut.[56] In the following month, a national forum on military writing convened in Beijing to further discuss the problem of upgrading literature.[57] Whether these actions will reverse the cultural patterns of past PLA literature and art or simply drive criticism into more subtle channels remains to be seen.

2. *Ethnic.* Since China's ethnic minorities constitute barely six percent of the PRC's population, one should not expect their impact on the PLA to be great. Actually, it is even less than their numbers might suggest. Official propaganda stresses the multinational character of the Chinese state, and voices the concern of Party government for the well-being of the country's fifty-five minority groups. The press regularly reports the military promotions of minority group members as evidence of this concern,[58] but the percentage of minority group members in the PLA is probably substantially below their proportion of the population, and most minority group members are in the lower ranks.

The chief factors behind the low percentage of minority group members in the military appear to be, first, the lower cultural and educational levels of many of minorities relative to the Han Chinese and second, Party and government suspicion of their loyalties. As it happens, the PRC's ethnic minorities with the best-developed martial traditions are precisely those groups who have been most opposed to Han Chinese rule: the Hui (Chinese Muslims), Mongols, Tibetans, Uygurs, and Kazakhs. Most of them reside in sensitive border areas, and may have relatives living on the other side. The Hui, reputedly China's best soldiers,[59] have no representatives at the higher levels of the PLA. Their native language is Chinese, and the educational level of Hui males, at least, is comparable to that of the Han. Two of the best Guomindang generals were Hui,[60] as were several outstanding warlords of the Republican period.[61] Evidence of the CCP government's reluctance to entrust military duties to Muslims may be found in a revelation of the early days after liberation: in one county in Gansu where the Hui constituted a majority of the population, the government decided to exclude them from the army and restrict them to one-third of the local militia.[62] The impression that members of traditionally restive minorities are still viewed with suspicion in the military is reinforced by interviews with refugee Tibetans and Kazakhs. Indeed, it would be surprising if they were not so regarded.

There has been one[63] minority group member in the highest echelons of the PLA: Wei Guoqing, a Zhuang. The Zhuang, numbering twelve million, is China's largest minority group, and one of its best assimilated. Wei, who was educated in Chinese schools and speaks Chinese as a first language, was a prominent commander in the Red Army as early as 1932.[64]

While simple ethnic prejudice does exist in the PRC, the above examples may illustrate a point: on the whole, a minority group member's chances of success in the PLA are less than those of the average Han Chinese. However, a minority group individual who speaks fluent Chinese, has an educational level comparable to the Han, and has demonstrated unquestionable loyalty to Party and state may actually have a somewhat better chance of success than a Han Chinese peer. In China, as elsewhere, it is considered desirable to place certain minority group members in positions of high visibility. In general, though, the impact of ethnic groups on the PLA has been negligible.

## Concluding Net Assessment

The conflict between military professionalists and revolutionaries within the Chinese military has proved enduring and is likely to continue. Personnel transfers and involuntary retirements initiated by Deng Xiaoping during the past several years have moved the military in the direction of increased regularization and professionalization. And a recent constitutional change placing the military more firmly under government control may reduce the role of the PLA in political decisionmaking. But there is a good deal of inertia in the Chinese system, as well as substantial resistance to Deng's reforms. The combination means that further changes in the direction of increasing military professionalization will require considerable pressure from above, and that they will come about slowly, if at all.

Economic constraints will further impinge on Deng's ability to create a smaller, younger, better trained, and better equipped fighting force. There is little money available for weapons and other equipment, few jobs for older demobilized soldiers, and little interest in an army career among younger people. In addition, Deng's efforts to obtain a smaller, more professional army would demand a reduction of the army's role in the civilian economy at a time when the civilian economy needs the PLA's contribution. Lean defense budgets have produced spare capacity in military-run industries, making it possible for them to manufacture much-needed consumer goods. It is, of course, possible to replace the military personnel in these factories with civilian workers. However, the replacement would entail a major and potentially destabilizing structural readjustment, and at a time when the PLA provides a steadying force against the economic and social strains caused by China's experiments with free market enterprises and liberalized social controls.

Despite the apparent wishes of Deng Xiaoping and the more professionally-minded elements of the PLA, the domestic societal imperative is the dominant force shaping the Chinese military. Should the perception of external threat grow, there would certainly be a significant alteration of the PLA's role in the direction of the functional imperative. This external threat is most likely to come from the Soviet Union, or from one of its client states situated near the PRC. Such a shift to the functional imperative of the PLA would, however, require the transfer of funds away from domestic investment. As shown by China's short and unimpressive invasion of Vietnam in February 1979, this shift would be militarily risky and would impose heavy costs on the PRC's already strained modernization program.

A weakening of the PRC's economy might, in the abstract, be welcomed by China's enemies. It is, however, highly unlikely that any of the them would choose to force the PRC into a defense buildup in order to weaken the Chinese economy. Despite the PLA's technological deficiencies, its large size and seemingly limitless manpower reserves are an effective deterrent against most forms of external provocation. Therefore, regardless of its shortcomings, the PLA aids both China's wellbeing and the PRC's standing in the international community.

Thus, while China's enemies have an interest in weakening the PRC's military, it is largely beyond their power to do so, short of an actual confrontation. The converse seems to be true as well: while it might be to the advantage of China's friends—or at least to the enemies of China's major enemy, the Soviet Union—to help modernize the PLA, the prospects for effecting significant change are beyond the resources available to any country. Current estimates place the cost of modernization of the PLA's weapons alone at U.S. $41–63 billion, and experts agree that no feasible volume of international transfers could conceivably diminish the disparity between Chinese and Soviet military capabilities.

Hence, one may expect that domestic forces will continue to be the major determinant shaping the role of the PLA, and that the military will continue to play a significant, although not the dominant, role in the political decisionmaking processes of the country, in its economy, and in its cultural patterns and ethical standards.

## Notes

1. See Alexander George, *The Chinese Communist Army in Action*. New York, Columbia University Press, 1967, for an account of this period. Harlan W. Jencks, *From Muskets to Missiles*. Boulder, Colorado, Westview Press, 1982,

p. 47, raises some doubts as to whether Lin Biao' was actually in command during this early period.

2. These reforms are covered in detail in Ellis Joffe, *Party and Army: Professionalism and Political Control In The Chinese Officer Corps 1949–1964.* Cambridge, Mass., East Asian Research Center, Harvard University, 1967.

3. Ibid., pp. 106–107.

4. The Gongzuo Tongxun, (GZTX) trans. by J. Chester Cheng, *The Politics of the Chinese Army: A Translation of the Bulletin of Activities of the People's Liberation Army.* Stanford, California, Hoover Institution, 1966.

5. GZTX 7 Jan. 1981 in Cheng, pp. 89–90; GZTX 11 Jan. 1961, in Cheng, pp. 116–123.

6. The PLA's involvement in the Cultural Revolution is summarized in Harvey W. Nelsen, *The Chinese Military System*, 2nd Edition. Boulder, Colorado, Westview Press, 1981, pp. 126–150.

7. Xinhua, Beijing, 18 Nov. 1980 in U.S. Department of Commerce, Foreign Broadcast Information Service, China, 1980, issue no. 224, p. L/1 (FBIS-CHI-80-224: L/1).

8. See Jencks, p. 114 for a convenient table detailing these changes.

9. The intent to reorganize the militia was first made public in a joint People's Daily (PD) and LAD editorial of 29 Sept. 1973. See FBIS-CHI-73-191: B/10.

10. *Beijing Review* (BR) 24 Jan. 1975, p. 15.

11. C. L. Sulzberger, "The Bear In The China Shop," *New York Times* (NYT) 10 Aug. 1975, p. IV-15.

12. See BR 9 April 1976, pp. 3–7.

13. In a recently published report entitled "Peng Dehuai's Account," Peng alludes to the existence of a "military club" at the time of the Lushan Plenum in 1959, saying that he refused to participate. See PD 30 Mar 1982 in FBIS-CHI-82-74: K/10-11. This author suspects that Peng's account may have been written recently, to present Peng, and Deng Xiaoping's conduct, in a manner consonant with the current party line. There is no corroborating evidence for such a military clique.

14. Xinhua, Beijing, 21 Aug 1981 in FBIS-CHI-81-166: U/1–2.

15. Xinhua, Beijing 4 June 1984 in FBIS-CHI-84-110: K/1.

16. Xinhua, Beijing, 10 Apr 1981 in FBIS-CHI-81-70: K/14–16.

17. Translated in FBIS-CHI-81-180: K/10-23.

18. Beijing Radio, 19 Apr 1981, in FBIS-CHI-81-75: K/1.

19. Xinhua, Beijing, 23 Dec 1981, in FBIS-CHI-81-247: K/3.

20. See Christopher Wren, "Deng Opens Drive On His Leftish Foes," *The New York Times*, (NYT) 3 October 1982, p. 3.

21. *Tung Hsiang*, Hong Kong, 16 Apr 1981 in FBIS-CHI-81-75: W/3.

22. See the table on the PLA budget carried in *The China Business Review.* July/August 1984, p. 44.

23. BR 27 Dec 1982, p. 24.

24. Fox Butterfield, "2,000 Students in Peking Protest Army's Use of Campus," NYT 11 Oct 1979, p. A2.

25. Guangzhou Radio, 31 Jul 1981, in FBIS-CHI-81-150: P/1.

26. Xinhua, Beijing, 4 Dec 1981, in FBIS-CHI-81-234: K/14–15.

27. See Dreyer, "Limits of the Permissible in China," *Problems of Communism*, Nov-Dec 1980.
28. Ma Zheng, "Two Nationality Disputes in Xinjiang," Cheng Ming, Hong Kong, 1 July 1981 in U.S. Department of Commerce, *Joint Publications Research Service* (JPRS) 78873, pp. 22–25.
29. *Wen Wei Po*, Hong Kong, 14 Jan 1982, in FBIS-CHI-82-14: W/2.
30. Beijing Radio, 11 Nov 81, in FBIS-CHI-81-225: T/1.
31. Beijing Radio, 21 Dec 81, in FBIS-CHI-81-245: K/1.
32. *Cheng Ming Jih Pao,* Hong Kong, 6 July 1981, in FBIS-CHI-81-128: W/6; FEER 17 Apr 1981, p. 17.
33. For example, PD 4 Apr 1981, in FBIS-CHI-81-70: K/18.
34. *Ban Yue Tan*, Beijing, 10 Aug 1981, in FBIS-CHI-81-165: K/20.
35. *Wen Wei Po*, 1 May 1982, in FBIS-CHI-82-87: U/1.
36. Kyodo, Tokyo, 20 Feb 1981, in FBIS-CHI-81-34: L/3.
37. Richard D. Nethercut, author's conversation, 17 March 1982.
38. Ibid.
39. In November 1984, it was announced that some units of the PLA's Capital Construction Corps would be reassigned to the Armed Police Force. Beijing Radio 30 Nov 1984, in FBIS-CHI-84-232: K/16.
40. For an account of the PLA's economic activities, see Dreyer, "The Role of the PLA ... the Chinese Economy," in *The Chinese Economy in the Eighties*, Joint Economic Committee, U.S. Congress, forthcoming.
41. See, e.g., *Guangming Ribao*, Beijing, 10 Feb 1981, in FBIS-CHI-81-43: L/3-7 and PD 30 MAR 1981, in FBIS-CHI-81-64: K/8-9.
42. Reuters, London, 20 Mar 1979 in FBIS-CHI-79-55: L/1.
43. See *Cheng Ming*, 1 Dec 1981, in FBIS-CHI-81-236: W/3–5 for a discussion of these problems.
44. Kyodo, Tokyo, 20 Feb 1981, in FBIS-CHI-81-34: L/3.
45. *Cheng Ming*, 1 Jan 1982, in FBIS-CHI-82-02: W/2–4.
46. Lhasa Radio, 23 Feb 1982, in FBIS-CHI-82-38: Q/5–6.
47. *Ming Pao*, Hong Kong, 13 Apr 1982, in FBIS-CHI-82-71: W/2.
48. *Cheng Ming*, 1 Mar 1982, in FBIS-CHI-82-43: W/5.
49. Beijing Radio, 11 Sept 1981, in FBIS-CHI-81-178: K/12.
50. *Ming Pao*, 22 Mar 1982, in FBIS-CHI-82-57: W/4–5.
51. Beijing Radio, 28 Mar 1982, in FBIS-CHI-82-60: K/12/13.
52. See, e.g., Beijing Radio, 7 Mar 1982, in FBIS-CHI-82-58: R/1.
53. *South China Morning Post*, Hong Kong, 4 Mar 1982, p. 3.
54. *Wanbao*, Beijing, 8 Feb 1982, in FBIS-CHI-82-36: K/12.
55. *Wenyi Bao*, Beijing, 7 Dec 1981, in FBIS-CHI-82-18: K/13.
56. Xinhua, Beijing, 26 Feb 1982, in FBIS-CHI-82-42: K/7.
57. PD, 21 Apr 1982, in FBIS-CHI-82-80: K/9–13.
58. See, e.g., Yinchuan Radio, 11 Jan 1982, in FBIS-CHI-82-17: T/1.
59. Robert Ekvall, *Cultural Relations on the Kansu-Tibetan Border.* Chicago, University of Chicago Press, 1939, p. 17; Harrison Forman, "China's Moslems," *Canadian Geographic Journal* Sept 1948, p. 140.
60. Li Zhongren and Bai Chongxi.
61. Ma Bufang and Ma Hongkui.
62. Sun Zuobin, "Some Opinions On Nationalities Work," *Xinhua Yuebao*,

Beijing, Feb 1950, p. 876.

63. Ye Jianying is a Hakka (Kejia, or "guest people"), a group of Han Chinese who moved from northern to southern China during the barbarian invasions of the Song dynasty. The Hakka speak a distinct dialect and retain certain cultural differences that set them off from other Han Chinese. However, they are not, and never have been, regarded as an ethnic minority.

64. See Wei's biography in *Who's Who in Communist China*. Hong Kong, Union Research Institute, 1966, p. 631.

# 2

# Taiwan's Armed Forces

*Edward W. Ross*

The derecognition of Taiwan on January 1, 1979 and the signing of the August 17, 1982 communique between the US and China sent major shock waves through the military establishment on Taiwan. These two events, in particular the August 1982 Communique, have led many to believe that Taiwan's military capabilities would inevitably deteriorate over time, weakening the island's security to the point that Beijing might be tempted to take military action to reunite the province with the mainland.

It is much too early to predict whether or not such forecasts will ever become reality. For the time being Taiwan's armed forces remain strong and the balance, or "imbalance," in the Taiwan Strait remains about what it has been for a decade. The United States continues arms sales to Taiwan, although it is on record as intending to abide by the terms of the August Communique. More important, Taiwan remains politically and economically healthy.

Taiwan's military forces play a key role in determining the future of the island and its 17 million inhabitants. The perception of its military strength, both at home and abroad, is an important factor in how Taiwan is approached by China, how foreign financial interests view the security of their investments in Taiwan, and how the people of Taiwan view themselves. This paper will examine the development of Taiwan's armed forces as an institution and as an element of Taiwan's society, and the contemporary and potential future impact of Taiwan's armed forces on the domestic political and economic systems, and the society. In addition, the influence of external factors on Taiwan and its military forces and their significance for the future will be assessed.

### The Formative Years

When the Nationalist (KMT) forces of Generalissimo Chiang Kai-shek first sought refuge in Taiwan following their defeat by the Chinese Communists in 1949, Taiwan's military forces ostensibly existed primarily for the purpose of one day "recovering the mainland." The current military establishment on Taiwan neither possesses the capability to recapture China, nor do its forces organize, train, or deploy to attempt such an adventure. Like most armed forces, Taiwan's military seeks to deter its primary adversary—China—and if deterrence should fail, to defend Taiwan. The early transition of Taiwan's armed forces from a mainland to a Taiwan-oriented force provides a starting point for understanding the role of the military on Taiwan.

The Nationalist Chinese Army's presence on Taiwan preceded its defeat by the Communists. At the Cairo Conference in 1943 the United States and the Allied Powers agreed that, following the defeat of Japan, Taiwan would be returned to the Nationalist Chinese government, ending nearly 50 years of Japanese occupation. After the Japanese surrender, US military ships began transporting elements of the Nationalist Army to Taiwan. Although the native Taiwanese population of the island was not saddened by the Japanese defeat and the subsequent deployment of Nationalist military forces to Taiwan, problems almost immediately began to emerge between the "mainlanders" and the Taiwanese. Rather than coming as liberators of their fellow Chinese, the Nationalists came as occupiers. Although Taiwan had been linked culturally and ethnically to China from the 17th Century, the separation of the island from the mainland during Japanese occupation had created many differences. Economically, Taiwan was considerably better off under Japanese administration and its economic and governmental infrastructure also was more developed. These differences, along with the exploitation of Taiwan by corrupt Nationalist civil and military officials after 1946, led to a confrontation between the Taiwanese and the Nationalist Army. In March 1947, between 10 and 20 thousand Taiwanese were killed by Nationalist soldiers during a series of riots and reprisals resulting from a Taiwanese student attack on Nationalist soldiers who had beaten an old woman to death.[1]

The Nationalist defeat in 1949 resulted in the bulk of their military forces, the Government, and many of the Chinese upper class, fleeing to Taiwan. There they reestablished the Government of the Republic of China, with its capital at Taipei. From then on, the political life of the island would be dominated by the mainland Chinese, who claimed Taiwan as the base from which the mainland would eventually be recaptured.

The immediate problem for the KMT, however, was not the recapture of the mainland but the garrisoning and defense of Taiwan, the Penghus, and the offshore islands of Quemoy and Matsu. A state of martial law, which continues to this day, was established in 1949 and construction of military facilities and a command and control network was begun.

The force with which the March 1947 uprising was suppressed discouraged further large scale resistance to KMT control of the island. In 1948 KMT internal security forces, under the direction of Chiang Ching-Kuo, the Generalissimo's son, began the suppression of dissident elements in Taiwanese society. Over the years, the Taiwan Garrison General Headquarters, the internal security organization of the armed forces, would imprison or force activist opponents of KMT rule to leave the island. By the 1960s effective and organized resistance to the KMT on Taiwan was virtually nonexistent.[2] In the 1950s both the military as an institution and the country as a whole were faced with serious problems. While the KMT clung to its goal of recovering the mainland it was confronted with the immediate tasks of defending Taiwan from Chinese attack, modernizing the military and developing the island province.

Early in 1950 the Chinese Communists designated the invasion of Taiwan as the principal task for the year. An assault force of some 300,000 men and an invasion fleet of barges, junks, and sampans assembled along the Fukien coast. Chinese airfields in the area had been reinforced with some 400 aircraft. Taiwan's defenses consisted of the 800,000 troops withdrawn from the mainland, of which some 300,000 were first-line combat troops, including a nucleus of men trained and equipped by the United States. Taiwan also had 750 tanks, between 300 and 600 fighter and transport aircraft, and perhaps 70 naval ships including 7 destroyer escorts, minesweepers, and LSTs. While the Chinese People's Liberation Army (CPLA) prepared its assault on Taiwan, Taiwanese forces conducted nuisance bombings of Nanking and Shanghai in an attempt to deny foreign ships entry to mainland ports.[3]

The outcome of a battle for Taiwan in 1950 would have been uncertain. On balance, neither side possessed a definite military advantage. Losses would have been massive on both sides but, had the Chinese persisted, Taiwan's limited supply of ammunition and deteriorating morale would probably have been the deciding factors. China likely would have prevailed.

The outbreak of the Korean War, however, prevented the planned invasion from taking place and set into motion forces which renewed KMT access to US military supplies and equipment. In 1949 the United States was attempting to distance itself from the Nationalist government on Taiwan on the postulate that it was beyond the US strategic line of defense in the western Pacific. The Korean War brought it within the area whose military defense the United States considered vital to its national interests. The Joint Chiefs of Staff soon recommended renewed military assistance to the Nationalists, and the US Seventh Fleet was deployed into the Taiwan Strait.[4] From 1950 to the early 1970s US naval and air forces served as the principal military deterrent to Chinese attack on Taiwan and the Penghus.

While a Chinese attack did not materialize in 1950, the threat of an attack broadened the KMT's base of support among Taiwanese. It reinforced what the Government had been saying all along—the civil war was continuing and there was a serious threat to Taiwan. The prospect of a Chinese Communist invasion and occupation loomed even more ominous to the Taiwanese population than the Nationalist occupation a few years earlier. Gradually, the threat from the mainland and the Government's growing ability to meet the needs of the island's people enabled the KMT to convince a growing number of Taiwanese that it could best provide for Taiwan's security.

As the immediate threat of Chinese attack diminished after 1950 Taiwan, with substantial US assistance and increasing support from the population, modernized its military forces. Military academies were established for each service and thousands of officers and men were sent to the US for military, professional, and technical training. With US advisers and equipment the military establishment on Taiwan began to resemble the US military. The major exception to this trend was the establishment throughout the armed forces of a system of political officers under the control of Chiang Ching-kuo. Chiang Kai-shek was convinced that the Nationalist defeat in 1949 resulted largely from the lack of such an apparatus of indoctrination and control.[5]

Another fundamental change in the armed forces concerned the recruitment and management of personnel. A universal military service system was instituted requiring each able-bodied, 18 year old male to serve either 2 years in the army or 3 years in the navy or air force. The troops evacuated from the mainland contained an unusually large proportion of older men, who had been in rear service units near the ports and were more readily evacuated than the younger combatants at the front. The traditional problem of unit loyalty to the commander rather than to the service also was eased as mainland enlisted men were replaced by Taiwanese conscripts. The military draft confirmed that within two decades native Taiwanese would comprise a substantial proportion of the military rank and file, eventually some 85 percent of the total military force. Other changes included a reform of the military finance system, which prevented corrupt commanders from stealing from the troops, and the retirement of many excess officers.

As Taiwan dealt with its many internal problems, the Taiwan Strait crisis of 1954 provided a catalyst for increased US assistance to Taiwan and the establishment of a formal US security commitment. Unlike the situation in 1950, Chinese action against Quemoy had significance beyond China's desire to integrate Taiwan with Communist Chinese society.

Chinese raids and artillery bombardment of Quemoy, and Nationalist sea and air attack on the mainland, were viewed in the United States in the wider context of US-China relations. In Washington, the bombardment of the offshore islands appeared to be a probing action intended to discover how far the United States might be prepared to defend the Nationalist regime and resist Sino-Soviet aggression. Secretary of State Dulles described it as a "horrible dilemma." To rush to the island's defense would involve the United States in the Chinese civil war, but to fail to do so might encourage the Communists to believe they could attack Taiwan with impunity.[6]

While the crisis simmered in the strait, Taiwan was engaged in negotiations to establish a basic commitment by the United States to defend Taiwan. The mutual security treaty between the United States and Taiwan, signed in Washington in December 1954, accomplished two objectives for the United States. First, it clearly signaled to China that the United States was committed to the defense of Taiwan. Second, in an exchange of notes between Secretary Dulles and Taiwan Foreign Minister Yeh, it was agreed that Taiwan would not resort to force (against China) except by agreement with the United States.[7] For Taiwan, however, the treaty provided a long term military relationship with the United States with continued access to arms and spare parts, military assistance, advice, and training, necessary if Taiwan were to strengthen its forces to the point that it might achieve a greater measure of deterrence or some day even be able to recover the mainland. Further, a formal security arrangement with the United States strengthened the legitimacy of the Nationalist government in the eyes of the island's inhabitants. The material and economic assistance pouring into Taiwan also demonstrated the Nationalist government's ability to provide for the general security and welfare of Taiwan.

## Force Development and Institutional Growth

With its military strength buttressed by US weapons and equipment, and the 1954 treaty, Taiwan embarked on a program of force development and engaged in a more aggressive deployment of its forces. Nearly 100,000 troops were stationed on Quemoy and Matsu and commando raids and deep penetration reconnaissance flights were conducted against the Chinese mainland. Military morale was strengthened as political and military leaders on Taiwan began talk more confidently about a "return to the mainland." This new Taiwan assertiveness, and mounting economic and political problems on the mainland, led China in 1958 to again conduct intense shelling of the offshore islands, this time accompanied by a naval blockade of Quemoy. Again the US Seventh Fleet was ordered into the Strait and the crisis cooled.

In the 1950s, US air and naval forces provided the principal military deterrent to a Chinese attack on Taiwan. Taiwan's primary emphasis during these years was to build up its ground forces. However, by 1961 the US security commitment to Taiwan specifically excluded defense of the offshore islands. Taiwan subsequently sought to develop its air and naval forces, and the United States began to provide modern aircraft and ships. Since the early 1960s most US military grant aid and later foreign military sales (FMS) to Taiwan consisted of weapons and equipment intended to strengthen its air and sea defenses. During the late 1960s, however, Taiwan managed to acquire many ground force items declared surplus to the needs of US forces in Vietnam.[8]

From about 1960, Taiwan built a relatively modern and well organized military force. As Taiwan's economy flourished, Taipei became less dependent on US military aid and increasingly capable of purchasing its requirements through FMS channels. While it occasionally purchases some weapons and equipment from third country sources, the United States has remained Taiwan's principal arms supplier. Taiwan now co-produces F-5E/F fighter aircraft and provides many end items and spare parts for its ground forces. Nevertheless, Taiwan remains heavily dependent on the United States for its military needs.

During the 1950s and 1960s another dominant trend was the growing prestige of the Taiwan armed forces as an institution. The military's effective propaganda apparatus and its relative successes, with US backing, in confrontations with China enhanced the military's reputation among the people. As more and more Taiwanese completed military service, the effects of their political indoctrination and acquired loyalty to the service were transmitted to the civilian population. Many Taiwanese also found that success in the military permitted a measure of upward mobility after they left the service. Technical training received on active duty enabled them to find better civilian jobs. Meanwhile, the Taiwan Garrison Command was continuing its suppression of dissident elements in Taiwanese society.

Beginning in the 1950s, Taiwan's military engaged in civil action programs to enhance its reputation and gain civilian support. Soldiers routinely went into the countryside at harvest time to assist farmers, and the military response in disaster relief has been recognized by all segments of Taiwan's society. The military had a monumental task in overcoming the effects of the 1947 uprising, but by the 1960s they had made great strides toward that end. Although the Taiwanese would never forget 1947, the incident no longer rankled as a major wedge between the younger Taiwanese and the military, itself increasingly Taiwanese.

While civil-military relations improved, many restrictions remained on the duties Taiwanese were allowed to perform in the armed forces. Many branches such as intelligence, for example, were not open to Taiwanese and promotions, especially within the officer corps, were limited. Taiwanese did not attend the elite political staff college in significant numbers until the late 1960s.

On balance, the military as an institution was successful in establishing itself as a stable fixture in Taiwan's society and in regularizing the modernization and development process. Taiwanese mainlander differences persisted but, by and large, the reality of KMT control and the increasing prosperity of Taiwan's economy were incentives for cooperation and support of the KMT by the pragmatic elements of Taiwanese society.

By the 1970s, Taiwan's armed forces had been transformed from the routed remnants of Chiang Kai-shek's Nationalist army to a modest but substantial, well trained, and efficient military force. Since 1949 the size of the armed forces has decreased overall from about 800,000 to about 350,000. This decrease reflects the transition of Taiwan's armed forces from a "Chinese" army to a military force with the primary mission of defending Taiwan. In addition, U.S. military assistance and Taiwan's expanding economy have provided the conditions under which the military are not only responsible for the island's defense but also permit it to play a role in the political, economic, and social development of Taiwan.

### The Armed Forces in Contemporary Taiwan

There are three significant dimensions to the impact of the armed forces on contemporary Taiwan politics, economy, and society. At one level, the military forces are a visible symbol and an extension of KMT legitimacy and authority. At another, senior military officers have considerable power and influence in the domestic political balance of power and the national decisionmaking process. At yet another level, the military makes a substantial contribution to the economic and social development of Taiwan.

First, the military is clearly a symbol to foreign investors and the local population of the Government's ability to defend Taiwan and to foster an environment for economic growth and social development.

A fundamental reality of Taiwan is that there exists a perpetual legitimacy crisis, external and internal. Both Beijing and Taipei acknowledge that there is but one China, and Taiwan is a part of China. The disagreement is, of course, over which is the legitimate government. Since 1971, the international community has come to recognize the

Chinese Communist government in Beijing as the legitimate government of all China. In December 1978, even Taiwan's closest ally, the United States, withdrew recognition from Taiwan and normalized relations with China. On Taiwan the KMT-led mainland minority dominates the political life of an island whose population is 85 percent Taiwanese. Despite winning a measure of Taiwanese support, the KMT minority is persistently faced with the task of demonstrating to the Taiwanese majority that it deserves to continue in power. Even though the KMT has a strong grip on the reins of power, it cannot afford any significant Taiwanese dissatisfaction.

Given the political circumstances that govern the situation in the Taiwan Strait region, a drastic weakening of the Taiwan defense establishment could threaten investor confidence and undermine the island's viability. It has long been realized that the key to Taiwan's viability is its flourishing economy. Over the past 30 years Taiwan has become one of Asia's most prosperous and dynamic economic systems. Its economy, however, depends largely on foreign capital and investment. Investor confidence, therefore, is an essential ingredient for continued prosperity and economic growth. The confidence of the people on Taiwan in their economic system also is vital, and would be affected by a general perception that Taiwan was less able to provide for its security. Precisely how foreign investors and the island's population might react in the face of a "weakening" of the military establishment is not clear.

Foreign and domestic investor confidence in the economy is also conditioned by the underlying enmity between Chinese mainlanders and the native Taiwanese. The overwhelming majority of Taiwanese support the KMT dominated government and its policies, so long as the economic health of the island is sustained. Nevertheless, the 1977 riot in Chungli and the 1979 riot in Kaohsiung demonstrated the animosity many Taiwanese hold for the Government because of its suppression of Taiwanese participation in politics and its limits on freedom of expression and human rights. These riots did not serve as a catalyst to broader political instability precisely because most Taiwanese were generally satisfied with their political and economic conditions.

The second dimension of the impact of Tawian's armed forces on the island's social-political system is the participation of senior military leaders in national decisionmaking.[9]

In a country that, in 1984, spent approximately nine percent of its Gross National Product (GNP) on national defense there is little doubt that the key senior military officers have power and influence in the domestic political balance of power and the national decisionmaking process. The military establishment is represented in the KMT Standing Committee by the Minister of National Defense, Admiral Soong Changchih, and by the Chief of the General Staff, General Hao Pei-tsun. General Wen Ha-hsiung, for twelve years the head of Taiwan's procurement mission in Washington, heads the Combined Service Forces, which also means that he is responsible for the armament industries. A special position is occupied by General Chen Shou-shan, Commander of the Taiwan Garrison Command, which is entrusted with internal security. General Hau is, as of early 1985, the most influential military personality and a power to be reckoned with in any struggle for succession to President Chiang.

The power and influence of the senior military leaders is not readily apparent in the daily political life of Taiwan. Their influence is primarily derived from personal associations and relationships with President Chiang and other senior political figures. Politics in the KMT is usually characterized in terms of "hardliners" and "moderates" and this difference generally holds true for the military. The hardliners are staunch anti-communists who believe that one day political conditions on the mainland will create a situation favorable for its "recovery." They oppose "Taiwanization" of the KMT and the military and favor harsh, repressive measures to deal with Taiwanese oppositionist elements. The moderates, like Admiral Soong, are inclined to emphasize the economic development of Taiwan and the need to open the political process to Taiwanese. The moderates have taken a less harsh stance toward those segments of Taiwanese society that have spoken out against KMT policies.

The generation of leaders now in power in the government and the military share the common experience of the Chinese civil war and the defeat of the KMT. They are acutely aware of the potential sources of political instability which could undermine Taiwan's economic and social progress. Although, as Asian societies go, Taiwan is a particularly stable society, senior military leaders have a voice in KMT policy because President Chiang and others realize how important they would be should political stability in Taiwan be threatened.

Perhaps the best example of the military's potential influence in Taiwan politics is its likely role in the succession process. Taiwan's constitution clearly specifies that, should the president die in office, the vice-president shall succeed him. The current vice-president, Lee Teng-hui, is a Taiwanese and widely recognized as without real political power. The second most powerful individual in Government is Premier Yu Kuo-hwa, and it is "understood" that Lee would serve as president only until elections were held. Sun would then most likely be elected as president to succeed Chiang. The military would most probably not oppose this chain of events. A problem would arise, however, if the military believed that the new president was diverging from past KMT policies. No likely president has either the personal following or the aura of legitimacy possessed by Chiang Ching-kuo. The determination of senior military leaders to ensure that Taiwan continues on course, and their power to act should the need arise, is recognized by the upper councils of the KMT.

Another example of the military's power is its role in internal security. Permanent martial law on Taiwan gives the military the right to arrest and detain civilians without formal charges, or without trial, for long periods. The Taiwan Garrison Command actively monitored the activities of dissident elements and, in the aftermath of the Chungli and Kaohsiung riots in 1977 and 1979, was particularly effective in suppressing oppositionist activity. Knowledgeable political observers reported that hardliners in the military were checked only by President Chiang's personal intervention. Even so, those put on trial following the Kaohsiung riot were given long prison sentences.

Finally, with regard to the political power of the military, previous associations of certain military leaders with their US counterparts provided opportunities for them to enhance their positions by being personally identified with weapons procurement and technology acquisitions. Such associations have been a valued power base. A general's ability to advance Taiwan's interests through US connections usually was instrumental in maintaining his position in the Taiwan power structure. These associations also provided opportunities for Taiwan to influence US policy. Through US advocates, Taiwan has been able to influence US decisions in ways beneficial to its interests. Since the US normalization of relations with China, the benefits of Taiwan's military association with the United States have diminished appreciably. Nevertheless, there remain many influential retired US military officers who support Taiwan and maintain unofficial relationships with Taiwan's military hierarchy.

The third significant dimension of the military's impact on Taiwan society is its contribution to the economic and social development of the island.

Taiwan's military forces operate sophisticated electronic and high-technology weapons and equipment which require many engineers and technicians. Taiwan's long association with the United States has made it possible for many of these military engineers and technicians to receive technical training in the United States. When junior noncommissioned officers and enlisted personnel return to civilian life after a tour in the military it is easy for them to find jobs in the growing electronics and high-technology sectors of industry.

Taiwan's defense industries provide jobs for a significant portion of the civilian work force. In past years nearly half the total government budget was spent on defense and defense related programs. Taiwan produces ground force weapons and equipment like artillery, armored personnel carriers, and infantry weapons, and co-produces, with US assistance, F-5E/F jet fighter aircraft. Although Taiwan depends heavily on the United States for high-technology weapons such as air-to-air and surface-to-air missiles, fighter aircraft, and military electronics, to name a few, it has made slow but steady progress in expanding its own defense production.

The military contribution to social development can be measured in terms of the basic ethical and spiritual values the military inculcates into Taiwan youth in the armed forces. Military training and education has a high political and social content. Recruits and inductees are taught Sun Yat-sen's "three principles of the people," and the goals and objectives of the government are explained to them. Pride in country, in the armed forces, and in traditional Chinese values are an integral part of every serviceman's daily life.

## The Future Role of the Military

Any discussion of the prospects for Taiwan's armed forces must embrace the broader context of US-China-Taiwan relations. Taiwan's dependence on the United States for arms and military equipment, and as the ultimate guarantor of its security, have become major issues in US-China relations. The future of Taiwan's armed forces and their impact on Taiwan's economy and society will depend in large measure on the resolution of those issues and the future policies of both Beijing and Washington toward Taiwan.

Ever since the US-China rapprochement of the early 1970s, Taiwan was an impediment to improving US-China relations but, in December 1978, the United States and China finally agreed to normalize relations. The Taiwan issues, specifically US arms sales to the island, were temporarily shelved so that a normalization agreement could be obtained. The United States agreed to terminate the 1954 Mutual Security Treaty with Taipei after a one-year moratorium, during which Washington also decided to make no new arms sales (although deliveries of previous sales continued). In 1980, arms sales to Taiwan were resumed.

Following President Reagan's election in 1980 China became concerned that the United States was attempting to strengthen its relations with Taiwan and was reneging on the understandings reached during the normalization process. Beijing evidently perceived that although the United States clearly indicated arms sales to Taiwan would continue after normalization, it believed that the problem would be resolved in the near term. President Reagan's statements during the 1980 campaign and subsequent actions by the new administration, however, contributed toward the Chinese taking firm action to head off improved US-Taiwan relations. Beijing threatened to downgrade relations with the United States if Washington acted favorably on Taiwan's request for the FX aircraft.

After a well publicized debate in the United States, during which both China and Taiwan attempted to influence public and government opinion, the President decided in early January 1982 not to sell the FX aircraft to Taiwan. Subsequently the United States and China opened discussions in Beijing over the future of US arms sales to Taiwan.

China opposes continued US arms sales to Taiwan because it believes these sustain Taipei's intransigence and unwillingness to enter into negotiations with Beijing on eventual reunification, and because China interprets US policy as evidence of a US desire to maintain the status quo in the Taiwan Strait. China wants the United States to eventually terminate military sales to Taiwan.

The United States has stated frequently that it expects the status of Taiwan to be resolved peacefully between the parties on both sides of the Taiwan Strait. Meanwhile, many argue that despite Beijing's peaceful overtures, the United States must continue to provide weapons to Taiwan.

All this is significant, not only for the future role of Taiwan's armed forces, but for Taiwan itself. The level of US military sales to Taiwan affects directly Taiwan's ability to maintain the relative military balance in the Taiwan Strait. In turn, Taiwan's military capabilities vis-à-vis China influence Beijing in its attempts to achieve the reunification of Taiwan. Finally, the political-military situation in the Taiwan Strait reflects domestic and foreign investor confidence in Taiwan's economy. It is significant that the perceptions of these variables are as important, if not more important, than the realities.

A gradual deterioration in Taiwan's military capabilities would not necessarily lead to increased Chinese belligerence in the short- to midterm. Over the long-run (10 years or more), however, Taiwan's vulnerability to Chinese military pressure could increase to where Beijing might be attracted to a policy of military action or even the announcement of a naval blockade, should its peaceful approach prove fruitless.

Certainly a Chinese decision to use military force against Taiwan would take into account considerations beyond Taiwan's defensive capabilities. China has come to recognize the value of a peaceful approach to Taiwan and realizes that belligerence toward Taiwan would adversely prejudice growing relations with the West and Japan. The degree to which Taiwan's armed forces deter Chinese military pressure, therefore, depends on the value one attaches to these external deterrent factors.

While the role of Taiwan's armed forces as a deterrent may be marginal, the implications of any reduction in Taiwan's military strength for its internal political stability may be more immediate. There are several results possible should Taiwan's access to US arms and spare parts be drastically reduced.

A perception that Taiwan's military strength was weakening could threaten the investment climate on Taiwan and concomitantly the economic viability of the island. Given Taiwan's current international status, foreign investors are very sensitive to the Taiwan issue in US-China and China-Taiwan relations. If foreign investors believed that a US security commitment to Taiwan, visible through continuing arms sales, was being drastically diminished, they would be considerably less willing to make long term investments. How long it might take for the impact of a withering investment climate to significantly affect the economic viability of Taiwan is, of course, subject to many other variables. Nevertheless, the incentive for those who could leave the island and remove capital savings would be stronger as the situation deteriorated.

A poor investment climate on Taiwan would likely be accompanied by a feeling of growing vulnerability on the part of senior political and military leaders. Hardliners in KMT and the military would probably feel the need for more repressive domestic policies to prevent domestic political debate over Taiwan's worsening situation from further wracking the country. This would be particularly true immediately following Chiang Ching-kuo's death. Then, hardliners in the military might call for greater restrictions on political activity of Taiwanese based opposition groups and for increased vigilance against "communist subversion." This would only further aggravate already strained relations between the KMT and several activist Taiwanese political groups and, in the extreme, could lead to political instability and domestic violence. As in the case of the Chungli and Kaohsiung riots, the Taiwan Garrison Command and other elements of the military would be called in to restore order and to suppress political dissent.

Further strains in Taiwanese-mainlander relations, coupled with a perception that the mainlander-dominated government was unable to stem the tide of deteriorating US-Taiwan relations likely would threaten the basic strength of the KMT. Even in the absence of domestic violence, the more vocal elements of Taiwan's society, such as the Taiwan Presbyterian Church, would increase their demands for discussion of Taiwan's options—specifically independence and a greater voice for Taiwanese in the Government.

In any event, the military would have to deal with domestic problems. Since 85 percent of its rank and file are native Taiwanese the military's ability to act would be complicated. No one knows how loyal these troops would be if called upon to use violence against large scale or countrywide political agitation against the Government. The military, out of necessity, would have to insure its own integrity while simultaneously taking measures to assure the political integrity of the nation as a whole.

The psychological impact of reduced military capabilities resulting from decreased US arms sales to Taiwan has many potential outcomes. Outlined above is a worst case scenario. Alternative scenarios include the possibility that China and Taiwan can indeed reach a peaceful solution to their longstanding differences. In recent years, indirect trade between China and Taiwan has grown steadily. Scholars, technical experts, and athletes from China and Taiwan have had increasing contacts in international forums, and there have been hopeful statements by both governments. Given sufficient time, there are indications that this process could result in a reconciliation between the two parties. Any meaningful rapprochement between Beijing and Taipei, however, is at least 10 years away. Meantime, most observers agree that the political and military strength of Taiwan's armed forces are major factors in determining which policies both China's and Taiwan's leadership pursue. It is difficult to assess the probability of any specific scenario but it is abundantly clear that the future role of the military is dependent on external influences beyond Taiwan's control.

## Summary and Conclusions

Taiwan's armed forces play a key role in Taiwan's political, economic, and social life. Despite underlying animosities between the mainlander minority and the Taiwanese majority, the armed forces have been transformed from an occupying army to the defenders of Taiwan's value system. United States military assistance and its security commitment to Taiwan have been significant factors in the development of Taiwan's armed forces as an institution, and the deterrence of attack by China.

Three dimensions of the impact the armed forces have on the politics, economy, and society of Taiwan can be readily identified. First, the military is clearly a symbol to foreign investors and the local population of government ability to resist China and to foster the conditions and environment on Tawian for economic growth and social development. Second, because of the military's strength and the relationships between political and military leaders, senior military officers participate in the national decisionmaking process. The military plays a pre-eminent role in internal security and stands ready to tip the balance of power in the struggle for succession to President Chiang Ching-kuo. Third, the armed forces make a large contribution to the economic and social development of Taiwan.

The prospects for Taiwan's armed forces and the future of the island, however, are clouded by external influences beyond Taiwan's control. Termination of the Mutual Defense Treaty and diplomatic recognition by the United States in 1979 permitted Washington to normalize relations with Beijing but continuing US arms sales to Taipei have made Taiwan a constant irritant in US-China relations. Taiwan's legitimacy and authority could be severely threatened if their principal manifestation—the armed forces—are weakened by a reduction in US military sales. Alternatively, growing China-Taiwan indirect trade and China's peaceful approaches to Taiwan suggest it may be possible for them to find a peaceful solution to their longstanding political and military conflict. Meanwhile, the political and military strength of Taiwan's armed forces are major factors in determining which policies both China's and Taiwan's leadership pursue.

## Notes

1. Peng Ming-min, *A Taste of Freedom*, New York: Holt, Rinehart and Winston, 1972, pp. 58-73. For an account of Taiwan's armed forces during this period also see, H. Maclean Bates, *Report from Formosa*, New York: Dutton, 1952. Bates, a journalist, born and raised in China, visited Taiwan in 1951. He provides a fairly good account of the general state of Taiwan's armed forces. Also see George H. Kerr, *Formosa Betrayed*, Boston: Houghton Miffin, 1965. Kerr was US Vice Consul in Taipei in 1947-48 and an eyewitness of the 1947 disorders.

2. Ibid, Peng Ming-min. For a somewhat different view of army-civilian relations on Taiwan also see, John C. Caldwell, *Still the Rice Grows Green*, Chicago: Regnery, 1955. Pages 119-122 noted that army-civilian relations on Taiwan were much better than they had been on the Chinese mainland in the 1940s, and claimed that on Taiwan they had improved greatly since 1951.

3. Ralph N. Clough, *Island China*, Cambridge: Harvard University Press, 1978, p. 97.

4. Foster Rhea Dulles, *American Policy Toward Communist China*, New York: Thomas Y. Crowell Company, 1972, Chapter 10.

5. Ibid, Clough, p. 103.

6. Ibid, Dulles, Chapter 10.

7. Ibid.

8. Ibid, Clough. Also see, Joyce Kallgren, "Nationalist China's Armed Forces." In *Formosa Today*, edited by Mark Mancall, New York: Praeger, 1964.

9. For a good overview of the dynamics of domestic politics on Taiwan see Jurgen Domes, "Political Differentiation in Taiwan: Group Formation Within the Ruling Party and the Opposition Circles, 1979-1980." *Asian Survey* (Berkeley), October 1981, pp. 1011-1028.

# 3

# Japan's Self-Defense Forces

*James H. Buck*

## Introduction

Japan has a long, illustrious military tradition of "such antiquity that it surely precedes history."[1] While military tradition is long, Japan's experience with national military forces is proportionately quite short, but not absolutely so in comparison with the armed forces of most other Asian countries. This chapter is concerned with Japan's contemporary armed forces but the historical development of Japan's armed forces as an institution must include two separate processes of development.

The first occurred with the Imperial Japanese Army (IJA) and the Imperial Japanese Navy (IJN) from 1870 to 1945. The second development was the evolution of the National Police Reserve (1950) into the tri-service, Ground-Maritime-Air Self-Defense Forces (1954), which constitute Japan's armed forces today. These forces have institutionally unique characteristics, and each has differed from the other in very fundamental ways.

Despite the obvious discontinuity caused by defeat and demobilization in 1945, followed by occupation until 1952, the institutional development of the Imperial forces merits brief discussion; not so much because the Imperial Forces are a model for the SDF but rather because they are a constant caution.

## Modern Historical Development (1870–1945)

Emerging in the 1870's from two and a half centuries of self-imposed isolation, Japan faced difficult problems: the development of an effective central government as free as possible from outside interference; forces to control domestic disorders; the study, selection and adaptive use of foreign military experience to form a national military force able to defend the nation; and deciding what criteria would govern civil-military relations.[2]

These tasks were accomplished more or less simultaneously over the first two decades of the Meiji Era (1868–1912). The national military force was manned through a conscription system (1872), a genuinely revolutionary event which destroyed the samurai monopoly on the profession of arms. The conscript IJA suppressed armed domestic rebellions during the 1870's. From this experience and from study of the French and Prussian military systems, the high command was reorganized to provide an independent general staff reporting, on operations and strategy, to the Emperor as Commander-in-Chief. Only the function of military administration (War Ministry) came under civilian control (1879). The Emperor's personal role as C-in-C (*Daigensui*) was specified in the "Imperial Precepts to the Soldiers and Sailors" (*Gunjin Chokuyu*) of 1882. These precepts encouraged loyalty, propriety, valor, fidelity, and simplicity for all military men and the Emperor promised never, as had been the case earlier, to relinquish his command prerogative to his ministers. Memorized and recited by millions of servicemen over three generations, they constituted a succinct code for the Imperial Forces that symbolized the military spirit of new Japan. It sanctified the unique position of the Emperor, focussed and reinforced the values of society and promoted the armed forces as a socializing force so that they became a "post-graduate" school for training conscript civilians in the ethics of society.

It was no accident that conscription and compulsory education were introduced almost simultaneously. The systems were complementary, each reinforcing the socialization of the individual. Respect for the Imperial Institution, patriotism, loyalty, and filial piety were common objectives. Japanese citizens were enjoined in the Imperial Rescript on Education (1890) "should emergency arise, to offer yourselves courageously to the state . . ."

By the 1890's, the Imperial Forces were ready to support national goals and performed effectively in wars against China (1894–95) and Russia (1904–05), in World War I, and in the late 1920's and 1930's on the Asian mainland.

The outstanding characteristic of pre-WWII civil military relations was the ability of the military, especially the IJA General Staff, to monopolize military affairs by a variety of administrative and constitutional devices, and to exclude civil officials, permitting the military to interfere in, and often control, broad areas of domestic and international policy.

It is commonplace to hold the military responsible for Japan's policies in the 1930's which led to defeat and enemy occupation in 1945. Maybe this was due to some constitutional deficiency. Or it may have been as Tojo testified, "We should have risen above the system in which we found ourselves, but we did not. It was the men who were at fault."[3] Perhaps the lesson of World War II, at least for Japan, was that imperial ambition, realpolitik and large military forces are what led it to Hiroshima and Nagasaki. Japan's experience with the institutional development of its armed forces during the first seventy-five years of the modern period is both unhappy and well-remembered.

## Contemporary Period (1945-   )

Allied Occupation policy directed the demobilization of the Imperial Forces, ordered the trial of major war criminals by an international tribunal convened in Tokyo, purged hundreds of thousands of Japanese officials from public office, and sought to eliminate ultranationalism and militarism. The 1945 Constitution imposed by the Occupation contains a unique provision (Article 9) whereby the "Japanese people forever renounce war as a sovereign right of the nation and the threat or use of force as means of settling international disputes." The same article literally obligates Japan never to maintain "land, sea, or air forces as well as other war potential." New constitutional controls were imposed to prevent a recurrence of "militarism": the Diet became the highest organ of state, only civilians could serve as ministers (or premier), and the Cabinet is collectively responsible to the Diet, which controls the budget.

By the late 1940's then, the Occupation denied Japan the right to establish armed forces, and Japan denied itself that right by accepting the constitution. This unprecedented circumstance was abruptly changed by the North Korean invasion of June 1950 and the dispatch to Korea of the four U. S. divisions stationed in Japan.

The Supreme Commander for the Allied Powers (SCAP) ordered Japan to establish a constabulary force (National Police Reserve) of 75,000 personnel in August 1950 to take over the public security function vacated by the departed U.S. troops. This is the origin of Japan's contemporary armed forces.

Augmented by a naval organization in 1952 and an air force component in 1954, the three services were designated the Self-Defense Forces in 1954.

## Organization, Missions, and Constitutional Status of the SDF

The 1954 law which established the Japan Defense Agency (JDA) assigned it the mission "to preserve the peace and independence of Japan, and to protect its security . . . to carry out the administration and supervision of the GSDF, MSDF and ASDF."[4] The JDA is one rank below Ministry and the civilian Director-General ranks as State Minister, not as full Cabinet Member, a significant departure from the prewar government hierarchy. He receives the right of command and control over the SDF from the Prime Minister and provides overall administration.[5] The JDA is organized into six bureaus, each headed by a civilian. Subordinate to the JDA are the three uniformed chiefs of service who constitute the Joint Staff Council (JSC), whose chairman is a fourth general/flag rank officer. This group is the highest military advisory body to the Director-General and is the executive body for carrying out his orders.

The two major missions of the SDF are to deter and/or defend Japan against external attack (*boei shutsudo*) and to assist in the preservation of public security (*chian shutsudo*). SDF public security missions differ from normal public peace preservation which is the responsibility of the police.

Provisions governing SDF mobilization (*shutsudo*) were widely discussed in the press in 1978 when the JSC Chairman, General Hiromi Kurisu, said that the SDF might have to take "supra-legal" action in case of surprise attack on Japan. His remarks seemed to cast doubt on the principle of civilian supremacy; in reality, they focussed attention on apparent defects in the SDF law which forbid the Prime Minister to mobilize them barring prior approval of the Diet.

As the public official with the right to mobilize the SDF for defense, the Prime Minister must, prior to mobilization, first consult with the National Defense Council (SDF Law Art. 62,2), then with the Cabinet, and finally get approval of the Diet. If the emergency arises when the Lower House has been dissolved, the Prime Minister may convoke the House of Councillors (a continuing body which is "closed" when the Lower House is dissolved) and take action with their consent (Constitution, Art. 54). Even this action is provisional pending Diet approval.

Given these procedures, under external attack, front-line commanders would be severely restricted in permissible actions. If foreign troops invade Japan without firing a shot and try to seize SDF weapons or equipment, SDF troops may use their weapons "to a reasonable extent," but are enjoined from "hurting human beings" (SDF Law Art. 95). Conversely, if SDF troops are killed by enemy fire, they then (Art. 37) could presumably return fire against the enemy, but only when "the harm produced by such act does not exceed the harm which was sought to be averted."[6] Not only is the SDF member required to make neat calculations of proportionality but he might later be charged with homicide. This hypothetical situation highlights both the rigid requirements for civil control and the ambiguity faced by the SDF. The matter is under intensive study.[7]

In mobilizing the SDF for its secondary mission of public security, the Prime Minister has no similar procedural restrictions: he may mobilize troops on his own initiative when ordinary police capabilities cannot preserve the public peace, or he may respond to requests from prefectural governors. The Prime Minister has never mobilized the SDF for either of its missions.

The constitutional status of the SDF is ambiguous. Article 9 prohibits the possession of war potential. Yet Japan maintains armed forces. However, according to Japan's 1980 Defense White Paper, "it is indisputably recognized that the provision (Art. 9) does not deny the inherent right of self-defense which Japan possesses as a sovereign nation," and the "government holds the view that there is no constitutional ban on the maintenance of the minimum military strength to exercise this right." It follows that any military strength exceeding the required minimum constitutes "war potential" and is therefore prohibited. Furthermore, weapons of a purely strategic offensive character (ICBMs, long range bombers) are prohibited constitutionally, as is the dispatch of armed SDF troops to a foreign country. Although Article 51 of the UN Charter provides that nothing in it impairs the "inherent right of individual or collective self-defense if an armed attack occurs," the government of Japan takes the position that "Japan is constitutionally banned from exercising the right of collective defense on the ground that the Constitution allows an act of self-defense as far as it is intended to defend Japan's own land and people." It bars Japan from aiding any foreign nation, with which it has close relations, against aggression.[8]

## Japan-US Security Arrangements

In line with these principles, the US-Japan Treaty of Mutual Cooperation and Security (MST) is not a "mutual defense" treaty: an attack on one party is not automatically an attack on the other. An attack against US forces outside Japan does not require Japan to do anything, although an attack against either party on Japanese territory requires both to act to meet the common danger "in accord with its constitutional provisions and processes" (Art. 5). This nonsymmetrical relationship had a sound basis in the political reality of 1952 when Japan was essentially defenseless and the US was militarily committed to containment of the Korean war. There was an implicit and perhaps moral obligation for the US to be responsible for Japan's security, an obligation tacitly undertaken by including Art. 9 in the 1947 Constitution. The MST was actually a *quid pro quo* for the peace treaty which restored Japan's sovereignty. It permitted, and still permits, the US to keep troops and base areas in Japan to provide for US security interests broader than the security of Japan.

According to the JDA, the purpose and value of the MST is deterrence, in that armed aggression by another nation against Japan "would lead to a direct confrontation with the enormous military potential of the US, resulting in substantial sacrifice, a consequence which actively deters aggression against Japan."[9] Japan's role included several successive buildup plans designed to enable the SDF to resist any conventional force invasion until US help could arrive. Authorized personnel strengths for the services are: Ground SDF—180,000; Maritime SDF—37,000; Air SDF—48,000. Defense expenditures rose steadily throughout the past 25 years, from about $800 million in 1957 to about $12 billion for 1984 while personnel strength over the same period increased about five percent.

## Strategic Rationale and Current Disposition

Japanese thinking about defense has generally been to defend Japan against conventional attack. The buildup plans have given the SDF modest capabilities for coastal security, air defense, and ground operation of limited duration. Japan has a tactical doctrine to accomplish these defensive tasks which find their justification in the belief that the Soviet Union constitutes a threat to its security. There are three distinct views of this threat.[10] The Japan Socialist Party and the Japan Communist Party hold that no such threat exists. A centrist view is that the USSR is a potential threat, but is so committed in Europe, Afghanistan and elsewhere that a significant military threat to Japan is unlikely. The third view, held by the government and most members of the dominant Liberal Democratic Party, is that the Soviet Union is a continuing threat, a view reinforced by the Soviet naval buildup in the Pacific and in the Northern Territories.

The ASDF and MSDF are deployed relatively evenly through the four main islands and Okinawa Prefecture. Ground forces (13 divisions composed of 46 infantry regiments) are deployed on the four main islands. This means mutual support and reinforcement of ground combat units would be hazardous and difficult. Therefore, there are relatively heavy ground concentrations in Hokkaido and Kyushu, the two islands most vulnerable to conventional amphibious attack from the Asian mainland.

The strength, organization, mission, and current deployment of the SDF must not be seen as characteristic of an independent free-standing force to deter external attack, or to defeat the attack if invaded but in the context of the MST which has served well the interests of both parties in providing for the security of Japan. The US objective to deter attack against Japan is pursued mostly by the combination of forward deployment in Asia and the strategic deterrent of missiles, bombers, and missile submarines. Japan serves as a rear base and support area for possible ground and air operations elsewhere, and for naval forces in the western Pacific and westward in the Indian Ocean.

Some fundamental problems trouble the generally satisfactory MST arrangements, partly from the different perspectives of the parties. Japan has taken a local or regional and narrow view of Japan's military security, while the US has always seen the defense of Japan in a global context. Japan insists that it must seek "comprehensive security" through political respectability, a by-product of a low-profile low-risk foreign policy, and through economic power.

### Economic Development

The growth of Japan's commerce and industry since the 1950's is one of this century's great success stories. Second only to the US among the non-socialist nations, Japan's GNP in the 1980's is well over one trillion dollars, and the economy sustained a real annual growth rate of 6.1 percent from 1969–1979.

This economic abundance can be traced, in part, to the postwar Occupation policies and to the resiliency and diligence of Japan's business leaders and work force. Others attribute this economic miracle to the fact that Japan, for 30 years, has got by "on the cheap" in defense. That is, by keeping defense expenditures under one percent of GNP, Japan has avoided spending what other nations must spend on defense because the US has provided for it. Nevertheless, Japan ranks about eighth in world defense expenditures.

Japan has the industrial base to produce a wide variety of military equipment. It now produces its naval vessels, including submarines, and ground support jet aircraft as well as the full range of support equipment. But production for SDF use is relatively unimportant according to the JDA, less than 1 percent of motor vehicles and less than 4 percent of ships manufactured in the early 1980's. At the same time 80 percent of aircraft production went to military use since Japan has no significant civil aviation production capacity.[11] Military procurement, perhaps $5 billion annually in the early 1980's, is not vital to its trillion dollar-plus economy. It is likely to remain small considering the domestic requirements and the prohibition of the export of military goods.

Japan could increase its defense expenditures above the "1 Percent Barrier" (of GNP) without harming the general economic welfare of its people. Pressure to do so is coming from members of the US government executive branch, e.g., Secretary of Defense Caspar W. Weinberger during his visit to Tokyo in March 1982.[12] Various resolutions were introduced in the US Congress in the fall of 1981 calling on Japan to "increase its defense expenditures to the level of at least one percent of that country's gross national product" (H. Con. Res. 213). A second resolution (H. Con. Res. 210) called for Japan "to pay an annual security tax to the United States Government equal to 2 per centum of Japan's annual gross national product, to more equitably compensate the United States for expenditures related to carrying out the provision of the United States-Japan Treaty of Mutual Cooperation and Security, and for the security of the free world."[13] Neither passed, and the second gained no Senate sponsor. Such congressional pressures are likely to remain a factor in US-Japan security relations until Japan adopts a more forthcoming defense posture.

## Domestic Political System

Japan's rise to global economic power has occurred in the context of the genuinely representative parliamentary democracy based on the 1947 Occupation-inspired Constitution. The majority party in the Lower House of the Diet selects the Prime Minister, provides all Cabinet Ministers and chairmen of Diet committees. It decides what bills shall become law and conducts Japan's foreign relations. With the consolidation of conservative political elements into the Liberal Democratic Party (LDP) and the coalescing of "progressives" into the Japan Socialist Party (JSP) in the mid-fifties, national politics settled into a pattern.

The LDP has had uninterrupted control of the government since 1955. For all practical purposes, therefore, the LDP has been the government. The LDP defense policy has been that of Japan, and the LDP has consistently supported the MST and SDF.

Japan's defense policy has not had bipartisan or multiparty support. However, the Democratic Socialist Party (DSP), a 20-year-old conservative splinter from the Japan Socialist Party (JSP), and the LDP's more conservative offshoot, the New Liberal Club, now support a "self-reliant defense system" and a vaguely "more responsible role commensurate with our (Japan's) national strength." On the other hand, the JSP, the largest opposition party, continues to advocate abrogation of the MST, although in a more gradualist mode than in the past. By the early 1980s the Komeito (Clean Government Party) seemed to be "shifting from its dovish position to argue that the SDF was not only constitutional but necessary for the protection of the territory."[14] The Japan Communist Party (JCP) favors the dissolution of all military blocs, denunciation of the MST, and advocates nonalignment and neutrality.

Election after election, the LDP has been attacked by its multiparty opposition on the defense issue. At times, the LDP ruled with only the slimmest of majorities, but its fortunes seem to have improved with the US return of Okinawa, termination of the Vietnam war, normalization of relations with the People's Republic of China, and the Soviet buildup in the Pacific coupled with the Soviet invasion of Afghanistan.

The general elections in the early 1980s were again victories for the LDP. The adroit LDP election strategy benefitted as usual from the bumbling opposition parties who speak of coalition against the LDP while revealing, by attacking one another, their inability to coalesce against the common enemy. More than half of the Japanese people were born after 1945, and voters in their 40's and younger have seen throughout their lives continued improvement in their material condition. The Japanese electorate is generally satisfied, without incentive to dismiss the LDP. It seems likely that the LDP will continue to control the government of Japan.

## Civil-Military Relations

Two aspects of civil-military relations need to be considered: (1) the relationship between the government of Japan and the SDF; and (2) the relations between the SDF and the Japanese people.

If the relationship between a government and its armed forces is seen as a continuum ranging from a government totally controlled by its military forces to one totally controlling its military forces, prewar Japan approached the former extreme. Contemporary Japan is close to the latter, and this is by conscious design. The Occupation was charged with two "ultimate objectives": to insure that Japan would not become a menace to the US or to the peace and security of the world, and to establish a peaceful and responsible government. The "authority of the militarists and the influence of militarism" was to be eliminated from Japanese life.[15] Measures to achieve these goals included the complete disarmament and demobilization of Japan, disestablishment of the state religion, enactment of the 1947 Constitution with its "no-war" article 9 and the statement that the Emperor derived "his position from the will of the people with whom resides sovereign power."

Constitutional controls on the military were given specific force with the enactment of the SDF Law in 1954. "Command and control" (*shikikantokuken*) of the SDF is vested in the Prime Minister. On military matters he is advised by the National Defense Council (NDC) which consists of the Deputy Prime Minister; Foreign Minister; Finance Minister; the Directors-General of the JDA, the Economic Planning Agency, and the Scientific and Technical Agency, the Minister of International Trade and Industry (MITI), Chairman of the Public Safety Commission and the Chief Cabinet Secretariat. The NDC is charged by law to consider changes in the authorized strength of the SDF, matters relating to the numbers and types of new equipment, and defense planning which extends over several years or involves large sums of money.[16] Thus, civilian control over defense policy formulation is assured.

Overall policy execution is supervised by the Director-General of the JDA, whose major subordinates are also civilians. The all-military Joint Staff Council is advisory to the Director-General. It may not, on its own initiative, issue orders directly to troop units in time of mobilization: it is the executive body through which the Director-General transmits his orders. Civilian control of the SDF is mandatory and extensive in its safeguards for both defense and public security operations.

The SDF has assiduously cultivated good relations with the people of Japan, most remarkably in disaster-relief missions. Japan is prone to such natural disasters as earthquakes, typhoons, heavy rains, heavy snow, and volcanic eruptions. From 1951 to 1980, the SDF carried out 14,000 relief missions, mobilizing nearly 4,000,000 personnel, to reinforce or repair levees, evacuate personnel, provide emergency medical treatment, and assure water supplies.[17]

Public opinion polls consistently show that SDF efforts in disaster-relief operations are widely recognized, appreciated, and enhance its stature. A 1977 poll[18] showed that 83 percent of the public supports the existence of the SDF, but this support seems to be based significantly on its performance in non-military roles.

## Decisionmaking Processes

Japanese government policy is the policy of the LDP. Decisionmaking is supported by research within the LDP structure, involving individual Diet members. As the policy item is more clearly defined and consensus grows, the idea is processed through the party's Policy Board and Executive Committee for introduction into the Diet. Defense matters are submitted to the National Defense Council whose membership assures that the bureaucratic and other interests of the major ministries are amply represented, both in the meeting and in subsequent public statements.

After consensus is achieved within the LDP, and among the many constituencies which comprise the entire conservative establishment, the defense bill is introduced into the Diet. Until 1981 the Diet had no committees comparable to the US House Armed Services Committee, and so defense legislation was handled by other committees, most importantly the Budget Committee of the Lower House. In 1981 a

Special Committee on Security in the Lower House was authorized and tasked with studying "problems relevant to the Japan-US security treaty and to work out the necessary measures,"[19] but does not have exclusive jurisdiction over defense policy, and the Budget Committee remains dominant.

Once introduced into the Diet, a defense bill becomes subject to direct opposition attack. Although the LDP has the votes to pass defense legislation, it must remain sensitive to opposition pressure and to public opinion. Frequently the opposition is able to impede or delay the passage of legislation.

The extent to which uniformed officers of the SDF directly influence drafting of defense legislation is not clear. No uniformed officer heads any of the six bureaus in the JDA, although uniformed personnel undoubtedly play an important part in drafting the details of policy once it is decided. Their subordination to party and JDA civilian bureaucrats is highlighted by the fact no SDF officer has ever been permitted to testify in the Diet.[20] Nevertheless, high-ranking officers have been able to focus wide public attention on specific defense problems by public statements just prior to "retirement."

Intra-military political dynamics, that is, competition among the services for allocation of resources, has been lacking, or is so well concealed, that it is not a matter of public discussion. It is likely that future allocations among the services will not be challenged publicly by uniformed officers.

### Foreign Policy Objectives

Japan subscribes to the principles of the UN Charter. Its foreign policy objectives include the preservation of peace and the cultivation of a world order in which Japan's development can be facilitated through interdependency, with secure access to raw materials and overseas markets required for its economic health. These objectives are sought through cooperation with or participation in a wide range of global and regional organizations, such as the UN, ASEAN and OECD, and by taking part in the regular economic summit meetings of the major Western democracies. Japan has diplomatic relations with 162 nations. It shares vital values with the Western democracies and their interests are more often congruent than not. Prime Ministers Suzuki and Nakasone, like their recent predecessors, have used the phrase "Japan will be increasingly required to play a role commensurate with its national power,"[21] but this role is likely to have no important military component.

## Defense Policy

Japan seeks global peace and stability under the concept of "comprehensive security," a concept made quite clear in the May 1957 Basic Policy for National Defense. It called for the promotion of international cooperation and efforts for peace, the establishment of a basis for national security through domestic political stability, the gradual establishment of an effective defense capability, and the maintenance of security arrangements with the US.[22]

This Basic Policy has survived major changes in the external environment, such as the US withdrawal from Vietnam in 1972, President Carter's partial withdrawal of US ground forces from Korea, and the abrogation of the US-Republic of China defense pact concurrent with diplomatic recognition of the People's Republic of China (PRC). Japan has been reminded of the role of military force in international politics by the Iran-Iraq war which threatened its oil supply, the Sino-Vietnamese War which threatened the stability of Asia, and Soviet military intervention in Afghanistan.

In assessing the relative power positions of the US and the USSR, the JDA concluded that the Soviet Union now surpasses the US "in certain areas of military strength, including strategic nuclear forces,"[23] and is vitally concerned about the Soviet's "unrelenting efforts throughout the 1960's and 1970's to build up its military power.[24] The JDA holds that Soviet activity "seems to indicate an increasing potential threat to Japan's security." Other areas of concern are Korea, whose "peace and stability have an essential bearing on the peace and stability of Japan which must continue to watch the situation carefully," and the Taiwan Strait about whose important sea lanes Japan is "keenly concerned."[25]

These statements about "potential" threats, "keen concern" and "essential bearing on the peace and stability of Japan" are tentative attempts to articulate some more or less specific reasons for having the SDF. The government has not identified a specific threat to Japan's security in the same way that Israel views the Arab states, or the PRC views the Soviet Union. The absence of generally recognized political and military purposes for the SDF has forced the LDP to proceed cautiously in defense policy. There is no general popular acceptance of the idea that a combat-ready SDF is needed to deter attack or to defend Japan in a real war.

Defense policy is constrained by this lack of a consensus on the proper role of the SDF, a situation attributed to the absence of a common perception of the external world and, following from this, lack of a common agreement on what if anything is needed in the way of a military component in Japan's comprehensive foreign policy.

Secondly, the constitutional status of the SDF remains a problem. Disputes relative to the SDF status have been adjudicated consistently in favor of the LDP position that the maintenance and use of armed force for self-defense is constitutionally permissible, albeit limited. The anomaly deserves public debate, but constitutional amendment comes hard in Japan, requiring approval by a two-thirds majority in both houses of the Diet followed by approval in a popular referendum.

A third factor limiting Japan's defense budget is the so-called "present Barrier," that is, that Japan's defense expenditures ought to be less than 1 percent of the GNP. Holding to such a guideline begs the question. "How much is enough?" is unanswerable so long as a strategy for employment of forces bought with these funds remains undefined. Japan has, indeed, made huge increases in its defense budget; an absolute tenfold increase from 1962 to 1979,[26] without breaking the "1 percent Barrier." This has been possible because of the enormous growth in Japan's GNP. One influential Japanese journalist believes the reluctance to break the barrier results from the Japanese distaste for military matters in general, a lack of strong leadership, a powerful Finance Ministry which holds down expenditures and the belief that the US will defend Japan—and Japan need only rely on the US for its security.[27] Yet powerful voices seek to rupture the barrier, for instance, the prestigious Research Institute for Peace and Security, partly financed by business groups in Japan and led by Masamichi Inoki, former President of the Japan Defense Academy.

Japan's weapons policy is a fourth restraint on the capabilities of the SDF. Japan signed the Nuclear Non-Proliferation Treaty in 1970 and ratified it in 1976. The nation has held fast to the Three Non-Nuclear Principles of no possession, no manufacturing, and no introduction of nuclear weapons into Japan. "Even when some nuclear weapons are considered to be permissible under the Japanese Constitution, Japan has decided never to possess them."[28] With regard to conventional weapons, the MITI in 1976 banned their export.[29]

A fifth constraint on Japan's defense policy is the Mutual Security Treaty. Japan relies on the US strategic deterrent and on the US for support in case of attack against Japanese or US forces on territory under the jurisdiction of Japan. This arrangement provides an "economical" defense for Japan and also increases the security of Japan's neighbors and former enemies to the extent that these nations fear a militarily resurgent Japan. By its very existence, the MST nullifies arguments for a substantially larger SDF with expanded missions, which are now prohibited: e.g., developing any capability to carry air or ground combat operations to foreign soil.

The MST, revised in 1960, was susceptible to revision in 1970 or annually thereafter with one year's notice by either party. Neither government has made any such overture. In March 1982, the "Committee of One Hundred for the Revision of the Japan-US Treaty" held its inaugural meeting in Tokyo. Among the 181 members are 58 Diet members, former diplomats, university professors and businessmen. They seek treaty revision because: (1) the US alone cannot maintain peace and security, nor must Japan continue to rely only on the US for its security; (2) the MST should reflect the growth in Japan's power— from 8 percent of the US GNP in 1960 to 50 percent of the US GNP today; (3) the MST keeps Japan in a protectorate status which is injurious to national pride; (4) increased Soviet power compels the Free World to strengthen its capacity for collective defense; and (5) Japan should shoulder the burden to defend jointly with the US its own sea lanes to the Mid-East.[30]

The government sharply denied any intent to revise the MST,[31] yet the announcement of the committee's program is evidence of the coalescence of some influential persons who want to expand Japan's defense capabilities as a "contributing member of the Western alliance."[32] It is unlikely that the MST will be revised in the next few years. Nevertheless, the committee and its supporters may well add impetus to the changes in US-Japan security arrangements contemplated in the "Guidelines for Japan-US Defense Cooperation" approved by the Japan-US Security Consultative Committee established in 1976.

These guidelines provide:

Japan, as its defense policy, will possess defense capability on an appropriate scale within the scope necessary for self-defense, and consolidate and maintain a posture to ensure the most efficient operation; and assure, in accordance with the SOFA, the stable and effective utilization of facilities and area in Japan by US Forces. The United States will maintain a nuclear deterrent capability, and the forward deployments of combat ready forces and other forces capable of reinforcing them.[33]

To fulfill these guidelines, joint studies are under way in combined operations, logistics, communications, and intelligence to ensure smooth coordination if undertaken. Public information on the substance of these studies is scant, but this consultation has resulted in a considerable increase in joint US-Japan training exercises.

## Net Assessment

The SDF has little effect on Japan's domestic well-being. It does not consume manpower or financial resources in amounts injurious to the domestic welfare. It is neither a divisive nor a unifying social force. The SDF has wide public support, yet there is no consensus on its proper mission or general role in Japanese life. There is highly vocal political opposition to the SDF on the national level, based more on ideological than on economic or social grounds.

In general the limited size and defensive capabilities of the SDF enhance Japan's standing in the international community. Its neighbors need not fear a weak Japan, and Japan has assiduously cultivated the image of a peace-loving people incapable of harming others. Probably Japan's image is enhanced by its defense ties with the US reassuring at least temporarily the ROK, the PRC, and others that the US continues its commitment to peace and stability in East Asia, yet also assuring that there is no rationale for an unsettling increase in Japan's military power. The memory of a militarily predatory Japan has not entirely disappeared from the memories of Asian leaders.

The contemporary role of the SDF in Japan seems likely to endure for several years. The Basic Policy for National Defense adopted in 1957 has served Japan well and the "buildup" plan running through 1987 continues emphasis on quality of manpower and equipment while ruling out significant strength increases. It is unlikely that the SDF will be allotted a much larger portion of the GNP, and its social impact will not differ significantly. This projection assumes no major changes in the domestic or external environment.

On the other hand, a significant alteration of the SDF's role is conceivable, depending on what specific events would cause a fundamental change in the distribution of political power within Japan. Internal events might include the favorite bugbear of the conservatives—natural catastrophe followed by economic crisis and the seizure of power by the leftists. Then a "progressive" government might eliminate the SDF, but it also might decide that a stronger SDF was needed for public safety and defense against another nation seeking to exploit Japan's crisis. Sample external events which might result in a more powerful conservative government and provide incentives for a more powerful SDF with offensive capabilities could include the withdrawal of the US from the western Pacific Basin; Soviet acquisition of an overwhelming naval force in the Pacific and in East and Southeast Asia; renewed war in Korea; or interdiction of the oil route from the Middle East to Japan.

Among foreign nations, the US has consistently favored strengthening the SDF, particularly since the Nixon Doctrine. A stronger SDF would mean a stronger partner under the US-Japan MST and presumably a less expensive commitment to Japan, coupled with greater flexibility for deployment to the Indian Ocean or to the Mid-East for instance, of US forces deployed in the western Pacific. The PRC and the ROK encourage a modest SDF and continuation of US-Japan defense ties, believing the US deterrent adds to their own national security vis-a-vis the Soviet Union and North Korea. Neither the PRC nor the ROK is likely to encourage an augmentation of the SDF to levels which could threaten them. In contrast, the Soviet Union and North Korea would surely prefer a demilitarized and neutral Japan, a circumstance which would enhance their security and lessen materially the power of the US to influence events in East Asia.

The major external influence on the SDF and its role in Japanese society has been the US. The Occupation established the overall "constitution" of contemporary Japanese politics as well as the principles of civilian control of the military. The US created, trained, and equipped the SDF and its predecessor forces. It provides selected individual training and education in the US for SDF officers and men, unit training (live fire practice of SAMs at Ft. Bliss), supplies selected antisubmarine warfare equipment and advanced fighter aircraft, and participates in joint exercises. Influence of broad policy nature can be exerted through the full range of US-Japanese diplomatic and other contacts, including the regular meetings of the Japan-US Security Consulative Committee.

All in all, US influence has been pervasive but Japan remains free to resist or accede to US influence. As the partnership moves closer to a partnership "between equals," we may expect Japan to pursue policies and courses of action selected increasingly on the basis of Japan's national interest.

## Notes

1. Leonard A. Humphreys, "The Japanese Military Traditions," in James H. Buck (ed.), *The Modern Japanese Military System*, Sage Publications, Inc., Beverly Hills and London, 1975; p. 21.

2. For a longer treatment of this topic, see my chapter "Japan," in Claude E. Welch (ed.), *Civilian Control of the Military*, SUNY Press, Albany, 1976.

3. Yale C. Maxon, *Control of Japanese Foreign Policy*, Berkeley, 1957, p. 218, quoting "Interrogation of Hideki Tojo," dated March 19, 1946, partly comprised in Exhibit 3336, Transcript pp. 20626–20632, *IMTFE*.

4. Boei Nenkan Hankokai, *Boei Nenkan 1974*, Tokyo, 1974, p. 201.

5. Ibid., p. 236.

6. Kiyoaki Murata, "Holes in SDF Law," *Japan Times Weekly* (JTW) 5 Aug 78, p. 3. "Joint Staff Council Head Ousted for Remarks on Defense Policy," *JTW*, 5 Aug 78, p. 1.

7. The Japan Times, Ltd., *The Defense of Japan 1980*, Tokyo. Originally published by Japan Defense Agency, pp. 159–161. At the same time "The Defense Agency thus considers that a surprise attack can be effectively countered under the existing law" (p. 160).

8. *Ibid.*, pp. 86-87.
9. JDA, *The Defense of Japan* 1978, p. 60.
10. Lee W. Farnsworth, "Japan in 1981: Meeting the Challenges," in *Asian Survey*, January 1982, Volume XXII, Number 1, p. 58.
11. Donald Kirk, "Japan Wary of Sharing How-To," *Atlanta Constitution*, April 6, 1982, pp. 1D, 3D.
12. "Weinberger Proposes Talks on Defense of Sea Lanes," *Japan Times Weekly (JTW)*, April 3, 1982, p. 1.
13. "Japan's Defense Spending: A Reaction from the US Congress" *JEI Report*, No. 4A Japan Economic Institute, Washington, January 29, 1982.
14. Farnsworth, *op. cit.*
15. "United States Initial Post-Surrender Policy for Japan," dated August 29, 1945.
16. Art. 62 of SDF Establishment Law, quoted in *Boei Nenkan 1974*, p. 200.
17. *Defense of Japan 1980*, pp. 217-222, 312-313.
18. JDA, "Opinion Survey for Analyzing Public Relations," *Defense Bulletin*, Vol. 1, No. 4, Tokyo, Jan. 1978, pp. 3-4.
19. *Defense of Japan 1980*, pp. 215-216.
20. Masaru Ogawa, "Our Times—SDF's Manpower Problem," *JTW*, April 4, 1981, p. 4.
21. For Suzuki's use of the phrase, see "Suzuki Foresees Greater Global Role for Japan," *JTW*, Jan. 9, 1982, p. 2.
22. Japan Defense Agency, "Defense of Japan—White Paper on Defense (Summary)," *Defense Bulletin*, Vol. V, No. 1, Oct. 1981, p. 14.
23. *Ibid.*, p. 7.
24. *Defense Bulletin*, Vol. IV, No. 2, Oct. 1980, pp. 2-3.
25. *Defense Bulletin*, Vol. V, No. 1, Oct. 1981, pp. 11-12.
26. *Defense of Japan 1979*, p. 228.
27. Nasu Kiyoshi, "Dilemmas of Japanese Defense," *Asian Affairs*, Vol. 6, no. 2 (Nov-Dec, 1978), pp. 112-113.
28. *Defense of Japan 1980*, p. 87.
29. John Endicott, "The Defense Policy of Japan," in Douglas J. Murray and Paul R. Viotti, *The Defense Policies of Nations*, The Johns Hopkins Press, 1982, p. 454.
30. Kiyoaki Murata, "Revising the Treaty," JTW, March 27, 1982, p. 3. "Security: It is Time for a Stronger Japan," *Wall Street Journal*, April 19, 1982, p. 27.
31. "Miyazawa Says Gov't Not Planning to Revise Security Pact with U.S.," *JTW*, March 13, 1982, p. 1.
32. Masaru Ogawa, "Our Times—Committee of One Hundred," *JTW*, March 20, 1982, p. 3.
33. See *Defense of Japan 1980*, pp. 287-294.

# 4

# The Societal Role of the ROK Armed Forces

*Edward A. Olsen*

How important is the role of the Republic of Korea (ROK) armed forces in South Korean society? The answer is so obvious the question seems rhetorical. Clearly it is very important. This is particularly true of the ROK Army, the institutional base for Seoul's two armed coups. The governments which emerged from those coups, the Park Chung-hee administration (1961-1979) and the Chun Du-hwan administration (1980-present), bear the clear imprint of the armed forces. The judgment regularly reached by both friendly and critical observers of the South Korean scene is that the Republic of Korea is under a military regime. While that opinion is largely true, it is overly facile because it implies the condition is long-standing and permanent. The former is not true and the latter is doubtful. These assertions will be examined in detail here in evaluating this chapter's main contention: the major role of the armed forces in South Korean society since 1961 is not in harmony with Korean traditions and may well prove to be a temporary phenomenon.[1]

### The Development of the ROK Armed Forces

When American occupation forces entered the Korean peninsula in 1945, liberating the area from Imperial Japan, the society it found was in disarray. Japanese colonial policy, aggravated by the exigencies of war, left Korean society plagued by political anarchy and economic backwardness. No segment of Korean society was more subject to this malaise than the armed forces.

In neither half of the Korean peninsula were there any appreciable indigenous armed forces. Japanese colonial policy discouraged Korean prowess in military affairs as a means to keep the Koreans subjugated. Only four types of military experience existed among Koreans: (1) individuals who had served with the Japanese armed forces and colonial police, generally at low levels; (2) those who took up small arms against the Japanese; (3) those who had served with either Chinese or Soviet forces; and (4) those possessing martial arts skills. Little of this "expertise" was of the sort needed by a modern armed force.

Reinforcing this existing weakness was the overwhelmingly civilian orientation of traditional Korea's Confucian culture. Only infrequently throughout Korean history had the armed forces played a major role, although there were wars and revolutions led by men in uniform. However, after they succeeded, these military leaders quickly donned mufti and ruled as full-fledged civilians. This role reversal was mandated by the accepted mores in Korean society. Its Confucian societal hierarchy prohibited the armed forces from playing a truly dominant role.

This combination of legacies from Korea's Confucian heritage and its colonial experience left Korea desperately unprepared for national security responsibilities at the end of World War II. The division of Korea into rival regimes by postwar international political decisions did nothing to improve either Korea's preparedness. Though mathematically illogical, the division of zero defense capabilities into two Korean halves seemed to produce less than nothing.

Since poor conditions existed in both Koreas, they started out on an apparently equal footing militarily. However, the North Koreans enjoyed some strategic advantages over the South Koreans. They possessed a better industrial infrastructure left by the Japanese, a smaller population which harbored fewer refugees and, therefore, was more easily disciplined, and had a foreign advisor with some reasonably well-defined goals for Korea.

Moscow's intentions in North Korea, and the ominous nature of developments there, quickly became apparent to officials in Washington and Seoul. However, the proper response was far less clear to either Washington or Seoul. Washington fostered the creation and tentative growth of the fledgling Republic of Korea, but was anything but solidly behind its protege. Washington's Korea policy was essentially a holding action and helped create a variety of governmental and societal institutions that a sovereign state should possess. None of the them were terribly successful, least of all the novice ROK armed forces.

When the Korean war erupted in 1950 the ROK armed forces were pitifully ill-prepared to cope with aggression from the North. The United States was even less ready to fight a war in Korea. Some would argue that American willingness to exclude Korea from the United States' regional security perimeter was a *de facto* invitation to communist aggression. Under pressure, Washington rapidly reassessed the situation in terms of a broader cold war threat to the United States' new national interest in Western Europe and Japan. Aggression could be neither tolerated nor rewarded, lest some pre-domino theory "dominoes" really be threatened. Washington's reassessment produced a set of American commitments to Northeast Asian security and, as a corollary, to bolstering South Korea's position in a network of regional alliances. A major part of Washington's effort was the crash program to create a truly viable and powerful set of armed forces in the Republic of Korea. The United States enjoyed great success in this endeavor.

Despite the pressures of war, the United States was able to train and equip substantial allied South Korean forces. From 1950 to the 1953 truce the armed forces of the Republic of Korea increased from about 100,000 to almost 650,000, accomplished by the most difficult sort of on-the-job training imaginable: military training under fire. The exigencies of the circumstances offered one invaluable advantage; they provided very tangible incentives to learn quickly and thoroughly. The imminence of external communist aggression tended to focus, rather acutely, the attention of both American advisors and South Korean students on the task at hand.

After the truce was signed in July 1953 the United States and the Republic of Korea entered a decade of even more pronounced and coordinated tutelage. The United States became South Korea's mentor and the American model—the paradigm for South Korean politics, economics, and security. From 1953 to 1961 the lessons seemed to be penetrating quite well. The Rhee government enjoyed a semblance of American-style democracy, kept its fiscal head above water (thanks to American economic assistance), and dispatched numerous uniformed Koreans for advanced instruction at U.S. military training facilities.

This scenario soured at the turn of the decade. Rhee's preoccupation with the false facade of American-style democracy was akin to rearranging the deck chairs on the Titanic. South Korea's economy had stagnated, aggravating a wide range of domestic social complaints. The first wave of successful dissent emanated from a traditional source, militant young intellectuals agitating for reform, backed discreetly by voices in the military. Their success in ousting Rhee with American tacit support produced another spontaneous and traditional response: the spawning of numerous political heirs apparent. During the short-lived Chang Myung government (August 1960–May 1961), there seemed to be some improvement on the political front, albeit often chaotic, but the economy faltered. In response to these developments the ROK military began to express more pointed criticism. In effect, certain elites in the South Korean armed forces perceived the disintegration of the national commonweal and tendered an ultimatum to Seoul's civilian political elite to "shape up or we will ship you out."

Had the civilian hierarchy had more time they might have been able to lead South Korea back from the economic-political abyss they confronted in 1961. However, some in the military perceived "time" as deadly momentum toward chaos. Led by Park Chung-hee and his key aide, Kim Jong-pil, a group of "young Turks" in the ROK Army decided to forestall the approaching disaster.

### Military Rule in South Korea

The Park coup ushered in the direct and indirect military rule in South Korea which persists to this day. Conventional wisdom, whether critical or supportive of Seoul, lends credence to two theories: (1) military rule was well planned from the outset; (2) military rule was influenced decisively by the United States, also from the outset. Though both theories enjoy periodic credibility, they are basically myths.

Military rule in South Korea can be considered well planned only with the benefit of hindsight. Park did not seize power or implement that power with a well-defined game plan. On the contrary, Park and his followers succeeded so well because of their relative lack of preconceived notions. They wanted for South Korea what the Rhee and Chang governments were unable to provide: stability, prosperity, and national strength. In pursuit of that goal Park, unlike his predecessors, was not preoccupied with means or methods mandated by either Korea's Confucian legacy or Seoul's American mentors. So, Park initiated experimentation in economics, politics, and administration. Initially, these experiments were ad hoc, pragmatic and incremental. If it worked, it was adopted; if it did not, it was not. That the most successful aspects of these experiments evolved into formal programs for modernization does not mean that the military elite had a clear vision at the outset.

Despite the satisfaction enjoyed by many U.S. officials at South Korea's myriad successes since 1961, objectively there is little reason for credit to accrue to Americans. Neither is the United States to blame for the shortcomings of South Korea since Park's takeover. Much of what South Korea has done since 1961 resulted from South Korean initiative and manipulation. The United States' role was supportive in many ways, but always tangential to the dynamic situation evolving in South Korea.

Though the tenuous nature of the U.S. inspiration for South Korean actions is evident on many fronts, nowhere is it more apparent than in the military model. There is little justification for assuming that the superficial similarities between the U.S. and ROK armed forces (in terms of uniforms, equipment, training, organization, and common strategic goals) translate into great U.S. intellectual or cultural influence over South Korea's military elite. On the contrary, there is much evidence that the ROK military elite behaves according to a largely un-American code of behavior.

The rigorous levels of discipline in the ROK forces bear no similarity to their American counterparts. The rigid sense of hierarchy and the blatant perquisites accorded to rank are quite un-American. Command authority is far more entrenched and sanctified in the ROK forces than in their ostensible U.S. mentor. Correspondingly, rank-and-file initiative is far less tolerated or rewarded in the ROK forces than their U.S. counterparts. These well-known characteristics of the ROK armed forces put them in sharp contradistinction to U.S. forces. Instead they bring to mind prewar Japan's armed forces,[2] and that similarity is not accidental. Despite the great material influence of the United States over the ROK armed forces, the preponderance of spiritual, ethical, and psychological influence derived from the training that many in the first generation of ROK military elite received from their Imperial Japanese military and colonial police mentors. That generation, including Park, transmitted their Japanese-inspired ethos to their successors. Clearly, the ROK armed forces are the last organized enclave of that *bushido* spirit. The impact of this ironic cultural transferal of military ethics has been pervasive. It enabled the ROK armed forces to do things and influence their society in ways that seemed unthinkable against the backdrop of traditional Korean culture. What they did and how well they succeeded will be addressed in the following sections.

## Strategic Rationale

The ROK armed forces could not have assumed the importance they hold in South Korea today if there had not been some valid reason for their existence. In their case, with the threat of North Korean aggression an ever-present reality, there is no doubt about the need for substantial armed forces. Unlike other Third World examples of a military elite perpetuating itself long after the rationale for its existence had atrophied, the ROK military elite's strategic rationale is alive and well.

Poised against the estimated 784,000-man forces of North Korea, the ROK has approximately 622,000 active duty personnel.[3] They are deployed almost exclusively in defensive and counterinsurgency postures against the Northern threat. Given the short distances involved (to use a well-known analogy; if Washington were Seoul, enemy forces would be in the Maryland suburbs), there is little trouble maintaining either the fighting spirit of the forces or popular backing for their military mission. Even South Korean critics of some of the ROK military elite's societal actions taken over the years are stalwart backers of that elite's strategic rationale. For virtually all South Koreans the logic of that rationale is beyond reproach.

## Political Relations[4]

The involvement of the ROK armed forces in a variety of political actions unquestionably has roused the greatest controversy surrounding their activities and is the clearest example of actions which emulate their pre-war Japanese model rather than their contemporary American mentors. Until the 1961 coup U.S. officials were inclined to view the ROK military as smaller versions of the American military. An incidental by-product of the extensive American training provided ROK forces in Korea and the United States was exposure to American-style civil-military relations. Numerous South Korean personnel experienced such contacts and there was a widespread assumption by American officialdom that the civic lessons had been absorbed by the ROK forces.

The 1961 coup d'etat confronted Americans with an unsettling reality: Seoul-style civil-military relations were not made in America. Official and popular U.S. reaction to the Park coup was a mixture of unhappiness and disappointment. Americans tended to feel let down by a group who seemed to have broken their implied promise. Only when the Park coup transformed itself into the more-or-less civilian Park government, with no signs of being a transitory phenomenon, did the United States adjust to the inevitable. In time, Washington became accustomed to the political prominence of military or ex-military figures in its South Korean ally. Some Americans even went so far as to praise the ROK military for their wisdom and skill in light of their subsequent accomplishments. However, despite a certain ambivalence, the enduring American view of South Korea's military-influenced leadership is that it would have been, and would still be, better for bilateral relations had the ROK military adhered to US-style civil-military relations. Out of this fundamental difference of opinion have grown a number of other bilateral controversies encompassed by the umbrella term "human rights."

The ROK military and ex-military have been quite willing to stand up to United States and other foreign pressures to reform South Korean civil-military relations and the military's role in domestic politics. In a perverse way, rejecting these external pressures on South Korea has evolved into a vehicle for Seoul's military-influenced elite to demonstrate its independence and nationalistic credentials. As a result of Seoul's rejection of these foreign pressures, South Korea's domestic political dynamics became increasingly complicated.

Since the Park coup the ROK army has been a key actor in South Korean politics. The ROK Air Force and Navy have remained far more apolitical. The ROK military grasped well the Maoist's political dictum that "power grows out of the barrel of a gun," conveniently ignoring the rest of that dictum, "and the party shall control the gun." Based on the ability of ROK Army units in the vicinity of Seoul to either take over the government by force, or threaten to do so, military or ex-military leaders connected to those powerful units exert tremendous direct and indirect influence over South Korean politics.

The direct influence of the military in ROK politics has taken one of three forms. The most glaring of these have been Seoul's two coups, led by Generals Park Chung-hee and Chun Du-hwan. Both men presented themselves as secular saviors, possessed of the correct ingredients to save the day and rescue South Korea from the cruel fate they saw on the horizon. Thanks to armed force and to an old-boy network of military and ex-military associates, both carried out successful coups. These military coups set the parameters for South Korean politics in the years since.

On several occasions in the 1960s, 70s, and 80s the Park and Chun governments resorted to martial law when political conditions seemed on the verge of getting out of hand. Most of the antigovernment unrest was civilian (students, clergy, labor, etc.) agitation protesting the actions and policies of the military-influenced government. Consequently, the periodic imposition of martial law by the "civilian" governments in Seoul is really just a reversal to a more basic mode of control characteristic of coups in their early stages. This tool and its ever-present availability serves to underscore the essential power of the armed forces in South Korean politics.

A widespread, if more benign, manifestation of the ROK military's direct role in South Korean politics is the large number of ex-military officers who became politically active either shortly after one of the coups or shortly after they retired from active duty. The career pattern of any of the ROK cabinets in the past twenty years underscores this very graphically. National Assembly membership rolls also bear out this pattern while in the "kitchen cabinets" of Park and Chun this trend is even more evident. The indirect influence of the military in South Korean politics is pervasive but more difficult to evaluate. The armed forces' presence on all fronts (strategic, political, economic, etc.) is so overwhelming that they appear to gain influence simply by sheer numbers and position. This might be considered influence by osmosis. A more purposeful form of indirect political influence in South Korean society occurs via the military's many paramilitary organizations. These take the form of ROTC, scouting, and rural-based home guards, organizations which serve legitimate purposes as well as indoctrinating impressionable sectors of South Korean society.

Critics of the ROK military's sometimes heavy handed presence tend to treat South Korea's military elite as a monolithic entity, single-mindedly bent on dominating the country. It would be easy, but probably unwise, to join those critics. Though it is difficult to get a firm reading of intra-military political perceptions, the Seoul rumor mill's frequent speculation about which military faction is up and which is down, which commanders are disgruntled enough to consider staging a coup, and the identities of hard-liners and moderates, clearly belies the image of the ROK military elite as even remotely monolithic. The fluctuations of specific factions are too time-sensitive to be germane to a study of this sort. Similarly, predictions about likely fomentors of political coups seem irrelevant, particularly since many rumors seem designed largely to undercut some faction's rival.

However, the repeated mention of hard liners and their rivals within the ROK military is worthy of analysis. This division can be traced back to Park's coup, when some Korean military leaders did seem to prefer the American-style civil-military relationships to which they had been exposed. Since then there have been numerous candid South Korean officers who told their American counterparts that they felt uncomfortable with the political activism of their seniors. Many, probably the great majority of the ROK armed forces, are distinctly apolitical. This is most obvious in the ROK Navy and Air Force. In large part, this can be attributed to prudence, but some of that reluctance to become involved may also reflect genuine doubts about the existing civil-military relations in South Korea.

There is also another, even less frequently mentioned, aspect of the hard-soft line divisions within the ROK military. Despite the image of Park and Chun and their followers as relatively hard-nosed characters, there is strong reason to consider them as centrists/moderates on the ROK military's scale of values. Evidence of this had been rumored before President Park's assassination. During his assassin's trial there was much discussion of the ultra hard liners. In fact, the assassination seems to have taken place in part to preempt the ultra hard liners from having Park crack down on political activists. The role of President Chun in the wake of the assassination and his accession to office remains controversial, but he appears not to have been either an ultra hard liner or a relative liberal, entering office as a self-chosen compromise.

Since neither the ROK military nor civilian elites encourage polling of their attitudes toward controversial issues, it is impossible to know where the current active duty and ex-military elites stand on these issues. However, from circumstantial evidence (i.e., persistent rumors that the government's main threat remains intra-military, supported by a number of personnel reshuffles) it is likely that President Chun is caught in the same political bind that enveloped President Park. Both leaders depended on the military for their access to power, their maintenance in office, and their prospects for successfully implementing a broad range of essentially civilian programs. In effect both Park and Chun were trapped by the system that produced them. Once they civilianized their regimes both Park and Chun discovered their continued reliance on a military power base was akin to riding on the back of a tiger. It is very difficult to control the beast or get off safely. It is in these terms that the ROK Army is frequently referred to as the only "party" that really counts in South Korean politics. President Chun, like Park before him, operates with ROK military leaders looking over his shoulder always ready to intervene if they are dissatisfied with the way things are going.

This aspect of the military's participation in ROK politics clearly needs further study. Having used their armed clout to foist themselves on a pre-existing civilian-oriented Confucian political system, altering that system in the process, how could any South Korean ex-military political leader undo what had been done? Though there is no single answer to that question, we shall return to it after reviewing other pertinent aspects of the military's role in contemporary South Korea.

## Economic Relations[5]

When the military first seized power in South Korea there was widespread concern about the country's economic prospects. Admittedly, the Republic of Korea was in dire economic straits at the time, but many feared the military would only make things worse, unable to visualize the highly bureaucratized South Korean military elite managing any economy effectively.

How did the ROK military manage to put the Korean economy on the track to the great success it has achieved in the intervening years? They did it by being pragmatic and using the best available to them regardless of the source. After a few false starts in the early 1960s the military-backed political elite under President Park admitted what their critics knew: the military did not have adequate economic skills for the stupendous task at hand. Having recognized that shortcoming they opted to bring on board, as a sort of second level elite, the first wave of economic technocrats—people who would resolve economic problems without regard for the political legitimacy of the military hierarchy. This is not to suggest that the elite took a hands-off attitude toward South Korea's economic problems. On the contrary, they became active senior partners, assigning themselves tasks they could manage. There were three essential tasks assumed by the elite: rebuilding a national commitment to succeed, helping to create the societal and material infrastructure so necessary to economic success, and maintaining the security necessary to enable everything else to proceed in safety.

The military-backed elite worked fitfully toward creating the national esprit needed to rebuild their country. When they found that capricious exhortational orders did not penetrate the ennui of a civilian society numbed by decades of abuse and mismanagement, the elite gradually revamped their approach in an attempt to rebuild the values of Korea's past. From the mid-1960s the elite stressed a variation of Korea's traditional Confucian virtues: diligence, frugality, loyalty, group identity, studiousness, and obedience to societal constraints. Following years of Japanese and American induced neglect of these traditional virtues, which had produced a certain amoral quality in Korean popular culture, the reemphasis on old verities amounted to reacculturalizing South Korean society by total immersion. Since Confucian values had never really atrophied, and the South Korean people were primed and starved for a measure of moral discipline, it is not surprising that these values met with a receptive audience.

Had the military-backed elite stressed Korea's true Confucian values they would have stirred trouble for themselves. Those values are largely civilian in orientation, relegating the military to the lower end of the well-defined and regulated pecking order, Korea's Confucian traditions being very orthodox. Instead of stressing this Confucian value system, the elite introduced a subtle change. Without fanfare, the elite put itself at the top of the new society's hierarchy. Two bases for this change are evident. One is an admission and acceptance by the military of the obvious; they are on top, so why not admit it, at least by implication.

The other basis for the shift is arguable and far more emotionally controversial. As part of its program to invigorate the ROK's economy the Park government certainly borrowed from Japan's developmental experience but the extent of the borrowing is debatable. The borrowing is far more extensive than many South Koreans are prepared to admit because of their antipathy toward Japan. The ROK's development model from the mid-1960s displays many parallels with both Meiji and postwar Japan. Perhaps the clearest expression of Park's intent was his usage of the term "Yushin" (revitalization) to symbolize Korea's moral and material renaissance. "Yushin" is the Korean pronunciation of "Ishin," as in Meiji "Ishin" (restoration). Though the English translation of this identical word differs in each context, Park's intention to revitalize or restore Korea's values by emulating Japan was clear. Park's plan for South Korea was an odd mixture of old and new Japanese developmental experiments, in a time-compressed form. Most of these borrowings are beyond the scope of this paper, but one is central to the role of the

ROK military in Korea. Along with many other imports from Japan since the 1960s, which South Koreans have been reluctant to acknowledge, Seoul borrowed a measure of Japanese-style Confucian theory, enabling the military-backed hierarchy to explain their societal and political prominence.

The extent to which this was planned or came about as an unavoidable part of a larger development model probably will never be known. The latter was likely the case. Despite the substantial training and influence received from Imperial Japan by the ROK's first generation military elite and their friendliness toward things Japanese (as compared to other groups in Korean society), they too remained essentially antagonistic toward Japan. It is doubtful that the ROK military consciously planned to emulate the prewar Japanese military by copying their view of the proper social order a state should enforce, yet that is what they have done. The ROK armed forces, and the government they back, bear a striking resemblance to their counterparts of the late 1930s in Japan. Clearly this analogy cannot be stretched too far, since there also are parallels with postwar United States and Japan. However, the analogy with prewar Japan and the volatility inherent in drastically altering civil-military values have some dangers associated with them to which we shall return.

Clearly, the military-backed political elite succeeded in rebuilding South Korea's ethic to succeed. An esprit, a drive, was infused in South Korean society that was not evident before President Park initiated his campaign combining moral rearmament with ethnic pride. Though this effort continues now that the ROK has made substantial progress, in the early stages of its development it helped in the massive rebuilding of the ROK's infrastructure. The less tangible aspects of that infrastructure, the societal and psychological network of supports that motivate any successful society, were the products of Park's spiritual campaign.

But the military also played an important role in bolstering the material infrastructure of the state. Armed forces generally are seen as a drag on the economy of the state that sustains them, which in a certain sense is true. However, there is another side to that story. Armed forces can play a very positive economic role, especially in developing countries. In the case of South Korea the armed forces initially played an important economic role by helping to construct facilities which contributed to the economic well-being of the country: railroads, roads and bridges. Perhaps even more important than the concrete artifacts they produced, were the training and confidence gained from these projects. Given the large numbers who have passed through the ROK's forces, many relatively skilled civilian workers have emerged from the uniformed ranks to help the ROK economy grow and prosper.

Still more important, if sometimes of questionable ethics, are the number of retired high-ranking officers who have become economic entrepreneurs. They adapted the technical and administrative skills they learned in uniform to the private sector. Ethical questions arise when these people use their former connections via old-boy ties and, in some cases, reportedly used ill-gotten funds to finance their entrepreneurial ventures. Still, on balance these contributions of the military and the ex-military to South Korea's material infrastructure are quite important to the ROK's economic well-being.

Finally, there can be no doubt that all the ROK armed forces have done their duty well in protecting South Korea from the dangers of a second North Korean attack. Despite North Korea's proximity and bellicosity, the ROK armed forces—helped by U.S. forces, but essentially on their own—have provided an atmosphere of stability sufficient to warrant solid foreign business confidence in the security of trade and investment. That is a very significant achievement, one to which the healthy South Korean economy owes a great debt.

### External Relations

In no sector has the impact of the ROK armed forces been greater than in South Korea's external relations. Since the ROK's creation, it has been known to much of the world as a client state of the United States. Since the Park coup, and despite the many bilateral disagreements when Seoul went its own way, the image persists of South Korea being an American "puppet." The periodic bilateral tensions attest to the spuriousness of those allegations. However, and despite South Korea's great economic success, the ROK is dependent on the United States to a substantial degree, largely attributable to the ROK military's role in setting the agenda for Seoul.

The essential factor for Seoul in the past, and for the foreseeable future, is keeping the American commitment to South Korean security as firm as feasible. This is the sum of Seoul's foreign and defense policies. Though Seoul's relations with Pyongyang and Tokyo are potentially more important, they are shaped by its need to keep the United States as a barrier fending off the North and a buffer moderating the influence of Japan.

If a purely civilian government existed in Seoul, there might be some incentive to explore new and innovative relationships with North Korea, Japan, and China which could guarantee South Korea's place as effectively—perhaps more effectively—than the current heavily armed stalemate. However, that government does not exist. The one in Seoul is heavily committed to preserving the status quo. Ostensibly, Seoul and

Washington support their stances for reasons of Realpolitik. There seems to be no other prudent choice valid today for Washington, though there are alternatives.[6]

For Seoul, however, the reasons to support the status quo are more complicated. As a government installed by force, supported in important ways by the military, and fearful and distrustful of alternative means of preserving the peace, it would be foolish, possibly suicidal, for Seoul not to reinforce the status quo at every opportunity. Only two outcomes could emerge from Seoul's turning against the status quo: either a new coup or a civilian government. Since neither outcome would include the powers that hold office today both are highly unlikely.

As long as the political and economic hierarchies in South Korea remain dependent on the military to retain their status there is little prospect of major changes in the ROK's foreign or defense policies. The external relations of South Korea are very static. When one hears of Seoul exploring new ties with China, the Soviet Union, or other heretofore off-limits states, it should always be viewed in the context of South Korea's essentially ultra conservative, military-oriented, and status quo world view.[7] Seoul may make a few incremental changes if it thinks such changes will not influence Washington's perception of bilateral commitments. The dilemma for Seoul is two-fold: not only can it not afford to violate the interests of its domestic military backers, it cannot do anything which might seem to authorize the United States to reduce its vigilance in Korea. If Seoul becomes too flexible, it fears signaling Washington that American flexibility on sensitive issues will be well received in Seoul. The military-backed political elite in South Korea is not prepared to do that any more than it is prepared to jeopardize its domestic support. However, none of these constraints on South Korean initiatives necessarily preclude greater flexibility and innovation in U.S. policy toward Korea should evolving U.S. interests suggest such a shift.

## Ideology and Decisionmaking

South Korea is a state which places great importance on its anticommunist and Confucian traditionalist credentials. Lumped together, these two strands of South Korea's contemporary value system make a potent combination. The conservatism of one reinforces the conservatism of the other. This combination also has produced a seeming anomaly: a dynamic society with great economic and social mobility, but constrained by the external and internal political realities of military-backed rule. There are substantial social freedoms in South Korea, certainly far more than in North Korea. Similarly, there are improving material rewards available to the industrious South Korean people. These, too, far surpass anything available to North Koreans. Seoul's political elite is fond of pointing out these disparities and the greater political freedoms enjoyed in the South than the North. This, too, is true, but it does not tell the whole story.

While other rights and privileges in South Korea have kept rough pace with the progress being made by South Korean society as a whole, the masses do not have significant access to the reins of power. Real power is essentially in the hands of a military-oriented hierarchy. This seemed to be shifting somewhat in the late 1970s as the Park government acknowledged tacitly the growing power of the civilian economic technocrats in the future of the country.[8]

Unfortunately, the Park assassination reversed what seemed to be an emerging trend. With the advent of the Chun government the military was again in ascendancy. Decisionmaking once more revolves around an oligarchy of ex-military old-boys whose chain of command stretches into both the uniformed ranks and the public and private bureaucracies. Despite the presence of numerous competent individuals from civilian backgrounds and some semblance of a credible political opposition, the core political figures and decisionmakers in Seoul today remain military-oriented. This centralized command and decisionmaking apparatus causes problems for South Korea's future that will be addressed in the concluding paragraph.

## Prospects and Options

The role of South Korea's armed forces is a paradox. Seoul is often criticized for being a military dictatorship. It is not, though it has verged on that condition during its coups. However, South Korean culture has spawned a strongly military-influenced authoritarian state. It is criticized with considerable justification on those grounds. Much of that criticism postulates models of how Korea should be if it could only reduce the influence of, or shed, its military-oriented leaders. This sounds fine and reads well until it is juxtaposed with the vital roles these same military-oriented leaders played and still play in South Korea. Without such leaders the ROK would not be what it is today, for better as well as worse. Consequently, it is hard to avoid concluding that the military in Korea have, on balance, served a useful purpose. This is not meant to justify their excesses but to be objective about their overall utility. Despite the significant domestic turmoil that has arisen sporadically in response to military-influenced rule in Seoul, the military has generally advanced the domestic well-being of South Korea.

They also have preserved South Korea's security and stability. Despite their effectiveness, and perhaps because of the means they used to be so effective, the overall image of ROK military rule remains negative. To many, South Korea is on a par with other right-wing military dictatorships around the world. Though South Korea does not deserve many of the epithets hurled at it (particularly if North Korea is left unscathed by those doing the hurling), it receives them anyway.

Much of this paradox and the dilemmas associated with it would be eliminated if South Korea reverted to truly civilian rule. If this happened gradually and at the direction of the existing power wielders, the impact probably would be salutary. In all likelihood the South Korean people are capable of managing their own political and other affairs with a more representative and pluralistic form of civilian government. There seems little real danger of South Korean society backsliding toward the quasi-anarchy feared by the military-backed elites. The South Korean people are too sensible and mature to permit that to happen. The best indicator of their maturity was the public calmness during the post-assassination period.

Despite this prognosis, there is little likelihood of the military-backed authorities yielding their power anytime soon. They do not recognize any incentives for such action. The only remote prospect I see of a dramatic change in the military's role in South Korean society is as a result of external intervention.

Such intervention could result from a coordinated decision on the part of one of South Korea's two major allies: the United States or Japan. Either could happen, but neither is likely. The United States does not want to risk tampering with success and Japan is very wary of doing anything to Korea. Moreover, both allies basically are content with the status quo.

Despite the high probability of continued military-based rule, there remains an undercurrent of discontent in South Korean society about the propriety of strong military influence in political and economic affairs. The incorporation of a very un-Korean intellectual concept with its roots in Japan (a military dominated Confucian hierarchy) is like a time bomb. Few Koreans, even in the armed forces, are comfortable with this aspect of existing political legitimacy. This dissatisfaction threatens the long term stability of any military-backed regime in Seoul. South Korean society cannot undo what the military has crafted without reassessing the entire nature of their society. This may never happen. If not, future historians probably will see Korean society as having forded a fundamental watershed in the 1960s.

However, never before in Korean history has the military been able to maintain such a tight and lasting grip on the reins of power. It seems unlikely to last this time either. Though making predictions is a risky business, I will venture that, if and when South Korean society rejects its military-backed leaders, it will come as a result of inadvertent "external intervention." I can visualize a scenario of recurrent anti-foreignism, focusing on domination by big powers. The United States might be the target, but this is unlikely given the fundamental necessity for the leadership in Seoul to keep on good terms with Washington. A far more likely and well-worn target is Japan.

Denouncing and attacking Japan is a longstanding and popular hobby of Koreans. Periodically the leaders in Seoul find it convenient to use frustration with Japan as a safety vent. The Japanese reciprocate in kind. There is no sign that the rapport created between President Chun and Prime Minister Nakasone in each's epochal visit to the other's country in 1983 and 1984 introduced any fundamental change. Kept within the well defined parameters established by Seoul and Tokyo, such mutual enmity is useful for bilateral reasons and as an excuse for U.S. consumption, rationalizing why closer ROK-Japan cooperation is impossible. There is, however, a danger that this tactic could backfire on Seoul's leaders. If anti-Japan sentiment, with memories stretching back to the colonial era, ever becomes identified in the Korean public's mind with the military's borrowing from the Japanese model and their cooperation with Tokyo in the 1960s, 70s, and 80s, there is no telling what reactions might be generated by the South Korean masses. Almost certainly, their reactions would be negative and destabilizing for the military.

Because the military cannot undo what they have done to South Korean society without a fundamental reassessment which could, and probably would, produce a volatile upheaval, changes are not likely to emerge. The potential for change is likely to be suppressed indefinitely. This likelihood is increased by the centralization of decisionmaking in the hands of a small oligarchy. However, if and when change occurs, it is likely to be explosive as far as the military is concerned. The only way this future confrontation seems likely to be avoided is for Seoul and its friends to take some steps while time permits to return South Korea to its civilian traditions via a process of transition. If the Korean peninsula and its tensions can be neutralized strategically, minimizing the need for real armed forces some day in the future, the armed forces of both Koreas will tend to lose their military reason for being. As this occurs and the people in uniform engage in more bureaucratic and administrative pursuits, there will occur a civilianizing of the military's role which will negate much that has been done to distort Korea's Confucian tradition in the last two decades. Only if this incremental civilianizing occurs can the constant themes of Korean history be reasserted, freeing South Korea from the conflict that otherwise awaits it.

## Notes

1. Readers interested in the earlier phase of military rule in the Republic of Korea will profit from Kim Se-jin's thorough study of that period: *The Politics of Military Revolution in Korea*, Chapel Hill: The University of North Carolina Press, 1971.

2. For an excellent description of the prewar Japanese armed forces, see: John M. Maki, *Japanese Militarism*, New York: Alfred A. Knopf, 1945; and Richard J. Smethurst, *A Social Basis for Prewar* Japanese Militarism, Berkeley: University of California Press. 1974.

3. International Institute for Strategic Studies, *The Military Balance, 1984-1985*, pp. 102-103.

4. See also: Ham Pyong-choon, "Korean Armed Forces and National Development" and C. I. Eugene Kim, "Armed Forces and National Development of the R.O.K.," papers presented at the 1st Wharangdae Symposium, September 21-23, 1981. See also C. I. Eugene Kim, "Civil-Military Relations in the Two Koreas," Armed Forces & Society, Fall 1984.

5. See also: Soon Cho, "Economic Development of Korea and the Armed Forces," paper presented at the Wharangdae Symposium.

6. The author explored alternatives toward North Korea in "North Korea: Another Candidate for Pingpong Diplomacy" in *The Christian Science Monitor*, June 30, 1982. A longer version of this alternative proposal entitled "Modifying the United States' Korean Policy" appeared in *Journal of Northeast Asian Studies*, Fall 1982. He also explored alternative US-ROK-Japan ties in "Northeast Asian Security: A Trilateral Alternative" in *Naval War College Review*, November-December 1984 and in *US-Japan Strategic Reciprocity* (Stanford: Hoover Institution Press, 1985).

7. See the author's assessment of South Korea's foreign policy shifts in "Evolution of ROK's Foreign Policy," *Washington Quarterly*, Winter 1984.

8. The writer examined that shift in "Korea, Inc.: The Political Impact of Park Chung-hee's Economic Miracle" in *ORBIS*, Spring 1980.

# 5

# North Korea: A Garrison State

*Gregory F. T. Winn*

The Korean Peninsula is one of the most heavily armed and fortified regions in the world and an area of vital concern to four of the world's major powers: Japan, the United States, the Soviet Union, and the People's Republic of China.

Much has been written but little is known about the Communist garrison state of the Democratic People's Republic of Korea (DPRK).[1] Winston Churchill once described the Soviet Union as a "riddle wrapped in a mystery inside an enigma." Applied to North Korea the analogy would require several more obscuring layers.

Nonetheless, this study, based on available evidence and conjecture, attempts to evaluate the institutional role of the North Korean military. It further examines that institution's present and possible future impact on the DRPK's society, politics, economics and international relations.

## Historical Evolution of the DPRK's Armed Forces

Before the modern era, the use of military means to achieve political ends was largely alien to Koreans. Belligerent behavior and militarism contradicted the traditional value system, which was heavily imbued with Buddhist non-violence and Confucian scholasticism. Korean history records some military campaigns and excursions. Struggles between rival kingdoms for domination of the peninsula occurred from time to time and armed factions contended over dynastic succession. Yet, none of this experience preserved for Koreans an enduring military tradition.

During the Japanese occupation of Manchuria, many Koreans served with Chinese Communist forces in Manchuria or under Soviet military tutelage in Siberia. From these came the cadres of North Korea's post-1945 army, as well as the partisan tradition which has since become official military legend.

The first armed force in post-World War II North Korea consisted of public security units activated in February 1946 by Soviet occupation authorities to assume the tasks of maintaining domestic order and security. By June 1947 these forces were estimated at between 120,000 and 150,000 men, including two Soviet equipped paramilitary divisions.

Formation of a conventional military force appears to have begun covertly from about mid-1946, shortly after the formation of the public security forces. Formal establishment of the Korean People's Army (KPA) was announced by public decree on February 8, 1948, seven months before the Democratic People's Republic itself.

Through Soviet sponsorship during this formative stage of the KPA, Kim Il Sung and his supporters secured a controlling position within the military establishment. This faction was made up mostly of officers who had fought with Kim against the Japanese, spent the war years with him in the Soviet Union, and returned to Korea with the Soviet occupation in 1945. The dominance which Kim Il Sung and the coterie of officers personally loyal to him secured over the armed forces proved crucial in the subsequent political development of North Korea. Only recently has the influence of Kim's "Manchurian Guerrilla Circle" diminished.

By the time Soviet forces completed their withdrawal from the North in 1948, the KPA (in comparison to the public security units) had a strength of some 60,000 men. From then until the Korean War in June 1950, referred to by the North Koreans as the Fatherland Liberation War, the KPA underwent a massive buildup in manpower and Soviet material. Troop strength grew to between 150,000 and 200,000 men.

The impact of the war on North Korea was devastating. The extent of devastation was indicated by the wartime comment of the head of the U. N. Bomber Command in the Far East, that "there are no more targets in Korea."[2] About 500,000 North Korean troops were killed and the destruction left a bitter legacy of anti-American hatred. Many of the military elite were killed, including officers close to Kim Il Sung.

Hostilities ended with the armistice agreement of July 1953, signed by the commanders of the KPA, the United Nations Command, and the Chinese People's Volunteers. South Korea, however, did not sign the armistice agreement, nor has any peace agreement been concluded since that time. Thus the peninsula remained technically in a state of war.

The Soviet Union and People's Republic of China (PRC) aided in post-war reconstruction but, as relations between China and the Soviet Union soured, North Korea was forced into an uneasy balancing act between allies. In October 1958, China completed its phased withdrawal. The Soviet Union continued substantial economic assistance and provided a military security screen behind which North Korea could concentrate on reconstruction and economic development. The armed forces that developed during this period had a strong peasant base rooted in loyalty to the Korean Workers Party and to President (then Premier) Kim Il Sung.

## The DPRK Military Institution

Kim Il Sung serves as President, Commander-in-Chief of the Armed Forces, and the General Secretary of the Korean Workers Party (KWP). The Military Commission of the Party's Central Committee has ultimate political control over the military structure. Normal operational control rests with the Ministry of the People's Armed Forces, a part of the regular governmental (non-Party) structure. Under the ministry is the General Staff which exercises operational control of the armed forces, and the General Political Bureau which directs all political activity and indoctrination in the armed forces.

In the command organization of the KPA, operational control rests with the Chief of the General Staff, subordinate to whom are the five armed service commands: the army; mechanized force; artillery; naval command; and air force command. Each of the service commanders has the concurrent rank of vice chief of staff. As in other socialist countries, to ensure party control of the armed forces there is a dual control structure of commanding officer and political guidance officer, the latter assigned at all echelons of command down to the company.[3]

Military officers play a prominent role in the upper echelons of the DPRK Government and KWP. Of the nineteen members of the Politburo, seven are military officers and eleven have military backgrounds. During the 1980s military officers serving as members or alternates of the Politburo have included the minister of the People's Armed Forces, General O Chin-u; the chief of the general staff, General O Guk-yul; the director of the General Political Bureau, So Chol; and the commander of the Worker-and-Peasant Red Guard, General O Paek-yong.[4] Even though a new generation is assuming prominence in North Korea, the relative proportion of military officers to party functionaries and government bureaucrats has remained constant.

While the armed forces provide an important element of the Party's power base, the Party leadership and Kim Il Sung personally hold tight control over the military establishment. For example, under article 100 of the 1972 Constitution the KPA is institutionally subordinate to the Supreme People's Assembly. In practice, control resides in the Military Commission of the party Central Committee headed, of course, by Kim Il Sung.

North Korean society is highly militarized. Approximately 4 percent of the population belong to the KPA, another 2 percent are in the military reserves, and an additional 11 percent belong to the Worker-

and-Peasant Red Guard (*Ronong Chokwidae*)—an organization originally conceived as a territorial militia for local defense but which increasingly assumed the role of an auxiliary military force. Thus, a large percentage of the citizenry is directly involved in some form of military activity through regular or auxiliary units.

## Raison D'être and Strategic Doctrine

North Korea's military doctrine has been rooted in its unique version of Maoist guerrilla warfare. The postulated conflict was seen as a protracted "people's war" in which "socialist" North Korea, the inner core and power base of a revolution on the Korean peninsula, would engage in mortal struggle with the "imperialist" forces in the south and their allies.

Looking back at the Korean conflict, Kim Il Sung concluded that the North's defeat stemmed, inter alia, from a lack of rear or reserve units, an inadequate air force, and immature and ill-trained troops, with respect both to strategy and tactics and in ideological preparation.[5]

Domestic military development has been tied to plans for reunification of Korea. According to a leading South Korean military analyst, Kim Il Sung followed Lenin's definition of "strategy":

> . . . strategy is the determination of the main blow of the proletariat at a given stage of revolution, the elaboration of a corresponding plan for the disposition of the revolutionary forces (main and secondary reserves), and the fight to carry out this plan throughout the given stage of revolution.

Therefore, Kim concentrated on four elements of strategy to successfully unify Korea: "policy objectives, main and reserve forces, direction of the main blow, and plan for deployment for forces."[6] In September 1961, Kim told the Fourth Party Congress that unification would follow in three stages: withdrawal of American forces, seizure of power by South Korean revolutionaries supporting a "revolution for democracy and national liberation," and linking of "patriotic democratic forces" North and South.[7]

In the mid-1960s there began a trend toward active guerrilla operations in the south. The 1967 defense budget allocation is estimated to have tripled. Substantial numbers of North Korean agents were captured or killed in the South, and in 1969 more naval violations of the armistice agreement occurred than in any previous year.

In January 1968 North Korea seized the USS Pueblo, imprisoned its crew, and dispatched a commando suicide squad which reached downtown Seoul in an unsuccessful effort to assassinate President Park. In November

1968, 120 North Korean commandos were killed or captured in a raid on the South Korean coast, and in April 1969, the North Koreans shot down an American (EC-121) reconnaissance aircraft.

Since 1969 the number of violent incidents and agent arrests has decreased, but the level of truce violations reportedly has increased. Serious incidents occurred in 1975 and 1976 at P'anmunjom (notably the axe murders of two U.S. soldiers in August 1976) and North Korean violations of South Korean air space in 1975 intensified its fears of invasion. In August 1981, North Korea unsuccessfully tried to shoot down an America SR-71 reconnaissance plane, and in the spring and summer of 1982 fire-fights occurred regularly along the demilitarized zone (DMZ) dividing North and South Korea. Since the armistice, at least 50 Americans, 1,000 South Koreans, and 600 North Korean agents have been killed along the DMZ. Most horrific of all, on October 9th 1983, North Koreans perpetrated a bombing attack in Rangoon, Burma, on South Korea's top leadership. President Chun Doo Hwan was unharmed, but 21 people were killed including four South Korean cabinet ministers.

## DPRK Armed Forces: A Brief Evaluation

Because of the close control North Korean authorities exercise over all information for internal and external dissemination, it is difficult to assess military capabilities. Estimates of North Korea's armed forces and its stock of major weapons vary widely and, in the general absence of independently verifiable evidence, remain highly uncertain.

Reassessments have produced sharp and sudden escalations of previous figures. In the late 1970s U.S. Defense Intelligence Agency analysts upgraded earlier estimates of ground force divisions from twenty-eight or twenty-nine to forty-one. Citing reasons for the new figures they noted, inter alia: the reconstruction of disconnected rear infantry squads as part of larger, dispersed divisions; a reevaluation of Kim Il Sung's rear forces strategic doctrine; and the location of previously undetected armed forces and weapons systems.[8]

Comparing DPRK military capabilities in 1985 with ten other nations in the world of approximately the same population (16 to 24 million) suggests that North Korea's military posture is not primarily defensive. With the exception of East Germany, which has approximately the same number of tanks, North Korea's military force is far superior to those of all nations of comparable size, with four times the number of men in uniform, and at least three times the average number of tanks and combat aircraft.

North Korean forces are formidable. The army numbered over 780,000 active duty troops. Ground weaponry includes approximately 2,800 tanks, 1,000 personnel carriers, 4,000 to 5,000 artillery guns and howitzers, 9,000 mortars, 3,400 various range rocket launchers, and 5,000 to 6,000 antiaircraft weapons.[9] South Korean experts argue that the North has artillery with a range of twenty to twenty-five miles, and between thirty-nine and 100 FROG 5 and FROG 7 surface-to-surface missiles, with a range of forty-two to fifty-six miles. The DPRK has also "dug-in" or "hardened" several bases and logistical supply areas for defense against aerial attacks.

Compared to South Korean forces, the North has more than twice as many tanks, artillery weapons, and armored personnel carriers. But, comparisons between North and South Korea can be misleading. For example, the Republic of Korea (ROK) has M-60 and M-48 tanks, while the North has T-54's and T-34's, of an older vintage and probably less reliable. The same is true in the sea and air: the South has destroyers and modern F-16, A-10, F-4 and F-5 aircraft; the North has a large number of coastal craft and older I128, MiG-15, and MiG-17 aircraft in its arsenal. Nonetheless, the DPRK has twice as many combat aircraft (even though many of these are outmoded); and in the event of war could probably control the sea lanes to South Korea with its naval forces (21 submarines, 33 large patrol craft, 338 fast attack craft, and 100 coastal and amphibious ships).

North Korea has also been building a munitions industry and modernizing its weapons systems. According to Stockholm International Peace Research Institute (SIPRI) reports, North Korea in 1975 received license to manufacture MiG 21 aircraft from the Soviet Union. By manufacturing its own or taking delivery on additional advanced "third generation" MiG 21's from the Soviets, it is possible that North Korea has as many as 150 of these planes rather than the 120 estimated by SIPRI (see notes). Some observers also expect that the DPRK will receive from the Soviets more advanced MiG models such as the MiG 23 or 25 to offset recent ROK acquisitions.

Besides the alleged assembly of MiG 21's, the North has a large munitions industry. It produces AK-47 rifles, mortars, rocket launchers, artillery, antiaircraft weapons, personnel carriers, patrol craft, submarines, and upwards of 200 tanks annually. The DPRK reportedly received some US $1,055 million in military grant assistance from the Soviet Union between 1961 and 1979.[10] Further, it received in 1978 and 1979 and again in 1982 and 1984 offers of more military aid, economic assistance, and oil deliveries on very favorable terms from the Chinese.[11]

In sum, the DPRK possesses a formidable military machine managed by a militant leadership driven by a revolutionary doctrine in pursuit of a reunified nation.

## Martial Spirit and Daily Life

The Korean People's Army is always cast in the role of defender of the Party and revolution as well as defender of the national territory. The broadly conceived role of the armed forces as an instrument of socialism is often reaffirmed as it was by Kim Il Sung in his 1981 New Year address. He said that the men and officers of the KPA and the security forces, with "boundless loyalty" to the Party and the revolution, must be ready at all times to firmly defend the country and its revolutionary gains.

The premise of protracted conflict between socialism and imperialism or capitalism provides the theoretical basis for a strong military capability. Of immediate and practical relevance to the importance of the armed forces is the continuing mutual distrust and hostility on the peninsula, rooted in the experience of the Korean War, subsequent internal and external political developments, and divergent reunification policies of the two Korean governments.

Through the enrollment of virtually all able-bodied men and many women between eighteen and forty-five in the Worker-and-Peasant Red Guard, military values and Party indoctrination have permeated the society.

North Korea is, and will be, a revolutionary society, owing to its fear of confrontation with South Korea and to its belief in the irreconcilable conflict between socialism and imperialism. Ideological doctrine is constantly emphasized, so that each citizen is prepared to support the garrison state and will unhesitatingly sacrifice his or her life for the "fatherland."

Calls for economic progress, social order, and political support are phrased and dramatized through such military-inspired slogans as "mount a speed battle" to meet economic targets, and "everybody to the battle to pull out weeds." Internal solidarity requires constant exhortation to vigilance, despite fluctuations in external threat perceptions.

Everyday life in North Korea takes on aspects of military life in the armed forces of other nations. For example, daily activities on the farm begin and end with a bell. Loudspeaker broadcasts commence as early as 0600, and there are even loudspeaker "economic guidance trucks" which travel about disseminating speeches, instructions, and encouragement in the countryside. Evenings are often filled with activities directed toward social-political education. During the lunch break period, "agitators" read newspapers and books aloud, and in rural areas "field propaganda teams" are often set up for education and rigid indoctrination.

Similarly, control over the individual's movement and personal activities is a conspicuous fact of life. Travel is restricted and requires special food ration coupons, and permission from local authorities. Itineraries have to be approved and the traveler is subject to identification checks on the road, at hotels, at any time. Among specific identification documents are a residence card, ration card, and military identification or discharge papers.

By definition, military regimentation and thinking also play a part in educational/cultural affairs. Military education and training systems are quite elaborate and the officer's higher educational structure includes approximately seventeen different universities, colleges, schools and academies, even a Korean People's Army Art Academy. A school of particular importance is the Kim Il Sung Military University for advanced officer education. The Navy and Air Force also have separate academies.

For the enlisted man, "class indoctrination" is part of military service. Members of the Worker-and-Peasant Red Guard also have similar training programs, and university students receive two to three hours of military training a week. Many North Korean films and stage productions focus on military themes.

Extensive efforts are made to militarize Korean society, thereby creating "fortress Korea." North Korea's society has suffered heavy psychological and financial costs in the creation of a garrison state.

### The Cost of Military Strength

Although difficult to quantify, the economic consequences of a large military establishment are substantial. On the basis of official defense budgets, between 1964 and 1975, North Korea's military expenditures exceeded those of the South by the equivalent of more than U.S. $1.0 billion. Between 1966 and 1967 alone, it increased its defense budget by 200 percent.[12]

In his November 1970 address to the Fifth Party Congress, Kim Il Sung observed that "our national defense power has been gained at a very large and dear price" and "frankly speaking, our spending on national defense has been too heavy a burden for us in light of the small size of the country and its population." Still, military budgets increased an average of 15 percent per year until 1972, when they declined sharply both in terms of absolute expenditure and proportion of total budget. Since the 1972 reduction, the North's defense budget increased at a slower rate than the South's (from US $532 million in 1972 to over two billion in 1984).[13]

Many analysts assume that the DPRK hides significant defense related expenditures such as military weapons production, military equipment, militia and paramilitary pay, and logistical supply expenses, under the other nondefense budget headings. Since the details of military expenditure have not been made public, total expenditures remain a matter of conjecture.

The DPRK's economic development focuses on heavy industrial production partly because their political objective is consistent, to strengthen military power. This commitment to a massive defense program and greater national self-sufficiency in arms and equipment, taken in the early 1960s, caused a major diversion of economic resources from development to military purposes. In turn, this led to sacrifices affecting the nation's standard of living.

The DPRK's growth rate slowed from an average 8-10 percent in the 1960s, to around 5 percent through the mid-1980s. Its economic credibility first suffered a setback in the 1970s when it failed to meet repayment schedules on several international loans. The 1973-74 oil crisis dampened demand for North Korean exports, and the oil crisis of 1979 had a similar impact. More recently, there are indications of a labor shortage, partly because of the large number of Koreans serving in the DPRK military.[14]

It is difficult to understand how the North, with one-half the South's population and one-fourth its GNP, can continue to match the ROK's military expenditures without adversely affecting its economic development. One remedy to this imbalance has been the elevation of many "technocrats" in the KWP hierarchy until the single most numerous group now in the Party's Central Committee is technocrats. Yet, simply increasing the number of economists and managers in the upper echelons of the government will not suffice. If the North hopes to keep up with the South, it needs knowledgeable and progressive leadership in the post-Kim Il Sung era.

**Military Leadership, Politics and the Succession Question**

Leadership succession in North Korea is a realm of Byzantine politics, of political intrigue and cabal. The military will play a pivotal role in the selection of Kim Il Sung's successor, but beyond that observation little is certain.

Since the early 1970s, Kim Il Sung has groomed his son Kim Chong Il to be heir apparent, but there is no precedent for dynastic succession in the Communist world. Nonetheless, Kim Il Sung has maneuvered his eldest son into prominence with the assistance of key party and military leaders.

Kim Chong Il was born in the Soviet Union in 1942, studied at an East German air force cadet academy for two years, and graduated from Kim Il Sung University with a major in political science and economics.[15] He entered the Korean Workers Party in the 1960s and became director of its Culture and Arts Department in 1970. In 1973, he became a candidate member of the KWP Politburo. Throughout the 1970s he was never mentioned by name in official publications but was identified only as "Party Center." In 1974 Kim Il Sung decided not to promote the succession of his younger brother Kim Yong-Ju, but turned to his son and began a series of purges in support of this effort. Several of Kim Chong Il's proteges including Generals Oh Kuk-nyol, Oh Paek-Yong and Yim Ch'un-ch'u received major promotions.[16]

The son's succession was apparently on course in 1977 when suddenly all media references to "Party Center" disappeared. No mention of Kim Chong Il or Party Center was made for almost two years, suggesting that the dynastic succession faced stiff resistance from within the party. During this period, unconfirmed reports indicated that Chong Il had suffered severe injuries either in a traffic accident or in an assassination attempt. However, he took part in the Sixth Party Congress (October 1980), and officially received prominent positions in the politburo, the central committee and the military commission.

Among the top five leaders of the DPRK in 1982, Defense Minister Oh Jin-U and Prime Minister Kang Song-San were seen as supporters and guardians of Kim Chong Il. Another prominent military leader, General Oh Kuk-nyol, apparently a classmate of the younger Kim's at the Mangyongdae Revolutionary Academy, was promoted to Chief of the General Staff in 1979.

Thus, given strong backing by the DPRK's top leadership, including the military, one might conclude that the "Son of the Sun's" succession is assured. Furthermore, in August 1984, Kim Chong Il's future succession was formally declared. Then again, other factors may preclude a smooth transition:

- During the Yi dynasty there was a long tradition of conflict between designated heirs, their incumbent kings, other family rivals and faction leaders.[17]
- Neither the Soviet Union nor China has found a simple formula for the transfer of leadership. Both country's leaders have basically accepted Kim Il Sung's plan for dynastic succession, but it is not clear whether they actually support it, or might intervene if the transition proves destabilizing.[18]
- After thirty-plus years of Kim Il Sung's iron fisted rule, there apparently are pockets of resistance and opposition to the son's

succession. Opposition in the Army to Kim Chong Il reportedly led to the dismissal of a dozen generals in 1982.[19]
- Kim Chong Il, unlike his father, has no military experience, not having fought in the prolonged "anti-Japanese" struggle or the Korean War.[20]
- There is a generational struggle involved. With the exception of a few older top leaders, Kim Chong Il's supporters are in their 40s and 50s. Yet, several of Kim Il Sung's original 1930s "Manchurian Guerrilla" group still have power and are unlikely to relinquish it.
- Little is known about Kim Chong Il, the man. Some reports indicate that he is a stylish aesthete, a film producer, a technocrat and peacemaker who opposes the use of force and was active in the 1972 reunification talks. Then again, Kim Chong Il is "credited" with the further intensification of the incredible "cult" of Kim Il Sung, has many "hard-core" military supporters, and may have been involved in the planning of the 1976 axe murders in P'anmunjom and in the Rangoon bombing.[21]

The longer Kim Il Sung lives, the more likely Kim Chong Il will be able to consolidate his position. The elder Kim is apparently convinced that the only way to safeguard his accomplishments and his "good" name is to insure his son's succession. As part of this effort, there has been an extensive media drive to insure that the military is absolutely loyal to Kim Chong Il. Kim Chong Il's attitude toward and support from the military will, in turn, directly affect the future course of the DPRK's foreign and defense policies.

### The Military, Foreign Policy and Defense

Heavy dependence on outside sources for military support has made North Korea highly vulnerable to shifts in the fluid regional environment. In 1965, Kim Il Sung convinced visiting Soviet Premier Kosygin that, in light of United States aggression in Vietnam, North Korea needed more advanced weaponry to bolster its defenses. Yet, the possibility of direct Soviet-U.S. confrontation, stemming from North Korea aggressive actions in 1968 and 1969, placed a strain on DPRK-USSR relations. In 1972 advanced military aid from Moscow was reportedly cut off. With the exception of the MiG-21 licensing agreement, no new major weapons systems were sent to North Korea during the 1970s. The axe murders of two American soldiers at the truce village of P'anmunjom in August 1976 and the October 1983 Rangoon bombing did little to relieve Soviet fears of North Korean unilateral adventurism. However, this situation could change, with the Soviets offering advanced military equipment and hard currency loans, especially as South Korean requests for U.S. weapons systems are approved.

As Soviet military support for the DPRK decreased in the 1970s China became P'yongyang's major supplier of weapons. Trips to Beijing over the last four years led to offers of more military aid, economic assistance and oil deliveries. A recurrent nightmare for China would be P'yongyang's clearly switching to Moscow, as the Vietnamese did. While on the surface ties are cordial and productive between Beijing and P'yongyang, diplomatic tensions exist.

North Korea's considerable military assets were countered by an impressive array of South Korean and United States weapons systems— many of which were viewed as life-threatening in the North. In the arms race, the DPRK's leaders added offensive capabilities, aware that as they did so, combined "enemy" forces were improving the quality and quantity of their own ground and air defense systems. In total capabilities, the North demonstrated a clear-cut *quantitative* advantage over South Korea, without its U.S. ally. However, the military balance was dramatically altered against North Korea when superior U.S. forces were introduced.[22] Similarly, should China or the Soviet Union, or both, directly support North Korea the balance would shift again.

Should the north decide to take advantage of its quantitative military advantage on the peninsula, it has several attack options. Off the coast of North Korea, northwest of Seoul, are five so-called western islands which are South Korean territory according to the 1953 armistice agreement. Some of these islands are close to shore and all were within the extended DPRK military coastal zone proclaimed in August 1977. North Korea could attack these islands, expecially the island farthest west, Paengyong, like China had attacked Quemoy and Matsu in 1958.

Between 1975 and 1978, three large tunnels were discovered under the DMZ, one of which was 246 feet below the surface, near the truce village of P'anmunjom. Two possible uses for these tunnels are as access channels for the infiltration of North Korean agents and for the rapid transfer of troops in the initial stages of an invasion. Other tunnels also apparently exist, their exact purpose unknown.[23]

A third military option would be an all-out "blitz" on Seoul, along three possible north-south attack corridors. ROK forces have constructed a fortified "FEBA-Alpha" line two to five miles south of the DMZ to counter such an attack. Seoul lies twenty to twenty-five miles south of this secondary defense line. If North Korean forces could advance south of the DMZ, FROG missiles could, at least initially, bombard and harrass the city. Conceivably, P'yongyang's leaders might believe that if Seoul were taken quickly, the North could then call for a ceasefire and negotiate a settlement to its advantage.

A more likely offensive scenario would be linked to political conditions in South Korea. In his speech to the Sixth Party Congress in October 1980, Kim Il Sung stated: "The tragic developments in South Korea and the disasters suffered by its people today immediately represent the distress of the entire Korean nation . . . Anyone who is of Korean blood cannot remain a passive onlooker to the unhappy state of affairs today . . . We must do away with the colonial fascist rule of the U.S. imperialists and their stooges in South Korea and reunify the country." Rather than invade the South, the DPRK might emphasize amphibious landings, paratroop deployments from low-lying AN-2 aircraft or other methods and routes of infiltration.[24] The potential for subversion in the South depends on the extent of deep-seated domestic discontent: the degree of anti-Americanism; political and economic disruption; and intellectual, religious, and student alienation.

From the North's perspective, South Korean military hardware, offensive attack options, ideology and strategic doctrine are a threat to their survival. North Korean leaders have been concerned by South Korean defense budget increases and weapons modernization programs; by American reconnaissance flights, tactical nuclear potential (to include neutron weapons), multi-billion dollar weapons transfer programs to the ROK, and by South Korean–American joint military exercises. In a June 1977 interview with *Le Monde*, Kim Il Sung argued "there is no threat of a southward invasion, rather it is we who are being threatened by invasion."[25] Recent western observers to North Korea report North Korean fears of South Korean aggression.

Perceptions of threat and the psychological ramifications of those perceptions affect and even control decisions for peace and war. Defensive arms are often considered offensive weapons by an opponent. A difficult decisionmaking problem for both North and South Korean leaders is how to reach decisions when there is only four minutes warning time of imminent aerial attack. Even with weapons parity, each side is aware of the advantages of striking first. Fear of attack could lead to plans for preemption in "defense." The enmity, mutual distrust, and legacy of conflict on the Korean peninsula reinforces and intensifies perceptions of threat. Consequently, problems of conflict management in the Korean situation are critical.

In a March 1976 *Sekai* article, Kim Il Sung argued that "huge" oil deposits had been discovered in South Korea, and this was a raw material the United States sought to control. He was inaccurate about the deposits, as in some respects North Korean leaders are ill- or uninformed about the outside world. Contacts with the outside world are expanding rapidly, particularly with nonaligned or developing states, but real knowledge of perceived adversaries is minimal. Given the DPRK conformist ideological "mind-set," new information contrary to preconceived concepts is likely to be dismissed. General guidance and subsequent decisional orders in their extensive bureaucracy emanate from "the leader" (or his son) down. Overly "literal" interpretations of Kim Il Sung's directives could lead to bizarre and unpredictable behavior.

North and South Korean "rules of engagement" and "counterattack" scenarios might also affect the probability of unintentional military escalation. For example, rules of engagement are predetermined procedures for combat situations in the event there is insufficient time to receive central decisionmaking authority. In air combat, these rules could vary from not firing unless directly fired upon, firing on sight, or firing within range of guided missile systems. In the dynamic conflict process, counterattack plans can range from meeting an attack at point of conflict with equal or slightly superior forces, or with overwhelmingly superior forces, or countering an attack at other locations of greater enemy vulnerability. Thus, in the Korean military situation, decisions prior to combat could directly affect escalation probabilities, regardless of whether broader conflict is desired or intended.

Despite recent efforts to broaden their contact with the Western world and to open up their economy, North Korean leaders retain a military siege mentality which dominates both their domestic and international affairs. Their belief in the "ultimate" victory of the DPRK system could lead to military rather than peaceful methods for reunifying the peninsula.

Then again, conflict is restrained by a combination of economic, psychic and international deterrents. After the Rangoon bombing, a number of high ranking North Korean leaders, including the Prime Minister and Foreign Minister, were replaced with technocrats interested in solving the North's economic problems. In 1983 and again in 1984, Kim Il Sung travelled to Beijing where the Chinese emphasized their economic modernization plan and insisted that the Koreans resolve their international problems through diplomatic means.[26]

During 1984, both sides, North and South, proposed a series of negotiations on economic trade and investment, divided families, and sports. In September 1984, the North Koreans, strictly following the Chinese example set in 1979, unilaterally declared a joint venture law to attract Western investment. At the same time, Kim Il Sung informed the visiting Chairman of the Japanese Socialist Party that he no longer required the immediate removal of U.S. forces from the South and wanted to conclude both a peace treaty to replace the Armistice Agreement and a non-aggression pact with the South. And during an October 1984 interview with Japanese parliamentarian, Tokuma Utsunomiya, Kim Il Sung reportedly praised the "one state and two systems" policy declared in the Sino-British joint declaration on the future of Hong Kong.[27]

Despite these positive signs, during this time period, the North also mobilized its attack forces closer to the Demilitarized Zone, greeted delegations from Cuba, Yemen, Libya, and the PLO, and continued its support for international revolution.

In his 1985 New Year's address, Kim Il Sung argued:

> Active dialogues and extensive cooperation and exchange between the North and the South will enable them to join efforts to develop the national economy in a coordinated way and attain national prosperity in all spheres. Our party and the government will make every sincere effort to ensure that the negotiations on economic affairs and Red Cross talks ... will bear good fruit and that extensive negotiations and many-sided cooperation and exchange between the two parts of the country will become a reality. If the North-South dialogues proceed successfully ... these will develop gradually into higher level talks, and culminate in high-level political negotiations between North and South.[28]

South Korean leaders have expressed the same objectives. However, past experience and conflicting forces within North Korean society lead to scepticism concerning these negotiations and prospects for rapprochement on the Korean peninsula. Although not proven, it is possible that Kim Il Sung's son and heir is not altogether supportive of joint ventures with the West and North-South rapprochement. After all, China's efforts both to modernize and improve their world status coincided with the renunciation of the cult of Mao Tse-tung and those associated with it.

## Notes

1. Some of the material in this chapter is an elaboration of an earlier study by the author: "National Security" in *North Korea: A Country Study*, Government Printing Office, Washington, DC, 1981.

2. Gavan McCormack and John Gittings, *Crisis in Korea* (London: Spokesman Books, 1977), p. 120; and Robert A. Scalapino and Chong-Sik Lee, *Communism in Korea*, 2 vols. (Berkeley: University of California Press, 1972), pp. 927-29 and 933-34.

3. Kim Il Sung speech, *Chojak Sonjip* Vol. V. (P'yongyang), pp. 494-523; and Ki-taek Lee "North Korean Military Policy Toward South Korea," *East Asian Review* (Seoul), (Vol. I., No. 2, Summer 1974), pp. 148-153.

4. Analysis of the Sixth Party Congress, Foreign Broadcast Information Service (FBIS), (October 14, 1980); and biographies of the KWP Central Committee in *Korean Affairs Report* (FBIS) (No. 149, July 27, 1981), translation from *Kita Chosen Kenkyu* (Tokyo) (November 1980), pp. 70-125.

5. Ki-taek Lee, *Ibid.* pp. 156-58.

6. Ibid.

7. Kim Il Sung speech, February 27, 1964, *Fourth Party Congress Report.*
8. U.S. Congress, 96th, 1st Session. House of Representatives Committee on Armed Services. "Impact of Intelligence Reassessment on Withdrawal of U.S. Troops from Korea." (Hearings before the Subcommittee on Investigations, June 21–July 17, 1979.) (Washington: GPO, 1980); and Franklin B. Weinstein and Fuji Kamiya (eds.) *The Security of Korea: U.S. and Japanese Perspectives in the 1980's* (Boulder: Westview Press, 1980), pp. 31–32.
9. The *Military Balance 1984-1985* (London: International Institute for Strategic Studies, 1984), pp. 102–103.
10. Ruth Sevard (ed.), *World Military and Social Expenditures 1981* (Leesburg, Virginia: World Priorities Inc., 1982), p. 7.
11. Edward A. Olsen, "The Political Implications of Resource Scarcity on the Korean Peninsula," *Korea Observer* (Seoul) (Vol. XII, No. 4, Winter 1982), p. 403. Dr. Olsen quotes a source who indicates that the North Koreans were supplied oil at well below OPEC market prices (Chinese oil at $4–5 per bbl. and Soviet oil at $8–10 per bbl).
12. *Pukhan Chonso 1945-1980* (Seoul: Kuktong Munje Yon'guso, 1980) p. 458, and *Pukhan Chonso 1974,* vol. II, p. 51.
13. Ibid. and "Budget Structure of Annual Revenues, Expenditures Analyzed," in *Pukhan* (Seoul: December 1981), pp. 74–85, and the IISS *Military Balance 1984-1985.*
14. "North Korea: The Camouflaged State" in *Far Eastern Economic Review* (Hong Kong: March 5, 1982), pp. 28–29; and, Robert A. Scalapino, "Current Dynamics of the Korean Peninsula" in *Problems of Communism* (Nov.-Dec. 1981), p. 23; and "North Korea Reaches Out" in *Asiaweek* (November 30, 1984), pp. 27–36.
15. "KWP Central Committee Members Cited" in the *Kita Chosen Kenkyu* (Tokyo, November 1980), pp. 11–68, *Korean Affairs Report* No. 149, JPRS (July 27, 1981) pp. 70–125.
16. *Ibid.* Yim Ch'un-ch'u was the head of military/infiltration operations against South Korea in 1967 and 1968, and was temporarily purged from the Party for his failure in this endeavor. A background evaluation of Kim Chong Il's military proteges raises concern because of their involvement in military activities directed against the South.
17. A large number of Kim Il Sung's relatives hold prominent positions in the DPRK hierarchy, Kim Chong Il's stepmother, Kim Song-ae, has been chairman of the Korean Democratic Women's Union and is a full member of the central committee. It is rumored that she opposes Chong ll's accession rather than her own childrens'. *Ibid.* p. 99, and *Chungang Ilbo* "North Succession Issue Viewed" (Seoul) February 1, 1982.
18. *Ibid.* p. 2, and *Far Eastern Economic Review* (February 19, 1982) pp. 16–17. Robert A. Scalapino has suggested that either the Soviet Union or China "might" intervene if political instability were to emerge. See his "Current Dynamics of the Korean Peninsula," in *Problems of Communism* (Washington: Nov.-Dec. 1981), p. 25.
19. *The Tongil Ilbo* (Japan), *South China Morning Post* (Hong Kong), and Kyodo news service all reported that revolts against the succession of Kim

Chong Il had occured in the spring of 1982. Reportedly workers and members of the Socialist Working Youth of Korea "rose up and destroyed Kim Il Sung's statues" and a sanctuary dedicated to Kim Chong Il's mother, Kim Chong Suk. See the Korea Herald (Seoul: June 13, 1982), p. 1; *Seoul Sinmun* (Seoul: June 15, 1982), the Seoul Domestic Service reported in the Foreign Broadcast Information Services "Asia and Pacific" Daily Report, February 24, 1982; and *Tong-A Ilbo* (Seoul: May 20, 1982), p. 2, and *Asiaweek* (November 30, 1984), p. 34.

20. Several members of Kim Chong Il's faction made a point of celebrating the 45th anniversary of Kim Il Sung's successful attack on a Japanese military stronghold at "Pochonbo." P'yongyang, KCNA in English, June 4, 1982.

21. Two summary biographies of Kim Chong Il, one pro-DPRK and the other pro-ROK, in a March 5, 1982 issue of the Far Eastern Economic Review, yield starkly different images. In the North's version, Chong Il was a child prodigy, has revised college textbooks, directed several films, curls his hair, is an enemy of regimentation, helped build the capital's subway and a "Disneyland-type park, and is a Yi Dynasty scholar. The other characterization suggests that Chong Il is behind the DPRK's military build-up, and if given the choice between "peace and reunification with war" would choose the latter.

22. U.S. weapons used by the Israelis in their invasion of Lebanon in June 1982 were proven, in most cases, qualitatively superior.

23. U.S. *News and World Report*, December 6, 1978; and *The Washington Post*, June 4, 1982.

24. The DPRK special "commando" force is estimated to be 100,000 men. *Washington Post*, June 4, 1982.

25. *Le Monde* (Paris, June 20, 1977).

26. *Korea Herald* (Seoul, October 24, 25, and December 2 and 6, 1984), also Xinhua Report broadcast from Pyongyang, October 25, 1984. In a meeting between Deng Xiaoping and former Japanese Prime Minister Zenko Suzuki (October 24, 1984), Deng told Suzuki that North Korea had begun "an open door policy" similar to China's. *Foreign Broadcast Information Service*, IV, Asia and the Pacific, 24 October 1984, p. E1.

27. *Asahi Shimbun* (Tokyo, September 12, 1984), on the joint venture law; *Sankei Shimbun* (Tokyo, September 29, 1984), on the Ishibashi visit; *FBIS*, IV, Kyodo News Service (Beijing), October 10, 1984, p. C2, on the Utsunomiya-Kim Il Sung interview.

28. "Comrade Kim Il-Song's New Year Address" (Pyongyang, KCNA, January 1, 1985), *FBIS*, January 2, 1985.

# PART TWO
## Southeast Asia

# 6

# The People's Army of Vietnam
*Douglas Pike*

The People's Army of Vietnam (PAVN), formerly the armed forces of North Vietnam and now, in effect, for all Indochina, is the third largest armed force in the world, outnumbered only by the People's Liberation Army (PLA) of China and the Armed Forces of the USSR.

PAVN is composed of two parts: a full military force, that is, a standing army, navy, air force, etc., and a paramilitary force made up of a half dozen various militia elements and what are called self-defense forces. Operationally it is divided into the more or less standard military theaters, corps, divisions and lower echelons.

A recent buildup increased the number of PAVN divisions to 51 (38 ordinary infantry divisions and 13 smaller units called economic construction infantry divisions). Nineteen of these regular infantry divisions are now in Kampuchea, three in Laos, and the remainder in Vietnam, chiefly near Hanoi and along the China border.

This brief study of PAVN is organized to permit comparative analysis with other armed forces in Asia. It is in three sections. The first deals with PAVN history and heritage. The second treats PAVN's relations with other institutions in Vietnamese society, its influence on these, and on political and economic decisionmaking. The third section assesses certain aspects of PAVN's existence and the meaning of these both internally and externally.

## Historical Development

This section surveys the historical development of the PAVN as an institution within Vietnamese society and discusses its strategic rationale.

The forerunner of the People's Army of Vietnam was a collection of self-defense forces used to protect Party officials and Party meetings in the 1930s. In the first decade after its founding in 1930, the Indochinese Communist Party had no organized military force, nor was there need for one.

There was, however, doctrinal thinking by Party officials about the type of armed force which should eventually be created. Out of these discussions emerged the basic notion of *dau tranh*. The term itself means "struggle," although the original in Vietnamese is more powerful and emotive than its English equivalent. Ho Chi Minh and General Vo Nguyen Giap created a military strategy out of the notion of *dau tranh*. Two types were developed: armed *dau tranh* (armed struggle) and political *dau tranh* (political struggle). Armed *dau tranh* roughly means military activity, although it includes actions normally not associated with an armed force, such as kidnapping and assassination. Political *dau tranh*, in effect, is politics with guns, including an aggregate of nonmilitary actions which involve social organization, mobilization of personnel and other resources, and motivation of military personnel and civilians alike to support the cause. The strategic concept envisions the two *dau tranh* as twin pincers closing on the enemy. Another metaphor used is hammer and anvil.

Other Vietnamese communist military concepts developed at the time include the notion of using the people as weapons of war, the correct meaning of the term "people's war"; the need to gear actions to international developments, including events in distant capitals, and a third was to harness nationalism and link it to the appeals of socialism and communism. Finally, there was the belief that passivity is the great enemy, that there always must be an aggressive mentality exhibited through constant offensive action, even when those actions are insignificant.

World War II was the great opportunity for Vietnamese Communists. A united front organization called the Viet Minh was formed, and it organized a series of guerrilla bands that were loosely referred to as the Viet Minh Army. During the next four years, Viet Minh guerrillas, many of them led by Vietnamese communist cadres, operated from bases in China into Indochina. They harrassed the Japanese occupying Indochina, spied for the Allies, rescued downed American airmen, and generally served the Allied cause.

Concurrently, the Vietnamese communists were developing their own separate but parallel military establishment. In the mountains of Cao Ban Province along the Chinese border of northern Vietnam, General Giap and a handful of cadres worked out the structure for a new type of military unit. From 1942 to 1944 they tested and, in late 1944, finally revealed their creation. It was called the Armed Propaganda Team, and although it did not appear to be significant at the time, eventually proved to have enormous impact. Formation of the first team on December 22, 1944, also marks the formal date now observed as the founding of PAVN.

The idea of the armed propaganda team should be more widely understood and appreciated than is generally the case, for it is a remarkable invention. It is well named if the term "propaganda" is accepted in its proper Leninist sense, not as usually employed in the West to refer to dissemination of repetitious, hackneyed ideas. Teams were armed but only for defense, or for some occasional spectacular military gesture to advertise the cause. The teams did not use their weapons to intimidate villagers, for this would have been self-defeating. Instead, the teams went into the villages of Vietnam to organize and mobilize the people. This was not easy as villagers were often suspicious and distrustful, and it took skilled cadres to break the communicational ice. The armed propaganda teams served the Vietnamese Communist Party cause well in the Viet Minh war. Years later, it was the initial institutional weapon in South Vietnam, with the formation of the People's Liberation Armed Forces (PLAF) of the National Liberation Front, or Viet Cong.

In its first years, the Viet Minh's armed forces was little more than a collection of guerrilla bands armed and equipped either by the allies during World War II or out of French and Japanese stocks captured after the war. The first regular units appeared in September 1950, and consisted of about 29 infantry battalions and eight heavy weapons battalions. In October 1950 these units, formed in China, drove across the border from which they were never dislodged. In September of the following year, the first full PAVN infantry division, known as the Vanguard Division, went into action. A year later PAVN heavy artillery began to appear frequently on the battlefield. The war dragged on for several years until its culmination at Dien Bien Phu resulted in a PAVN victory, and the Geneva talks, where the two sides wrote an end to French colonialism in Indochina.

At the end of the Viet Minh War, PAVN was still a united front military force. There were, for instance, Catholic battalions operating in the South under the Viet Minh banner. But the basic structure of PAVN as a national armed force for North Vietnam had been established and, gradually over the next few years, it became less a united front army and more a Party-controlled army.

There then began a developing and enlarging process that has continued to this day. PAVN by 1955 had about 200,000 men. By 1965 it had about 400,000; by 1975, 650,000, and by 1985 there were nearly one million men in its regular army. In addition, there are a half dozen paramilitary elements which total perhaps an additional million. This makes PAVN probably the largest army per capita of any country in the world.

In 1959 the Communist Party decided to begin armed struggle in South Vietnam, and created the National Liberation Front, the united front organization with its People's Liberation Armed Force (PLAF). In the early years of the Vietnam War, the burden of combat was on PLAF, not on PAVN. Because of attrition, buildup of the army of the Republic of Vietnam (ARVN), and arriving American and other Allied troops, gradually the balance of forces began to tip away from PLAF. At that point, Hanoi began to send PAVN units South. The first of these went as "filler packets" into the PLAF units. Then came smallish PAVN units, and finally whole PAVN divisions. By the 1972 Easter offensive, about 90 percent of the day-to-day combat in the South was by PAVN, that is, North Vietnamese regulars in uniform. The toll on PAVN/PLAF for this Vietnam War was extraordinarily high; the estimated number of dead ranges from about 650,000 to nearly one million.

After the Vietnam war, virtually all 18 PAVN divisions were sent to the South for occupation duty and to establish a military government.

PAVN troops were also assigned the task of dealing with the resistance in the South. There were four major sources of resistance. In descending order of significance, they were: first, the Montagnards in the Highlands, some associated with the organization called FULRO. Second, the Hoa Hao sect, a militant element centered in the Seven Mountains area of Cahu Doc Province. Third, the National Salvation Movement made up of remnants of the VNQDD (Viet Nam Quoc Dan Dang) and the Dai Viets, both nationalist Vietnamese movements dating back to the 1930s. Fourth, ARVN holdouts and recently formed ex-ARVN resistance elements located in the Nha Trang area, in Phuoc-Tuy and Vinh Long Provinces, and also in the Highlands along the Kampuchean border. The Catholics form a fifth passive resistance element in Vietnam, for they are generally unarmed. The Catholics are important, however, because they are socially organized. In general, this resistance is widespread, but low-grade, poorly organized and poorly led. Virtually no outside observers believe it can significantly affect the internal situation in Vietnam, at least not as long as the Vietnamese army remains united and coherent.

After the Vietnam War, debate arose in the Politburo over the demobilization of PAVN. Politburo members in the economic sector wanted to demobilize large numbers of PAVN troops and transfer them to that sector. This was opposed by the generals, who offered a compromise: PAVN troops would perform economic duties but remain in uniform. PAVN units were then assigned agricultural tasks and such duties as building roads, bridges, building, and other construction. PAVN's first post-Vietnam War test came in late 1978 with the invasion of Kampuchea—a highly visible Soviet-type attack with tank-led infantry plunging across the border, driving to the Thai border, then fanning out over the country and occupying, if not controlling, all of it in a matter of days. Pol Pot and his followers of Democratic Kampuchea (DK) fled to the Cardomom Mountains between Battambang and the sea to continue the war. Resistance to PAVN was soon joined by what was called the Third Force, including troops under Son Sann and Norodom Shihanouk, the former Cambodian ruler. The Chinese began quietly to underwrite this opposition and the war in Kampuchea bogged down.

In retrospect, the Vietnamese invasion of Kampuchea appears to have been a disastrous mistake. Apparently, it was a decision taken in the belief that a quick victory was possible; the calculation was that Pol Pot had neither political depth nor military staying power, and that a traumatic assault would shatter his capability to resist and cause the Khmer people to rally to the new government, to be called the People's Republic of Kampuchea. But from the start, the enterprise was misbegotten, assumptions proved wrong, and PAVN's strategy did not work.

The first major repercussion from this invasion came in February 1979—the 17-day Vietnam-China border war. The Chinese attacked north of Hanoi, moved through the mountains to stop just short of the plain that leads to Hanoi, and then withdrew. The Chinese assault did not go well, chiefly because of logistic and transportation problems. This brief war was a military defeat but a political victory for China.

China's attack and the subsequent quagmire in Kampuchea threw the PAVN logistics into heavy dependency on the USSR. There are no arms factories in Vietnam and all military hardware must be imported. Vietnam is also dependent now on the Soviet Union for about 10 percent of the rice it consumes and for other vital commodities such as oil, spare parts for its transportation system, and chemical fertilizer. In the 1980s, the USSR and Vietnam moved closer toward a systematic military arrangement, an alliance in all but name.

PAVN's rationale for its existence today is threefold. First, its duty is to defend Vietnam, the basic duty of every army in every society. Second, it must insure the continuation of the present sociopolitical system in which the Communist Party monopolizes all political power. In theory, this duty must be performed even if it means the sacrifice of PAVN. PAVN has a third, socioeconomic, duty to society, that of contributing to the restructuring of society. In the North this means the never-ending effort to create a classless society. In the South, it means helping to "break the machine" of the southern social structure. PAVN also has purely economic duties: producing goods, helping solve the country's many economic problems, and generally contributing to the nation-building process. The latter task was neglected in the last few years because PAVN has been preoccupied with its war in Kampuchea and with preparing to defend the country against China.

## Impact of PAVN on Vietnam

This section considers the contemporary and potential impact of PAVN on nine aspects of the Vietnam scene, and is a brief description and assessment of PAVN's sociological influence on Vietnamese society.

### Domestic Political System

Political control within the Vietnamese political system is exclusively reserved for the Communist Party. The Party monopolizes power and any political activity in which the ordinary Vietnamese engages is merely participatory. The National Assembly, for instance, serves as a mobilizing force to harness the political energies of the people through major social organization, but is not a power broker as in noncommunist societies.

The style of politics is factionalism, since Vietnam is a Sinic-based system. Day to day political activity at the top, within the upper reaches of the Party, consists of struggle between factions, and *bung di,* or "faction bashing," is the chief mode of political conduct.

Similar politicking goes on within PAVN, at the High Command and upper cadre level. The mechanism here is the Party within PAVN. There is, as a result, a dual command structure within the Vietnamese armed forces, one Party and one PAVN, which is standard in communist military organizations everywhere. However, these two elements should not be regarded as separate institutions but as an integrated entity.

There is a good deal of overlap between the PAVN High Command and top Party posts within the Political Bureau or the Politburo. There is also considerable dual functioning or "wearing of two hats" by single military figures. For instance, the top defense position on the State side is the post of Minister of Defense, held by General Van Tien Dung. The top Defense position of the Party side is in the Central Party Military Committee, also chaired by General Dung. Finally, the top operational post within PAVN, commander-in-chief, is also held by General Dung. In reality then, the highest level of the Vietnamese military defense establishment consists of about 12 to 15 generals and a few civilians who make all of the decisions, representing the State and the Party in a single entity. There is no true hierarchy or chain of command, or even a superior-subordinate arrangement within this upper level; rather there are various sets of organizational boxes occupied by the same few individuals and organized in this fashion for division of labor only.

## Civil-Military Relations

The relationship of PAVN soldiers and officers with civilians is highly complex, sometimes contradictory. It is as integrated as an armed force can be into a social system. It cannot be said of Vietnam that at some certain point the "military" ends and the "civilian" begins. The Party is distinctive from the State, but the military transcends both. There is no such thing as a "military mind" among PAVN officers, and it would be impossible for a "military industrial complex" to emerge in Hanoi.

This integrated, multifaceted role that PAVN plays cannot help but give rise to certain contradictions and cross purposes. At times PAVN seems simply confused, like an actor trying to play several roles at the same time. Its members often attempt to be all things to all people and special things to the Party. It attempts both to serve and to lead the people under a political line laid down by the Party that is contradictory to one or both of these efforts.

Since 1980 there have been indications that factionalism is developing at the Politburo level that could divide it into military vs. civilian. The Party, like communist parties elsewhere, has always feared the rise of separate military influence and consistently taken stern and careful measures to prevent it. Nevertheless, in the last few years have come indications of a sharp divergence of interest within the Politburo that has caused military members to behave as a group and take policy stands against those of the civilians.

## Intra-Military Political Dynamics

For reasons having to do with the 1954 Geneva Accords, PAVN technically is an army but actually is the Armed Forces of Vietnam. This means that organizationally, there is neither a Vietnamese Air Force nor a Vietnamese Navy, only a PAVN Air Force and a PAVN Navy. Since the Vietnam War however, there has developed a trend toward a separation of services which is apparently encouraged by Soviet advisers in Vietnam. Thus although organizational charts still list only PAVN, in actuality there is a separate Vietnamese Air Force and a Vietnamese Navy. Since the war there also has been muted but growing intraservice rivalry, particularly on the part of Air Force personnel, and in the last few years the Air Force and the Navy have increasingly taken on separate identities, that is, distinct uniforms, insignia, and other military trappings. Of course, in sheer numbers these two services still are microscopic; PAVN stands at about 960,000 men, whereas the Vietnamese Navy is about 12,000 and the Vietnamese Air Force is about 15,000. As far as is known, there is no separation of general officer rank yet; all generals are PAVN generals. Even the Navy is commanded by a PAVN general.

The prospect for the future is growth and intensification of intraservice rivalries manifested by competition in the allocation of resources, particularly manpower, as well as by rivalry at the ego level among senior officers but such rivalry is unlikely to become extreme or prove destructive for PAVN.

*Economic Development*

Vietnam can be regarded as an economic basket case. Because of a series of bad policy judgments by the Politburo since the Vietnam War, it has one of the most seriously mismanaged economic systems in the world. It is, as a result, deeply dependent on the USSR to keep its economy running.

Many of these economic ills however, do not appear to fall heavily on PAVN. It is as if PAVN lives in its own economic world where things work better than in the society's economic system. All military aid of course is imported, mostly from the USSR, and PAVN seems to lack for little. PAVN also has its own sources of food, in direct imports from the USSR, from Kampuchea, and from state farms which it runs for its exclusive benefit.

PAVN has long had what are called economic duties, like communist military forces elsewhere. During the Viet Minh War, and again during the Vietnam War, most military units had additional economic duties. They were obliged to feed themselves for two or three months of the year. They could do this either by raising food for consumption or engaging in some other economic enterprise such as lumbering from which they would derive income and use the money to purchase food. After the Vietnam War and until the war in Kampuchea and rise of the China threat, there was a distinct move by PAVN into economic enterprises. For a brief period a sizeable proportion of PAVN was engaged in construction work, running state farms and similar work. This triggered a factional dispute among professional generals within PAVN who objected to this kind of activity, while the political generals felt it was proper. Still others held it was PAVN's answer to those who, in the first years after the war, wanted demobilization. In any event, both in theory and in practice, PAVN is assigned a central role in the economic development of Vietnam. It contributes little to this effort at the moment, being preoccupied with military mattters and military preparation. But if Vietnam were at peace PAVN would represent a sizeable and well-trained labor force that could be converted to the civilian economy and make a major contribution to nation building and economic development.

## Decisionmaking Process

All major decisions within the Vietnamese political system are made by the 15 men of the Politburo. This is a unique political arrangement for of no other country can it be said that so much political power is held in so few hands. In Hanoi there is no outside institutional challenge to Politburo authority, as in the USSR; nor outside geographic challenge as in China. Some of these 15 Politburo members are military and among the most influential. Thus decisionmaking is concentrated in a civilian structure, but with strong armed forces representation there is no reason to believe that Politburo decisions are not compatible with the needs of the armed forces.

Once a major decision is taken by the Politburo, it is then communicated to the State structure through the Party's mechanism, a series of central committees that go from Hanoi down to village level and are filled with cadres whose task is to see that those decisions are fully implemented. Within PAVN there is this pervasive Party influence, but of course there is also influence in the opposite direction, that of the military on the Party system.

## Foreign Policy Objectives

Vietnam is virtually isolated in the international realm. It is surrounded by enemies, with no close friends in the entire Pacific region. Worldwide it has only two close foreign supporters, the USSR and Cuba. Vietnam does not have a fully determined, fully enunciated operating foreign policy. Thus while the influence of PAVN on foreign policy potentially could be quite great, its actual impact is slight because Vietnamese foreign policy is amorphous and unformed.

Vietnam's chief foreign policy objective at the moment appears to be to maintain intimate relations with the USSR to protect itself from China, and because the USSR is a necessary source for both economic assistance and military aid. Obviously, PAVN generals fully concur with this objective for they are totally dependent on Moscow for arms and need both the military and psychological support of the USSR against the threat of China. This is not to say that PAVN generals, particularly the professionals, approve of the way the Politburo has handled foreign relations since the Vietnam War. Probably neither they nor others in the leadership like this close relationship with the USSR, but all accept it as a necessity. There remains, however, the possibility that in the upper echelons of the armed forces are generals with the profound conviction that Vietnam's foreign relations are being so badly handled that rectification could be required should things get worse. They sense that the Pol Pot problem could have been handled either through engendering factional infighting with the Kampuchean commune Communist Party system or by steady erosive diplomatic pressure. Also that the Chinese—admittedly difficult to get along with—could have been handled in a more skilled manner which would have prevented relations from rupturing.

If there do exist any serious policy differences within the Hanoi decisionmaking structure, it would be over the China issue. However, because of Chinese counter-policy—maximum pressure on Vietnam, attempting to bleed it in Kampuchea and isolate it internationally—it is virtually impossible for anyone within the ruling group to advocate a policy other than implacable opposition. Something of the same thing can be said for better relations, which cannot be improved until the Kampuchea issue is settled satisfactorily. This, in effect, excludes improved or even changed relations.

*Defense Policy Objectives*

The influence of PAVN on defense matters, effected through the political generals in the Politburo, is virtually unquestioned. What PAVN wants or needs is what it obtains. There may be defense policy debates at the Politburo and High Command level but only on a narrower, technical level. Even then however, because of the overlap of membership, it is almost a case of PAVN arguing with itself.

One defense policy issue which existed earlier was how best to solve the Pol Pot problem in which the slower older strategy was cast aside in late 1978 in favor of a western (or Soviet) type strategy. This was chiefly a quarrel over means, not goals, however. The objective of ridding Vietnam of the Pol Pot problem was one to which all members of the Vietnamese leadership subscribed, and the argument continues over how best to pacify Kampuchea.

The overwhelming influence on Vietnam's defense planning is the Sino-Soviet dispute. China represents a threat, hence the strategic problem of how best to deal with it. The USSR represents assistance in meeting this threat—even though Hanoi cannot be sure how committed Moscow actually is—and a necessary source for military supplies to pursue the war in Kampuchea. Probably all in the leadership in Hanoi would prefer more amicable relations with China, but they also may have concluded there is little than can be done to effect this in the short run.

The unity of Indochina is still another factor in determining Hanoi's defense policies and objectives. All top military and party leaders accept the idea that the proper political configuration for the Indochina peninsula is a Federation of Indochina, to include Vietnam, Laos and Kampuchea. In the early years this was a stated goal, one North Vietnam long pursued. Indeed, one of the reasons for the present hostility with Kampuchea is that the Indochina federation triggered fear and anxiety within the Khmer Rouge and turned Pol Pot, as early as 1970, to a confrontational stance. Vietnam will pursue this goal although not necessarily by military means. Nor is it in any hurry to accomplish federation.

*Ethical/Spiritual Standards*

One of PAVN's enunciated duties is to serve as a moral example for Vietnamese society. This includes communicating a value system to the civilian society. In the North it has always taken the form of the endless drive to establish a classless society, rooting out the remnants of class structure, which seem to endure regardless of effort. In the South the PAVN task was to help "break the machine" of the southern society, which meant replacing the former social system with an equalitarian, classless structure.

Vietnam's major ethical problem appears to be moral corruption. It has always plagued both the society and PAVN, although earlier outsiders' impressions were that PAVN was less susceptible to such blandishments, and thus less corrupt than the general society. Now it appears the two are equally guilty. PAVN troops, particularly in the South, have been seduced by *cai luong* or the "yellow wind" of the South, symbolized by popular southern music but also implying the entire gentler nature of life as compared with the harsher North. Thus while the temptations of corruption spread and intensify, PAVN increasingly becomes the practitioner of wrongdoing rather than the model of propriety which society is to emulate.

*Cultural/Ethnic Patterns*

Vietnamese society is overwhelmingly (more than 90 percent) composed of ethnic Vietnamese. PAVN is even more Vietnamese, at least 95 percent, with the small remainder being ethnic minority highlanders called Montagnards.

Previously the other major ethnic minority in Vietnam and PAVN was Chinese. In earlier years in North Vietnam, Vietnam-Chinese relations were fairly amicable, although perhaps tinged with a certain hostility on the part of the Vietnamese. With the deterioration of Sino-Vietnamese relations the place of the ethnic Chinese in Vietnam society in general, and in PAVN in particular, began to deteriorate. After the 1978 Chinese border war, relations hit rock bottom. Ethnic Chinese were expelled from PAVN and many of them, as well as civilian ethnic Chinese, were expelled from the country—driven overland into China or taken to the coast, put aboard vessels and pushed out to sea. PAVN treatment of ethnic Chinese officers was particularly brutal, and for a period it became actively racist.

Treatment of the Montagnards generally was better. Many of the first members of PAVN, in the guerrilla days of World War II, were Montagnards, as were some of the first generals. Attitudes within PAVN may have changed some since the Vietnam War, since much of the resistance in the South now comes from Montagnards. This cannot help but have some effect within PAVN ranks.

## Net Assessment

In this third and concluding section we attempt to make a net assessment of PAVN which we address as questions.

Do PAVN actions contribute to Vietnam's standing in the international community?

It is difficult to separate Communist Party influence from PAVN influence in this respect. Even within PAVN there are differing factors that involve political generals and professional generals. Official pronouncements come from the political generals.

It would appear that PAVN should be regarded as a potential bellicose force, a disruptive element within the region on the basis of past performance, and could pose a future threat to Thailand.

Many of the initial postwar developments within PAVN, as within the Vietnamese society, were born of overconfidence stemming from the outcome of the Vietnam War. The Hanoi leadership believed that a militant stand towards China, called a "high posture" in Asia, was the proper way to restructure the Sino-Vietnamese postwar relationship. This also proved to be an error.

Has the Hanoi leadership, the 15 men of the Politburo who made the decisions, learned from these mistakes? Probably not, because of the nature of that leadership. Vietnam is and will be a praetorian state, communist-style. It is deeply militaristic, not in outward appearance but in mindset. Its leaders treat all external phenomena—foreign relations, for example—as military campaigns. That this should be so, that these leaders should take such a martial approach to affairs, could hardly be otherwise in light of history. The men who run Vietnam are more experienced in warfare, have been at it longer, than any other ruling group in the world. They may appear in mufti, their official photo captions may omit military titles, but they come from a world of military affairs. They think in terms of campaigns, combat, victories. All that they are, all that they have achieved, has been the fruit of war. Their victories, first in the Viet Minh War and then the Vietnam War, were battlefield victories. Each ended in the same manner, with flower-draped tanks rolling into the prostrate capital, into Hanoi, into Saigon. Other communist leaders might come to power through revolution (Russia), or courtesy of a foreign military occupation force (East Europe), or coup d'etat (Czechoslovakia) or elections (Chile), but not the North Vietnamese. Power is the barrel of a gun. Their military thinking may be unorthodox but it is still military.

However, the men of this mindset are destined soon to pass from the scene. The average age of the Politburo is 71; of the ruling Central Committee about 68. Eventually, and perhaps soon, there will come a generational transfer of power in Vietnam. We cannot be sure what the next generation of rulers will be like but we can be sure they will differ, as son always differs from father.

There is reason to believe that even now, among the professional generals, there exists considerable unease about the anachronistic sort of leadership provided by the Politburo. What is not known, however, is the direction this attitude might take.

How durable is the contemporary role of PAVN?

It is likely that PAVN will play a central role in Vietnam decisionmaking regardless of changes of government, including generational transfer of power. The sheer numbers involved would assure this. The presence of PAVN or ex-PAVN, that is the veteran population, is nearly overwhelming. Probably one out of every three males in what was North Vietnam either is in PAVN or served in it at one time. There is a dominating quality about the armed forces in Vietnam, reflected in the martial quality of the society itself, which will continue.

What, however, would be the impact of significant alteration of the armed forces role in Vietnam? The chief prospect to suggest itself here is assumption by PAVN of responsibility for a significant portion of the nation building effort. This would have to be preceded by settlement of the Kampuchean issue, which would permit withdrawal of most of the 190,000 PAVN troops now engaged in pacification efforts there, and a diminution of the China threat—neither of which seems likely in the near future. Given these changed conditions, however, the pressure quite logically would develop from forces in the Politburo, and on down— for PAVN either to demobilize or to transfer its energies *en masse* to the economic sector. The latter is more probable, since a number of arguments were raised at the end of the Vietnam War as to why PAVN should not be demobilized but be reassigned, as military units, to the economic sector. Military elements would then manage state farms, become construction companies, etc. Obviously this would have a profound effect both on PAVN and on the society.

What external entities have an interest in perpetuating, or in changing, the present role of PAVN? All of Vietnam's neighbors would strongly prefer a smaller PAVN, one turned to economic development of the country. This is particularly true of the ASEAN countries and the Chinese, who have nothing to gain from permanent hostility. Japan, and the more distant United States, would also prefer a Southeast Aisa in which there was a smaller and more benign PAVN.

The key factor here of course is China, with which unfortunately there is a circuitous force at work: because China offers a threat to Vietnam, PAVN must continue to be large and formidable, and because PAVN continues large and formidable (allied and made so by the USSR) the China threat remains. What must happen of course is to break the circle and reverse direction. This may happen eventually but it is unlikely for at least a decade.

The USSR, on the other hand, has a vested interest in seeing that PAVN's present major size and role does not change. Indeed, the basis of Moscow's presence in Indochina, and its foothold in Southeast Asia, rests on the continued need by PAVN for Soviet assistance and alliance. A PAVN hostile to China serves as a useful threat for the USSR.

One other influence should be noted in conclusion, a small cloud on the horizon, yet one with enormous potential. It is the worldwide phenomenon of the possible militarization or "martialization" of communist societies. We have seen the rise of direct influence of the military in Moscow, and even more so in Warsaw. If the trend continues, it will have profound effect on East Europe and the USSR, one that could spread to Vietnam where the preconditions are present for a similar development.

What then is the prognosis for these external influences on the future of PAVN's role?

For the near future, the prospect is that Vietnam will remain in intimate embrace with the USSR. This is assured by the Vietnamese dependency. As long as Vietnam is unable to feed itself, and as long as the China threat to Vietnam remains, this condition will prevail. However, Vietnam should within a few years be able to solve its "grain problem." There is no reason why it cannot produce all the food it requires and even some for export. It is probable that in the longer run relations between Vietnam and China will return to a normal level, despite Soviet counter efforts. Most Vietnamese, leaders and rank and file alike, privately would agree that Vietnam must get along with China, that China is simply too large and too near to permit permanent hostility. Improved Sino-Vietnamese relations, however, are not likely until the present Politburo leadership passes. Nor is there a great deal that outsiders, such as the ASEAN countries or the U.S., could do to hasten this process.

Probably the Soviet-Vietnamese relation is neither as close nor as durable as most outsiders believe, lasting only as long as Vietnam's dependency exists. Other nations, particularly the ASEAN countries, can best serve their interests by communicating to Hanoi that it is in Vietnam's interest eventually to distance itself from the USSR, and that they stand ready to improve their relations with Vietnam once this happens.

# 7

# The Political Dynamics of Military Power in Thailand

*David Morell*

For fifty years, since the military's intervention in 1932 brought to an end several centuries of absolute monarchy, the armed forces—especially the army—have exercised dominant political power in Thailand. With occasional brief lapses after World War II and again in the mid-1970s, Thai political dynamics have revolved around the army: its infantry and tank battalions, its generals and colonels, its dominance over and yet cooptation of the civil bureaucracy, the business community, political parties, and even nascent labor, farmer, and student organizations. The military has been in charge. Only its internal factional squabbles over leadership and personal power, and over access to the spoils of rampant corruption, have threatened its continued hegemony.

Yet beneath this superficial stability, the Thai armed forces were far more vulnerable as a political organization than appeared on the surface. This vulnerability increased immeasurably in the 1970s, and is burgeoning today. Indeed, while the military straddled the center of the Thai political stage, its fundamental weakness derived from this position. For though they were masters of both control and cooptation, Thailand's armed forces desperately lacked the basic political legitimacy essential to stable rule. Instead, traditional legitimacy continued to emanate from the nations' centuries-old monarchy. The Great Revolution of 1932 had replaced rule by the princes with rule by the generals, but as an institution, the military remained dependent on the royalty for prestige. By the early 1970s, however, this uneasy alliance was increasingly in disarray; and by 1981 the monarchy was openly (and dangerously) supporting one military faction against another. Lacking political legitimacy of their own, certain top military leaders (including the Prime Minister, General Prem Tinsulanonda) dragged their nation's most revered institution into the midst of the political fray.

The Thai military's problems with legitimacy over the past five decades have also come from a very different direction, as the country's political system tried to cope with the introduction of western concepts of representative democracy, political participation, "power to the people." While the 1932 coup replaced princes with generals as the nation's rulers, the coup's leaders had to justify the enormity of their decision to end Siam's absolute monarchy by citing western political doctrines. These had little relevance to the practical political realities of Thailand circa 1932, but they were essential to rationalize the military's seizure of power. In essence, democratic political theory was the only explanation the coup leaders could offer to themselves and their countrymen. Ever since, each group of military rulers has felt compelled to pay homage to participant political parties, elections, and so on. Without such a facade, their claim to rule would become tenuous, based solely on raw coercive force rather than on ideology and on traditional norms of Siamese legitimacy. While the power equation was tilted heavily toward the army and its closest allies, the people's basic legitimacy as sovereign was perceived as the only alternative to the overwhelming potential of the monarchy to legitimize all political actions—or to fail to do so.

A complicated balancing of the military's sheer power with the monarchy's classic legitimacy saw the system through the 1950s with relative success. The height of effective, mutually reinforcing interaction between palace and garrison came during the rule of Field Marshal Sarit Thanarat, Prime Minister from 1957 to 1963.[1] Since then, however, several factors rendered the old pattern of consensual rule increasingly anachronistic. Those army leaders who followed Sarit, such as Field Marshals Thanom Kittikachorn and Praphat Charusathien, were less adept than their predecessor, and the monarchy increasingly asserted itself into the power quotient, shifting the balance gradually but inexorably closer to the palace. Simultaneously, rapid social and economic change in this Southeast Asian nation and its involvement in the expanding Indochina conflict injected new claimants into the stagnant political scene. Students, labor unions, farmer groups, young monks, teachers, young army officers—all were mobilized into political activity, many for the first time. These groups claimed access to power; they demanded that the political rhetoric of 1932 and thereafter now be matched by a reality of dispersed political power. The period from 1973 to 1976 witnessed an enormous upsurge in open political confrontation.[2] While the military and monarchy reasserted their control over the chaos in October 1976, latent political pressures have remained evident.

During the 1970s, Thailand's armed forces entered an era of unprecedented challenge to their political dominance. Traditional attitudes and previous norms of action no longer sufficed. Neither coercion nor cooptation worked as it had only a decade or so earlier. A resurgent politicized monarchy and a covey of new political actors all asserted their right to the mantle of legitimacy. None of these groups recognized the military any longer as their surrogate in this role. New concepts were rampant; traditional and modern principles were in direct competition. Conflict had replaced consensus as the basic dynamic of Thai politics, posing difficult new choices and dilemmas. In response, the armed forces and other institutions began to search for their own revitalized political identity, a difficult task which is still underway in 1982.[3]

## The Military in Historical Perspective

Military power has traditionally been very important in the Thai political system. The growth of the Sukothai and Ayudhya kingdoms depended on how effectively the rulers could maintain their manpower base and, when possible, add to it by capturing population from their rival neighbors. Early militarization of the state expanded the importance of military leaders, and allowed the rulers to build grandiose temples and palaces to glorify their power and enhance their legitimacy. During the 417 years of the Ayudhyan kingdom, there was an average of one war every nine years.[4] In the early years of the Chakri dynasty, beginning in 1782, military power was an important though less dominant component of the state's authority.

The dominance of the armed forces since 1932 is apparent: over 5 decades, 6 army prime ministers held power altogether for almost 39 years, while their 9 civilian counterparts were in office for some 11 years. Moreover, several of the nine civilians were simply puppets of one faction or another within the armed forces. The institutional turmoil of this half-century is witnessed by the need to proclaim 13 constitutions, hold 14 elections, stage 15 coups (9 successful in attaining power), and install 42 different cabinets.[5] Each military intervention typically resulted in abrogation of the previous constitution (a practice David Wilson has termed "factional constitutionalism"),[6] abolition of the existing parliament, dissolution of all political parties, and suspension of all participant political activity. Each time, though, the new military leaders sought popular legitimacy by reestablishing parliamentary institutions of some kind. But these institutions eventually threatened the military leadership group's control over power and wealth, leading to yet another coup in what Dr. Chai-anan Samudavanija has termed "the vicious cycle of Thai politics."[7]

Compared to other nations, Thailand ranks quite high in the frequency of military intervention. Data on its 15 coups are presented in Table 1. Until the 1970s, this volatile political system retained surprising overall stability. An understanding of this unusual pattern of military

TABLE 1
Military Interventions in Thailand, 1932-1981

| Coup # | Date | Interval | Result |
|---|---|---|---|
| 1 | June 1932 | | Successful |
| 2 | June 1933 | 1 year | Successful |
| 3 | October 1933 | 4 months | Failure |
| 4 | November 1947 | 14 years, 1 month | Successful |
| 5 | October 1948 | 11 months | Failure |
| 6 | February 1949 | 4 months | Failure |
| 7 | June 1951 | 2 years, 4 months | Failure |
| 8 | November 1951 | 5 months | Successful |
| 9 | September 1957 | 5 years, 10 months | Successful |
| 10 | October 1958 | 1 year, 1 month | Successful |
| 11 | November 1971 | 13 years, 1 month | Successful |
| 12 | October 1976 | 4 years, 11 months | Successful |
| 13 | March 1977 | 5 months | Failure |
| 14 | October 1977 | 7 months | Successful |
| 15 | April 1981 | 3 years, 6 months | Failure |

leadership in an Asian state can be enhanced by exploration of some of the dynamics of Thai politics between 1932 and 1976.

Those army officers who, along with several civilian colleagues, staged the June 1932 coup were composed of senior and junior factions. Members of both groups had been educated in Europe. In June 1933 the junior faction, led by Major Phibun Songkram, mounted a second coup to oust the conservative civilian Prime Minister Phya Mano, installing in his place senior military leader Phya Bahon. Five years later, the junior clique took over, with Phibun the Prime Minister from 1938 to 1944. His seven cabinets contained an average of more than half military officers.

Civilians took control of the government toward the end of World War II, as it became evident that Thailand's wartime ally Japan was headed for defeat. By November 1947, however, the situation was ripe for another military intervention. This coup group was far more traditionalist than its predecessors; its leaders lacked exposure to western concepts, education, and culture and consequently had little interest in or tolerance for parliamentary processes. Colonels Sarit, Thanom, and Praphat were this group's three principal younger figures. Phibun again became Prime Minister, however, holding this position until 1957 despite three coup attempts by disaffected army and navy officers and by progressive civilians led by Dr. Pridi Banomyong, intellectual leader of the 1932 intervention.

During the early 1950s the leaders of the 1947 coup group involved themselves in hundreds of profitable commercial ventures, accruing enormous wealth for themselves, their families, and their political allies.[8] As Chai-anan summarizes:

> ... from 1947 to 1957 the young professional army officers corps was quickly transformed into politico-economic interest groups; these officers had become "commercial soldiers" whose companies gained privileges in trading as agents or compradores of government organizations.[9]

This pattern of interlocking relationships between top military leaders and the business/banking/commercial sectors has continued. According to Chai-anan: "It is quite clear that the Thai military-politicos in the past were primarily concerned with political-economic power and status more than the "corporate interest" or "professionalism" of the armed forces."[10]

By 1957, Sarit had amassed sufficient strength to overthrow Phibun and assume control himself. The period from then to Sarit's death in December 1963 was characterized by what Dr. Thak Chaloemtiarana has termed "despotic paternalism."[11] Sarit was a stern ruler, authoritarian in image and action. He thus appealed to the public's desire for stability and order. Yet Sarit also appealed successfully to his public's desires for a more responsive monarchy. In sharp contrast to Phibun, a 1932 coup promoter, Sarit forged the military-royal alliance so evident thereafter. He also initiated programs of national development in both Bangkok and the countryside, setting Thailand on the path of accelerated socio-economic change. Trends stemming from both of these actions by Sarit, so fundamental to his pattern of leadership, would by the 1970s undermine the armed forces' ability to rule Thailand successfully.

Contemporary military politics in Thailand can best be understood by looking more closely at the sixteen years from September 1957 to October 1973, when the country was ruled by a single group of men: the officers who rose to power in Sarit's coup. The character, personalities, and ruling style of these men, who called themselves simply the military group (*khana thahan*), are crucial to understanding events since 1973.

By the early 1970s, three of them shared rather uneasily the leadership of the military group: Thanom, Praphat, and General Krit Sivara. In 1957, all three had been among the nine members of the group's inner core.[12] Each had risen to power through the classic route: commander of the First Army (garrisoned in Bangkok) and later commander-in-chief of the Army. In 1973, Thanom was prime minister and supreme commander of the armed forces; Praphat was deputy prime minister, deputy supreme commander, minister of interior, and commander of the Internal Security Operations Command; and Krit was commander of the army. Following Sarit's death in 1963, Thanom became prime minister and the overtly top figure in Thai politics. Yet his political control over the army was fragile because he no longer held any actual command position. Praphat was the strong man, but the charges of massive corruption frequently directed at him constrained his potential to achieve the topmost position. Of all the senior military leaders, Praphat was the most heavily involved in financial and commercial activities.

The Thanom/Praphat alliance benefited both men. Praphat was the ultimate in a strong, decisive leader. His keen perceptions of the realities of domestic political dynamics and his vast resources of authority and wealth allowed him to operate successfully within the networks of military-politicos and their factional groups. And where he was weak—reputation, relations with the palace, and expertise in dealing with foreign governments—Thanom was strong. This alliance worked well for over a decade, providing stable leadership for the military group and for the nation. Praphat's poor reputation but immense personal power epitomize the paradox of Thailand's leadership dilemma, an issue which has troubled Thai politics for over twenty years. The political system is founded both on the sheer power of the army and on the consensus between different patron-client factions achieved through participation in shared corruption. These areas were Praphat's forte, a characteristic shared by several other contemporary army leaders. Yet the political system also depended on royal-based legitimacy, and therefore on the reputation with which the monarch held key military leaders. This is the area in which other generals, such as Prem Tinsulanonda, excelled. Not since Sarit has one man combined these two sinews of control; thus the military's vulnerability has remained.

This vulnerability became apparent to the world in October 1973, when a series of student-led demonstrations exploded unexpectedly into massive protest (500,000 demonstrators in the streets of Bangkok at one point) and then into ugly violence. Thanom and Praphat were forced into exile. The army was driven from power. To restore order, King Phumpiphon appointed respected civilian judge Sanya Thammasak as the new Prime Minister, responsible for leading the nation in a new direction. Sanya was the first civilian Prime Minister in 15 years (when an army-sponsored appointee held brief tenure), and the first civilian in 27 years to hold this position without explicit army backing.

Before examining civil-military politics after the 1973 uprising, it may be useful to examine the sources of the military's power during the several decades it did rule. One factor was the absence of organized, effective competition. The Thai armed forces were successful in preempting or crushing all potential opponents. In the 1930s, after a rebellion led by Prince Bowaradej was crushed by Phibun, the army eliminated potential opposition from the palace. Rather than challenging the military's authority, the monarchy reached a tacit agreement with the military regarding political equilibrium. The army was satisfied to see a continuation of the dynasty, under a constitutional monarchy. They allowed royal performance of religious and cultural activities. In return, the monarchy agreed to refrain from explicit political activities and provided legitimacy to army leaders. The palace recognized the army's monopolistic control over authoritative rulemaking.

The civil bureaucracy, while huge, is fragmented and relatively unorganized, and did not seriously threaten the military's power. Indeed, the country's rapid economic progress under military rule was characterized by a high degree of cooperation between soldiers and civil bureaucrats.

Similarly, the armed forces dominated important contacts with foreign elites. In this way, the generals affirmed their role of representing their country's national interests. Foreign recognition was particularly important following the military's return to power in November 1947 (and again in October 1976).

When political parties were allowed to function, many were dominated by military leaders. During 1969-1971, for example, Thanom, Praphat, Krit, and other top generals controlled the government's United Thai People's Party.[13] Control over the press has also been evident.

The economic, commercial, and business community in Thailand is dominated by Chinese (Sino-Thai) enterprises. The military elite has participated actively in these organizations over the past three decades, preempting the growth of any autonomous political power by Chinese businessmen, and thereby coopting another potential competitor.

For years the student community was also coopted. Most university students believed that the desirable careers were in the bureaucracy; thus good behavior in school was essential. In addition, Thai cultural traditions of respect for elders, patience, and rectitude acted to preclude major student demonstrations against the regime, at least until 1973.

The Buddhist monkhood, by virtue of its numbers and the respect accorded by the rest of Thai society, represents a potentially powerful force. But until 1973 the church remained pacifist, contemplative, and apolitical.

Finally, effective challenges to the military's monopoly of political power from the rural sector have emerged only in recent years in the form of the revolution being led by the communist party. The rural populace as a whole has not challenged the military's control of political power.

Thus, until the student-led activism in 1973, no competing institutions had emerged to contest military dominance of the political process. In the absence of other sources of political organization, the armed forces continued to be the only segment of society willing and able to occupy chief positions of authority.

The military's basic institutional cohesion has been another factor in its political prowess. To be sure, powerful factions have specific spheres of influence in which they operate; and membership in particular groups shifts somewhat with the flow of events. Nevertheless, on major issues (continued military rule, especially) the armed forces showed great cohesion until the 1980s.

The political skills of individual military leaders were also important. Unlike many other developing countries in which the military frequently intervenes in politics, the dynamics of the Thai political process require that the military be analyzed as a political machine, with many of its senior officers functioning as politicians. Military leaders here have not exhibited the professionalism frequently discussed in the literature on the military and political development.[14] Rather, they have acted as politicians skilled in bargaining, negotiation, compromise, and patronage.

The military structure in recent decades produced officers with a high degree of political skill, men whose political capabilities far exceeded their military effectiveness. The system rewarded the politically astute officer with rapid promotions and early access to the economic assets that allow him to develop his own set of followers (his personal political machine). In response to these incentives, skilled politicians such as Phibun, Sarit, Thanom, Praphat and Krit progressed to the top of the political hierarchy. The military has also offered an attractive career for young men from lower middle-class backgrounds and thus provided extensive opportunities for upward mobility. Young men, by attending the military academy, were able to enter a career system that placed no limits on their advance. Skills and diligence as military-politicos permitted them to attain powerful positions. Though Thailand's civil bureaucracy has also provided opportunities for high achievers to advance rapidly,[15] the armed forces have been especially striking in this regard.

The military has also been successful in coopting civilian specialists to implement and manage the national development effort. Over the past few decades, the bureaucracy has been controlled by the assignment of military officers to crucial positions of authority over civilians and by the continual process of coopting bureaucrats to work amiably for the military regime. The many cabinet and bureaucratic positions held by senior military leaders give them access to budgets, personnel, and the other sinews of power.

## Contemporary Politico-Military Dynamics

Traditional analyses of Thailand's politics emphasized consensus; they described a profound coalescence of interests and values. Conflict and competition over political power, while never completely absent, as in the many military interventions, were seen as subordinate characteristics of political life, annoying aberrations from stability and order.

In the 1970s, however, conflict replaced consensus as the dominant modality of Thai political behavior. Individually, each of the country's basic institutions, including the armed forces, is now under intense pressures. Institutional fragmentation characterizes the army, the Buddhist monkhood, the monarchy, the labor and student movements, and even the communist party. The clash over profound values and expectations led to polarization and bloodshed in the 1970s. While the 1980s have remained comparatively quiescent, no lasting rearrangement of political forces has yet occurred to recreate the basis for traditional Thai consensus. Nor should such a rearrangement necessarily be expected. Instead, the Thai political system is undergoing a deep-seated identity crisis. The relevance to modern realities of traditional institutions—preeminently the monarchy—is coming under growing scrutiny, and the fundamental legitimacy of military rule and of the political system itself is now questionable. As Professor John Girling said:

> "Thailand cannot return to the old "accepted" system because the consensus on which it was based has been lost. It is to be hoped that a new consensus can still be created, bringing in the previously neglected and repressed elements of Thai society; otherwise a harsher conflict than has yet appeared will surely take its place."[16]

This domestic political turmoil is taking place, of course, in a country immediately exposed to Vietnamese military power along the Kampuchean and Laotian borders. This combination of factors represents an enormous challenge to Thai military leaders.

The characteristics of Thailand's institutional fragmentation are clearly visible within its armed forces. Thailand's politically involved armed forces have typically witnessed competition for power between various factions and their individual leaders. Nevertheless, the military's institutional fragmentation in the 1980s has been of unprecedented severity. Starting in 1977, a group of young military officers challenged their superiors' ideology, their values, and their very control over Thai politics. Terming themselves the "Young Military Officers Group" (*khana thahan num*) or, more popularly, the "Young Turks" (a phrase used in Thai as well as in English), all were 1960 graduates of the Chulachomklao

Royal Military Academy. This group's pressures on top military leaders from 1977 to 1981, and their ultimately unsuccessful coup on April 1, 1981, are the most significant and intriguing developments in contemporary Thai politico-military dynamics.

According to Dr. Chai-anan Samudavanija, who studied this movement, the group "was formed . . . as a reactive and defensive mechanism against the growing tension and conflicts in Thai society."[17] While explicitly supportive of the three preeminent national institutions—"the nation, the religion, the monarchy"—the Young Turks also expressed deep concern over the pervasive corruption and obvious military incompetence of their politicized army superiors. As one of the group's leaders, Colonel Manoon Rupekajorn, explained to newcomers joining the group in 1980:

> . . . we could not let national security remain in the hands of those dirty politicians or even senior officers who are irresponsible to the nation and allowed themselves to be subservient to the rotten political system just to live happily with benefits handed to them by those politicians.[18]

This group of Army Colonels, most assigned to key troop command positions in and around Bangkok, or along the Kampuchean border, played a decisive role in the October 1977 coup which overthrew the reactionary civilian government of Thanin Kraivichien. They then became the primary component of General Kriangsak Chomanand's power base in his tenure as prime minister in 1977-78. Yet they were closest in ideology and personal ties to Lt. Gen. Prem Tinsulanonda, whom Kriangsak promoted to Assistant Army Commander in 1977. Leading Young Turks called Prem "papa," having served under his command.[19]

By late 1977, the Young Turks had expanded their role from safeguarding the military's institutional interests to arbitrating disputes within the political system as a whole. As Chai-anan concludes:

> Long years in the remote countryside had given these young army officers a highly politicized perspective. They lost patience with and expressed disdain for the decadent air-conditioned comfort of the traditional Bangkok military power elite. They believed that corruption had to be suppressed and more equitable national development accelerated if the real threats to the nation, both international and internal, were to be met successfully.[20]

As battalion commanders in key army units, the Young Turks differed from their predecessors not only in their unique ideology but in their autonomy. They were not simply junior clients of senior officers as their former counterparts had been under Sarit, Thanom, and Praphat.

In February 1980 the Young Military Officers Group withdrew its support from General Kriangsak's government, forcing the Prime Minister to resign. General Prem became the new Prime Minister. Later that year, however, conflict emerged between the Young Turks and their "papa." Like Thanom in the early 1970s tension arose over Prem's pending mandatory retirement from active military service at age 60 (in September 1980). While General Prem as a retired officer could have continued to serve as prime minister, his political power base derived from his position as Army Commander-in-Chief. As Dr. Chai-anan put it:

> There were feelings from certain quarters *especially the palace* that General Prem should remain in his army position for at least another year in order to stabilize both the army and the government.[21]

Major General Arthit Kamlangek, Commander of the First Army Division and reportedly a special favorite of Queen Sirikit, collected about one thousand signatures from army officers supporting Prem's extension of tenure. Although the Young Military Officers Group opposed this move as unprofessional, the King granted Prem a one-year extension on active duty. A deep fissure emerged between the group and Arthit, who they felt had involved the monarchy too deeply in political maneuvering.

By early 1981 the Young Turks were confronted by two complex and interrelated issues: a crisis in military leadership, including questions about the army's future role; and a crisis in political leadership, including questions about the future of Thailand and the identity and legitimacy dilemmas facing it. Prem needed the support of the Young Turks, since he lacked the financial resources of a Praphat or a Krit. But factional tension was intensifying between the Young Turks and Arthit's supporters. Prem and Arthit, however, also had the option of relying more explicitly on their close links with the palace in the growing conflict.

By February 1981, Prem's coalition cabinet faced a crisis from conflict between its two principal political party components: the Social Action Party and the Thai Nation Party. As so often happens in Thai politics, the issue involved political corruption. Cabinet changes in March brought in Generals Prachuab Suntharangkun and Sudsai Hasadin, both openly opposed by the Young Turks as "political opportunists." To the colonels, Prem's credibility as their leader was increasingly at stake.

On the night of March 31, the young troop commanders acted. They successfully moved their troop units into Bangkok and seized control of the city. This was not to be just one more Thai coup, however. The Young Turks at first tried to have Prem lead the coup himself, using it to purge "opportunistic and corrupt" elements from his cabinet and thereby shift the balance of power within the army toward a more professional footing. Prem apparently agreed at first to the urgings of his younger colleagues. When he changed his mind under pressure from the palace, Prem's Deputy Commander, General Sant Chitpatima, assumed leadership of the coup forces. Meanwhile, General Arthit had gone to the palace to see his patron the Queen, urging her to take whatever steps were necessary to counter the now successful coup. The Queen apparently demanded that the coup leaders allow Prem to come to the palace. Prem and the Royal Family then fled together from Bangkok to the town of Korat, in the Northeast. Here they used radio and television to express their open opposition to the coup.

This was the first time in nearly fifty years that the King and Queen of Thailand had openly opposed a successful military coup. Forty-eight hours later, without bloodshed, the Young Turks acquiesced. In Chaianan's words:

> "Without the tacit approval of the King, who openly supported Prem, the Young Turks automatically became a rebel group. Their power and influence based on control of coercive forces in society thus ended abruptly."[22]

These events were the most explicit involvement of the monarchy in Thai politics since the end of absolute monarchy.

By the early 1980s, the crisis of royal legitimacy thus was evident for all to observe. While coercive force was still perhaps a necessary element of power, it was no longer a sufficient basis for political authority in Thailand. The April 1981 coup group had seized control of Bangkok, but the King alone had the power to sanction their action. His legitimacy proved superior to their tanks and troops. The armed forces had become squeezed inexorably between two alternative patterns of legitimacy: one emanating from hierarchical traditions, the other based on popular sovereignty. For forty years, Thai political institutions failed to institute a viable participant political system. Instead, army coups had become institutionalized as the means of changing governments. But by the late 1970s these swings of the political pendulum had become more violent, more dangerous. The locus of frustration and discontent shifted to a new group, the Young Turks in the army, first as arbiters of conflict and then as an activist force for profound change. These dedicated officers responded to the intense forces of socio-economic change sweeping Thai society, shifting their own actions from an internal army pressure group concerned with military decisions to a powerful political element concerned with far larger political themes. Eventually they saw no alternative but to try to reform the corrupt, decadent system which until then they had served. At the critical moment, however, they stopped short of irrevocable defiance of the nation's traditional locus of legitimacy: the monarchy. Unwilling to go all the way to popular sovereignty by founding a republic, they instead chose to surrender control over Bangkok.

Several aspects of this complicated set of events in 1981 are vital to an assessment of the institutional fragmentation within the Royal Thai Army, and its future political role. First, in terms of sheer military power, it is important to highlight the coup group's success on April 1, 1981. Prem's opponents controlled Bangkok and most otner critical locations. Interestingly, in terms of army priorities, vital army units commanded by the Young Turks had been moved into the metropolitan area to take part in the coup, far from their normal positions facing the Vietnamese army along the Kampuchean border. From a military (though not from a psychological) perspective, it seems unlikely that the Korat-based forces aligned with General Prem could have dislodged the country's new military rulers. This makes the royalty's explicit intervention even more significant.

Second, the extent to which the King, Queen, and royal family intervened in this event was unprecedented in modern Thai politics, and crucial to the defeat of the successful coup. Never before had the leaders of one army faction been forced to drag the monarchy so blatantly into the political arena. All educated Thai observers of these striking events, and many westerners, whatever their personal political persuasions, were stunned by the extent to which the army's institutional coherence had been shattered. Prem's ability to continue as his nation's leader had been tarnished by his obvious need to rely on the nation's most revered institution. And the monarchy's own institutional vulnerability was apparent as never before (at least since the early 1930s).[23] Finally, massive bloodshed was avoided in the spring of 1981 primarily by the decision of General Sant and the Young Turks to accede to their monarch's wishes and surrender peacefully from their powerful positions in and around Bangkok. Once the Prem/palace coalition made its demands explicit from its new base in the Northeast, Thailand tottered on the brink of violence. There could have been massive conflict approaching civil war, as army units fought one another, followed perhaps by a republican form of government if the militarily stronger group had prevailed. Instead, of course, the coup's leaders decided to give up. For this, Thailand owes these pragmatic and nationalistic men a debt of gratitude.

In any event, the phenomenal split within the Thai Army was now evident for all to see. The apparent, if occasionally illusory, consensus of the recent past would be difficult to reestablish. Military leaders would continue to search for renewed legitimacy through their tenuous relations with the monarchy, and through tentative attempts to move toward popular sovereignty. Military rule in Thailand in the 1980s is far more difficult than in the past.

## Notes

1. See Thak Chaloemtiarana, *Thailand: The Politics of Despotic Paternalism* (Bangkok: Social Science Association of Thailand, 1979).
2. David Morell and Chai-anan Samudavanija, *Political Conflict in Thailand: Reform, Reaction, Revolution* (Cambridge, MA: Oelgeschlager, Gunn & Hain, Publishers, Inc., 1981).
3. Ibid., pp. 309–315.
4. Ibid., p. 12.
5. Chai-anan Samudavanija, *The Thai Young Turks* (Singapore: Institute of Southeast Asian Studies, 1982), p. 1.
6. David Wilson, *Politics in Thailand* (Ithaca: Cornell University Press, 1962).
7. Chai-anan, *The Thai Young Turks*, p. 2.
8. Ibid., pp. 14–21 and Fred Riggs, *Thailand: The Modernization of a Bureaucratic Polity* (Honolulu: East-West Center Press, 1966).
9. Chai-anan, *The Thai Young Turks*, p. 18.
10. Ibid., pp. 19–20.
11. Thak, *Thailand*.
12. Ibid., pp. 122–171.
13. David Morell, "Power and Parliament in Thailand: The Futile Challenge, 1968–1971," Ph.D. dissertation, Princeton University, 1974, pp. 175–225.
14. See Morris Janowitz, *The Military in the Political Development of New Nations* (Chicago: University of Chicago Press, 1964).
15. Opportunities for social mobility in the Thai civil bureaucracy may be coming to an end, with new recruitment restricted almost entirely to holders of foreign university degrees, most of whom are the children of the present bureaucratic elite. See Hans Dieter-Evers and Thomas Silcock, "Elites and Selection," in *Thailand: Social and Economic Studies in Development*, T. H. Silcock, ed. (Canberra: Australian National University, 1967).
16. John Girling, *Thailand: Societ and Politics* (Ithaca: Cornell University Press, 1981), p. 12.
17. Chai-anan, *The Thai Young Turks*, p. 31.
18. Quoted in Ibid.
19. Ibid., p. 34.

20. Ibid., p. 35.
21. Ibid., p. 50; emphasis added.
22. Ibid., p. 55.
23. See Kenneth Landon, *Siam in Transition* (Chicago: University of Chicago Press, 1939).

# 8

# The Role of the Armed Forces and Police in Malaysia

*Robert L. Rau*

In 1957 Malaya (now West Malaysia) was granted independence within the British Commonwealth. Sabah and Sarawak (East Malaysia) were managed by the British North Borneo Company and the Brooke family, respectively, until 1942 and were British colonies between 1946 and 1963. When Malaya was granted independence in 1957, the political superiority of the Malays and the economic strength of the Chinese were validated in the new constitution. Movement toward the Federation of Malaysia by 1963 was fueled by the need to provide a governmental framework for Sabah and Sarawak and use their indigenous populations to balance the 75% Chinese population of Singapore. The Federation of Malaysia, composed of Malaya, Sabah and Sarawak was formed on September 16, 1963. Singapore was a member of the Federation until 1965.[1]

Malaysia is divided into two regions separated by 400–1000 miles of South China Sea, a distance significant in the administration and political give and take of a nation composed of three races.[2] Recognizing the barriers that the population and cultural differences represented, London worked to accommodate the desires of both Malays and Chinese.

### Armed Forces and Royal Malaysian Police in the Security of Malaysia

The Royal Malaysian Police were added to the Malaysian Armed Forces because of their central role in the security apparatus. Since World War II Malaya has been combatting the Malayan Communist Party (MCP). The MCP challenged British control of Malaya and Singapore in 1948 through 1957 with terrorism (the "Emergency"), armed attacks on military and police installations, small unit combat in the jungle, and a very effective propaganda and psychological warfare campaign designed to exploit racial divisions in the society. Soon after 1957 Indonesia confronted Malaysia with a major dispute but limited military activity (1963-1966). "Confrontation," demonstrated the need for flexible armed forces, an upgraded Navy, and a newly established Air Force. The Police played a major security role during the "Emergency" as well as "Confrontation." They functioned not only in the traditional role but also in international intelligence, counterespionage, and jungle oriented infantry units from squad to battalion size.

The Malaysian government refers to the army and police as "security forces" (SF). The Internal Security Act [Malaysia, 82/1960: Part 1] States:

> Security forces include the Royal Malaysian Police, the Police Volunteer Reserve, the Auxiliary Police, persons commissioned or appointed under the Essential (Special Controlling) Regulations, 1948, the armed Forces.[3]

The Malaysian government has linked the armed forces and police in security matters in response to the threat of the MCP. The linkage is the joint nature of operational planning and field activities. The Joint Army and Police are organized by task according to the situation and have developed over nearly thirty-seven years (1948-85).[4] A largely successful method of combatting the armed units of the MCP developed, characterized by the mobilization of both police and army units. The National Security Council and the State Security and District Committees provide strategic direction.

Although faced with the task of nation-building, and important questions concerning political and economic progress, security and stability became the primary goals.

Two other considerations are of considerable importance:

- Civilian control of the government has been established and unbroken since independence in 1957.
- The civil service plays a major role in the direction and control of the armed forces and police.

Besides the "Emergency" and "Confrontation," the communal riots in 1969 and the continuing challenges of the MCP, the Islamic fundamentalist movement and the separatist political movement in the Malaysia-Thai border area have tested the political and social fabric of the country. The political leadership (the Alliance Party, now the National Front) has not changed since 1957.

They acknowledged that Malaysia would have to provide for its national defense and security by joining a military alliance with the United Kingdom (The Anglo-Malaysian Defense Agreement of 1957). The Internal Security and defense portfolios have been closely controlled and "a political-military-police matrix has been established in the administrative politics of Malaysia."[5] The role of the civil service in police and military matters is important because of their balance which counters the influence of police and armed forces officials.

## History of Armed Forces and Police

Police units were formed soon after the British colonized Malaya in 1786, and many were used in a paramilitary role.[6] Building a Malay defense corps was discussed in 1913 by the British colonial government but not until 1932 was formal approval granted. Support for the Malay Regiment was expressed by the Royalty as well as the common citizen.[7] This unit accepted only Malays as recruits. In 1958 it was designated the Royal Malay Regiment by the King with the intent that it provide the services with infantry. During the Emergency, the Federation Regiment was established by the British to provide a unit in which other races could enlist. It merged with the Federation Armored Car Regiment in January 1960 to become the Federation Reconnaissance Corps, equipped with armored cars to support infantry and police field units, and served with distinction as the reconnaissance unit of the Malaysian Army in Sarawak and Northern Malaysia.[8]

The development of the armed services was slow prior to independence, since British, Australian and New Zealand units were responsible for the external defense and internal security of Malaya in 1947 and the early fifties. The Naval service began in 1934 as the Malay version of the Royal Navy, officered by Malayans with British commanders. In 1952 it became the Royal Malayan Navy.[9] The Royal Malayan Air Force (RMAF) was formed in June 1958, its first local officers commissioned in January 1959. The first RMAF pilots flew STOL aircraft, for resupply in jungle areas.[10]

In the post war period, the police developed both the functional and paramilitary roles. The Emergency in 1948 caused them to establish jungle squads, whose units were increased in size in the early years into jungle companies. During the Emergency, the police were waging an effective campaign to win the "hearts and minds" of people living in the rural areas of Malaya. Police units could identify the communist terrorists (CT) and their location (Special Branch). The police field forces (PFF) were then employed to find and pin the CT units and military units were called if the number of CTs made it necessary. Police units operating and working the same locations could provide security for people living in the area.[11] The guarantee of security frequently produced information which was used to induce surrender or capture of the CTs. Use of military air and artillery fire to harass and interdict was found to be effective by the authorities in Malaya. The use of civic action, new villages, and increased detective work evolved in response to the lack of success of purely military means.

Independence in 1957 and the end of the Emergency in 1960 ended the assured defense by the United Kingdom, Australia and New Zealand. Had "Confrontation" not developed it is probable that Malaya and Singapore would have been left to their own defense solutions in the early sixties.

## ANZAM

In 1949 the Governments of Australia, New Zealand and the United Kingdom agreed to coordinate defense planning in the "ANZAM" region. This included the Australian and New Zealand home territories and the British territories in Malaya (to include Singapore) and Borneo.[12] The agreement also covered adjacent sea and air spaces. Initially it was to protect the communications routes and consisted of coordinated efforts between the military services of the country involved. It did not encompass political commitments. Later, in 1955 the ANZAM arrangement was expanded to cover the defense of Malaya.[13] The same year, Australia and New Zealand agreed to an enlarged military commitment in Malaya; they joined British and other Commonwealth forces in counter-terrorist operations against the Malayan Communist Party (MCP) and formed the core of the Commonwealth Strategic Reserve.

In September 1951, Australia, New Zealand and the United States signed the ANZUS Treaty which provided security protection for Australia and New Zealand in the event of aggression. It also formalized United States interest and military support in the event of an armed attack on their metropolitan territory, island territories, or armed forces, public vessels or aircraft in the Pacific. The political and security implications of ANZUS provided the ANZAM group with political influence and potential military force in its dealings with MCP.

Australia and New Zealand's participation in ANZAM and subsequent security arrangements with the United Kingdom relative to Malaya have been loosely knit "understandings" which have provided Britain with selective military assistance, when necessary. These commitments were accepted by both countries as evidence of their concern for the security of Southeast Asia and their backing of British policy.

## AMDA

When Malaya attained independence in 1957, it sought defense protection against subversion from within and from an external attack.

Australia and New Zealand agreed to contribute limited air, naval and ground forces in support and the relationship was formalized in the Anglo-Malayan Defense Treaty of 1957 (AMDA).

AMDA was originally structured to apply only to Malaya. Singapore, in 1957, was the major British military base in Southeast Asia and still a Colony. Britain was reluctant to relinquish political control and wished to retain the freedom to station troops in Singapore to insure political stability and to house its strategic reserve forces, committed to SEATO. AMDA did not permit Britain to station its strategic reserve in Malaya and required Malayan permission to use British troops stationed there anywhere else in Southeast Asia. The Federation of Malaya, mindful that its population was more than forty percent overseas Chinese, disassociated itself from the SEATO pact. From the Commonwealth view, these restrictions limited the usefulness of troops stationed in Malaya and made the military facilities in Singapore much more important.

AMDA worked satisfactorily for all parties and Malaya was able to devote its fiscal resources to economic development, not for defense purposes. Britain was able to maintain a security presence in Malaya/Singapore which protected its investments, provided training areas for its military forces and contributed to the security of Southeast Asia.

## Defense Arrangements—Federation of Malaysia, 1963

In 1961, during negotiations which culminated in the establishment of the Federation of Malaysia in 1963, the United Kingdom and Malaya agreed that the AMDA Treaty of 1957 be extended. This permitted the British to continue ground, air and naval units in Singapore for use in Malaysia or throughout Southeast Asia.

The separation of Singapore from Malaysia in August 1965 left Malaysia protected under the Joint Statement of 1961 but placed Singapore in the untenable position of not having a formal treaty for defense. The British Government indicated that, in practical terms, its defense commitments to Singapore remained unchanged. An unpublished agreement between Singapore and the United Kingdom in June 1967 pledged Singapore a voice as to the number and strength of British troops adequate for Singapore's defense. Great Britain and Malaysia concluded a like agreement in July 1967.

The announcement in January 1968 of Britain's accelerated military withdrawal plans for Singapore and Malaysia left both countries to provide for their individual and "indivisible" defense.

In June 1969 representatives from Great Britain, Australia, New Zealand, Malaysia and Singapore met in Canberra, Australia, to discuss efforts to provide joint security for Singapore and Malaysia after the termination of the AMDA Treaty of 1957.

### Five-Power Group Political and Military Negotiations, 1968–1972

The British Government's decision to reduce or withdraw its military forces from Malaysia/Singapore was evident in 1966. The January 1968 announcement of the British withdrawal of all forces by 1971 left Malaysia and Singapore with little time to expand their small military forces. The withdrawal also implied cancellation of the AMDA defense treaty.

In August 1967 the Prime Minister of Malaysia suggested that a Five-Power Conference be convened to discuss mutual security concerns. Australia, Britain, New Zealand and Singapore agreed to discussions in August 1967 but it was apparent that little unanimity existed among the powers regarding commitments replacing AMDA.

The British Labor Government's decision to retrench east of Suez left Australia the only viable military power able to shoulder the British security commitment.

Representatives of the Five-Power group met in Kuala Lumpur, Malaysia in June 1968, expressing interest in developing future cooperation by all concerned. It was agreed to replace AMDA when the following substantative matters were settled:

1. Singapore and Malaysia agreed that the defense of both states was indivisible and they resolved to improve their individual defense postures. This declaration was welcomed by the other three Governments.[14]
2. Singapore outlined plans to establish an air force which would supplement the Five-Power integrated air defense system being established to protect Malaysia/Singapore air space.
3. Australia promised air support to the integrated air defense system until 1971. In 1968 Australia had not determined whether it would preserve a defense commitment in Southwest Asia after 1971, let alone assume the major security responsibility upon the departure of the British.
4. The conference agreed to hold joint ground exercises in the Malaysia/Singapore area after 1971 and to establish a multinational joint exercise planning staff and a jungle warfare training school.
5. Britain stated that a major exercise should be held in 1970, the forerunner of joint exercises to be held regularly after 1971. These would enable Britain to test and refine its ability to rapidly deploy troops from the U.K. to Singapore, if necessary after 1971.

In May 1969 communal rioting between Malays and Chinese and later between Malays and citizens of the Indian Community in Kuala Lumpur threatened the establishment of the Five-Power defense group.[15]

Communal riots in Malaysia or Singapore have always affected racial relations in the other state. The May rioting in Kuala Lumpur had immediate consequences in Singapore where limited numbers of Chinese and Malays were arrested, and incidents in that city restricted, due to quick riot control procedures and impartial and strict justice for violators regardless of race.

Australia perceived the stationing of its troops in Singapore or Malaysia as an invitation to involvement in possible communal disturbances.

In June 1969 representatives of the five nations met in Canberra for further discussions, alert to the May riots in Kuala Lumpur and the Philippine claim to Sabah, East Malaysia.

Military aspects of the Five-Power relationship proceeded smoothly. Advisory Working Groups established after the 1968 conference focused on logistics, force levels and a large scale joint exercise in Spring 1970, which would test the British ability to airlift troops from Britain. Other topics of importance involved the Jungle Warfare School at Ulu Tiram in the southern part of Malaysia and billets for Australian and New Zealand troops. Both countries insisted that their units be moved from Terendak, near Malacca in West Malaysia, to Singapore. Lee Kuan Yew stated that Australian forces would be better employed in West Malaysia as a token of Australian commitment to maintain "forces of sanity and stability there." This remark referred to the plight of Chinese living in Malaysia who suffered considerable losses in the May 1969 riots. It is probable that the Australian/New Zealand decision to move to Singapore took into consideration the possibility of communal conflicts as well as cost factors and facilities. The ANZUK states encouraged Singapore-Malaysian defense cooperation, including scheduling joint training exercises. The prevailing mutual distrust in the Singapore-Malaysian relationship, however, precluded that form of joint defense relationship.

The Australian decision to move its troops to Singapore and its vacillation concerning defense of Malaysia moved Tunku Abdul Rahman to state in August 1969 that the "Five-Power defence arrangement was useless now as far as Malaysia is concerned." He added that Malaysia would upgrade its relations with its neighbors. Malaysia had been quietly negotiating bilateral security arrangements with Thailand and Indonesia involving coordination and logistics assistance in joint campaigns on their mutual borders against communist terrorists.

In April 1970 the Five-Power nations staged Bersatu Padu (Malay for complete unity), a joint military exercise in north Malaysia. Approximately 25,000 troops of all five countries participated. The scenario called for the Five-Power forces to repel invasion of Malaysia by conventional forces from the mythical state of "Ganesia." Bersatu Padu reflected the desire of the ANZUK nations to avoid committing their troops to anything other than an external attack. Singaporean and Malaysian units worked together in this exercise, with troops from Singapore operating in Malaysian territory for the only time.

The relative success of this operation encouraged political and fiscal support in the Five-Power nations. On April 21, 1971 the Five-Power group agreed on defense arrangements to take effect on November 1, 1971. The agreement stressed that, in the event of any armed attack, the member countries would "hold immediate consultations" and decide what measures would be taken "jointly or separately" to meet the threat. Implicit in the understandings was that no ANZUK state was obligated to come to the aid of Singapore or Malaysia. Also, no ANZUK forces would be used in case of internal aggression or communal strife in either country.

On November 1, 1971 Britain and Malaysia terminated the Anglo-Malaysian Defense Agreement. Letters were also exchanged by Australia and New Zealand with Malaysia terminating their association with AMDA. Letters were exchanged between the ANZUK states and Singapore and Malaysia setting out the arrangements which would apply after November 1.

ANZUK forces numbered approximately 6,000 men, with Australia the largest contributor. ANZUK military force in 1971 included three battalions of infantry, five to six destroyers or frigates, two submarines and a supporting air contingent of fighter bombers, helicopters, long-range reconaissance and transport aircraft. This force, backed with available infantry, amphibious personnel carriers, tanks and artillery from Singapore and Malaysia, adequately symbolized the interest and desire to help of the ANZUK states. It was probably inadequate to defend either Singapore or Malaysia from an external attack.

The military components of the Five-Power group were in three categories: ground, air, and naval. The effectiveness of ANZUK ground units were limited by a scarcity of training areas, and their mission. They represented the nonutilitarian aspect of the Five-Power pledge. They would either be reinforced or withdrawn in the event of an attack on either Malaysia or Singapore.

The integrated Air Defense System made little progress due to its highly technical equipment. Malaysia and Singapore are approaching competence in developing their air and missile systems. ANZUK attached units are rotated into Malaysia and Singapore from home airfields.

The ANZUK naval contribution is the most functional in that its ships patrol the Strait of Malacca and adjacent waters, showing their flags and limiting the pirate and smuggling activities rife in the area.

ANZUK forces operate largely independently of the military forces of Malaysia and Singapore. Small groups of instructors function within units of the Malaysian and Singaporean military but, with the exception of Bersatu Padu, little joint training has been accomplished. Five-Power cooperation and mutual assistance, and joint planning and training, have evolved better in the Air and Naval areas. The Malaysia-Singapore impasse in some aspects of joint defense planning (involving ground operations) illustrates the difficulties in planning and training for defense against attack on either of the countries or upon both at the same time.

Politically, the Five-Power arrangement has been limited by clashes of national interest and differences in objectives and perceptions of the participating states.

Malaysia's position is ambivalent. The last British military unit left in 1976. One Australian Air Force Squadron remains in Malaysia until 1986 when it will be withdrawn. In early 1985 New Zealand, alone, continues to guarantee a military presence, an infantry battalion in Singapore, for the future. Malaysia's basic foreign policy premise, however, is its non-aligned stance and its concept of the neutralization of maritime Southeast Asia (ZOPFAN) and its recent doctrine of comprehensive security.[16] The formulations highlight ASEAN resiliance, exclusion of the superpowers from the region and regional security. Malaysia is on record that, should the neutralization proposal eventuate, it would dissociate itself from the Five-Power arrangements.

From 1964 to 1985 the armed forces and police have expanded in manpower as well as quality and quantity of weapons, aircraft and ships. The May 1969 riots in West Malaysia and the apparent breakdown in leadership in the Royal Malay Regiment during incidents in Kuala Lumpur forced further consideration of the racial composition of the armed forces and the police.[17] The opposition clamored for an explanation from the government, which triggered a review of management, administration, and recruiting procedures in the armed forces and police. The 1969 riots had considerable impact on purchases of equipment, training of officers and enlisted, composition, location and mix of forces.

After 1971, emphasis was placed upon a gradual buildup of the security forces and the initiation of bilateral relations with both Indonesia and Thailand. The fall of South Vietnam in 1975 and the invasion of Kampuchea by Vietnam in 1978 forced still another defense review. The perceived Vietnamese threat, either by conventional attack or increased guerrilla pressure, caused a change in emphasis to conventional war tactics. In 1980 the government accelerated recruitment of officers, and established a staff college. The June 1980 Vietnamese incursion into Malaysia's border territory highlighted the changing security balance in the region, especially as Malaysia was an active bilateral security partner with Thailand. During 1981, the Malaysian government committed itself to a massive buildup of equipment and manpower in the armed forces and the police. Much of this expansion was included in the Fourth Malaysia Plan, completed by 1981. Conventional warfare training exercises followed the purchase of modern, heavy weapons.

Signs that the government of Dr. Mahathir might be concerned less with security, and more with management and economies in military expenditures, became apparent in December 1981. Six months later the Defence Ministry cut between 800 and 1 billion dollars from the 1982 defense budget and closed recruit training centers in Johore and Sabah. The RMAF base in Gongkedak was deferred, as were forward RMN bases in Johore Baru, Labuan, and Kuching. These retrenchments mean that the manpower buildup since 1979 is slowed but weapon purchases were not reduced.

## Strategy and Disposition of the Armed Forces and Police

Malaysia seeks to combat internal economic and social challenges and communal instability, as well as possible external threats, by promoting economic and social development for its people in order to guarantee political stability. Malaysia enjoys substantial success as an authoritarian democratic system with an excellent record of internal defense against a thirty-four year insurgency.

Affiliation with ASEAN and the Five-Power group provide limited security benefits and the larger possibility for substantial diplomatic assistance in time of need. The security forces of the country are structured and operate to support this policy.

## Security Problems

*Internal Threats*

Communist Party of Malaysia (MCP)—The MCP is no longer a military threat in West Malaysia, isolated from the mainstream of political life. It endures because it has exploited communal grievances among the Chinese and smaller numbers of other races. A pernicious problem is the MCP's ability to infiltrate trade unions, schools and political parties. Other successful ventures have converted or corrupted editors, publishers and government officials.

North Kalimantan Communist Party (NKCP)—The NKCP is very small (perhaps 150), on the jungled Sarawak-Kalimantan border. Joint Task Forces of Malaysian and Indonesian soldiers pursue these individuals. The defection of more than five hundred members of this party in 1973 left a limited structure and terrorist force in the field. Malaysian and Indonesian forces cooperation and joint operations have demonstrated the effectiveness of bilateral security cooperation against these communists. The NKCP is denied sanctuary on either side of the Sarawak-Kalimantan border.

Pluralism—Malaysians of Chinese race believe that government policies are unfair to them and are designed to economically advance Malays at their expense. The Malay government intends to give Malays equal status through its "New Economic Policy." The MCP takes advantage of this policy and friction will exist because of it.

Islam—A 1984 government White Paper, entitled "Threat to Muslim Unity and National Security," named the Pan Islamic Party (PAS) and the Communist Party of Malaya (CPM) as guilty of exploiting the Islamic religion for their political ends. Other concerns related to security and politics involved continuing problems with the continuous export of religious influences and doctrine from Iran.[18]

*External Threats*

"Soviet Hegemony" (Vietnam and Kampuchea)—The Malaysian government is concerned about the USSR becoming involved in Southeast Asia, yet established relations with them because the Soviet bloc had become an important market for primary commodities such as rubber. The Soviets use naval bases in Vietnam and Kampuchea and in return provide considerable financial and security assistance to Vietnam. Malaysia perceives an enlarging Soviet interest in the loosely organized region, and is concerned that Soviet military and economic assistance make it easier for Vietnam to threaten Thailand, bordering Malaysia, with invasion.

"PRC Hegemony"—Malaysia normalized diplomatic relations with the PRC in 1974 but is apprehensive about the long-term interests of the PRC. The relationship has been correct but the PRC's recognition and support of the MCP hinders closer ties. The Communist Party of China supports the MCP in its unique form of party-to-party relations but has moderated its support. In 1981 Chinese Premier Zhao Ziyang attempted to distance the government of the PRC from the MCP.

"Vietnamese Hegemony"—The perception of threats from Vietnam includes but is not limited to a "worst case scenario," an invasion. Yet Malaysia has boldly come to terms with the Vietnamese, and has maintained a dialogue with them without appearing to challenge the more formal understanding by ASEAN and Vietnam to disagree. Current Malaysian equipment purchases and military training are directed toward repulsing a conventional invasion, coming through Thailand or over the beaches used by the Japanese in 1942. Other problems caused by Hanoi are increased funding for Thai communists, or those of the MCP or its splinter, the Revolutionary Malay Nationalist Party (RMNP).

*Other External Security Related Issues*

Protection of Malaysia's Two Hundred Mile Economic Zone—In 1980 the government declared a 200-mile exclusive economic zone along its coasts, including Malaysian waters in the Strait of Malacca, the Gulf of Thailand and the South China Sea. Maritime issues and problems have become prominent: examples are greatly expanded economic pressures to exploit oil and fisheries; smuggling, piracy, and the broader question of the boat people. In November 1977 the RM Navy intercepted a Thai smuggling vessel loaded with electrical goods. In April 1982 the RM Navy sent two minesweepers to protect Malaysian fishermen in Indonesian waters. A potentially serious incident involved Vietnamese troops on Amboyna Island north of Sabah. Amboyna is considered by Malaysia within its continental shelf.[19] Vietnamese troops were discovered on the island in 1978.

## Security Solutions

*Equipment, Manpower and Bases*

The July 1982 slowdown in buildup probably does not alter the government estimates. Base construction has not been deleted, only deferred. New equipment purchases continue as do increases in manpower in the armed forces and police, the only delay being officer selection and training. Malaysia's security lies partly in more sophisticated equipment, additional manpower, and new bases in strategic areas.

Emphasis will continue on providing permanent internal security in the north and northeast states of Kedah, Perlis, Kelantan and Trengganu with economic development an additional goal. A highway across Malaysia from Penang to Kota Baru, and the MS2OO Trengganu hydroelectric dam must be protected. Communist threats to security in Sarawak have abated: the limited number of terrorists pose a minor security problem. Emphasis in east Malaysia is on naval patrols, such as the protection of its 200 mile economic zone.

## Five-Power Defense Arrangements, Bi-lateral Relations in ASEAN and Malaysia-Singapore Security Relations

External treaties have limited utility to Malaysia in terms of guaranteed security assistance in time of need. The lesson of the 1970s is that England, Australia, New Zealand, and the United States are not in political or economic positions to always assist under a treaty commitment. Malaysia recognized these realities.

The Five-Power arrangement was moribund because little was demanded of it. Two beneficial aspects spanned the 1970s, the Integrated Air Defense System (IADS), which controls the air defense of Malaysia and Singapore, and infrequent training opportunities in Australia for army units. Malaysia has benefited from the Five-Power relationship in diplomatic and political associations. In the security calculations of any power threatening Malaysia the probable early involvement (politically, militarily, or both) of Australia, New Zealand and the U.K. must be considered.[20] Under ANZUS, any attack on Australian or New Zealand forces would trigger consultation with the United States, resulting in the possibility of assistance. The resurgence of the Five-Power concept in the early 1980s may be credited to Australia. The Soviet invasion of Afghanistan, the Vietnamese invasion of Kampuchea, were partially responsible. Any Five-Power agreement in the 1980s may have "a new look," since Singapore asserted that the arrangements were "outdated" and what was needed was a collective defense arrangement based on U.S. involvement.[21]

Malaysia is an active member of the Association of Southeast Asian Nations (ASEAN Brunei-Indonesia-Malaysia-Philippines-Singapore-Thailand). A major Malaysian foreign policy concept long endorsed by ASEAN is the declaration of the Southeast Asia region as a Zone of Peace, Freedom and Neutrality (ZOPFAN). Whenever some ASEAN members suggest that the organization be "enhanced" into a security organization, Malaysia vetoes the suggestion. Malaysia has quietly opted for bilateral security cooperation with other members of ASEAN: Malaysia-Thai cooperation on their joint border against MCP terrorists; Malaysia-Indonesia cooperation in the Sarawak-Kalimantan border area, Malaysia-Singapore Special Branch cooperation against the MCP, and in other police matters. Malaysia's rejection of an ASEAN security pact stems from the belief that it would cause dissension and lend credence to Hanoi's claim that it is threatened by ASEAN.

## The Impact of the Armed Services and Police on Politics, Policy-Making and Communal Relations

In a region where the military has frequently assumed political control the Malaysian example is noteworthy. Neither the military nor the police has ever attempted to play a political role or sought political power.

The structure of the armed services and policy provides that civilians control personnel selection for senior ranks, the purse strings for all of the services, and the decision making procedures for operations. The leadership of the armed forces and police, the political world and civil service is all Malay, from the same language stream and social strata of Malay society and with similar values and view.[22] An officer's misuse of his position is a serious offence, and officers have been asked to resign while others have retired.

Concerns for an over-powerful military aristocracy have been expressed by the opposition in the House of Representatives since the 1960s.[23] The military has not elected to exceed its traditional duties because the usual rationale is nonexistent in Malaysia. The political system has functioned, although not without stress, especially in the area of equal access to education and some economic opportunities.

Malaysia has both an internal and external security threat. The CPM insurgency has been the focus of its military planning, and the Army and RMAF have been employed in counter-insurgency roles for the past thirty-five years. Government strategy is to contain the CPM guerrillas and prevent them from spreading into the heavily urban areas on the peninsular west coast.

The uniformed services are well paid, well taken care of on retirement, and enjoy commercial opportunities when no longer on active duty.

The military and police have had no glaring grievance or necessity to justify the assumption of power. Too, the police with their paramilitary capabilities, manpower, equipment, and control of the intelligence apparatus of Malaysia tend to balance the army. The army and police have made major social and economic contributions in the rural areas. Military auxiliaries such as the Territorial Army (reserves) and the Peoples Volunteer Corps have served in community development tasks, natural disasters and other emergencies, as well as security related duties.

In the armed forces and police some units are more effective than others in dealing with the civil populace. In Malaysia the police are trained to enforce the law and protect the people, whatever racial group they may be dealing with, while the army is trained in the use of force as a first priority.[24] In Malaysia both police and military are aware of the importance of good civil-military relations. The MCP has striven to separate armed terrorists from their supporters in the cities and rural areas. With the exception of the 1969 riots, all civil disorders have been handled by specially trained Federal Reserve Units or Police Field Forces. Few of these disputes have had overtly racial overtones.

The ethnic or racial composition of the armed forces/police is important mainly in terms of their perception by various racial groups. The Chinese and Indian communities harbor fears resulting from the 1969 riots. Ethnic and cultural differences abound in Malaysia. The probability of Royal Malay Regiment (all Malay) troops being used against Chinese citizens has been greatly reduced although not eliminated. The police are tasked with riot control responsibilities, and are traditionally multi-ethnic (40% Malay, 40% Chinese, 20% Indian) with a greater number of non-Malay officers than other military units. The government is properly concerned about the possibility of racial clashes developing into full scale rioting and works to reduce the probability that such rioting would recur.

Most enlisted are Malay in the army, police and other services. A more multi-ethnic cross section exists within the officer ranks (with the exception of the Royal Malay Regiment), especially in the Navy and Air Force. There are ethnic and cultural complexities in recruiting for all the security services. Cultural factors are especially important. The Chinese are not usually interested in serving in the army and police. They gravitate to the Special Branch, technical positions and office billets in the Navy and Air Force. The most dire predictions regarding the "racial factor" stemming from the 1969 riots, have not materialized. Overt racial friction in Malaysia is not commonplace and the military has not attempted to assume control of the government.

## Overall Net Assessment of the Armed Forces and Police in Malaysia

Malaysia's success in political-security terms is attributed to its ability to cope with internal challenges to its governmental system. The insurgency provided the justification for internal security policies and procedures which are, in many ways, Draconian. One cannot predict what may evolve in communal relations. The Malay position is that the economic injustices of the colonial past must be eradicated and the Malay "bumiputeras" be given equal opportunity with Chinese and Indians for economic advancement.

Malaysia's police field forces are employed in cooperation with Thai forces in Thailand. Malaysian police and army units have also operated with Indonesian forces. Special Branch and other police units cooperate on a daily basis with their counterparts in Singapore. The security services of Malaysia are increasingly relied upon within ASEAN.

Islamic fundamentalist activity is presently on the rise in Malaysia, presenting new security ramifications. Strong and stable security forces in Malaysia are vital to Malaysia's State security and its role in ASEAN.

The Malaysian political leadership, in its direction and control of the security services, has been impressive and prudent. They have structured the armed forces and police to deal with pragmatic and perceived internal and external threats.

## Notes

1. Racial, political differences and issues in Malaysia are discussed in the following works: Stanley S. Bedlington, Malaysia and Singapore, the Building of New States (Ithaca, NY: Cornell University Press, 1978); Karl von Vorys, *Democracy Without Consensus Communalism and Political Stability in Malaysia* (Princeton, NJ: Princeton University Press, 1975).

2. Approximate population statistics as of 1978: 45.2% Malays, 35.1% Chinese, 10% Indians, 9.7% other racial groups in Sabah and Sarawak. A census taken in 1980 tentatively showed the numbers of Chinese decreasing in West Malaysia Department of Statistic (K.L., 1978), also 1981 *Asia Yearbook* (Hongkong: Far Eastern Economic Review, 1981), p. 191.

3. See Zakaria Haji Ahmed. "The Bayonet and the Truncheon: Army-Police Relations in Malaysia," *Journal of Asian Affairs*, Vol. 3, No. 2 (February 1978), p. 103.

4. Ibid., p. 106.

5. Ibid., p. 105.

6. Ibid., p. 107.

7. See, "Early Years of the Malaysian Armed Forces," *Asian Defense Journal*, Kuala Lumpur (April 1982), p. 23.

8. See, "The 3rd Regiment Royal Malaysian Reconnaissance Corps," *Asian Defense Journal*, Kuala Lumpur (Sept/Oct 1978), pp. 68–69.

9. See, Chandran Jeshurun, *Malaysian Defence Policy* (Kuala Lumpur: Penerbit Univeresiti, Malaya, 1980), p. 2.

10. Ibid.

11. The term "Emergency" is used to describe a war which lasted from 1948 to 1960 and continues today in much reduced scope. The London insurance market paid for losses of equipment, stocks, etc. through riot and civil commotion in an "emergency"; but not in a war.

12. During the early phases of the Emergency (1949–1955) both Australia and New Zealand committed small air units in support of the ground forces deployed by the United Kingdom and other Commonwealth countries. See Derek McDougall, "The Evolution of Australia's Defence Policy in Relation to Malaysia-Singapore, 1964–1971," *Journal of Southeast Asian Studies*, Vol. III, No. 1 (March 1972), p. 97; Keith Jackson, "Because it's there ... A consideration of the decision to commit New Zealand troops to Malaysia beyond 1971," *Journal of Southeast Asian Studies*, Vol. II, No. 1 (March 1971), pp. 22–23.

13. The commonwealth Strategic Reserve force was established as a task organized mobile force to be used on a regional basis and in support of SEATO contingency plans. It was to have included military units from all of the Commonwealth countries in Southeast Asia and Australia. It failed to develop into the type of organization originally envisioned. The British, Australian and New Zealand units remained tied up in the campaign against the Communist Terrorists (CT's) in Malaya until 1960. See Jackson, pp. 22–23.

14. In part of the 1965 Separation Agreement, Singapore and Malaysia had pledged to cooperate in defense matters. Little cooperation and consistent low level bickering had occurred up to the shock of the British announcement to withdraw its military forces. The ANZUK states were relieved to see Singapore and Malaysia showing evidence of defence cooperation. Instituting a joint defense command with all of its inherent political aspects would have been impossible with two members hostile to each other.

15. A detailed discussion of these riots and their political and social complications may be found in Derek Davies, "Some of Our Best Friends. . .," *Far Eastern Economic Review*, Vol. LXIV, No. 26 (June 26, 1969, pp. 700–705, and Dr. Felix V. Gagliano, *Communal Violence in Malaysia, 1969: The Political Aftermath* (Athens: Ohio University Center for International Studies, Southeast Asia Program, 1970).

16. Datuk Musa Hitam, "Malaysian Doctrine of Comprehensive Security," *Asian Defense Journal*, (August 1984), pp. 14–16.

17. Among the many accounts of the riots and their impact on the concept of Malay superiority and political control of the government, two accounts are worthy of note: the first is Chandran Jeshuran's analysis, *Malaysian Defence Policy*, which relies heavily on the printed record of the debates in the Dewan Rakyat or House of Representative. In this forum the government was much more forthcoming than is usual. Malaysia is noteworthy for its "lid" on security issues, data, events, etc. The second account is Von Vorys *Democracy without Consensus*, which is as unbiased as possible.

18. "New Straits Times," Kuala Lumpur, in *Foreign Broadcast Information Service-Asian and Pacific*, hereafter cited as *FBIS*, 14 November 1984, p. 01. For reportage on alleged Iranian efforts to export revolution to Malaysia, see *FBIS*, 18 November 1983, p. 01 and 17 December 1984, p. 01.

19. See *FBIS*, 3 March 1980, p. 01.

20. Britain's capacity to respond in the Falklands dispute has been enlightening and thought provoking in the Five-Power context.

21. For an excellent analysis of the Australian motivation and Five-Powers generally in the 1980s, see P. Lewis Young, "What Future for the Five-Power Defence Arrangement?—A Personal View from Australia," Asian Defence Journal (October 1981), p. 35–39.

22. See Stanley S. Bedington, *Malaysia and Singapore*, p. 167.

23. See Chandran Jeshuran, *Malaysian Defence Policy*, pp. 1b and 2b.

24. See Zakaria H. Ahmad, "The Bayonet and the Truncheon," pp. 112–113.

# 9

# The Role of the Military in Singapore

*Patrick M. Mayerchak*

**Introduction**

Singapore is a multi-ethnic island ministate of 237 square miles located off the southern tip of the Malay peninsula. The population of 2,413,900 is predominately Chinese with smaller Malay and Indian communities.[1] Within Southeast Asia, Singapore is unique not only in size, but also in standard of living. In 1983 the island's per capita GNP was almost four times that of Malaysia and twelve times that of Indonesia.[2] In economic terms the state of Singapore is an unqualified success, and far ahead of its Southeast Asian neighbors.

In other terms, this success has been problematic. It can be argued that there is no nation of Singaporeans. Factors of race, religion, language and culture weigh heavily on the diverse immigrant population. Relations between the dominant Chinese community and the Malay minority have posed the greatest challenge for Singapore's political leaders. Ethnically related issues have not, however, threatened the society as in neighboring Malaysia, where relations between the dominant Malay community and Chinese minority deteriorated into uncontrolled violence after the 1969 elections. Any serious ethnic crisis in Singapore, remote as it seems, is likely to be externally generated from Malaysia, and not as a result of unmanageable internal problems.

Size, economic success, and a multi-ethnic society are three realities which confront Singapore's leaders, which, with the exception of the latter, differentiate Singapore from its neighbors. The armed forces of Singapore, like the society itself, differ from the military establishments of other Asian states. The role of the armed forces is perhaps less critical to the nation building process. At the same time, some of its problems are akin to those of the armed forces in some Western states. While Singapore possesses one of the smaller military forces in Asia, its citizen-soldier army and professional air force and navy constitute one of the best conceived military establishments in the region.

The challenges confronting Singapore's armed forces in the 1980's are the product of a successful development process which is likely to continue. How the military planners meet these challenges will determine the future role of the armed forces. The following pages describe the role of Singapore's armed forces today, its historical development, and the significant challenges ahead.

## Historical Background

While the defense of Singapore prior to independence rested largely in the hands of British colonial forces there has been significant participation by local voluntary organizations in the defense of the island. In 1854 the Singapore Volunteer Rifle Corps (SVRC) with sixty-one European expatriates was established to respond to clashes between rival clans. The SVRC augmented the regular garrison and functioned primarily in internal security matters. It was not until 1902 that sufficient Chinese had joined the SVRC to allow for the creation of a separate Chinese Singapore Volunteer Infantry No. 2. This was followed in 1910 by the formation of a Malay Volunteer Unit.[3] Then, in 1924, the army volunteers were augmented by the 200 man Malay Straits Settlements Royal Naval Volunteer Reserve ("the Malay Navy") and in 1926 by the Straits Settlements Volunteer Air Force at Seletar.

In the battle for Singapore (December 1941-February 1942) the Straits Settlements Volunteer Forces suffered heavy casualties. When Singapore fell, on February 15, 1942, the volunteers were ordered to disperse and return to their homes.[4] Not until 1949 were the Volunteers reorganized. Then, in 1954, the National Service Ordinance was passed, the first attempt by the colonial government to establish a defense force built on conscription. This policy was discontinued after only one year during which some 400 servicemen had been inducted. While the government of Singapore attributes the failure of this attempt at conscription to the unpopularity of the colonial government, it is safe to conclude that equally important was the lack of enthusiasm among the Chinese community for military service.

Over the next ten years the Volunteers continued to play an active role in the defense of Singapore. Volunteers were used to combat industrial strikes and riots in the late 1950's. At the time of Confrontation with Indonesia, Volunteers were mobilized to protect strategic locations on the island. During Singapore's participation in Malaysia (July 9, 1963–August 9, 1965) the Singapore Volunteer Corps (SVC) was sent to the jungles of Johore state in West Malaysia to combat guerrillas. SVC forces were used in other off-island operations including building roads and maintaining communications in Sarawak in East Malaysia. After Singapore separated from Malaysia and became independent on August 9, 1965, the SVC was renamed the People's Defense Force

(PDF). Though the PDF continues, several factors have contributed to the blurring of its mission, among them the reintroduction of conscription in 1967 by the newly independent government, and the withdrawal of British forces from Singapore which accelerated the arrival of a modern military establishment.

Another citizens organization of more recent origin was the Vigilante Corps, organized in 1964 to maintain community security. As a purely voluntary organization the Corps was short lived. In 1967 it was made an arm of the National Service, accepting national servicemen as well as volunteers. By 1980 the Vigilante Corps had only 670 volunteers and 51,000 part-time reserves functioning in the following organizations: Community Security Force, 5,640; Civil Defense Unit, 32,390; fire service, 1,690; and life guards, 420.[5] In 1983, the last year for which figures are available, the Vigilante Corps took in 14,000 enrollees during the April-May recruitment period.[6] The Corps continues to be overwhelmingly composed of national servicemen.

Voluntarism has been a part of Singapore's military history for over a century. At the outset, these forces had a large Eurasian flavor. Malays joined, as did Chinese. Nevertheless, acceptance by the Chinese community was slow in coming. This was to carry over into the conscript armed forces of modern day Singapore and has been overcome only with considerable effort on the part of the government.

## The Growth of Singapore's Armed Forces

Singapore's professional armed forces had their genesis in 1957 when, with British finances and officer personnel, the First Battalion, Singapore Infantry Regiment (1 SIR) was raised. As with the Volunteer Corps, the emphasis for 1 SIR was on internal security. In 1961 this force was used to control a severe Public Works Department strike. A similar second battalion was established in 1962. Both battalions had a high percentage of Malay personnel.

When Singapore became part of Malaysia, 1 and 2 SIR were joined to the Malaysian Armed Forces. In 1964, 1 SIR was sent to Perak state as part of Malaysia's response to Indonesian confrontation. This force also served in Sabah, East Malaysia, and on Sebatik Island, which was divided between Malaysia and Indonesia. In February 1965, 2 SIR engaged Indonesian infiltrators in combat on the southeastern coast of Johore state.[7] These activities constitute the combat experience of the armed forces of Singapore.

By the early 1960's Singapore was taking seriously the possibility of a British withdrawal of its defense forces. In July 1967, the Labor Government in Great Britain announced its intention to withdraw troops east of Suez. This decision was based on a defense study completed early in the year which called for a one-half reduction in forces east of Suez by 1970–1971, and for a complete withdrawal by 1975. The timetable was shortened to 1971 by Prime Minister Harold Wilson in a speech before the House of Commons on Janauary 16, 1968.[8] While this shortened timetable for withdrawal was not met, it served to accelerate Singapore's efforts to achieve an independent defense capability.

The concerns of Singapore and Malaysia over defense of their territories in crisis were alleviated by the Five Power Ministerial Meeting in Kuala Lumpur, Malaysia in June 1968. This conference eventually led to the Five Power Defense Arrangement between Australia, Malaysia, New Zealand, Singapore, and the United Kingdom, and to the first and only joint military operation involving all five powers. Exercise Bersatu Padu was undertaken to demonstrate the willingness and ability of the three extraregional powers to come to the aid of Malaysia and Singapore should they be threatened by hostile forces.[9]

In spite of British reassurances, Singapore moved rapidly in the sixties to develop its own defense forces. Several alternatives for an independent military force were considered. One possibility was to develop a small, highly trained, professional armed force. However, a small military force was not considered adequate for Singapore's needs. At the same time a large force on the same order was beyond its resources. The possibility of a regular corps supplemented by a volunteer reserve was also considered. In the end, Singapore's small size, and its multi-ethnic society dictated the creation of a citizen-soldier military establishment consisting of a regular corps supplemented by a conscript reserve. Initially all males over eighteen served a two-year term in the Singapore Armed Forces (SAF). The length of service was later extended to thirty months. Reserves serve on active duty for forty days each year up to age forty (fifty for officers.)[10] In this manner, over a decade, Singapore built up a substantial reserve force of well trained personnel.

In theory, this system of compulsory national service would aid Singapore in achieving a nation of Singaporeans. National service would develop patriotism and help create a national identity through a multi-ethnic army with no communal loyalties but a commitment to defend the Singapore nation-state.

In its quest to rapidly develop a citizen-soldier military, the Singapore government searched for appropriate assistance. The Israeli model of the citizen army with its highly compressed training system was deemed appropriate to Singapore's needs. Ministry of Defense personnel were sent to Israel, and eventually concluded several agreements for the purchase of equipment and training. In 1969, SAF personnel went to Israel for instruction in the use of the AMX-13 tank which the Singapore government intended to purchase. Additional personnel from infantry, signals and logistics were also sent to Israel in 1969. Israeli personnel conducted training related activities in Singapore until 1975.[11]

The actual withdrawal of British Forces stationed in Singapore under the Five Power Defense Arrangement, and the ANZUK (Australia, New Zealand, and United Kingdom) defense force (established separately from the Five Power Defense Arrangement) occurred in stages. British air bases at Seletar, Changi, Sembawang, and Tengah, and a radar station at Bukit Gombok were turned over to the Singapore government by 1972. Singapore became a participant in the Integrated Air Defense System (IADS) which included the ANZUK countries, Malaysia, and Singapore, and provided for the cooperative defense of the two latter countries. On December 3, 1974, the British Minister of Defense, announced the withdrawal of "our forces stationed under the Five Power Defense Arrangement in Southeast Asia, with the exception of a small group which we will continue to contribute to the integrated air defense system."[12] The consultative provisions of the Five Power Defense Agreement were left intact.

Australia withdrew its battalion of army personnel and naval unit in 1973. The ANZUK command was dissolved on January 1, 1975.[13] However, New Zealand's presence has continued in Singapore to the present in the form of one infantry battalion.

## The SAF Today

By the mid-seventies Singapore's armed forces had achieved the buildup deemed so necessary as the 1960s drew to a close. Today, Singapore has a modern military establishment adequately prepared for its tasks of maintaining internal security and providing limited protection against outside aggression.

The role of the military in Singapore is considerably different from those of military establishments in a number of neighboring political systems. Many of its problems are more akin to those often associated with the military in more highly developed states.

The SAF did not play a significant role in the domestic politics of Singapore until the mid-1980s. And, the significance of such changes is, as yet, unclear. There have not been, nor are there now, any military strongmen to challenge civilian political authority. There has been no appreciable inter-service rivalry, which is often the root of political instability in politically weak states. By Asian standards, the armed forces of Singapore are fairly young and the services have yet to produce any military heroes or a large number of high ranking careerists. That nationalist sentiment did not require the military as a vehicle for

TABLE 1
The Armed Forces of Singapore

| | | |
|---|---|---|
| Army (excluding reserves) | 45,000 | (30,000 conscripts) |
| Air Force | 6,000 | (1,000) |
| Navy | 4,500 | (3,000) |
| Reserves | 150,000 | |
| Paramilitary Forces: | | |
| Police/Marine Police | 7,500 | |
| People's Defence Force | 30,000 | (app.) |

Source: Figures are adapted from The Military Balance (London); International Institute for Strategic Studies, 1984, pp. 108-109. Slightly different figures appear in "The Citizen Soldier," Far Eastern Economic Review (January 13, 1983), p. 26.

expression on the independence issue also affects the position of the armed forces in society. And, while ethnic difficulties have arisen within the SAF, they have not inhibited the development of a modern integrated military force to any great extent. Lastly, while defense expenditures have become a serious concern for Singapore's leaders, the economy is not burdened with lopsided defense expenditures which could drain the economy of its vitality.[14] Concern for scarce resources led to the adoption of the citizen-soldier concept for the SAF, and today checks military expansion.

From 1983-85, two high ranking SAF officers entered civilian government service. Brigadier General Tan Chin Tiong was appointed second permanent secretary in the Ministry of Home Affairs. Equally impressive was the meteoric rise of Lee Hsien Loong, eldest son of the prime minister. In September 1982, at age 30, Lee was named Chief of Staff, making him the number three man in the SAF. In 1984 he became Minister of State for Defense and Trade. These changes, and similar ones that are sure to come, do suggest a role for the military in the political arena. The government intends to encourage the SAF's best and brightest to move into the civilian public and/or private sectors as a means of demonstrating the value of career military service. Whether there will be any negative side effects for the SAF or the political process, remains to be seen.[15]

While ethnic cleavages within the military do not threaten the society, the representation of Singapore's minorities (particularly the Malays) within the SAF has been a problem which Singapore shares with other third world political systems. The SAF is depicted as one of the primary mechanisms for nation building in Singapore. It provides an environment in which national ideas can be inculcated into diverse ethnic groups. In the past, the Malay minority used the military as a means of self-improvement and for upward mobility. The problem stems from the ethnic makeup of the military which Singapore inherited from the British. Prior to 1959, Malays constituted 80 percent of the army and police.[16] In the 1970s a survey showed that 80 percent of Malays questioned on the merits of national service strongly supported it.[17] Clearly Malays look on the military as a means of improving their economic lot within the competitive Singapore environment.

Singapore's leaders have extolled an ideology of state building based on multi-ethnicity and meritocracy, interpreted to mean that there shall be no favoritism for any group over another. Here is where a conflict between ideology and reality arises. In the late 1960s Singapore's military establishment was heavily dependent on the Malay minority and when national service was introduced in 1967, many Chinese families sought exemption for their sons. Because of the racial problems between the Malays and Chinese in neighboring Malaysia, from which Singapore had been ejected, Singapore could not accept a Malay dominated military establishment. Thus, while preaching multi-ethnicity and meritocracy, the government prevented Malays from entering the military service by not calling them up. This put many Malay youths in an awkward position. They had not been inducted for national service, yet they were unable to find employment because they could not produce certificates of exemption.[18] Thus, the policy designed to increase the proportion of ethnic Chinese within the SAF created rather serious problems within the Malay community.

This situation continued into the 1970s, though some adjustments were made to allow for the enlistment of Malays into the SAF. Nevertheless, the proportion of Malays in the armed forces had dropped considerably from the colonial period so that today the ethnic composition of the military approximates that of the society as a whole. While this has not been popular within the Malay community it should be noted that Malay participation in the public sector (excluding the military) has been more than proportional and has increased significantly since the 1960s.

While the need for an ethnically proportional military establishment worked against the armed forces as a positive factor in the nation building process, it by no means eliminated it from this task. The military does follow policies designed to accommodate different ethnic groups and to foster understanding between them.

The armed services maintain special dietary policies to meet the needs of Malay servicemen. Servicemen are encouraged to learn the language of their comrades. Numerous other duty and after hours training

TABLE 2
Singapore Government Employees by Ethnic Group and Division, 1967 and 1977

| Ethnic Group | Division 1 1976 | 1977 | Division 2 1976 | 1977 | Division 3 1976 | 1977 | Division 4 1976 | 1977 | Average % 1976 | 1977 |
|---|---|---|---|---|---|---|---|---|---|---|
| Malay | 2.4% | 2.5 | 3.7 | 9.5 | 10.9 | 16.5 | 37.5 | 41.2 | 17.1 | 19.7 |
| Chinese | 73.5% | 83.3 | 79.2 | 79.3 | 75.5 | 73.2 | 41.9 | 40.3 | 66.3 | 67.3 |
| Indian | 11.5% | 8.7 | 9.0 | 7.6 | 8.0 | 8.2 | 14.3 | 14.9 | 10.1 | 9.7 |
| Other | 12.6% | 5.5 | 8.1 | 3.6 | 5.6 | 2.1 | 6.3 | 3.6 | 6.5 | 3.3 |

Source: Data abstracted from People's Action Party: 1954-1979 (25th Anniversary Issue (Singapore: People's Action Party), pp. 83-84.

programs enhance the career potential of the servicemen and foster the spirit of the Singapore nation.

In addition to Singapore's need to create a more ethnically balanced military establishment there is another reason for the military's secondary role in the nation building process. While Singapore is classified as a developing nation-state it is, in comparison to other states in this category, a highly differentiated society which has a number of mechanisms in addition to the military for fostering a sense of nation. These include: the educational system, the urban resettlement scheme, the series of Community Centers in virtually every neighborhood, the Citizens Consultative Committee, MP's Meet-the People sessions, the People's Action Party Malay Affairs Bureau, and the government controlled trade union movement.

The role of the military in the economic development of Singapore has been positive. In general terms, the armed forces of Singapore contribute to the economic development process by producing trained personnel who, on leaving the service, are prepared to assume a productive line of employment. This concept of the military as a training institution for Singapore's citizen soldiers is stressed throughout Ministry of Defense (MINDEF) literature and is often a central theme in the speeches of Singapore's leaders. The following comments are from the former Minister of Defense, Mr. Howe Yoon Chong.

> Our national service or citizens' army should allow technical skills to be taught to both NSF's and to regulars to widen the individual's choice of jobs in civilian life and to improve his capability to contribute to our industrialization effort ... Whatever useful skills are learned in the army can only improve the soldier in his work (in civilian life).[19]

The SAF participates in the national development process in more specific terms as well. When the Singapore Vigilante Corps and Special Constabulary were disbanded in 1981, they were replaced by a civil defense corps and several construction battalions. The announcement of this action stated that "the construction brigade is being set up to augment national defense and not primarily to ease the acute labor shortage in the booming building industry."[20] There is, however, clearly more than a military need being met by this new organization. The construction battalions call up 1,500 to 2,000 men each year for training in the building trades. Personnel in the battalions undergo a three month modified military training program and a construction trade course, followed by nine months of on-the-job training at Housing Development Board (HDB) sites. For this initial year, personnel are paid at national service rates. Those performing satisfactorily are then "disrupted" from national service and deployed to HBD construction projects for the next eighteen months during which they are paid at market rates.[21]

To the extent that Singapore's survival depends on the strength of its business community, the construction battalions are justifiable as being in the national defense. More specifically, however, the SAF has become a direct participant in the development process. It is perhaps another indication of the pragmatic nature of Singapore's leaders that such a scheme could be so easily established without visible objections from the professional military establishment.

## Problems for the Eighties

If the military role in the development of Singapore as a nation and an economically prosperous state is to remain positive (even if qualified in the former), there are several problems which must be solved by Singapore's leaders. How these problems are resolved will also affect the military's role in the achievement of Singapore's defense and foreign policy objectives.

In the eighties, Singapore faces an aging population, a need to attract and retain better-qualified persons in the armed forces, and rising defense expenditures.

Singapore slowed the growth of its population to slightly over one percent a year, a goal which many third world countries covet. This has been accomplished through an intensive government campaign which saturates the media with the message that "two is enough." One result has been an aging population. The average age in 1970 was 24.7 years whereas in 1980 it was 27.9 years. The population under fifteen years of age in 1970 was 38.8 percent of the total. In 1980 only 27.1 percent of the population was under fifteen years of age.[22] As early as 1977 this problem was noted in a speech by the Minister of Defense before the parliament.

TABLE 3
Percent of SAF Senior Officer (Major and above) and Selected Government Service Employees with Graduate Degrees (High School)

|  | 1966 | 1981 |
|---|---|---|
| SAF Regular Officers | 2.0 | 19.6 |
| Administrative Service | 90.0 | 97.9 |
| Economic Development Board | 87.5 | 98.8 |
| Public Utility Board | 90.5 | 100.0 |

Source: Abstracted from a widely circulated speech by Prime Minister Lee Kwan Yew.

> As a result of successful family planning in the past years, the number of young men available for national service in the future . . . will show a steady but relentless decline. In ten years time (1987) the number available will be nearly 30% less . . . It will certainly be necessary to trim down manpower establishments and to reduce or even abolish vocations which do not contribute much to the combat efficiency of army units. It will be necessary to increase the number of regulars . . . (and) . . . it is more than likely that national service will have to be extended to women.[23]

The implications are clear. A more combat oriented army will mean less development oriented activities and may also lessen the emphasis on career development for national servicemen. Meanwhile, an increase in the number of regulars, and a consequent decline in national service conscripts may reduce the military's already limited role in the nation building process.

Given the pragmatism of Singapore's leaders, the problem of numbers will be overcome. The quality of available manpower may pose a far more serious challenge to the government. A substantial percentage of the Singapore population has completed high school. Consequently, the country has a pool of relatively well educated professionals who fill the private sector and government service. Unfortunately, statistics suggest that SAF officers do not possess the educational qualifications to match the individuals in these groups. Thus, the typical SAF officer is often less qualified educationally than the reserves he commands, many of whom are from the public sector, or who are managers or other professional men.[24]

The Ministry of Defense has attempted to raise the quality of SAF officers. One program was begun in 1974 with the title of "Project Wrangler." This program seeks out the best and brightest incoming officers and establishes a career plan for them which allows for optimal development. The program identifies officers with the potential for senior command and staff appointments. It is anticipated that "Wrangler Officers" will reach senior command positions by the mid-1980s.[25]

Such programs have not eliminated the problem of SAF officers with education inferior to those of the men they command. Singapore's booming economy provides opportunities for young professionals seeking the good life. A military career is not as financially rewarding as careers in the private sector. Only recently the government reacted with a substantial increase in pay for military careerists. In April 1982, the Ministry of Defense announced the first-ever comprehensive pay revision for the military which will result in a pay raise averaging twenty-eight percent for officers in the SAF.[26]

In addition, a military career does not command the respect within the society which the government feels it should. Given the government's recognition of this problem it is likely that other steps in addition to pay increases will be taken to change the public's perception of a military career.[27]

Financial considerations will also weigh heavily on the overall future of the military in Singapore. Given the relatively open nature of the political system, by Asian standards, it is understandable that there are competing claims of a very legitimate nature on the island's scarce resources. Were Singapore a military dominant system, the SAF would have an easier time of it.

The cost of keeping men under arms in Singapore will undoubtedly increase since countries with booming economies have to pay more for their servicemen. In addition, while Singapore has developed a substantial defense industry, the country still imports much of its military hardware, the cost of which continues to rise. From 1976 to the early 1980s, MINDEF's (Ministry of Defense) share of the FY expenditures of the government of Singapore has exceeded fifteen percent. For 1984–85, defense expenditures equalled 13.7% of the budget. This is an underestimate, however, since it does not include special appropriations which are granted MINDEF to cover unforseen costs and arms purchases. If the SAF is to remain essentially the same in size, configuration, and mission, defense expenditures must be kept under reasonable control. On the other hand, the government might have to increase its defense expenditures if the Thai-Vietnamese problem escalates and with it increased communist activity in Malaysia. The perception of such a threat in 1976 was probably responsible for substantial increases in hardware purchases in 1976 and 1977.

## Strategy for Survival

The survival of Singapore as an independent nation-state depends on at least three factors: 1) the existence of an adequate defense force capable of providing internal security and protection against external aggression, 2) the execution of a foreign policy which can provide security through political means, and 3) the continued success of the economic modernization process which provides technological, financial, and business leadership for Singapore among the ASEAN states. If Singapore is to be protected from external threats, the military alone cannot provide this protection.

Singapore's leaders acknowledge that the country's military is not capable of protecting the island from a determined extraregional aggressor or from a hostile power within the region, without the cooperation of its immediate neighbor, Malaysia, and preferably Indonesia as well. The country's size ultimately inhibits the military's defense capability. Singapore's leaders hope that the military can inflict a high price on any potential aggressor.

There is no immediate threat to the country. As long as Malaysia and Indonesia remain friendly and maintain their internal stability, the SAF can deal effectively with more distant threats. It is possible that the SAF would participate in the defense of the Malay peninsula in the event of a concerted communist resurgence or should there be a direct threat to Malaysia initiated by Vietnam.[28]

Singapore thus seeks an independent though limited defense capability within the framework of ASEAN cooperation. The equipment expansion of the SAF over the last half decade was not an attempt by Singapore to establish self sufficiency in defense capability, but a contribution to the balance of defense forces in the region with ASEAN on one side and Vietnam on the other. This buildup became necessary in Singapore's view because of its perception of Vietnam as a threat to regional stability.[29]

Important to the survival of Singapore is an articulate and aggressive foreign policy. The country has benefitted from the presence of one of the Third World's most dynamic leaders, Prime Minister Lee Kuan Yew. Under his leadership, Singapore has created an important niche for itself as an intermediary in global politics connecting the ASEAN states with other regions of the world. Singapore has been dubbed the "cool headed interpreter of ASEAN" by one regional analyst.[30] The obvious question is whether or not future leaders will be able to maintain the status and viability of the present leadership in international circles?

Within the region, Singapore has been one of the hardline states on the issue of Vietnam. The polarization in the region between the ASEAN states and Vietnam has been a positive factor for Singapore. While there have been disagreements within ASEAN between Singapore and Thailand, and Malaysia and Indonesia over the question of how best to deal with Vietnam and its occupation of Kampuchea, the general cooperation among the five ASEAN states has probably eased debate on other issues of more direct concern to Singapore.[31]

Singapore's security is enhanced by its political leadership within the region. It would be more difficult for an aggressor to contend with a well known and respected political leadership than to push aside a weak and unskilled administration.

The role of the military in Singapore's foreign policy is that of a legitimizer. The limited but adequate defense capability of the SAF reaffirms the independence of the state and makes possible an active, and at times, aggressive posture of political leadership. Were there no credible defense force, questions of neutrality and/or protectorate status under the wing of some power would eventually arise. The military cannot be used to threaten or even force an unwilling state into an acceptable policy but this does not diminish the military's importance to foreign policy.

The third factor in Singapore's equation for survival is the continued success of the economy. Singapore must remain attractive to regional and extraregional states as a center for financial and economic activity.

Lacking adequate port facilities and economic dynamism of their own to attract foreign investment, Singapore's neighbors rely on it to act as a magnet to attract outside investment. Singapore is also an entrepot for various regionally produced or imported commodities. In sum, Singapore is important to Southeast Asia. Further, so long as Singapore is not dominated by any extraregional power, its dynamic economy remains a valuable asset to all states with an economic interest in Southeast Asia.

This modern state in the developing Southeast Asian region is the headquarters from which many nonregional states, corporations, and international agencies conduct their regional activities. Western oil companies operating in Indonesia have their base facilities in Singapore, as do several national and international relief agencies. The U.S. Department of Agriculture conducts agricultural assistance programs for the region from Singapore. The greater the number of states, corporations, and international organizations with an interest in Singapore, the more secure the tiny state will be.

## Conclusion

Singapore's fate, unlike that of several of her neighbors, does not rest heavily on the military. That Singapore is a true mini-state makes a military defense improbable against any but the least of aggressors.[32] This may be in the best interest of the state for the long term. Not being able to afford a one dimensional solution has forced Singapore to explore other avenues for guaranteeing the existence of the state. Singapore cannot afford the luxury of shoving internal problems under the carpet. Nor can external problems be ignored. This cannot be attributed to the democratic political system, for any head of Singapore's political mechanism would be forced to seek solutions to serious problems or see the state fail.

Singapore's fate is tied to the attractiveness of its economy to the outside world, to the success of its foreign policy, and to an adequate but limited defense capability. While Singapore's size limits its options it also makes the state less suspect and perhaps affords a kind of security which many larger states do not enjoy.

If manpower and financial constraints force the SAF to concentrate on wholly defense related tasks Singapore would be the loser for, while the obvious function of a military establishment is to defend the state's territorial integrity, the SAF could contribute more to the overall progress and advancement of the Singapore nation-state.

The true citizen soldier concept is an admirable one. It envisions a people imbued with the feeling of nation and prepared with skills adequate for the defense of the state. Singapore cannot afford to rest on its accomplishments. All of its institutions should be utilized to the fullest in the processes of nation building and economic development. Ideally, one would hope for the continued role of the military in these processes.

## Notes

1. In 1981 the population of Singapore was broken down into the following ethnic groups: Chinese, 1,850,000 (76.1%); Malay, 351,500 (14.5%); Indian, 154,600 (6.4%); and others, 51,600 (3.0%). See *Singapore 81,* (Singapore, Ministry of Culture, 1982), pp. 206-207.

2. Figures provided by the East Asia and Pacific Regional Office, The World Bank, Washington, D.C. 20433.

3. *The Singapore Armed Forces,* (Singapore, Public Affairs Department, Ministry of Defense, 1981), p. 34.

4. Ibid, p. 40.

5. *Singapore 81,* pp. 122-123.

6. *Straits Times,* (Singapore) September 10, 1981.

7. *The Singapore Armed Forces,* pp. 40-43.

8. Harold Wilson, *The Labour Government 1964-1970, A Personal Record,* (London, Michael Joseph Ltd., 1971), p. 483.

9. *The Singapore Armed Forces,* pp. 45-48.

10. Under the Enlistment Act Reservist Officers are liable for service up to age fifty, while Reservist Other Ranks serve until forty. Reserves may be called up for Reserve Service up to a maximum of forty days a year. In practice the

duration of annual in-camp training is usually three weeks. Reservists are usually informed six to twelve months in advance of the dates they have to report for in-camp training. No exemptions are granted on hardship grounds. This matter was recently covered in the *Parliamentary Debates Singapore (Official Report)*, (Singapore, Singapore National Printers, March 26, 1981), cols. 1233-1234.

11. *News Release*, (Singapore, Ministry of Culture, September 15, 1975), p. 18.

12. Ibid., p. 18.

13. For the Singapore government's view of these events see the comments of Goh Keng Swee, former Minister of Defense, in *The Mirror*, (Singapore, Ministry of Culture, July 22, 1974).

14. Defence expenditures for 1984-1985 fiscal year are projected at US$1.09 billion, equal to 13.7% of the national budget and 6% of the GNP.

15. Patrick Smith and Philip Bowring, "The Citizen Soldier," *Far Eastern Economic Review*, (January 13, 1983), p. 27.

16. The problem of Malays in the Singapore military is thoroughly explored by Stanley S. Bedlington, "Ethnicity and the Armed Forces in Singapore," in DeWitt C. Ellinwood and Cynthia Enloe, *Ethnicity and the Military in Asia*, (New Brunswick, Transaction Books, 1981).

17. Stanley S. Bedlington, *The Singapore Malay Community: The Politics of State Integration*, (PhD Dissertation), (Ithaca, Cornell University, Department of Government, 1974), p. 246.

18. Stanley S. Bedlington, "Ethnicity and the Armed Forces in Singapore," p. 259.

19. *The Singapore Armed Forces*, p. 6.

20. *Straits Times*, (Singapore), September 10, 1981.

21. Ibid.

22. *Singapore 81*, p. 168.

23. Addenda to (the) Presidential Address, *Parliamentary Debates Singapore (Official Report)*, (Singapore, Singapore National Printers, February 8, 1977) cols. 112-114.

24. *Straits Times*, (Singapore), April 30, 1978.

25. *News Release*, (Singapore, Ministry of Defense, September 9, 1981), p. unknown.

26. *Straits Times*, (Singapore), April 1, and April 5, 1982.

27. President's Address, *Parliamentary Debates Singapore (Official Report)*, (Singapore, Singapore National Printers, February 3, 1981) cols. 11-12.

28. Cooperation between police officials of the two states is an established fact. Of greater significance was the mid-1983 participation of seven Malaysian F-5 fighters in the first bilateral exercise with Singapore's air force from Singapore air fields since the island became independent. On the other hand, it is still difficult to foresee the day when Singapore army personnel would be used in Malaysia in a cooperative arrangement.

29. The Singapore Armed Forces, p. 188.

30. Derek Davies and Susumu Awanohara, "Lee Kuan Yew, 20 Years On," *Far Eastern Economic Review*, (Hong Kong, October 26, 1979), p. 18.

31. The ASEAN-Vietnam problem has been covered thoroughly in a number of thought provoking pieces authored by Gareth Porter. For example, see "Negotiating Kampuchea: Scenario for a Settlement," *Indochina Issues*, no. 24, March 1982 (Washington, DC, Center for International Policy).

32. The implications of being a ministate are clear when one considers that the SAF cannot even train on its own territory. Agreements to allow the army to train abroad have been concluded with Australia, Brunei, New Zealand, Taiwan, and Thailand. The air force trains in the Philippines.

# 10

## The Role of the Indonesian Armed Forces

*Harold W. Maynard*

**Introduction**

Indonesia is the largest country in Southeast Asia; and, with over 150 million people, it is the fifth largest country in the world. It occupies a strategic position astride the sea-lanes between the Pacific and Indian Oceans, and it is rich in human potential and natural resources—oil, natural gas, nickel, copper, tin, rubber, and lumber.

Indonesia is not an easy country to govern. It stretches 3,200 miles from west to east, 1,200 miles from north to south, and consists of over 13,600 islands. About 75 percent of the population lives on Java, one of the world's most densely populated areas and a natural location for outbreaks of catalytic violence. Though most Indonesians are literate in the Indonesian language, the population is still divided by 30 regional languages and scores of dialects. The country is 90 percent Muslim, but differences between strong and nominal believers are so great that religion, a potentially unifying force, has often been a source of friction.

Politically and economically, Indonesia leans toward the West. Nonetheless, as a founding member of the Nonaligned Movement, it is the only ASEAN member without formal defense ties to the major English speaking countries. Like other Southeast Asian countries, Indonesia has been hesitant to turn ASEAN into a military pact, preferring instead to rely on informal bilateral arrangements. While accepting ASEAN unity as a touchstone of foreign policy, it has been careful to maintain constant dialogue with the Government of Vietnam. Indonesia's size and independent orientation have occasionally led some Southeast Asian leaders to suspect it of long-term aspirations to dominate the region. Indonesia has done its best, however, to allay such fears by persuasion and by preaching "regional resilience," a concept based on self-sufficiency and the ability to withstand outside political, economic, and military pressures.

Decisive political power in Indonesia is in the hands of the Armed Forces. The military is the only group capable of governing the country effectively. This chapter provides an overview of the Indonesian military, with special emphasis on the social, political, and economic roles it plays.

## Historical Overview—Before Independence

Though Indonesians trace their history to the ancient empires of Srivijaya and Majapahit, little is known about the military in pre-colonial times. By the nineteenth century, the small kingdoms in the Indonesian Archipelago had exhausted themselves with internecine warfare, thus facilitating the divide-and-rule approach of European colonial powers. Indonesian princes and popular leaders fought futilely against the Western onslaught. National military heroes like Iskandar Muda, Hasanuddin, Diponegoro, and Pattimura now live on only in history books and in the names of the Indonesian Army's Area Commands.

In the early years of colonial rule, Dutch authorities experimented with small auxiliary infantry and cavalry units composed of Indonesians, by recruiting the sons of the indigenous gentry and conscripting peasants. Though thousands of Indonesians were given rudimentary military training, few were promoted into leadership positions. The Dutch finally suppressed the last major Indonesian resistance in the early 1900's, after a bloody 30-year guerrilla war waged by radical Muslims in North Sumatra.

During World War I, Indonesian nationalist groups were divided on whether the Dutch should conscript Indonesians into military service. Sarekat Islam leaders in East Java contended that unless native Indonesians were provided a representative body, in which they could freely express their political opinions, they should not be conscripted for defense purposes. Boedi Oetomo leaders in West Java, however, basically favored conscription and hoped that military service would help the nascent nationalist movement by instilling discipline in otherwise unruly Javanese youth.

By World War II, the Dutch had organized Indonesians into a 30,000-man police Army known as KNIL (Koninklijk Nederlands Indisch Leger). Leadership of KNIL was in the hands of Dutch officers. KNIL forces were comprised of companies from different regions. Thus, troops from Menado and Ambon could be used to put down disturbances on Java, while Sundanese and Batak troops could be used in eastern Indonesia. Many Indonesians viewed KNIL as a caste set apart from, and occasionally against, Indonesian nationalist aspirations.

Indonesians fared no better under the Japanese. Indonesian conscripts, pressed into service by the Dutch at the onset of the war, performed poorly—largely because they did not believe wholeheartedly in the Dutch cause. At first, Indonesians openly accepted the Japanese, but nationalist hopes were soon dashed by Japanese decrees that forbade display of the Indonesian flag or discussion of the country's political structure. The Japanese then suggested some form of military "participation" by Indonesians.

In 1943 the Japanese created two large organizations to provide manpower badly needed for the war effort. Heiho, established in April, organized indigenous personnel as auxiliary troops for transport, road building, and antiaircraft defense duties. Though occasionally armed, Heiho troops were more often used as servants and conscript labor than as independent soldiers. They received only two months of training, and all officers were Japanese. Nonetheless, by 1945 some 25,000 Javanese and 15,000 other Indonesians received military experience in Heiho.

More important for the future Indonesian Army was Peta, the Army for Defense of the Fatherland. Started in late 1943 by Japanese military intelligence, Peta was designed to assist 10,000 Japanese troops defend Java from Allied attack. Although Peta eventually provided impetus to the nationalist goal of independence, when it was formed talk of full autonomy was forbidden by the Japanese. By war's end 38,000 Peta troops had been recruited, though weapons were provided to only half this number. The Japanese trained approximately 1,600 Peta officers, mostly at Bogor. Soldiers were recruited and trained locally. Peta units were organized as territorial defense forces rather than as maneuver battalions. Arms and uniforms came largely from captured Dutch stocks.

Though Peta was supposed to consist entirely of indigenous personnel, it never reached autonomous status. The Japanese appointed Indonesian battalion commanders, but these men received only a few months training. Communication between Peta units was prevented by the Japanese, and there was no central indigenous Peta leadership above battalion level. Because the Japanese suspected the fighting ability and loyalty of Peta, virtually no effort was made to train Indonesian staff officers. At the end of the war, there were still 350 Japanese officers assigned as advisers and staff officers with Peta. Peta never saw combat except in rebellion. A noteworthy revolt occurred in Blitar in February 1945, caused in large part by Japan's abuse of conscript labor, excessive rice taxation, arrogance of Japanese noncommissioned officers, and totalitarian tactics of Japanese police.[1]

## 1945–1965

Notwithstanding KNIL and Peta, the Indonesian Armed Forces (ABRI) were actually formed in the 1945–1949 Indonesian struggle for independence. This is fundamental to understanding ABRI's role; it explains

ABRI's struggling spirit, territorial warfare doctrine, current leadership, and abiding suspicion of civilian rule. Though Independence was declared on 17 August 1945, it was not until 5 October that the new government officially designated a People's Security Army. This date is now celebrated as Armed Forces Day.

ARBI takes pride in having sprung spontaneously from the Indonesian masses. It was not created by civilian politicians, nor by the Dutch or Japanese. Armed bands gathered, elected their own officers, and fought the Dutch—all without benefit of centralized political leadership or logistic support. Because of this, the army perceived itself less an instrument of the state than as a reflection of the will of the people. Inasmuch as the Army was built from the bottom up, it was difficult for the central government to enforce orders.

In 1948, at the height of the struggle against the Dutch, a communist-supported revolt occurred in Madiun. Today the Madiun Affair is viewed by the Indonesian military as the first example of communist betrayal, subverting the country even during its War of Independence. Later in December 1948, Dutch forces captured most of Indonesia's civilian leadership, and the military had to fight alone. Regrouping in rural areas, military commanders created subdistrict-level governments with political, economic, and social staffs, in addition to their combat organization. During and after the war for independence, military leaders leveled accusations against the country's civilian leadership for delay and mismanagement in forming the Army, ill-timed ceasefires and negotiations with the Dutch, and excessive politicization of the Armed Forces.[2]

In 1950, shortly after achieving full independence, Indonesia adopted a parliamentary constitution in which the military was clearly subordinate to civilian authority. The first major political crisis involving the Army came in 1952 during the 17 October Affair. Army officers organized a protest in front of the Presidential Palace in hopes of forcing Sukarno to dissolve Parliament, which they believed was interfering in the Army's reorganization and demobilization plans. This "half coup" failed.

During the early 1950's, Indonesian officers came to view civilian politicians as selfish, ineffective, irresponsible, immature, and corrupt.[3] Some politicians tried to indoctrinate the officer corps with particular political philosophies, while others harrassed military leaders and intervened in spheres that officers regarded as their own. Even President Sukarno did not hesitate to instigate minor military mutinies to undercut his political opposition. Then, in 1955, senior officers banded to reject a political appointee as Army commander, signaling a new political assertiveness by the military. In 1957, military officers were involved in nationalizing Dutch holdings as part of the campaign to liberate

West Irian. Thereafter they played a significant role in managing semi-public economic ventures, projecting the military into a national economic management role.

During the late 1950s and early 1960s Indonesia's military leadership concentrated on eliminating "warlords" in the provinces, centralizing control in Jakarta, suppressing various secessionist rebellions, and combating attempts to transform Indonesia into an Islamic state. Some of ABRI's most deeply felt threat perceptions can be explained by the revolt of radical Muslims in West Java (Darul Islam) and by secessionist movements in the outer islands (PRRI-Permesta) during the late 1950s. When the parliamentary system collapsed in 1957, martial law was declared, enabling military officers to take on broad political, administrative, and economic functions.

In this era, Army Chief of Staff Nasution formulated the "Middle Way" concept by which the military would neither remain politically inactive nor attempt to take over the government. In 1959 he was instrumental in convincing President Sukarno to return the country to the Constitution of 1945 and begin an era of "Guided Democracy," with strong presidential leadership. The Army's role further expanded in 1961-1963 when the military's involvement in West Irian helped pressure the Dutch to transfer sovereignty of this territory to Indonesia.

By 1963 the Muslim and secessionist threats were under control, military unity was largely restored, West Irian (now Irian Jaya) was in Indonesian hands, and military leaders focused again on the growing threat posed by communist groups. The communists appeared determined to ally themselves with President Sukarno against the army, while courting communist sympathizers within the Armed Forces. Tension rose, especially during 1963-1965, as Sukarno's foreign policy turned against the West and as communist groups expanded their front organizations, eventually boasting at least three million followers.

When the Indonesian Communist Party (PKI) provoked the hypernationalistic Sukarno government into an armed campaign to crush Malaysia in September 1963, Indonesia's military leadership felt ambivalent. The campaign proved useful for acquiring massive quantities of military equipment from the Soviet Union for increasing the role of the military in national politics. Nonetheless, ABRI clearly did not want war, and military leaders did not want the confrontation with Malaysia to justify arming communist paramilitary troops with Chinese weapons for use as a "fifth force" outside ABRI. Senior military officers became particularly suspicious when Nasakom (Nationalism, Religion, and Communism) was pushed as an ideologic distillation of Indonesia's Panca Sila philosophy, and they rankled when attempts were made to establish Nasakom advisory committees within the Armed Forces.

## 1965-1975

By mid-1965 Army leaders decided to stand firmly against the challenge of the PKI's alliance with the President and the PKI's increasing penetration of ABRI. Before action could be taken, however, radical elements, allied with two Army battalions and elements of the Air Force, launched a coup on the night of 30 September 1965. Half a dozen key Army generals were viciously killed. It took several days for the Army's Strategic Command (Kostrad), under General Suharto's leadership, to put down the attempted coup, and another six months to purge the military and gradually wrest power from Sukarno. Over one-half million people were slaughtered as Muslim and military groups took vengeance against suspected communists and ethnic Chinese.

After months of turmoil, on 11 March 1966 President Sukarno was convinced to transfer to General Suharto formal authority to take "all necessary steps" to reestablish stability. The next day Suharto banned the PKI, and within a week he dismissed 14 government ministers and set about establishing a new cabinet. Suharto's new authority was confirmed by the National Consultative Assembly (MPRS) in June 1966, and he was appointed Acting President by that body in March 1967. Though General Suharto was named President in March 1968, it was not until 1971 that nationwide elections provided him with a clear popular mandate.

During the late 1960's Suharto and the military made noteworthy changes in the government. Confrontation with Malaysia ceased, and in September 1966 Indonesia resumed its seat in the United Nations. In December 1968 President Suharto launched Repelita I, Indonesia's first five-year development plan. Repelita was implemented with the beginning of the new fiscal year on 1 April 1969, a date the Indonesian military leadership views as the beginning of its efforts to rehabilitate the country's economy and pursue national economic development.

Important changes were also made in ABRI's command structure in 1969. The Ministry of Defense and Security (Hankam) acquired command of all combat and territorial forces, operating through a newly created echelon consisting of four regional headquarters (Kowilhans), sixteen Military Area Commands (Kodams), and throughout the Army's Strategic Command (Kostrad), Special Forces Command (Kopassandha), and National Strategic Command (Kostranas). Service commanders were downgraded to chiefs of staff. Although they kept their administrative responsibilities, they lost their command authority and had their political staffs emasculated. Hankam's sociopolitical staff (Staf Kekaryaan) assumed responsibility for assigning military officers to nonmilitary functions and for management of military representatives in Parliament.

The Army also lost its Command for Restoration of Security and Order (Kopkamtib) to Hankam, a step that both revitalized this important organ of political and social control and increased the involvement of other services. These changes significantly increased Hankam's authority over the military's involvement in social and political affairs.

ABRI's next major challenge came with the 1971 parliamentary elections, the second in Indonesia's history. Of the DPR's 460 seats, 75 were to be filled by military officers and 25 by other presidential appointees. The military wanted a large share of the remaining seats to go to Golkar, the alliance of functional groups that serves as the government's political party. Though Golkar lacked a grass roots organization, Lt. Gen. Ali Murtopo managed a successful campaign that netted 236 of the remaining 360 seats for Golkar. Nine regular political parties were left with only 27 percent of the seats. After the election, the government formed these parties into two new political constellations (the PDI and PPP) so that national politics could be more systematically managed. A similar trend occurred at the regional and local levels where there were increased appointments of military officers as governors and mayors.

In January 1974 a series of anti-Japanese riots erupted in Jakarta during the visit of Prime Minister Tanaka. Two military factions, one led by Lt. Gen. Ali Murtopo, the other by General Sumitro, bitterly differed over whether the events signified a devious plot to discredit the government and overthrow the Suharto regime or reflected genuine popular discontent with foreign domination of Indonesian trade and investment. After the riots were quelled, General Sumitro retired from his position as commander of Kopkamtib. Significantly, this serious dispute between senior generals did not result in military disorders in the streets by the contending ABRI factions. Few combat units were aware of any behind-the-scenes maneuvering until well after the event.

## 1975–1980

ABRI's most recent combat experience has been in Timor. In 1974 Portugal indicated its intention to withdraw from Timor. The next year, a radical group (Fretilin) declared independence. As a result of leftist disturbances, ABRI sent combat forces to Timor. The military operation did not go smoothly, but East Timor was declared Indonesia's 27th province in July 1976.

Jakarta has faced three problems related to East Timor—lack of recognition from other states that Timor is now part of Indonesia, establishment of economic and social development programs, and festering Fretilin insurgency in the highlands. In these problem areas, ABRI has cause for optimism.[4] Economic dislocation and famine have been largely overcome. Social services have been established, and a local government structure is being filled with trained Timorese. Hence, local residents and UN diplomats are increasingly inclined to accept Indonesian rule in East Timor as a reasonably benevolent *fait accompli*. Occasional combat operations are still necessary against some two hundred Fretilin resistance fighters. ABRI tried to separate rebels from the populace by relocating some Timorese to Atauro Island and by regrouping other Timorese into secure villages.

ABRI plays a more direct role in East Timor than elsewhere in Indonesia. Hardship duty pay has been insufficient to attract some types of civil servants, and the province is administered by a special military team rather than by the Ministry of the Interior. Though this leaves an impression that the province is under tight military rule, most residents are convinced that substantial development has taken place and that there are more opportunities than during the era of Portuguese rule.

In 1978-1979 several other events prompted a revitalization of the Indonesian Armed Forces. President Suharto appointed a new Defense Minister, General Jusuf, who quickly gained a reputation as an activist reformer. General Jusuf was obviously determined to control corruption and ostentatious living of senior officers, while increasing the pay, housing, morale, and general welfare of enlisted troops, especially in remote areas. ABRI began a new five-year strategic development plan with an emphasis on updating the military's equipment inventory, especially in infantry weapons, combat aircraft, and naval vessels. Meanwhile, the threat from the north appeared more ominous because of the Vietnamese invasion of Kampuchea, China's border clashes with Vietnam, China's support of Khmer communist resistance forces, and increased Soviet military aid to the states of Indochina. Indonesia showed increased interest in patrolling its northern flank and reacting rapidly to incursions into its territorial waters. The government was determined to ensure its archipelagic territory (Wawasan Nusantara), as defined in the Law of the Sea Treaty. This concern was heightened by conflicting claims with Vietnam over the potentially rich natural gas seabed located north of Natuna Island. Finally, skyrocketing oil prices gave Indonesia the means to undertake a major construction program, large-scale equipment purchases, and a revamp of military pay and benefits. These factors, along with ABRI's experience in Timor, converged to stimulate a more active and professionally competent military force as ABRI entered the 1980s.

## Contemporary Issues—Military Upgrade Program

In 1978, ABRI was underequipped and poorly trained. Improvements had to be made in organization, personnel, and armament. The Army upgraded the equivalent of 100 combat battalions by issuing new equipment and instituting a rigorous program of unit level combat training, including a series of publicized amphibious landing exercises. Efforts still are being made to improve Army mobility, with the goal of developing an airlift capacity for deploying, on short notice, a brigade anywhere in Indonesia.[5]

Indonesia's Navy is also modernizing, acquiring the capability to patrol the archipelago and its 200-nautical mile Exclusive Economic Zone. Of great concern is attainment of sea control in the South China Sea near the Natuna Islands' petroleum deposits and near contested territorial claims with Vietnam. The fleet has acquired more frigates, corvettes, patrol boats, hydrofoils, and submarines—with major purchases from the Dutch, Germans, and South Koreans. Three dozen French Exocet surface-to-surface missiles were added to the fleet's weapons inventory, and Mark 46 torpedoes are on order from the United States.[6] Antisubmarine warfare helicopters (Wasps) and Australian-built reconnaissance aircraft (Nomads) have been added to the Navy to supplement the surface fleet patrolling key straits and to watch for foreign fishermen poaching in Indonesian waters.

The Indonesian Air Force has focused on American combat and transport aircraft. First-line planes include squadrons of A-4's, F-5's and OV-lO's. Now the Air Force is searching for fighter aircraft such as the F-16. The Indonesians use Spanish CASA-212's and Dutch Fokker F-27's for normal airlift, and rely on American C-130's for heavy transport operations. In keeping with ABRI's attempt to broaden its coverage of the Archipelago, the Air Force plans to improve airbases in Sumatra, Sulawesi, and West Irian; to upgrade facilities on Natuna Island; and to establish an effective radar network along major approach routes from the north.

## Defense Industries

Indonesia is improving the output and technological sophistication of its defense industries. Presidential Decree No. 40/1980 established a high level team, headed by Research and Technology Minister Habibie, to reduce dependency on imported weaponry and increase indigenous maintenance capabilities.[7]

Over the next 10 years, emphasis will be on small arms, rockets, ammunition, propellants, communications equipment, and mobility elements. This last category includes transport and armored vehicles, fast patrol boats, transport vessels, transport aircraft, and helicopter gunships. More sophisticated equipment—such as heavy artillery, guided missiles, tanks, combat ships and submarines, fighter aircraft, and electronic warfare equipment—must be imported for the foreseeable future.

In Bandung a newly expanded aircraft factory (P.T. Nurtanio) assembles helicopters (Bo-105 and Super Puma) and transports (CASA-212), and is developing a new transport, the CN-235. The Navy shipyard in Surabaya (P.T. PAL), home of most ship repair and overhaul facilities, has begun building a fleet of fast patrol boats. The Army's small arms and ammunition plant in Turen (P.T. Pindad) produces ammunition and small arms and the firm's plant in Bandung has reserve capability to produce agricultural equipment, and automotive and railway components. In these ventures, the government's aim is to use imported technology and assistance only when necessary and to acquire skills to establish a reasonably autonomous arms industry.

## Budgets

Indonesian defense expenditures are not easily analyzed. Some information is available on the national budget, but this does not reflect funds from nonbudgetary sources. Ten years ago extrabudgetary funds represented as much as 30 to 40 percent of actual military expenditures.[8] Today this figure is undoubtedly less. The defense budget, like the national budget, depends on fluctuating oil revenues, which are derived from the state petroleum monopoly, Pertamina. About 70 percent of the Indonesian national budget depends on revenues from oil and natural gas. For many years Pertamina funds were also tapped for major military equipment purchases, development of defense industries, or lesser projects such as building military hospitals and assembly halls. However, since Pertamina's mid-1970's financial crisis, oil revenues are channeled to the Ministry of Finance where they enter regular budgetary channels and are more closely controlled. Other nonbudgetary funds are generated by ABRI from a variety of military-run economic enterprises and business ventures. Statistics are not available on the magnitude and uses of these nonbudgetary funds.

In his annual speech to the Parliament in January 1978, President Suharto announced that the growing financial capacity of the state allowed a reorientantion of defense expenditures to better respond to foreign threats.[9] General Jusuf's term as Defense Minister largely coincided with increasing military budgets during ABRI's 1979–1983 Strategic Plan. His successor, General Moerdani, has faced far tighter restrictions during the 1984–1985 period.

Between Fiscal Years 1978–79 and 1981–82 the total national budget reportedly rose from $11.62 billion to $22.24 billion, while the military budget rose from $1.69 billion to $2.76 billion. Though this meant real growth in the defense budget, in percentage terms it reflected a slight drop in the military's share of the national budget—from 14.5 percent to 12.4 percent. Significantly, that portion of Hankam's budget devoted to new equipment purchases and force infrastructure more than tripled between 1978 and 1982, from $236 million to $909 million.[10] Whereas the military's development budget accounted for 4.3 percent of the country's development budget in FY1978–79, its share rose to 6.4 percent in FY1982–83. During 1984–1985, however, national economic austerity measures caused by depressed oil markets (and the declining value of the Rupiah) had taken their toll on the military budget. In dollar value, Hankam's budget was just over $2 billion, roughly two-thirds of which was slated for routine (as opposed to development) expenses.

## Populist Element

During the early 1980s substantial progress was made in improving military housing and troop morale. General Josuf often visited remote small units, not only to examine military preparedness but also to check on the living conditions of common soldiers. Inquiries were made into individual pay, equipment, housing, and dependent care, and on-the-spot directives were issued to improve pride and morale among enlisted troops.

Efforts have also been made to improve ABRI's public image. Officers have been told to sharply curtail displays of conspicuous consumption. Lavish hotel weddings, luxury cars, and sumptuous airconditioned offices are discouraged. Civic action type projects have given the military a more favorable image and have put it into the villages (ABRI Masuk Desa). ABRI builds bridges, digs wells, erects schools, and extends small feeder roads into remote areas. These programs positively reinforce the thousands of noncommissioned officers assigned to leadership roles at the village level (Babinsa). Their mission is to demonstrate and reinforce ABRI's unity with the people, in support of the military's system of Total Peoples Defense and Security (Hankamrata).

## Generation Transfer

Indonesia's most senior military leaders joined the armed forces during the 1945–1949 struggle against the Dutch. Because most of these men have reached the mandatory retirement age of 55, only a handful of the country's colonels and generals come from the "1945 Generation."[11] ABRI's leadership also includes a small group of about 40 senior officers who joined the military during the early 1950s, and they too will soon reach mandatory retirement age.

Leadership responsibility is shifting to a younger generation of officers who graduated from the Military Academy (Akabri) at Magelang. Akabri graduates comprise about 10,000 men, roughly twenty percent of the ABRI officer corps and less than two and a half percent of ABRI's total strength. Though they fill most principal staff positions in the Kowilhans and Kodams, only in 1983 did they begin taking over key leadership positions at Service headquarters and Hankam. Within this Akabri group, the focus is clearly on the first several graduating classes (1960–1963), for it is from these classes that the greatest percentage of new generals will be chosen. In recent years, the number of general officer billets has been halved, and promotions for the "Magelang Generation" come slowly. Younger officers occasionally have not been promoted in rank, even when given responsibilities and positions previously requiring general officers.[12] Today, only a few new generation officers have been promoted to Major General.

Several problems are associated with generational transfer. First, the 1945 generation has been slow to give up power. Senior officers argue that they are still young enough to perform well and are far more experienced than Akabri graduates. The younger generation was, after all, school trained in professional military values after the older generation had fought the Dutch, communists, radical Muslims, and outer island separatists. Second, some older officers who formally retired from active duty, find it difficult to secure prestigious and reasonably lucrative jobs for their remaining productive years. Third, the older generation is concerned that younger officers may deviate from the course already chosen for the nation and armed forces. Specifically, they are concerned whether the younger generation will "withdraw to the barracks"—leaving most government functions in the hands of civilian technocrats, bureaucrats, and politicians—or will continue the military's dual function, as a defensive force and as a socioeconomic political force.

For the past dozen years a major effort to pass on the "values" of the 1945 generation (Dharma Pustaka 45) to younger officers has occurred, especially through classes and seminars at the staff colleges. Ideological training has also been implemented through government-wide P4 training (Pedoman Penghayatan dan Pengamalan Panca Sila), consisting of several weeks of lectures, discussions, and papers devoted to inculcating Panca Sila values in seminar participants. The P4 curriculum is now included in Indonesian military schools and training programs.[13]

Related to generational transfer within the military is the question of Presidential succession. General Suharto has been President since 1967, and was reelected in 1983 for another five-year term. Speculation on a successor to Suharto normally centers on another Javanese general to be chosen by the military elite. Such speculation is, however, discouraged by the government, and little attempt has been made to establish the procedure for selecting the next President. Presumably the man will be chosen informally, behind closed doors, by senior officers. The decision may then be validated by an ABRI Commanders Call and Golkar Supervisory Board meeting prior to being formally legitimized by the People's Consultative Assembly. Meanwhile, the ruling coalition of military men, technocrats, bureaucrats, and middle-class professionals can be expected to support the Vice President, in accordance with the 1945 Constitution.

### Pledged Norms

ABRI, the government, and Indonesian society take as their political touchstones the Panca Sila philosophy and 1945 Constitution. In addition, military personnel are specifically pledged to uphold two creeds—the Seven Pledges (Sapta Marga) and the Soldiers Oath (Sumpah Prajurit).

The Panca Sila is expressed in the preamble to the 1945 Constitution as follows:

> We believe in an all embracing God; in righteous and moral humanity, in the unity of Indonesia. We believe in democracy, wisely guided and led by close contact with the people through consultation so that there shall result social justice for the whole Indonesian people.

The Panca Sila—belief in one God, humanitarianism, national unity, consultative democracy, and social justice—is repeatedly invoked by military officers as criteria to judge the efficacy of particular programs or the dangers posed by specific social groups. For the military, the Panca Sila is above politics. It is not subject to public debate or ridicule; however, it may be invoked, explained, and discussed to ensure better understanding and greater implementation.

Unlike the Panca Sila and 1945 Constitution, which military leaders view as applicable to all Indonesians, the Seven Pledges and Soldier's Oath apply only to military personnel. The Seven Pledges follow:

I. We are citizens of the unitary Republic of Indonesia based on the Panca Sila.

II. We are Indonesian patriots, bearers and defenders of the state ideology, who are responsible and know of no surrender.

III. We are Indonesian knights, who are devoted to the One God, and who defend honesty, truth and justice.

IV. We are soldiers of the Indonesian Armed Forces, guardians of the Indonesian state and nation.

V. We soldiers of the Indonesian Armed Forces uphold discipline, are obedient and observant to our leadership, and uphold the soldier's attitude and oath.

VI. We soldiers of the Indonesian Armed Forces set ourselves to perform our task with courage, and are always ready to devote ourselves to the state and nation.

VII. We soldiers of the Indonesian Armed Forces are loyal and keep our word and the Soldiers' Oath.

The first three points regulate individual conduct, while the last four relate the individual to society. The third pledge is particularly interesting. Indonesian officers and soldiers view themselves as "satria" (knights). This ancient Javanese concept asserts that a satria has both the right and duty to involve himself in any segment of society to help solve social problems. The satria earns his status through noble deeds and is always present in crisis. He carries a weapon that confers both real and mystical powers. Politeness and self-control are regarded as essential for a true satria.[14]

In the Soldier's Oath, Indonesian officers and enlisted personnel pledge:

> To be faithful to the Government and obedient to the Laws and Ideology of the State. To obey military law. To execute my duties with full responsibility to the Armed Forces of the Republic of Indonesia. To firmly uphold military discipline, meaning to be obedient, faithful and subordinate, as well as devoted to superiors without questioning their orders or decisions.

Usually the Seven Pledges and Soldier's Oath are mentioned just after the Panca Sila and 1945 Constitution as fundamental tenets of the Indonesian Armed Forces. Article 13 of the May 1982 Draft Law on Voluntary Military Service provides for dishonorable discharge of personnel who violate the Seven Pledges or Soldier's Oath.

## Threat Perceptions

The Indonesian military has long been more concerned about threats to internal security than the possibility of external attack. ABRI remembers well the 1948 Madiun revolt and the 1965 coup attempt by the communists. Military officers, almost none of whom are ethnic Chinese, fear that communism may have sympathizers among Indonesia's Chinese community. Though the ethnic Chinese are only about two percent of the population, they are viewed as a potentially subversive fifth column. In the major cities of Java the Chinese are often suspected for their capitalist ties to Singapore and Hong Kong, but in more rural areas (such as West Kalimantan, the Riau Islands, and Eastern Sumatra) the Chinese community is looked upon as a breeding ground for pro-Beijing subversives. Nonetheless, PKI remnants are seldom uncovered; released communist political prisoners rarely cause further problems; and little evidence exists of external support for communist subversives.

Of greater concern, therefore, are the threats posed by radical Muslims. This concern is reinforced by zealous and doctrinaire Islam in its recent resurgence throughout the world. Although most ABRI personnel are Muslim, fanatic Muslims who advocate an Islamic state, or press for secession, are viewed as threats. Until 1982, when government officials were pressured by Islamic leaders to drop the term, ABRI officers spoke of the threat posed by the "Holy War Command" which some believed was dedicated to toppling the government. Because conservative Muslims are respected in society, are contestants in elections, and are represented in Parliament, they are more apparent than communists as a potential internal opposition group.

Besides the communist subversives and radical Muslims there is a constellation of possible internal tensions: a small but active insurgency in East Timor, separatist cells in Irian Jaya, unbalanced development, underemployment, unfair income distribution, liberal democratic ideas, Western culture, Presidential succession, corruption within the governing elite, and splits between the older and younger generations of officers. The list is long, but none of these potential threats appears either large or imminent.

Clearly, the greatest long-term external threat perceived by ABRI comes from communist China. The PRC has not been forgiven for supporting the PKI during the early 1960s. China's proximity to Southeast Asia, and the Overseas Chinese who play major roles in the economics of the region, guarantee a continuing role for Beijing. As one Indonesian general expressed it, "The Chinese, like the poor, are always with us." That China is over 1,000 nautical miles from Indonesia and has little conventional force projection capability reassures ABRI. Nonetheless, China's support of Khmer resistance fighters reminds ABRI of Beijing's continued willingness to support insurgencies in Southeast Asia should it fit Beijing's foreign policy interest. Indonesia's military leaders are ambivalent on formal diplomatic relations with Beijing, and they hope that the United States will not move too quickly to provide economic and military assistance to China simply as a means of offsetting Soviet power in Asia.

Next in the hierarchy of external threats is Vietnam, supported by the USSR. Again, however, there is some ambivalence. Though concerned over Vietnam's political and military strengths, Indonesia has been less critical than other ASEAN countries of Vietnam's 1979 invasion of Kampuchea. Within ABRI there is a certain admiration for the Vietnamese Armed Forces, who gained their country's independence through a revolutionary anticolonial war. Although admired for their nationalism and anticolonial independence struggle, the Vietnamese are suspected for their communist ideology, close ties to Moscow, and forcible occupation of Kampuchea. Overlapping territorial claims in the South China Sea and fleeing Vietnamese refugees are still causes for concern. Indonesia's large population, more stable economy, and distance from Vietnam are, however, reassuring.

ABRI has shown less concern over the Soviet military presence in Vietnam than over its subversive activities in Indonesia. For many years the Soviets have been suspected of financing certain publications (*Topik, Merdeka, Indonesian Observer*) that espouse a consistently pro-Soviet and anti-Western editorial policy. In early 1982 an Indonesian Navy officer was caught handing detailed marine charts to a KGB agent in exchange for cash. ABRI is also concerned by corrupting influences from the West, such as ads that stimulate consumer demand for luxury goods and Western writers who extol the efficacy of tumultuous elections and advocate civilian control of the military.

## Kopkamtib

Indonesia's Operational Command for the Restoration of Security and Order (Kopkamtib) is a unique, feared, and poorly understood military institution. It is more an organizational arrangement than a regular organization, with only a small permanently assigned staff and few, if any, exclusive duties. Though its form is not fixed, Kopkamtib's mission is clear: to guarantee national stability and public order by quickly suppressing outbreaks of social unrest. Its task is internal security, and its powers are great.

Kopkamtib was formed immediately after the abortive 30 September communist coup attempt[15] to "restore order and security." In August 1967, its authority was officially spread to the regions when Kodam commanders were appointed Kopkamtib Special Executors. As the communist threat subsided in the late 1960s, Kopkamtib's role declined. In 1969, however, new life was breathed into this unique institution when its responsibilities were switched from Army headquarters to Hankam as part of a general centralization of control in the Ministry of Defense. Formal command now rests with the Armed Forces Commander, General Moerdani, but it is clear the President can directly pick up the reins whenever he so desires.

When founded in 1965, Kopkamtib's mission clearly focused on restoring order and eliminating communist "remnants" in the wake of the coup attempt. This mission was expanded in late 1965 by a Presidential Decision instructing Kopkamtib "to restore the authority and integrity of the Government through physical military and nonmilitary operations."[16] Another expansion of Kopkamtib's function, in a 1969 Presidential Decision, authorized it "to surmount other extreme and subversive activities" and "to take part in securing the authority and integrity of the Government and its apparatus from the Central to the Provincial Administration in order to safeguard the preservation of the Panca Sila and the 1945 Constitution."

Since 1969, several Presidential Decisions have further delineated Kopkamtib's operations, but the official mission is unchanged. This technicality notwithstanding, Kopkamtib's role expanded throughout the 1970s. In 1974 President Suharto designated it the instrument to carry out the Consultative Assembly's mandate to "safeguard and maintain the unity and integrity of the nation" and to safeguard national development.[17] The latter responsibility has now become part of Kopkamtib's statement of its own goal, wherein its peace and order functions are explicitly identified as absolute requirements for the country's five-year development plans. Thus, to the question of "Which comes first, security or development?" Kopkamtib answers clearly—"Security!"

Kopkamtib has acquired wide-ranging tasks, asserting it is responsible for destroying elements that endanger integrity of the state, raising the level of national stability, securing the authority of the Government, restraining cultural influences that conflict with Panca Sila values, and generating greater public participation in peace and security matters. Specifically, it has had responsibility for securing national elections, cleansing the government of corrupt officials, suppressing communist rebels in Kalimantan, combating Papuan separatists, putting down political disturbances in Jakarta, monitoring the activities of former political prisoners, and canceling the publication permits of newspapers and magazines that incite social unrest.

Kopkamtib effectively controls and censors Indonesia's media to prevent publication of information that would either undercut the authority of the Government or incite social unrest. Though presses in Indonesia can operate only with permits from the Information Ministry,

Kopkamtib can force revocation of such permits on a moment's notice, without right of appeal. Many publications that were temporarily closed in the wake of the 1974 riots have never been reopened. Kopkamtib officials often provide editors with advice on proscribed subject matter. Not coincidentally, a senior military officer serves as general manager for Antara, the government's news agency. The military, directly or indirectly, publishes several newspapers.

Kopkamtib does not assert, however, that its powers are unlimited or that it has rights to act arbitrarily. After the 1974 riots, it adopted four principles which were designed to constrain its misuse of power. These obliged Kopkamtib to: 1) provide guidance to the people but also allow them to develop their own initiatives, 2) act as protector of society, 3) take repressive measures only to prevent undesired or unstable situations, and 4) use force only as a method of persuasion.[18]

Kopkamtib may be viewed as a quick-reaction nonroutine chain of command that bypasses most normal military staff agencies. Technically, its command line goes from the President to the Deputy Commander of the Armed Forces (Pangab), who also carries the title of Kopkamtib Commander (Pangkopkamtib), thence to the Defense Region Commander (Pangkowilhan), who serves as Regional Special Executive (Laksuswil), and finally to the Army Area Commander (Pangdam), who serves as Area Special Executive (Laksusda). Notably missing from this official chain is the Minister of Defense. The Kopkamtib command chain is not, however, invariably used. At critical moments, Kopkamtib is inclined to rely on informal and skip-echelon communications, so the importance of the chain of command decreases as situations become more critical.[19]

The effect of the Kopkamtib command line is to substantially elevate the power of the Commander of the Armed Forces. As Kopkamtib Commander he can use all instruments of the Armed Forces and state apparatus to ensure security in accordance with the Panca Sila philosophy and 1945 Constitution. He also has legal access to all government and nongovernment offices and the authority to detain or arrest virtually anyone in Indonesia, if that person is determined to be threatening the principles of the Panca Sila and 1945 Constitution.[20]

At the national level, Kopkamtib has both a regular and special staff, though neither is dedicated full time to Kopkamtib matters. The regular staff consists of five assistants—intelligence, operations, territorial affairs, social order and security, and sociopolitical affairs. The special staff consists of another five key elements, which constitute the central implementation echelon of Kopkamtib—Intelligence Task Force (Satgas Intel), Social Communications Information Service (Dispen Humas),

Communications Unit (Sat Hub), Central Investigative Team (Teperpu), and the Central Prosecution Team (Tod Sapu). While Kopkamtib's intelligence, information, and communications functions are performed by regular Hankam staffs, the investigative team (director generals and inspector generals from several departments) and prosecution team (attorneys) exist on a more ephemeral basis, depending on the situation.

At the implementing level (Laksusda), Kopkamtib functions are carried out by the Military Area Commander, so the Army has dominant power. The Laksusda does not have a separate Kopkamtib staff but normally relies on the Kodam Chief of Staff to assemble special teams of military and civilian personnel in the Kodam. The operations and intelligence assistants are responsible for organizing, preparing, and summoning operational elements for combat operations or other special Kopkamtib roles. The Kodam Commander, as Laksusda Kopkamtib, also has a special staff that includes the local Air Force and Navy chiefs and the commander of the local Intelligence Task Force (Satgas Intel) detachment. Intelligence Task Force duties at the Kodam level include investigations, security, and "influence by persuasion." Also on the special staff is an Area Investigation Team (Teperda), for interrogating personnel suspected of subversive activities; a team of judges and prosecutors (Todsad), for bringing suspects to trial; and a screening unit (Satgas Ningda), whose role is unclear.

Given Kopkamtib's extensive functions, powers, and implementing network, one may conclude that it has martial law powers even when a State of Emergency has not been formally declared. Kopkamtib has denied this, asserting that its responsibilities for internal security and countering subversion must be continuous in "normal and ordinary" circumstances. Kopkamtib publications acknowledge, however, that Kopkamtib may be eliminated if a State of Emergency is declared under Article 12 of the 1945 Constitution.[21]

One may, of course, question the distinction between the powers of Hankam and those of Kopkamtib. Kopkamtib and ABRI headquarters are clearly colocated and, by and large, share the same staffs and perform the same functions. The basic distinction between ABRI and Kopkamtib is the focus of the threat and the speed with which duties are performed. ABRI is responsible for external defense and internal security; Kopkamtib handles only internal security. Koptamtib responds to crisis situations with telephone hot lines and skip-echelon communications. Its authority is tremendous once a threat to security has been declared; however, its implementing agents are regular assets—territorial commands, intelligence units, and the national police. For specific operations, Hankam provides the prime assets and the logistics support for Kopkamtib.[22]

## Civil-Military Relations

The study of civil-military relations is not alien to Indonesian officers, but they are uncomfortable discussing it with Westerners because of the implied legitimacy often attached to civilian control of the military. Civilian control and civil-military relations are not concepts embodied in the 1945 Constitution. They were borrowed from the West and invoked on a regular basis in Indonesia only between 1950 and 1959.

Officers of the 1945 generation argue that they were not set apart from the people during the revolution. Military leaders created the modern state and have fought repeatedly to secure it from both internal and external threats. They ask rhetorically, "Who is better qualified or more responsible for governing Indonesia?" ABRI bases the vast scope of its role on the Dual Function doctrine that authorizes both military and sociopolitical functions. The military dominated regime that came to power in 1965-1967 did so with the blessing of the constitutionally supreme Peoples Consultative Assembly (MPRS). Although the regime rules legally, only in a very limited sense does Indonesia have separation of executive, legislative, and judicial power.

Under the 1945 Constitution, the President and cabinet are not responsible to the Parliament (DPR), which is in session almost continuously, but to the Consultative Assembly (MPR), which is only required to meet once every five years. The major tasks of MPR members are to elect the President and pass the Broad Outline of State Policy (GBHN), which establishes the government's administrative and legislative guidelines for national development. Significantly, the defense portion of the GBHN is drafted by the National Defense and Security Council (Wanhankamnas), a group that consists almost entirely of senior military officers.

Indonesia's military elite has been instrumental in creating Golkar, a federation of functional groups (e.g. youth, farmers, women) that effectively serves as the government's political party. Though active-duty military personnel are not allowed to take leadership positions in Golkar, an advisory council of senior retired generals directs Golkar election strategy from behind the scenes. Golkar was not founded on the Western principle that political support should spontaneously arise from below, or that the national good is served by vigorous public debate of emotional issues. Rather, ABRI believes society can be conditioned and consensus arranged from the top. For example, General Ali Murtopo acknowledged in the 1971 elections that the task of ensuring a Golkar victory was the "greatest mission" and "greatest role" ever given him by the Army.

Since the New Order began, ABRI had overseen three national elections—in 1971, 1977, and 1982. Whereas in 1971 ABRI and Golkar were often indistinguishable, in more recent elections an effort was made to differentiate the two structures and to set ABRI more above politics. ABRI participation in Golkar councils is now restricted, and officers who wish to spend all their time on Golkar matters should resign and pursue their political interests through Pepabri, an association of retired military personnel. Increasingly, Golkar affairs will be conducted from outside Hankam, though still managed by retired military officers.

Civil-military relations in Indonesia are illustrated by the operations of the ABRI faction in Parliament, which essentially serves as a national sounding board. Military officers do not highly value the semiautonomous role of Parliament and political parties. In the opinion of many officers, these institutions should support rather than lead. They are tolerated by military officers as long as they endorse the government's economic development plans and do not provoke political turmoil. In addition to Golkar representatives, 75 military personnel are regularly appointed to Parliament. To encourage turnover, military officers sometimes serve only half of the regular five-year term before being replaced. Appointment of officers to both the DPR and MPR is ostensibly to compensate military personnel for their nonvoting role in elections. Not surprisingly, with Golkar and military representatives predominant in the DPR, ABRI leaders stress that popular dissent must be channeled through legal parliamentary means. Protests may take the form of petitions to the DPR or appeals to the bureaucracy, but complaints may not take the form of strikes or street demonstrations.

The Indonesian military does not expect civilian ministries to be fully autonomous. Senior officers are often placed in key billets outside Hankam, much to the chagrin of civil servants who are thereby denied promotions and independent decisionmaking power. The ABRI staff, under the Chief of Staff for Sociopolitical Affairs, selects an appropriate man, obtains ministerial agreement, and arranges training. When assigned to another ministry, an officer wears civilian clothes and reports through his new chain of command, but his performance is monitored by ABRI, and he is expected to uphold military standards. No ministry is authorized to relieve or reassign these men, even for cause, without ABRI approval.

Retired military officers hold key positions in many of Indonesia's social institutions—trade unions (FBSI), boy scouts (Pramuka), political parties (PPP and PDI), civil defense (Hansip), intelligence (Bakin), and, universities. Retired military personnel often get jobs in the personnel or security sections of private commercial concerns. Other retirees become part of Indonesia's transmigration effort and move to remote areas on the outer islands where they become pillars in their new communities.

## Scope of Military's Bureaucratic Role

Senior military officers clearly dominate the centers of political power in Indonesia. In 1982 active and retired military personnel occupied roughly half the top positions in the country's central bureaucracy.[23] President Suharto was a retired general and seven of his eight principal aides in the State Secretariat were military men, active or retired. Two of the three coordinating Ministers and eight of 17 Department Ministers were either active or retired military. Sixteen of 18 Secretary-General level positions and 11 of 17 Inspector-Generalships were held by military or former military men.

Critical positions held by the military elite deserve special mention: President, State Secretary, Coordinating Minister for Political and Security Affairs, Coordinating Minister for Social Affairs, Minister of Internal Affairs, Minister of Defense and Security, Minister of Justice, Attorney General, Head of the Supreme Court, Minister of Information, Head of the Parliament, Head of the Supreme Audit Board, Head of the Logistics Affairs Board, and the Head and Deputy Head of the State Intelligence Coordinating Agency.

The three government organizations that are most critical to maintaining social order and government authority—the Defense Ministry, Ministry of Internal Affairs, and the State Intelligence Coordinating Agency—have the highest percentage of military leadership. Military control of the Ministry of Internal Affairs rose from less than 30 percent of the key positions in 1966, to 70 percent in 1971, and 90 percent in 1982. Significant increases in military personnel were noted in the Ministries of Information, Social Affairs, Religion, Foreign Affairs and Justice. Though military men are less prominent in ministries dealing with finance, mining, energy, and public works, there is no ministry where the military is not well placed, at least in the key oversight positions of Secretary-General or Inspector-General.[24]

The military's influence is not confined to the peak of the bureaucratic pyramid. Two-thirds of Indonesia's 27 provincial governors are retired flag-rank officers. By virtue of its territorial organization, the Army has an administrative organization that virtually parallels that of the Ministry of Internal Affairs, all the way down to the village level.

Except in emergency situations, ABRI officers are not inclined to rule by fiat. Instead they rely on "musyawarah," the traditional Indonesian practice of reaching decisions through mutual consultations. At the provincial level this practice has been institutionalized into the Area

Leadership Conference (Muspida), consisting of the Kodam commander, Provincial Governor, Provincial Attorney, and senior Navy, Air Force and Police Commanders. At the district level the military and civilian authorities meet in a more abbreviated forum, known as Musda, and at the sub-district level the group is known as Tripida. Regardless of whether it is a Muspida, Musda, or Tripida, important government decisions are made by these civil-military councils which serve as coordinating bodies for representatives of the Army, Police, Ministry of Internal Affairs, and Attorney General's Office.

The number of military men in government outside the Ministry of Defense is not known with certainty; most current estimates run between 12,000 and 20,000, although occasionally one hears an old figure of 40,000.[25] The military is unlikely to soon abdicate its prominent political role. President Suharto will likely remain in office for several more years and it is reasonable to expect him to retain much the same group of senior officers in key government posts.

### The Military and Foreign Policy

Indonesia's Department of Foreign Affairs (Deplu) is headed by a civilian, but several of Deplu's most senior positions are occupied by retired officers. President Suharto tends to select Indonesian Ambassadors from among his former military colleagues, and today about 40 percent are from the military. Most key ambassadorships, including all those in Southeast Asia, are filled by former flag officers. The practice is so commonplace that it has given rise to a verb in ABRI's lingo, "didubeskan," which means to be posted abroad as ambassador as a form of honorable retirement. Many Indonesian consular officers, especially in Southeast Asia, also come from the ranks of retired ABRI officers.

The military's heavy involvement in the Foreign Ministry has not eliminated tension between Foreign Affairs and Defense. Key issues such as the Middle East, Law of the Sea, Indochina, and Timor occasionally see the two Ministries vying for the President's ear, thus placing a military ambassador in the uncomfortable position of serving two ministries. His formal allegiance is to the Foreign Minister, but his career friendships and affinities lie in the Department of Defense.

ABRI has a major role in foreign policy formulations, but its policy preferences are hard to differentiate from the Indonesian government's general approach to international relations. It advocates an independent, active and nonaligned foreign policy that maximizes ASEAN solidarity and regional "resilience." ABRI would clearly like to limit great power military activity in Southeast Asia. The military is inclined to accept the fait accompli of Vietnamese occupation of Kampuchea but would like to wean Vietnam away from excessive and continuing dependence on the Soviet Union.

## Economic Impact of the Military

Though ABRI assumed power in 1965 and General Suharto became Acting President in 1967, the New Order dates its economic development program from 1969 when Indonesia's First Five-Year Development Plan was initiated. Economic progress, measured by most conventional indicators, has been impressive. Oil exports have guaranteed a favorable balance of trade and gross national product has increased by an average of about 8 percent per year. Inflation, which skyrocketed in the early 1960s has been brought under control, and the country has basically realized self-sufficiency in rice production.

These successes notwithstanding, military rule has not eliminated poverty. Though the percentage of people living under the poverty line is decreasing, average income is only about $600 per year. The gap between rich and poor appears to be widening. Underemployment and unemployment are serious and may be worsening. Only one-third of the population has safe drinking water, and the country has only one doctor for every 13,000 inhabitants. Infant mortality is high. Though 90 percent of school age children attend primary school, less than 25 percent go on to secondary school. Despite family planning, the population of 160 million increases by about 3 million per year. Congestion is acute on Java despite the government's sponsorship of an ambitious transmigration effort. Finally, the country's economic health is excessively dependent on oil and natural gas exports. Fluctuating prices, declining reserves, and increasing domestic consumption make such dependence precarious. Despite admirable economic progress under military rule, Indonesia faces the normal problems of an underdeveloped country. The mid-term prognosis is only moderately favorable.

Though military men occupy a number of key positions in national economic planning, President Suharto has entrusted this responsibility primarily to civilian technocrats, many of whom are graduates of Berkeley or the University of Indonesia. Nonetheless, military men head Indonesia's three most powerful independent state corporations—Pertamina (oil and gas), Bulog (rice, sugar, flour), and Tambang Timah (tin). Major financing has been arranged for these military dominated corporations through low interest state loans, tax credits, revenues from government-authorized monopolies, and the sale of contracts, licenses, leases, and distributorships.[26]

In addition, the Ministry of Defense is directly involved in a variety of economic enterprises that are not state corporations. The best known and probably largest military enterprise is Tri Usaha Bakti. This vast holding company, founded by the Army to provide employment for retired servicemen, now has shares in at least 38 companies. Most of these companies are in partnership with regional military commands, Chinese businessmen, or foreign investors.[27]

The Indonesian Army, Navy, and Air Force are involved in major consumer cooperatives (Inkopad, Inkopal, and Inkopau) at the national, regional, and district levels. Their joint venture activities include shipping, storage, forestry, fishing ship repair, banking, logging, construction, and air transport. The Army's Strategic Command sponsors at least a dozen companies, including an airline (Mandala) and auto assembly plant (Volkswagen).[28] Each regional military command has its own network of affiliate companies, often managed by Chinese businessmen. These provide military units with income in addition to funds available through normal budgetary channels. The scope and magnitude of such military related enterprises is huge, but their complexity defies accurate assessment of their contribution to either military funds or national economic development.

### New Defense Legislation and Organization

For many years Hankam's defense role was defined primarily by a 1954 Consultative Assembly law (No. 29), based on the Provisional Constitution of 1950. Noticeably missing from the 1954 Defense Law was mention of ABRI's sociopolitical role and the Dual Function doctrine. After the country returned to the 1945 Constitution in July 1959, legal consistency required a new law. The government, however, delayed efforts to formulate such a bill until passage of MPR Decision No. IV in 1978, on the Broad Outlines of State Policy, required a basic national defense and security law. The MPR's 1978 call for new legislation made it clear that ABRI's dual function should be enshrined in the new bills. Senior military officers obviously wanted to avoid the distinctions between strict civilian and military spheres and preferred to rely on Panca Sila democracy, which is based more on "family" principles.

Brainstorming on the new defense legislation began at the Army Staff College in 1979. Four draft bills were submitted to the Parliament shortly after the May 1982 national elections, but only the main bill (Number 20) passed prior to the end of the legislative session.

Significantly, the new legislation specifically allows separation of the Minister of Defense (Menhankam) from the Commander of the Armed Forces (Pangab). The Minister of Defense assists the President in managing the execution of state defense and deciding policies concerning ABRI service as an element of the social force, oversees efficient use of national resources for national defense, and plans and implements the strategic defense plans of the state. By contrast, the Commander of the Armed Forces assists the President in executing command authority for state defense. Pangab heads "Armed Forces Headquarters" (as opposed to Ministry of Defense), using the armed forces both as a defense and social force.[29]

In addition to the legislation discussed above, Government Regulation NO. 31 of 5 October 1981 has had significant impact on Hankam reorganization plans and on the issue of generation transfer in ABRI.[30] It facilitates the voluntary reemployment of retired military personnel, as military reserves, for tasks requiring particular skills and experience. The President selects flag-rank officers and the Minister of Defense selects other officers for reserve duty. More importantly, the Defense Minister decides which reservists will be recalled to active duty and what compensation they will receive. The government's explanation of Regulation 31 argued that extension of selected senior officers on active duty past mandatory retirement at age 55 is "necessary for promoting the performance of tasks and for inheriting or transferring skill and expertise to the future generation." Though the government stated that reemploying retired military members should be reserved for "matters of great urgency," younger ABRI officers are concerned. Key billets into which they had hoped to be promoted may now be filled by extended-duty officers from the 1945 generation. Just as importantly, Regulation 31 facilitated the separation of Defense Minister and ABRI Commander, allowing the creation of a significant Hankam staff manned with retired military personnel.

With the beginning of the new fiscal year in April 1985, ABRI implemented a major reorganization that has been long discussed. The military's territorial organization has been reduced to 10 Military Areas (Kodams), 2 Air Force Operational Commands (Koops), and 2 Fleets. At Air Force and Navy headquarters the staffs have been streamlined into three main directorates—operations, personnel, and logistics. While there has been this major reduction and streamlining of headquarters, efforts have been made to find meaningful jobs for younger generation officers who have been displaced by the reorganization. Many Military Reserve Commands (Korems) and bases are acquiring new staff officers. Other officers are being routed to new sociopolitical jobs on the Kodam staffs, and younger active duty officers are now being trained to replace retired officers who represent ABRI in the national and regional parliaments. Concomitant with the reorganization, noticeable efforts are being made to improve the professional standards of officers serving in both mainstream military units and sociopolitical roles.

## Net Assessment

The Indonesian military can be proud of its past. It secured the country's independence and maintained national security against threats from communists, radical Muslims, and assorted secessionists. ABRI has achieved its goal of military unity, while centralizing and rationalizing its command structure. Since 1965 ABRI has dominated the country's political and economic life, bringing far more stability and development than Indonesia experienced under civilian rule. Much of the country's economic success, however, has been built on petroleum exports, the future for which is uncertain. Major economic problems still face the country: overpopulation, underemployment, limited industrialization, corruption, and an inefficient bureaucracy. ABRI also faces two distinct leadership problems in the 1980s, transitioning to a post-revolutionary generation of officers and eventually selecting a replacement for President Suharto.

One's evaluation of the Indonesian military depends on the criteria chosen. ABRI judges its own success by two measures—security and development. By these criteria, the military is doing quite well. Foreign journalists and academics, however, often put more emphasis on how well ABRI implements Western concepts of political democracy and how equitably it allocates the country's resources. By these criteria, ABRI does less well. Whatever the evaluation, ABRI will dominate Indonesian politics for years to come. The military dominated government faces no major or immediate political challenge. Potential opposition groups have been coopted or penetrated, while others find their ability to organize frustrated by the military's control of both the legislature and the media. ABRI is the only institution in Indonesia which is both dedicated to national unity, stability, and development, and capable of effectively governing the country's multifaceted society.

## Notes

1. Joyce Lebra, *Japanese-Trained Armies*, (Hong Kong: Heineman Educational Books, 1977), pp. 146–149. See also Nugroho Notosusanto, *The Peta Army During the Japanese Occupation of Indonesia*, (Tokyo: Waseda University Press, 1979).

2. This theme comes through very strongly in the various writings of General Abdul Haris Nasution. See A. H. Nasution, *The Indonesian National Army,* (Washington: Joint Publications Research Service Report No. 19, 185, May 1963).

3. Ulf Sundhaussen, "The Military: Structure, Procedures, and Effects on Indonesian Society," in Karl D. Jackson and Lucian W. Pye *Political Power*

and *Communications in Indonesia*, (Berkeley: University of California Press, 1978), p. 45. Though now somewhat dated, this Sundhaussen article is a good short description of ABRI. See also Sundhaussen's book, *The Road to Power: Indonesian Military Politics, 1945-1967*, (London: Oxford University Press, 1982).

4. For a balanced summary of ABRI's involvement in Timor, see Susumu Awanohara's "Falling Into Step" and "Flooded with Funds" *Far Eastern Economic Review*, 6 August 1982, pp. 19-25.

5. For a useful discussion of ABRI's upgrade program see Khalid Abdullah "Nation's Armed Forces Examined," *Asian Defense Journal* (Kuala Lumpur), May 1982, pp. 36-44. This article, however, contains some factual errors. See also "Revitalization of Armed Forces Noted," *Asian Defense Journal*, March 1982, pp. 23-27.

6. James Hazlett, "Strait Shooting," *Proceedings*, June 1982, p. 72.

7. This entire section comes from "Indonesia's Defense Industry," undated handout provided by members of BPPT team (Agency for Development and Application of Technology) while in Washington during early 1982, pp. 1-6.

8. Richard Robison, "Capitalism and the Bureaucratic State in Indonesia: 1965-1975," PhD Thesis at University of Sydney, November 1977, pp. 228-289.

9. As cited in Donald Weatherbee, "Indonesia's Armed Forces: Rejuvenation and Regeneration," *Southeast Asian Affairs 1982* (Singapore: Institute of Southeast Asian Studies, 1982), pp. 152.

10. *Indonesian Financial Statistics* (Jakarta, Bank Indonesia, 1982).

11. *Tempo*, 26 June 82, p. 12.

12. In October 1981 there were about 320 active duty flag rank officers in ABRI, but this number has been whittled dramatically since then by scores of retirements by 1945 generation officers.

13. See especially *Buku Materi Pelengkap Penataran* (Bandung: Seskoad Gravida, July 1979) pp. 167-197.

14. Harold Maynard, "A Comparison of Military Elite Role Perceptions in Indonesia and the Philippines" (PhD Dissertation available from Xerox University Microfilms, No. 76-19,448), p. 266.

15. Harold Crouch, *The Army and Politics in Indonesia*, (Ithaca: Cornell University Press, 1978), p. 160, 355.

16. *The Role and Function of Kopkamtib*, (Jakarta; Kopkamtib, January 1977), p. 3, (Keppres 179/1965 and Keppres 19/1969).

17. Ibid., p. 3 (Keppres 9/1974 to carry out MPR 10/1973).

18. Ibid., p. 5.

19. "Organization and Procedure of Laksus Kopkamtibda Irja" (Mimeographed handout, presumably from Kodam 17, circa 1981), p. 3.

20. *The Role and Function of Kopkamtib*, op. cit., p. 6. It appears that this vast power excludes the President who, by definition, supports the Panca Sila and 1945 Constitution, and it excludes foreign diplomats, who are protected by diplomatic immunity.

21. Ibid., p. 6.

22. *Vademecum, Pengetahuan Pertahanan Keamanan,* Cetakan Kedua (Bandung, Indonesia: Markas Besar Tentara Nasional Indonesia, Angkatan Darat, Sekolah Staf dan Komando, 1982), p. 406–410.

23. John A. MacDougall, "Patterns of Military Control in the Indonesian Higher Central Bureaucracy" *Indonesia* (Cornell), Spring 1982, pp. 129–148. MacDougall analyzed the backgrounds of incumbents in 145 central government positions during early 1982. The military justifies its wide-ranging involvement in political, social, and economic affairs under the Dual Function Doctrine (Doktrin Dwi Fungsi). An active duty or retired officer who plays a predominantly social and political role—as opposed to a strictly military or defense role—is known as a "Karyawan." This term became especially popular after President Sukarno's 22 April 1959 speech concerning Guided Democracy and the military's role as a functional group in Indonesian society. The term "Karya" means work, as well as the service such work performs for society. Karyawan Angkatan Bersenjata (Armed Forces Workers) may be on active duty and assigned to the Ministry of Defense, but in many cases they are not. Whether or not organic to the military, they are expected to work for prosperous and just social development. A fuller explanation of the Karyawan concept can be found on page 41 of Major General Sokowati's *Amalkan Tri-Ubaya-Cakti* (Jakarta, 1965).

24. MacDougall, op.cit., p. 90.

25. David Dodwell, "Indonesia: So Much to Gain by Firm Handling," *Financial Times Survey,* 21 December 1981, p. 1.

26. Robison, op.cit., p. 238.

27. Ibid, p. 260–261.

28. Ibid., pp. 271–275 and Maynard, op.cit., pp. 224–225.

29. Articles 20–21 of Draft Bill on Principles of Indonesian State Defense.

30. Titled innocuously (Reenlistment of Members of TNI Who Have Completed Their Terms of Service as Members of TNI Reserves), this short document has been overlooked by many outside observers of Indonesian military affairs. Not coincidentally, Regulation 31 is dated 5 October 1981, Indonesian Armed Forces Day.

# 11

## The Changing Role of the Philippine Military During Martial Law and the Implications for the Future

*William E. Berry, Jr.*

In September 1972, Philippine President Ferdinand Marcos declared martial law. Since then, Marcos has increased the powers he wields in the Philippines through different means. The significance of increased presidential power is that Marcos has used the military as a primary means to exercise his political power and, as a result, the Philippine military has become a dominant actor in domestic politics. Even before the declaration of martial law, Marcos had been closely associated with the military and this association became closer over the past ten years.[1] The purpose of this chapter is, first, to analyze the increased presidential powers exercised under martial law; and second, to determine how these increased powers have affected the military, particularly concerning increased resources and manpower, roles and missions, and the politicization of the military.

When he declared martial law, President Marcos indicated that such action was necessary to control lawlessness and threats of subversion within the country.[2] The lawlessness referred to corruption within the government and the wanton acts of violence which were common occurrences in the Philippines during the late 1960s. The subversive threat was perceived to come primarily from the New People's Army (NPA), the military arm of the Maoist-oriented Philippine Communist Party. Marcos specifically charged that the NPA was responsible for the bomb explosion at a political rally in August 1971, and for the attack upon Defense Minister Juan Ponce Enrile shortly before martial law was declared.[3] In addition, there had been student demonstrations in the late 1960s and early 1970s, some of which had become violent, which President Marcos believed were orchestrated by the left.[4]

The declaration of martial law was controversial at the time and has remained so.[5] Marcos attempted to attenuate the controversy by stating that his declaration was constitutional and did not represent "a military take-over of civilian government functions."[6] Some opposition political leaders voiced concern that martial law would result in a military dictatorship and be used to continue Marcos in power.[7] Fears of a military dictatorship resulted, at least in part, because the Philippine military was based on the American model—that is, subordinate to civilian control. The President was the commander-in-chief of the military, but only the Congress had the authority to declare war.[8] Those opposed to martial law were concerned that civilian control over the military could be destroyed by martial law. These fears were exacerbated by the tremendous increase in presidential power which developed as the martial law period commenced and the President's dependence on the military became established.

Immediately after he declared martial law, President Marcos began to secure his political position. He adjourned the legislature, censored the free press, established military tribunals to try civilians, and imprisoned many of his political opponents, including Benigno Aquino, who was generally believed to be the President's most likely successor. Even more important to his consolidation of political power was the influence Marcos exercised over drafting a new constitution. A Constitutional Convention was convened in June 1973 to consider a revision of the 1935 Constitution and change the form of government from a presidential to a parliamentary system. Under a parliamentary system, Marcos could run for a seat in the legislature and, as the leader of his party, become Prime Minister as long as his party remained in the majority. In this manner, the President could circumvent the two-term restriction of the original Constitution.

The convention bogged down over this effort to change the form of government, as both the Congress and the courts became involved with some of the issues being raised. Nonetheless, on 7 July 1972, the convention voted 158 to 120 to change the form of government.[9] Article VII of the proposed Constitution provided that the President would become the "symbolic head of state" but would not exercise any real political power. The provision for a National Assembly was included in Article VIII. Members of this unicameral legislature would serve six-year terms, and the power to declare war remained with the legislature.

Article IX addressed the role of the Prime Minister and Cabinet. The Prime Minister would be the head of government, elected by the members of the National Assembly. He or she would be commander-in-chief of the military and would appoint all officers from the rank of brigadier general up. After martial law was declared, a convention committee drafted a series of "transitory provisions" to provide for an orderly transition from a presidential to a parliamentary form of government. These provisions were incorporated into Article XVII by the full convention. This article is extremely important as far as the increased political powers available to Marcos under the new Constitution are concerned. An interim National Assembly was to be created until such time as the National Assembly could be elected. However, the incumbent President, meaning Marcos, was given the authority to convene the interim National Assembly. Section 3, paragraphs 1 and 2, are quoted because of their significance to Marcos' increased power.

> Section 3 (1). The incumbent President of the Philippines shall initially convene the interim National Assembly and shall preside over its sessions until the interim Speaker shall have been elected. He shall continue to exercise his powers and prerogatives under the nineteen hundred and thirty-five Constitution and the powers vested in the President and Prime Minister under this Constitution until he calls upon the interim National Assembly to elect the interim President and the interim Prime Minister, who shall then exercise their respective powers vested by this Constitution.
>
> Section 3 (2). All proclamations, orders, decrees, instructions, and acts promulgated, issued, or done by the incumbent President shall be part of the law of the land and shall remain valid, legal, binding, and effective even after the lifting of martial law or the ratification of this Constitution, unless modified, revoked, or superseded by subsequent proclamations, orders, decrees, instructions, or other acts of the incumbent President, or unless expressly and explicitly modified or repealed by the regular National Assembly.

The significance of this article is that Marcos would determine when both the interim and regular National Assemblies would convene. Meanwhile, he would be the sole political power in the country, exercising the powers of both President and Prime Minister. His decrees, proclamations acts, etc., were legalized by the new Constitution. On 29 November 1972, the full Constitutional Convention voted in favor of the new Constitution and forwarded it to Marcos for submission to the electorate in a plebiscite.[10]

President Marcos initially announced that the required plebiscite would be held on 15 January 1973, after a period of free debate on the merits of the Constitution. Subsequently, the President stated that the scheduled plebiscite would be replaced by nationwide "citizens' assemblies." He argued that elements in the society were taking advantage of the free debates to cause confusion which would lead to further deterioration in the country.[11] Every citizen fifteen years of age and older was allowed to vote in rural, town, and city neighborhoods across the country. The voting was conducted by a show of hands or voice vote. No ballots were cast. The voting was completed, under these conditions, and on 17 January 1973, Marcos issued Presidential Proclamation 1102 announcing that the 1973 Constitution had been ratified.[12]

In reaction to this proclamation, several concerned citizens including five former senators, filed suit before the Supreme Court, charging that the President's action violated the requirement for a plebiscite to ratify the Constitution.[13] In April 1973, the Supreme Court rendered a rather complex decision regarding the legality of the new Constitution. Significantly, in a six-to-four decision, the Court ruled that the Constitution had not been ratified in accordance with constitutional provisions. However, in a separate vote, the Court attempted to determine if the new Constitution was in effect even if not properly ratified. Four justices voted that the new Charter was in force, two voted that it was not, and four abstained.[14] In his summary, Chief Justice Roberto Conception stated that "there is more than *prima facie* evidence showing that the proposed Constitution has not been ratified in accordance with the 1935 Constitution or acquiesced in by the people." He concluded that "there were not enough votes to declare the new Constitution not in force."[15] In effect, the Court ruled that the Constitution had not been properly ratified, but accepted its being in force because Marcos had presented the justices with a *fait accompli*, the legality of which the Court was unable to resolve.

Following the precedent established in January 1973, the Constitution was amended in 1976 further strengthening the President's political power. The first amendment stipulated that an interim Batasang Pambansa would serve as the legislative branch instead of an interim National Assembly, even though the latter body had not come into being since the 1973 Constitution went into effect. The interim Batasang Pambansa was limited to 120 members, one of whom was to be the incumbent President. The third amendment was very important because it strengthened the executive in relation to the legislature. The President was to convene the interim Batasang Pambansa within thirty days of the date the legislature was elected. However, there was no date specified for this election, the decision being left to the incumbent President.[16]

More important, this amendment allowed Marcos to exercise all the powers provided in both the 1935 and 1973 Constitutions, even after the interim Batasang Pambansa was elected. The fifth amendment granted Marcos the right to continue exercising legislative functions until martial law was lifted. These executive powers were further extended into the post-martial law period by the sixth amendment. If the President determined that the interim Batasang Pambansa or the regular National Assembly failed to meet their responsibilities in times of emergency or crisis, he was authorized to issue decrees, orders, or letters of instruction "which shall form part of the law of the land." These amendments provided President Marcos with the authority to exercise both executive and legislative powers even after the legislature was elected. Marcos issued Proclamation Number 1595 on 27 October 1976, specifying that these amendments were approved by the Philippine people at a referendum-plebiscite conducted on 16 and 17 October 1976.

On 17 January 1981, President Marcos terminated more than eight years of martial law. There was speculation at the time that Marcos ended martial law to impress the Reagan Administration and improve relations with Washington, and to foster a better atmosphere for the visit of Pope John Paul II scheduled for February.[17] The lifting of martial law resulted in little more than the restoration of the right of *habeas corpus* and the termination of the military tribunals. President Marcos still retained overwhelming political power.

The Constitution was amended by a series of legislative resolutions passed in early 1981 and ratified in another referendum-plebiscite on 7 April 1981.[18] These amendments once again changed the form of government to one similar to the French government in the Fifth Republic. Resolution Number 2 provided for a strong President as chief executive, elected directly by the people for a six-year term, with no limitations on the number of terms served. The President would be commander-in-chief of the armed forces and appoint all military officers in the rank of brigadier general/commodore and above. Section 15 provided immunity to the incumbent President for any acts committed during his tenure and to others acting under his orders. This immunity extends to the President and his assistants, even after their tenure in office has ended. Further, all the powers vested in the 1935 and 1973 Constitutions were to continue in effect "unless the Batasang Pambansa provides otherwise." Specifically, this resolution enables presidential rule by decree or proclamation, as stated in the third amendment to the 1976 Constitution. The President could dominate the legislature, and still be immune from current or future adjudication.

The interim Batasang Pambansa was replaced by the National Assembly elected in May 1984, with elections scheduled every six years thereafter. The legislature retained the authority to declare war, but in the event of war or other national emergency, could grant to the President "powers necessary and proper to carry out a declared national policy."[19] The Prime Minister would head the Cabinet, but the President nominates the Prime Minister who must be a member of the National Assembly. This nomination then must be approved by a majority of the legislature before the Prime Minister can assume office. In July 1981, President Marcos selected Cesar Virata, who served as Finance Minister during the martial law period, to be Prime Minister; and Virata subsequently was approved by the Batasang Pambansa. In 1984, the Constitution

TABLE 1
Philippine Military Spending and Manpower

| | $ Million | % Government Expenditures | % GNP | Number in Army, Navy, Air Force | Philippine Constabulary |
|---|---|---|---|---|---|
| 1972 | 136 | 22.1 | 1.7 | 31,000 | 23,000 |
| 1973 | 172 | 22.6 | 2.1 | 42,700 | 34,900 |
| 1974 | 312 | 24.2 | 3.6 | 55,000 | 34,900 |
| 1975 | 407 | 19.3 | 2.6 | 67,000 | 35,000 |
| 1976 | 410 | n.a. | 3.0 | 78,000 | 40,000 |
| 1977 | 680 | 18.3 | 3.4 | 99,000 | 40,000 |
| 1978 | 793 | 17.2 | n.a. | 99,000 | 47,000 |
| 1979 | 793 | 16.0 | n.a. | 103,000 | 43,500 |
| 1980 | 962 | 13.0 | 2.0 | 112,800 | 43,500 |
| 1981 | 863 | n.a. | n.a. | 112,800 | 43,500 |

Source: International Institute for Strategic Studies, The Military Balance 1975-1976, pp. 76-79; The Military Balance 1978-1979, pp. 88-91; The Military Balance 1980-1981, pp. 96-97; and The Military Balance 1981-1982, pp. 112-113.

was amended again to provide for a Vice President. However, this position will not be restored until the presidential election in 1986.[20]

It is clear from both the constitutional revisions in April 1981 and the actual governmental activities since the new Prime Minister was selected that President Marcos remains the dominant political figure in the Philippines. He determines what the short- and long-term programs will be, and the Prime Minister and his Cabinet then are responsible for implementing these programs. The importance of President Marcos' increased power since 1972 is that the military has become the primary means by which Marcos exercised this power. The role of the military has changed most significantly in resources and manpower, roles and missions and, perhaps most important, politicization of the military, particularly as the latter will affect the succession struggle in the post-Marcos period.

## Resources And Manpower

The Armed Forces of the Philippines (AFP) benefited during the martial law period, both through increased military budgets and manpower allocations. President Marcos initially increased the base pay of all commissioned officers by 150 percent after declaring martial law in an attempt to guarantee their loyalty to him.[21] The data included in Table 1 clearly indicates the increases in both resources and manpower. The military budget increased from $136 million in 1972 to $863 million in 1981. The Army, Navy, and Air Force quadrupled from a force of 31,000 in 1972 to a force of 112,800 in 1981; and the Philippine

TABLE 2
Individual Service Growth

|      | Army   | Navy   | Air Force |
|------|--------|--------|-----------|
| 1972 | 16,000 | 6,000  | 9,000     |
| 1975 | 39,000 | 14,000 | 14,000    |
| 1981 | 70,000 | 26,000 | 16,800    |

Source: International Institute for Strategic Studies, The Military Balance 1972-1973, p. 53; The Military Balance 1975-1976, pp. 58-59; and The Military Balance 1981-1982, pp. 86-87.

TABLE 3
Other Asian Military Spending and Manpower

|          |      | $ Million | % Government Expenditures | % GNP | Number in Armed Forces: Army, Navy, Air Force |
|----------|------|-----------|---------------------------|-------|-----------------------------------------------|
| Thailand | 1972 | 289       | 19.7                      | 3.8   | 150,000                                       |
|          | 1975 | 542       | 25.7                      | 3.7   | 204,000                                       |
|          | 1980 | 1,092     | 20.5                      | n.a.  | 230,800                                       |
|          | 1981 | 1,279     | 18.7                      | n.a.  | 238,100                                       |
| Malaysia | 1972 | 212       | 14.5                      | 4.5   | 50,500                                        |
|          | 1975 | 385       | 17.3                      | 4.0   | 61,100                                        |
|          | 1980 | 1,465     | 14.3                      | n.a.  | 66,000                                        |
|          | 1981 | 2,250     | 23.0                      | n.a.  | 102,000                                       |

Source: International Institute for Strategic Studies, The Military Balance 1975-1976, p. 77; The Military Balance 1978-1979, p. 89; The Military Balance 1980-1981, p. 97; and The Military Balance 1981-1982, p. 113.

Constabulary, primarily involved with internal security, increased from 23,000 to 43,500 during the same period.[22] The Army and Navy were the major benefactors, increasing from 16,000 to 70,000 and from 6,000 to 26,000, respectively, while the Air Force increased from 9,000 to 16,800 during the martial law years, as indicated in Table 2.[23]

It is informative to compare these figures with the manpower and military expenditures for two Philippine neighbors in Southeast Asia—Thailand and Malaysia. As the figures in Table 3 indicate, these countries also increased substantially their military budgets and forces since 1972. Both have military budgets greater than the Philippines, with Thailand having over 100,000 more personnel in its armed forces than does the Philippines, while Malaysia and the Philippines are roughly equal in this category.[24] Both Malaysia and Thailand spent greater percentages of their government budgets for defense than did the Philippines in

1980, as a comparison of Tables 1 and 3 illustrates. The trend in the Philippines during the past several years has been to reduce military expenditures as a percentage of both government expenditures and the Gross National Product.

Nonetheless, two other factors must be considered in this comparison between defense expenditures in the three countries. These factors are the perceived external threats to each country and their security relationships with the United States. The external threat to Thailand appears to be the most serious, primarily because of the Vietnamese presence of approximately 200,000 troops in neighboring Cambodia, which began in December 1978. There have been a number of border incursions, the most serious being in June 1980 when Vietnamese forces crossed into Thailand and hostilities ensued. As many as 130 Thai soldiers reportedly were killed during the ten hours of fighting before the Vietnamese withdrew into Cambodia.[25]

The threat from the Soviet Union is also an important factor in Thailand's military planning. This threat is perceived both indirectly because of the alliance between the Soviet Union and Vietnam, evidenced by the reported 5,000 to 6,000 Soviet advisors in Vietnam, and directly by Soviet naval exercises in the Gulf of Thailand. Four Soviet warships, including the helicopter carrier Minsk, were observed approximately 50 miles off the Thai coast in November 1980, the day after Thai Prime Minister Prem Tinsulanonda returned from a trip to China.[26] Because of the closer Thai-Chinese relationship, Thailand finds itself involved in the Sino-Soviet dispute, which causes concern in Bangkok.

Both the United States and Thailand were signatories of the Manila Pact in 1954, which created the Southeast Asian Treaty Organization (SEATO). However, when SEATO became a casualty of the Vietnam war, serious questions were asked by Thai leaders concerning the viability of the United States as an ally in case of an attack on Thailand. In response to the Vietnamese incursion in June 1980, the U.S. increased military supplies to Thailand, particularly tanks, artillery, recoilless rifles, and ammunition, but doubts still remain.[27] These doubts help explain the closer Chinese-Thai relationship which has developed in response to the Vietnamese-Soviet threat. Thailand also is confronted with a communist insurgency which has been waging guerrilla warfare against the government for several years.[28]

Because of its geographical location as a "front-line" nation-state, and because of questions which have developed involving American military assistance in times of crisis, it can be argued that Thailand's increases in defense spending and military manpower reflected in Table 3 are the result of a perceived external threat which warrants such expenditures. The same argument can be made in regard to Malaysia, although to a lesser degree. Malaysian leaders are worried about the situation in Cambodia but, perhaps because it does not have a common border with either Cambodia or Vietnam, the Malay position has been somewhat different from that of Thailand. In March 1980, then Prime Minister Datuk Hussein Onn met with Indonesian President Suharto and a statement of views on Cambodia known as the Kuantan Principal resulted.[29]

The two leaders attempted to take a more evenhanded approach than Thailand's to superpower involvement in Indochina. They called upon both China and the Soviet Union to stay out of Indochina so that regional differences could be resolved by those countries directly involved. Malaysia also has attempted to keep the lines of communication open to Hanoi to improve relations with Vietnam. Perhaps a major reason for Malaysia's apprehensions about China is the large ethnic Chinese population in Malaysia which caused domestic difficulties on occasion.

The defense of the Strait of Malacca is a major preoccupation of the Malaysian military because of the importance of this waterway between the Indian and Pacific Oceans. The Malaysian Air Force and Navy are primarily responsible for the defense of this waterway since Malaysia does not have extensive military ties with other countries. The Australian Air Force maintains two squadrons in Malaysia, but one of these was withdrawn in 1983. There is an Integrated Defense System which includes Malaysia, Great Britain, Australia, New Zealand, and Singapore, but this organization functions more to coordinate military training among the members.[30] Malaysia is also confronted with a domestic insurgency, but coordinated efforts with Thailand to deny safe sanctuaries along their common border have met with success in reducing the insurgent threat.[31]

This brief review of the external threat and security relationships in both Thailand and Malaysia indicates that there are valid fears in both countries over the external threat they face, although Thailand is in a more tenuous position than Malaysia. Because of these perceptions of the external threat, as well as domestic insurgencies in both countries, increased defense expenditures appear justified. The Philippines is not confronted with an external threat as serious as either Thailand's or Malaysia's, and the security relationship with the United States is well established. This conclusion is important in determining what the increased military budgets and manpower have been used for in the Philippines.

The Philippines is an archipelago of over 7,000 islands. Its geographical location is important as far as security issues are concerned. Unlike Thailand, or even Malaysia, the Philippines is not threatened directly by other Asian countries. When Vietnam and the Philippines normalized relations in July 1976, each pledged respect for the territorial integrity of the other.[32] More important from the Philippine view is that Vietnam does not have the military capabilities to threaten the Philippines because of the intervening sea. The People's Republic of China has been interested in improving its relations with Southeast Asia because of its fears of an increased Soviet presence in Asia. During a visit to Manila in August 1981, Prime Minister Zhao Ziyang specifically stated that China had no intention of creating spheres of influence in Southeast Asia.[33] Like Vietnam, China does not threaten the Philippines.

The only country with such capabilities is the Soviet Union. President Marcos, like the other political leaders in Southeast Asia, is worried about the growing Soviet military presence in Asia, particularly the Soviet Navy.[34] Soviet access to Vietnamese bases at Danang and Cam Ranh Bay increased these concerns.[35] Yet, it is inconceivable that the Soviets would conduct overt aggression against the Philippines unless it was part of a larger confrontation with the United States.

There are two local issues which could pose a threat to the Philippines, although both appear unlikely. The first is a long-standing dispute with Malaysia over the eastern Malaysian state of Sabah. Tensions increased to such an extent over this issue in the early 1960s that diplomatic relations were broken for a short time between Malaysia and the Philippines. However, statements by President Marcos in 1978, that the Philippines was taking steps to renounce its claims to Sabah, have attenuated the differences between the two countries.[36]

A potentially more troublesome issue involves the Spratly Islands. Located approximately 250 miles west of the Philippines, these islands became a focus for controversy because of their strategic location, the possibility of oil deposits, and the claim by four countries to all or portions of the islands. Besides the Philippines, the other claimants are Vietnam, the Republic of China (Taiwan), and the People's Republic of China (PRC). The Philippines occupies six of the islands encompassing some ninety hectares. Vietnam occupies three islands, totaling twenty hectares. Taiwan has forces on one island of forty-two hectares. The PRC claims all the islands, but does not have military forces on any of them.[37]

The situation is contentious and the chances of conflict are greater because of the possibility that large deposits of oil and natural gas are located near the Spratlys, and because of the strategic location of the islands in the center of one of the world's most heavily traveled waterways. The Philippines began deploying military units on the islands it claimed in 1971 and has nearly 1,000 men stationed there. An airstrip was built on Pegasus Island, capable of handling C-47 transports and T-28 fighters. Plans were made in 1978 to expand this runway to 6,000 feet so that more modern aircraft, such as F-8s and F-5s, could land and take off. The Vietnamese maintain approximately 350 men on their islands, one of which is only 200 yards from Parola Island, claimed by the Philippines. Taiwan has almost 600 men on the island it controls.[38]

As suggested, the Philippines is confronted with a minor external threat, certainly less than those confronting Thailand and Malaysia. To counter this threat, the Philippines has the United States as a major alliance partner. The basis of this relationship with the U.S. was established by two documents after World War II. The first of these was the Military Bases Agreement (MBA) of 14 March 1947, and the second was the Mutual Defense Treaty (MDT) signed on 30 August 1951.[39] The MBA has been amended several times, most recently in 1979 and 1980,[40] but it remains the source of legitimacy for the American military bases in the Philippines. Clark Air Base and Subic Bay Naval Base are the two most important of these bases. Clark is the headquarters for 13th Air Force, which includes two fighter squadrons consisting of forty-eight F-4Es, one aggressor squadron of ten F-5s and four T38s, a tactical airlift wing with sixteen C-130s and three C-9s, and an aerospace rescue and recovery squadron which maintains three HH-3D helicopters and one CH-3 helicopter. In June 1979, there were 7,992 U.S. military personnel assigned to Clark.[41]

Subic Bay Naval Base is the home port for the U.S. Seventh Fleet. In 1979, there were over 5,800 U.S. military personnel assigned to the base. The carrier task forces based here are the most important elements of the defense of the Philippines. Aircraft launched from these carriers, in conjunction with fighters from Clark, would attempt to provide air superiority in the airspace surrounding the Philippines. In addition, P-3C Orion aircraft, primarily designed for submarine detection, fly out of Cubi Point Naval Air Station, adjacent to Subic, to monitor Soviet submarine activity in the region.[42]

The MBA and MDT are important to the defense of the Philippines because of their provisions and also because of the spirit of cooperation which developed between the two countries as a result of being allies. The Philippines benefited specifically through various military assistance programs which provided equipment and training. The 1979 MBA amendment serves as an example.[43] For the continued use of the military bases, the U.S. agreed to pay $500 million over a five-year period. This payment would be divided into three types: Military Assistance Program—$50 million; Foreign Military Sales Credits—$250 million; and Security Supporting Assistance—$200 million. It is clear that the first two programs are important as far as the Philippine military is concerned. Although the funding for the training of Philippine military personnel in the U.S. has declined in recent years, $600,000 was provided in FY

77, $700,000 in FY 78, and $650,000 in FY 79. In 1983, the U.S. agreed to pay $900 million over five years with $475 million in economic assistance; $125 million in military aid grants; and $300 million in Foreign Military Sales credits carrying concessional interest rates for twenty years.[44]

After the unification of Vietnam in 1975 under a communist regime, President Marcos raised serious questions concerning the validity of the American security connection.[45] Each American administration from Gerald Ford to Ronald Reagan attempted to convince the Philippine President that the U.S. intends to remain an Asian power and will meet its obligations, particularly those included in the MDT.[46] In July 1981, Vice President George Bush traveled to Manila and pledged continued American support for the Philippines.[47] Secretary of Defense Caspar Weinberger made similar comments during his visit to Manila in April 1982.[48] These officials and others have tried to overcome concerns among American allies and friends in Asia about U.S. resolve. A primary means to accomplish this goal is to stress the importance of the American military presence in the Philippines, and that this presence will continue.

It is clear that Philippine military budgets and manpower allocations increased dramatically during the martial law period. Yet, because of the relatively low external threat and the American security connection, it does not appear that these increased resources and personnel have been employed primarily to protect the Philippines from foreign aggression. The actual roles and missions of the Philippine military illustrate how these funds and manpower have been used.

## Roles And Missions

The Philippine military performs a variety of roles and missions. In the martial law period, some of these roles and missions were extensions of earlier roles. Others, however, were greatly expanded, and some have developed during martial law since 1972.

The civic action mission falls into the first category. There is a long history in the Philippines of military civic action programs dating to the presidency of Ramon Magsaysay, 1953-1957. Magsaysay desired to reduce economic hardships, particularly in the countryside, to reduce peasant unrest and eliminate a source of recruitment for the Hukbalahap (Huks), a strong anti-government dissident group.[49] He established the Economic Development Corps (EDCOR) to resettle and rehabilitate former dissidents. Military engineering battalions constructed new settlements to accomplish these functions.[50]

Magsaysay's successor, Carlos Garcia, continued the military's civic action role by establishing the Socio-Economic-Military Program (SEMP) in 1958. This employed military personnel for public works projects, food production, and rural development campaigns.[51] President Marcos continued this civic action tradition. Speaking to a military audience in 1970, he praised their efforts in "administering to the health and welfare of the citizenry" and developing a "social conscience."[52] In an earlier speech, he described the dual role of the military as being a "defender" of the country and an "achiever" of social progress for the people.[53]

During the Marcos regime, the military was involved in civic action programs in addition to the normal response to natural disasters such as typhoons and floods, which plague the Philippines. In 1966, President Marcos agreed to send a Philippine military contingent to Vietnam, at the request of Lyndon Johnson. In return for these forces, the U.S. promised financial assistance to the Philippines for specific purposes, which Marcos defined. One of these was equipping three engineering construction battalions employed in various civic action programs, including road building, construction of schools and hospitals, and irrigation-flood control projects, among others.[54]

More recently, the military undertook other civic action projects. Part of the 1979 amendment to the Military Bases Agreement involved the payment of $200 million designated as Security Supporting Assistance. A stipulation imposed by the U.S. Congress is that this assistance can not be used directly for military equipment, etc.[55] Interviews with Philippine military personnel at Clark Air Base revealed that one program, in effect was using funds from the Security Support Assistance allocation to relocate squatters surrounding the base to another location where small homesteads would be provided. These officials hoped that such efforts would reduce the economic deprivation of these individuals and, thereby, the possibility of them joining dissident groups who exploit effectively dissatisfaction among the people.[56]

While civic action programs are more a continuation of previous military activities, the military's role against subversive and dissident groups increased dramatically during martial law. When President Marcos declared martial law, he specifically referred to the threat of subversion, and he used the military, including the Philippine Constabulary, in the attempt to control two major insurgent organizations: the New People's Army (NPA) and the Moro National Liberation Front (MNLF). In 1968, the Communist Party of the Philippines (CPP) was formed. This was different from the previous communist party in that it was Maoist, while its predecessor had a Soviet model. The NPA became the military arm of the CPP in late 1968, and clashes between the NPA and government forces increased steadily from 1969 to 1972.[57]

Despite intensive efforts after 1972 to destroy the NPA, the Ministry of Defense reported that the NPA actually increased in size from approximately 2,000 armed men in 1972 to over 5,000 by 1981, and these estimates did not include supporters thought to be several times that number. By early 1985, Philippines government officials stated the NPA had increased to approximately 11,000 and was operating in all 73 provinces. As evidence of this increased concern, President Marcos, in a speech to the National Assembly in January 1985, described the NPA as a "menace to our society." In previous references to the NPA, he generally downplayed the insurgency.[58] Particular gains have been realized in areas such as Samar where the government had been ineffective in meeting the needs of the people, or in areas where development efforts have disrupted the lives of the people, as in the Cagayan Valley in northern Luzon where a proposed dam threatens the ancestral home of the valley inhabitants.[59]

Whereas the NPA has been increasing in size and the scope of its operations, the MNLF was more of a threat in the mid-1970s than it is in the middle of the 1980s. Conflict between portions of the Muslim population in Mindanao and the Sulu Archipelago and the Christian central government in Manila is not new as the conflict has occurred off and on for the past four hundred years.[60] In short, a significant percentage of the Muslim population does not believe that their government respects Muslim religious and cultural traditions and has demanded greater autonomy from the government. Because of Mindanao's natural resources and agricultural productivity, political leaders in Manila have resisted efforts for increased autonomy and have vigorously supported relocation of Visayan and Luzon Christian farmers into the largely Muslim regions, depriving Muslims of title to their farms.

Although this conflict has been going on for hundreds of years, it increased in intensity after martial law for two primary reasons. First, military authorities attempted to collect firearms to reduce the lawlessness rampant in 1972. For cultural reasons, as well as concern over self-defense, this effort was resisted by the MNLF and clashes with military authorities increased. Second, Christian migration, primarily from Luzon, which began after WWII, grew after 1972. This migration was perceived by many Muslims as a threat to their way of life and they resisted. Military forces became more active in protecting the Christian settlers, most of whom came to Mindanao through government sponsored programs.[61]

For the Philippine military, this conflict has been extremely costly in terms of casualties, forces deployed, and resources. At the height of conflict in 1974-1975, it was estimated that seventy-five percent of the Philippine Army ground forces were fighting in Mindanao and Sulu.[62]

The major cause for the increase in military manpower and resources evident in Table 1 was the conflict with the MNLF. In addition to the economic and human costs described, this fighting has also caused disaffection among junior officers, especially graduates of the Philippine Military Academy, because they have been deployed to the combat zones and casualties have been high.[63]

According to Ministry of Defense estimates in 1981, MNLF strength was 16,000, with a support base of approximately 500,000. Although the level of fighting has decreased in recent years, sources have speculated that more than 24,000 Army personnel, 7,500 Philippine Constabulary, 5,000 sailors, 3,000 Marines, and 6,000 airmen were still stationed in the southern war zone in 1981.[64]

The Philippine military and Constabulary also have been active attempting to control an element in the Catholic Church which remains opposed to the Marcos regime. In a country which is eighty-five percent Catholic, the Church can exert a tremendous influence. The Church hierarchy was somewhat ambivalent when martial law was declared, but the leadership, or at least parts of it, have become more vocal, particularly as some local priests and nuns were incarcerated allegedly for association with the NPA, MNLF, or other dissident groups.[65] Perhaps ten percent of the Church could be classified as sympathetic to radical economic and social reforms, and works in pursuit of such goals. Nonetheless, they are a vocal minority, and particularly effective in those areas of the country where the government's performance in meeting the people's needs has been unsatisfactory.[66] When Pope John Paul II visited Manila in February 1981, elements of the hierarchy supporting a more activist role for the Church urged him to speak out on economic and social inequities in the Philippines, which again brought the Church and the government into confrontation.

Among the unfortunate results of the increased military involvement against domestic groups, whether the NPA, MNLF, Church or others, have been frequent reports by both Philippine and international groups of human rights violations by the military.

Much of the goodwill generated by the civil action programs has been negated by charges of persecution of political prisoners, forced relocation of individuals, and murder.[67]

While the use of the military against subversive or dissident groups increased during martial law from previous periods, the military also performed completely new roles. Among the most important of these was the judicial one involved with military tribunals. President Marcos established these tribunals by issuing Presidential Decree Number 39 on 7 November 1972.[68] Twenty military commissions were set up with five members each. These commissions heard cases, involving both military and civilian personnel, where the penalty for conviction would be jail for six years or more. Since many members of these tribunals had no formal legal training, critics complained that decisions rendered were arbitrary. Although the military tribunals were abolished with the termination of martial law in January 1981, this judicial experience most likely has had long-term effects, both on those citizens who were tried under such circumstances and possible future military roles.

President Marcos used the military to consolidate his political position, especially early in the martial law period. He effectively removed many of his political opponents on the national level by incarceration or other forms of intimidation. But there remained local opposition to the centralization of power in Manila. By using the central command structure of the AFP, the President could extend his influence into local communities, avoiding and isolating those politicians who opposed him. National political leaders had never before used the military in this fashion or to this extent.[69]

The military role in the declaration of martial law also is important as far as government decisionmaking is concerned. In 1974, President Marcos revealed that he consulted closely with twelve high-ranking military officers in the five days preceding the declaration of martial law. This is important, because several of these officers continued their service during the first few years of martial law.[70] This reliance on military advice continues with one important modification. President Marcos has tended to promote those individuals to the highest positions of authority and responsibility who are either related to him or his wife, or who are from the Ilocos region, Marcos's home area. A 1980 World Bank Report noted that, of the twenty-two generals in the Philippine Constabulary, eighteen were from this region in northern Luzon.[71] The Ilocano connection also is evident in the backgrounds of the two most powerful military men in the Philippines. General Fabian Ver, suspended AFP Chief of Staff, is from Ilocos Norte and is an old Marcos friend. Lieutenant General Fidel Ramos, Acting AFP Chief of Staff, is also from Ilocos Norte and his wife is a Marcos' cousin.[72]

The increased resources and manpower, as well as roles and missions, which the Philippine military acquired since 1972 led inevitably to a politicization of the military to an extent unknown in the Philippines prior to martial law. The most significant ramification of this increased politicization is likely to become evident in the post-Marcos period, during the succession.

### A Politicized Military, Succession, And Aquino's Assassination

Who would succeed President Marcos was a major question during the martial law period. The 1973 Constitution established a procedure for presidential succession, but Marcos confused the issue by indicating he had written a secret decree stipulating his successor. The decree would be made public only on the president's death.[73] The 1981 constitutional amendments reduced the ambiguities of the succession process. Article VII, Section 7 stipulated that a fifteen-person Executive Committee, under the Prime Minister, would exercise executive powers in the event of death, permanent disability, or removal of the President until an election could be held. The date of the election must be set by the National Assembly within thirty days of the vacancy. The election then would be held no sooner than forty-five days nor later than sixty days from the date of the legislative call.[74]

Although the 1981 constitutional amendments appeared to resolve the succession process, Marcos' actions indicated he was not confident these procedures would be followed. In March 1982, President Marcos traveled on a diplomatic mission to Saudi Arabia. On his departure from Manila, he reportedly instructed General Ver to use the AFP if necessary to insure that the Executive Committee fulfilled its constitutional role in case something happened to him while he was out of the country.[75] The specifics of this instruction are unclear, but it is evident the AFP would have been involved in preventing any assumption of power not provided for in the Constitution. In January 1984 the Constitution was amended again. The Office of Vice President will be restored in 1987, but in the meantime the succession procedures have changed. The Executive Committee is no more. The Speaker of the National Assembly, Nicanor Yniguez, would become the caretaker chief executive upon the death or incapacity of the President. Within three days of the presidential vacancy, the National Assembly must meet and enact a special election law within seven days of its first meeting. This law will set an election date between forty-five and sixty days after its date of passage.[76] However, because of changes to the Constitution involving succession procedures, none of which have ever been implemented, serious questions remain concerning the post-Marcos succession and what role the military will play. Marcos was re-elected in 1981 so his six year term of office will last until 1987, if he is physically capable of completing his term.

In the past it seemed unlikely the AFP would participate in a coup against Marcos, because the President selected military leaders intensely loyal to him and rewarded them handsomely. The military as an institution also benefitted from the increased budgets and manpower allocations, and individual service personnel received substantial pay increases and other incentives. For these and other reasons, it appeared likely the military would remain loyal. A more likely prospect was that the AFP would perform what Eric Nordlinger termed a "moderator" function.[77] In this role, the military would attempt to protect the status quo to the extent possible. The implications for those who would succeed Marcos are obvious. Any attempt to reduce the budgetary allocations, roles, and missions of the AFP likely would be resisted.

President Marcos has used the military frequently to intimidate his political opponents and dissident groups who wanted to remove him from office. Some of his closest advisors are military officers, particularly General Ver and Lieutenant General Ramos. Consequently, the AFP has become politicized to the extent that the established tradition of civilian control is not necessarily a given in the post-Marcos period. The next President may not have the political skill that President Marcos has accumulated over the past eighteen years to keep the military in check. Because of the obvious increased AFP role in the political process, many Filipinos are worried about the implications for democracy and the peaceful transfer of political power. In addition, the economic strains caused by increased military spending during a decline in the Philippine economy, and reports of human rights violations by the military, contributed to an estrangement in the early 1980s between the military and civilian components of Philippine society. Two events exacerbated the tension between the military and civilians particularly on the possible roles of the military in the post-Marcos succession.

The first was the assassination of former Senator Benigno Aquino as he returned to the Philippines on 21 August 1983.[78] No event in recent Philippine history has affected the Philippine political and economic systems to the same extent. But the emphasis here is on the effects of Aquino's murder on the Philippine military. A commentator wrote that the assassination dealt the popular standing of the military "its severest single blow in the Marcos era."[79] The official government explanation of the assassination was that a lone gunman shot Aquino just after he left the airplane in the custody of the military.[80] It was not until several days later that the killer's identity was released—Rolando Galman, a reported gun for hire, with the strong implication that "leftist subversives" had hired Galman.[81] Opposition political leaders immediately challenged the government's story—questioning how a lone gunman could know which plane Aquino was on, and how he could get close enough to fire the shot before being stopped by Aquino's military escort. They suggested that the military was involved in the assassination and only used Galman as a scapegoat. Since Galman was killed by the military escorts immediately after Aquino was shot, there was no way to question him about his motives.[82]

After two abortive attempts, President Marcos appointed a board of inquiry chaired by former judge Corazon Agrava. In October 1984, this board delivered two important findings concerning the Aquino assassination and the identity of those reponsible. The minority report was signed by Agrava and indicated there was a military conspiracy to kill Aquino, but the conspiracy was limited to seven military men and did not include General Ver, AFP Chief of Staff and confidant of President Marcos. The majority report, authored by the other four members of the board, recommended the prosecution of twenty-five military men and one civilian. Among the military contingent was General Ver. Shortly after the latter report was filed, General Ver took leave of absence from his post and was replaced on a temporary basis by Lieutenant General Ramos, who retained his position as head of the Philippine Constabulary.[83] Subsequently, in January 1985, the Philippine government filed official charges against all twenty-six men. Seventeen are accused as "principals" in the case, meaning they were directly involved with the murders of both Aquino and Galman, the man the government initially accused as the killer. Eight individuals, including General Ver, are accused of being accessories in the plot. This means they are not believed to have participated in the conspiracy, but had knowledge of the plot and attempted to conceal it after the murders occurred. The final man was indicted as an accomplice, allegedly because he identified Galman as a person the military could use as a scapegoat in the Aquino assassination.[84] The trial, held in 1985, acquitted General Ver and all armed forces personnel.

The involvement of the AFP in the Aquino assassination and the indictment of General Ver and the others had a devastating influence on the military. Even before the murder, the AFP was on the defensive because of accusations of brutality against suspected dissidents and charges of graft, corruption, and inefficiency.[85] Because Marcos was in power so long, and the military is such a political force, a dichotomy developed in the AFP officer corps between those who were loyal to the president as an individual rather than to the country and constitution they were sworn to protect and defend. General Ver, a captain when Marcos came to power in 1965, attained the rank of full general and was appointed AFP Chief of Staff in 1981 primarily because of his loyalty to the President. In 1982, Ver reorganized the military into 13 Regional Unified Commands directly under his control through the appointment of loyal regional commanders. Ver not only consolidated his power over the military but also insured that the regional commanders were loyal to him and the President.[86]

As the power of the Marcos loyalists increased, that of the more independent professional officer declined somewhat. Lieutenant General Ramos is generally considered a representative of the latter category rather than the former.[87] Ramos, a West Point graduate and experienced commander, indicated during his brief tenure as AFP Chief of Staff that he intends to initiate reforms. However, as long as he is acting

Chief of Staff, he may be limited in these efforts. It will be interesting to see if Ramos attempts to change the regional unified command system and the retirement dates of general officers. The regional command system allowed Ver to consolidate his power, but it sapped the authority of local commanders over their areas of responsibility. The retirement schedule is controversial because thirty-eight of the eighty-three AFP general officers have been extended by President Marcos beyond their scheduled retirement date.[88] This not only allows Marcos to keep ranking officers loyal to him on active duty but also restricts the promotion opportunities of other officers. Whether Ramos will attempt such reforms, or succeed if he does, will be instructive in evaluating his performance and relationship with President Marcos.

In the wake of Aquino's assassination and the turmoil that followed, the declining health of President Marcos raises serious questions about the future role of the military in the political process. Clearly, the Marcos succession will be influenced by the manner in which the incumbent passes from the scene. In the latter part of 1984 and early 1985, Marcos experienced declining health, with widespread rumors that he visited the United States for major surgery.[89] While the rumor about surgery apparently was nothing more than a rumor, Marcos' long absences from public view indicate he has health problems. If he dies suddenly, the chances for violence are more probable. If violence does occur, it seems likely the military would be involved, and could play a direct role in determining the future political leadership. On the other hand, in a peaceful transfer of political power through the electoral process, the military is less likely to become involved. Important in all these considerations is how effectively Ramos can initiate the necessary reforms in the AFP and combat the growing strength of the NPA.

The Reagan administration encouraged the Marcos regime to reform the military; an important example being comments by Assistant Secretary of Defense Richard Armitage and Assistant Secretary of State Paul Wolfowitz during visits to Manila in January 1985.[90] They also recommended that Ramos be retained as Chief of Staff. Although the United States exercises influence in the Philippines on political, economic, and military issues, this administration is wary of pushing Marcos too hard because the Philippine-American relationship is generally viewed in the larger context of Soviet-American competition in Asia. The U.S. military bases in the Philippines are viewed as extremely important to protecting American interests in this competition. Therefore, present leaders must cope with the increased politicization of the Philippine military. This will not be easy, nor without risks for those involved and the country itself.

## Notes

1. When martial law was declared, one observer noted that President Marcos was closer to the Philippine military than any of his predecessors. See John H. Adkins, "Philippines 1972: We'll Wait and See," Asian Survey, Vol. XIII, No. 2, February 1973, p. 143.
2. Presidential Decree 1081, dated 22 September 1972. The text of this decree is in the Foreign Broadcast and Information Service Bulletin, 25 September 1972, pp. 1–6.
3. Justus M. van der Kroef, "Communism and Reform in the Philippines," Pacific Affairs, Vol. 46. No. 1, spring 1973, pp. 39–42.
4. For specific examples, see the Philippine Free Press, 9 August 1969, p. 71: 7 February 1970, p. 6; 3 June 1972, p. 14; and 24 June 1972, p. 14.
5. For a view supporting the declaration of martial law, see Beth Day, The Philippines: Shattered Showcase of Democracy, pp. 15–25. For negative views, see Raul S. Manglapus, Philippines: The Silenced Democracy, pp. 16–17, and Primitivo Mijares, The Conjugal Dictatorship of Ferdinand and Imelda Marcos.
6. Foreign Broadcast Information Service Bulletin, op. cit., p. 1. The 1935 Philippine Constitution provided in Article VII, Section 10, paragraph 2, that "In case of invasion, insurrection, rebellion, or imminent danger thereof, where the public safety requires it, he [the President] may suspend the privileges of the writ of habeas corpus, or place the Philippines or any part thereof under martial law.
7. Manglapus, op. cit., pp. 39–40, and the author's interview with former Senator Jose Diokno in Manila, 14 September 1979. The Constitution limited the incumbent President to eight consecutive years in office. Since Marcos was first elected in December 1965 and reelected in December 1969, he would have had to step down in December 1973. See Article VII, Section 5, of the 1935 Constitution.
8. Article VII, Section 10, paragraph 2, and Article VI, Section 25, respectively.
9. Adkins, op. cit., p. 144.
10. Article XVII, Section 16, stipulated that the new Constitution would not take effect until it was ratified "by a majority of the votes cast in a plebiscite called for the purpose."
11. Rolando V. del Carmen, "Constitutionality and Judicial Politics" in David A. Rosenburg ed., Marcos and Martial Law in the Philippines, pp. 90–91.
12. Mijares, op. cit., pp. 451–452. Mijares was a close associate of Marcos until 1975 when he became disaffected. He came to Washington and testified before a Congressional committee and stated that the votes from the "citizen assemblies" were manipulated to give Marcos the legitimacy he needed to concentrate his power. See pp. 29–38 for more details.
13. A copy of this suit can be found in Enrique M. Fernando, The Constitution of the Philippines, Appendix C, pp. 857 ff.
14. The New York Times (hereafter NYT), 3 April 1973, p. 3.
15. Ibid., p. 3.
16. In fact, the election for the interim Batasang Pambansa was not held until April 1978. Marcos convened the legislature in June of that year. For a

summary of the election, see *Asia 1979 Yearbook*, published by the *Far Eastern Economic Review* (hereafter *FEER*, particularly pp. 279-283.

17. *NYT*, 18 January 1981, p. 1, and *FEER*, 23-29 January 1981, pp. 8-9.

18. For copies of these resolutions, see "Constitutional Amendments Proposed by Batasang Pambansa and Ratified 7 April 1981," in Albert P. Blaustein and Gilbert H. Flanz, eds., *Constitutions of the Countries of the World*, pp. 9-26. For an evaluation of these constitutional changes, see Tae Hoon Kang, "Analysis of Constitutional Amendments of April 7, 1981," in the Philippines supplement to the Blaustein and Flanz book, pp. 1-11.

19. Batasang Resolution Number 2, Section 15.

20. *FEER*, 31 July-6 August 1981, pp. 8-9 and *NYT*, 28 January, 1984.

21. David Wurfel, "Martial Law in the Philippines: The Methods of Regime Survival," *Pacific Affairs*, Volume 50, Winter 1977, p. 24.

22. These figures were compiled from the International Institute for Strategic Studies, *The Military Balance 1975-1976*, pp. 76-79; *The Military Balance 1978-1979*, pp. 88-91; *The Military Balance 1980-1981*, pp. 96-97; and *The Military Balance 1981-1982*, pp. 112-113. For more information on the *Philippine Constabulary*, see John G. Jameson, Jr., *The Philippine Constabulary as a Counterinsurgency Force, 1948-1954*, U.S. Army War College, 8 March 1971. Since December 1970, the AFP has consisted of four services: the Philippine Constabulary, Army, Navy, and Air Force. The AFP Chief of Staff is the highest ranking military officer in the AFP. In 1975, an Integrated National Police Force was created, with the Philippine Constabulary "as the nucleus" and local law enforcement agencies serving as operating units. See Jose M. Crisol, *Marcos and the Armed Forces*, pp. 179-185, and Robert B. Stauffer, "Philippine Authoritarianism: Framework for Peripheral 'Development,'" *Pacific Affairs*, Vol. 50, No. 3, Fall 1977, p. 371.

23. Ibid., *The Military Balance 1972-1973*, p. 53; *The Military Balance 1975-1976*, pp. 58-59; and *The Military Balance 1981-1982*, pp. 86-87.

24. The figures for the Thai and Malaysian military expenditures and manpower were compiled from The International Institute for Strategic Studies, *The Military Balance 1975-1976*, p. 77; The *Military Balance 1978-1979*, p. 89; *The Military Balance 1980-1981*, p. 97; and *The Military Balance 1981-1982*, p. 113.

25. For a series of articles on the Vietnamese incursion, see the *NYT*, 24 June 1980, p. 1; 25 June 1980, p. 3; and 26 June 1980, p. 3.

26. *Philadelphia Enquirer*, 4 November 1980, p. 3; and *The Economist*, 15 November 1980, p. 49.

27. *NYT*, 28 June 1980, p. 3.

28. For a recent article on the guerrilla war, see *NYT*, 22 April 1982, p. 3.

29. *FEER, Asia 1981 Yearbook*, pp. 191-192. The subsequent discussion of the Kuantan principle is taken from this source.

30. *NYT*, 11 July 1982, p. 4.

31. *FEER*, 2 September 1977, pp. 38-40.

32. *NYT*, 14 July 1976, p. 6.

33. *NYT*, 9 August 1981, p. 14.

34. For two timely articles on the Soviet military presence in Southeast Asia, see Sheldon Simon, "The Soviet Union and Southeast Asia: Interests, Goals, and Constraints," *Orbis*, Vol. 25, No. 1, Spring 1981, pp. 55–88; and Richard H. Solmon, "Choices for Coalition-Building: The Soviet Presence in Asia and American Alternatives," P-6572, The Rand Corporation.

35. For an evaluation of Soviet capabilities, particularly relating to the Vietnamese bases, see *U.S. News and World Report*, 19 July 1982, pp. 59–60.

36. For an historical article on the Sabah issue, see Lela Garner Noble, "The National Interest and the National Image: Philippine Policy in Asia," *Asian Survey*, Vol. XIII, No. 6, June 1973, pp. 560–576. For a shorter article referring to more recent times see *The Asia Record*, January 1982, p. 12.

37. *FEER*, 24 February 1978, pp. 11–12. See also Martin H. Katchen, "The Spratly Islands and the Law of the Sea: 'Dangerous Ground' for Asian Peace," *Asian Survey*, Vol. XVII, No. 12, December 1977, pp. 1167–1181.

38. Geofrrey Kemp, "Threats from the Sea: Sources for Asian Maritime Conflict," *Orbis*, Vol. XIX, No. 3, Fall 1977, pp. 1042–1043; and *FEER*, 24 February 1978, pp. 11–12.

39. The Military Bases Agreement can be found in Treaties and Other International Acts Series (hereafter TIAS) 1775 (1947–1948). The Mutual Defense Treaty is in TIAS 2529 (1952–1953). For detailed accounts of both the MBA and MDT, see William E. Berry, Jr., *American Military Bases in the Philippines, Base Negotiations, and Philippine-American Relations: Past, Present, and Future*, and unpublished Ph.D. Dissertation, Cornell University, 1981, particularly pp. 162–185.

40. TIAS 9224; *Washington Post*, 2 June 1983, p. 23; and *FEER*, 16 June 1983, pp. 30–32.

41. "13th Air Force, A Quick Look," a brochure published by 13th Air Force and available at Clark Air Base. These figures are found on p. 17. No C-141 or C-5 transport aircraft are assigned permanently to Clark Air Base, but aircraft of this type are temporarily assigned to bring in equipment and move it as required.

42. "Fact Sheet," a document published by the Public Affairs Office at Subic Naval Base, pp. 1–5.

43. TIAS 9224. In addition to tangible rewards such as military hardware and training opportunities, American support is important to the Marcos Administration psychologically as well, both as far as the Administration's legitimacy at home is concerned and for its international reputation, particularly among Southeast Asian countries.

44. These figures were provided by Lt. Colonel Herbert G. Thoms, Joint U.S. Military Advisory Group (JUSMAG), Manila, in an interview with the author on 19 September 1979. See also *The Washington Post*, 2 June 1983, p. 23.

45. For some of Marcos' 1975 speeches, see the *Philippine Official Gazette*, 24 April 1975, p. 2423; 28 April 1975, pp. 2429–2430; and 2 June 1975, pp. 3195–3205.

46. For a speech given by then Secretary of State Henry Kissinger, see *Department of State Bulletin*, Vol. LXXV, No. 1938, 16 August 1976, pp.

217-226. For the Carter Administration, see the testimony of then Assistant Secretary of State for East Asia and the Pacific Richard C. Holbrooke before the House Committee on International Relations in March 1977, *Department of State Bulletin*, Vol. LXXVI, No. 1971, 4 April 1977, pp. 322-326.

47. *NYT*, 1 July 1981, p. 13. Bush's toast to President Marcos became controversial after the latter's inauguration. Bush stated, "We stand with the Philippines. We love your adherence to democratic principles and democratic processes. We will not leave you in isolation." See the *Washington Post*, 1 July 1981, p. B-13. For then Secretary of State Alexander Haig's comments after Marcos' election victory, see the *Washington Star*, 19 June 1981, p. 12. For a critical comment on the Bush statement, see *NYT*, 10 July 1981, p. 23.

48. *NYT,* 3 April 1982, p. 3.

49. For two books on the Huks, from different perspectives, see Benedict J. Kerkvliet, *The Huk Rebellion*; and Eduardo Lachica, *The Huks: Philippine Agrarian Society in Revolt*.

50. Harold W. Maynard, *A Comparison of Military Elite Role Perceptions in Indonesia and the Philippines,* unpublished Ph.D. dissertation, American University, 1976, pp. 328-329.

51. *Ibid.*, p. 331.

52. Crisol, *op. cit.*, p. 20.

53. *Ibid.*, pp. 78-79.

54. Lachica, *op. cit.*, pp. 245-246. For more on the Philippine contingent to Vietnam and the quid pro quos involved, see U.S. Congress, Senate Committee on Foreign Relations. *U.S. Security Agreements and Commitments Abroad: The Philippines*, Hearing Before the Subcommittee on U.S. Security Agreements and Commitments Abroad, Part I, 91st Cong., 1st Session, 1969, pp. 355-358.

55. Author's interview with John L. Wilkinson, Assistant Desk Officer, Philippines, Agency for International Development (AID), Department of State, Washington, D.C., on 13 November 1979.

56. Author's interview with Brigadier General Oscar Alejandro, Commander, Clark Air Base Command, 20 August 1979.

57. For the background of the NPA, see van der Kroef, *op. cit.*, pp. 34-38. For information concerning CPP programs, see Joel Rocamora, "The United Front in the Philippines," *Southeast Asia Chronicle*, Issue No. 62. May-June 1978, and *FEER,* 21-27 August 1981, pp. 17-24.

58. The Asia Record, April 1982, pp. 1 and 11; *The International Herald Tribune* (hereafter IHT) 15 January 1985, p. 5; and *FEER,* 27 December 1984-3 January 1985, pp. 26-27.

59. *The Asia Record*, Ibid., p. 11.

60. For a history of the MNLF and the prospects for the future, see Peter Gordon Gowing, *Muslim Filipinos: Heritage and Horizon.*

61. Lela Garner Noble, "The Moro National Liberation Front in the Philippines," *Pacific Affairs*, Vol. 49, No. 3, Fall 1976, pp. 405-412.

62. U.S. Congress, Senate Staff Report to the Subcommittee on Foreign Assistance of the Committee on Foreign Relations, entitled "United States-Philippine Base Negotiations," 95th Cong., 1st Session, 7 April 1977, p. 10.

63. This insight was provided by Raul Manglapus, former Foreign Minister and now a leading opposition leader in the U.S. in an interview with the author in Washington, D.C., on 11 July 1979. See also Wurful, *op. cit.*, p. 25.

64. *FEER*, 8-14 May 1981, pp. 36-42. The particular figures on AFP strength are found on p. 42.

65. Robert L. Youngblood, "Church Opposition to Martial Law in the Philippines," *Asian Survey*, Vol. XVIII, No. 5, May 1978, p. 505. The Marcos government also has attempted to control foreign missionaries, particularly American Catholic priests and nuns, in the Philippines. These efforts resulted in the expulsion of missionaries. For one of the most recent examples of this, see the case of Reverend Edward D. Shellitio outlined in the *NYT*, 16 June 1981, p. 12.

66. *FEER*, 13-19 February 1981, pp. 16-17. See Belinda A. Aquino, "The Philippines Under Marcos," *Current History*, Vol. 81, No. 474, April 1982, p. 162.

67. One of the best chronicles of alleged human rights violations is *Report of an Amnesty International Mission to the Republic of the Philippines, 22 November-5 December 1975*. For a recent report to the U.S. Congress, see "Country Reports on Human Right Practices for 1981," 97th Cong., 2d Session, February 1982. The section on the Philippines is found on pp. 661-674. See also *FEER*, 12-18 March 1982, pp. 39-40; and 19-25 March 1982, pp. 21-22. For a government response to charges of human rights violations, see *The Asia Record*, March 1982, p. 9. Because of the important role that the village (barrio) priests play in the lives of Philippine peasantry, military actions against these individuals have alienated part of the population.

68. For this discussion on the military tribunals, I am indebted to the research and conclusions found in Maynard, *op. cit.*, pp. 375-378.

69. Stauffer, *op. cit.*, p. 369.

70. Maynard, *op. cit.*, pp. 374-375.

71. A copy of this World Bank Report is available in *The Asia Record*, December 1980, pp. B 1-4. The particular reference to the Ilocano presence in high positions of authority is on p. B-4. See also Carl H. Lande, "Philippine Prospects After Martial Law," *Foreign Affairs*, Vol. 59, No. 5, Summer 1981, p. 1150. Although President Marcos relies on the advice of his senior AFP commanders on both foreign and defense policy issues, it would be a mistake to assume that Marcos doesn't make most of his decisions based on his own instincts and counsel. An example of this decisionmaking style is evident in the last base negotiations. General Romeo Espino, then AFP Chief of Staff, was the primary Philippine negotiator, but he was on a very short leash and had to consult with Marcos frequently. For more on this, see Berry, *op. cit.*, pp. 349-350.

72. For two good articles on Ver and Ramos, and Ver's selection as AFP Chief of Staff, see *FEER*, 7-13 August 1981, p. 12; and 1-7 January 1982, pp. 8-11.

73. For more on this, see Berry, *op. cit.*, pp. 476-477.

74. *FEER*, 31 July-6 August 1971, pp. 8-9.

75. *FEER*, 2–8 April 1982, pp. 26–27.
76. *FEER*, 29 November, pp. 16–17.
77. Eric A. Nordlinger, *Soldiers in Politics: Military Coups and Governments*, pp. 22–24.
78. For a series of articles on various aspects of the Aquino assassination, see *FEER*, 1 September 1983, pp. 10–15.
79. Ross H. Munro, "Dateline Manila: Moscow's Next Win?," *Foreign Policy* No. 56, Fall 1984, p. 185.
80. *NYT*, 22 August 1983, p. 1.
81. *NYT*, 31 August 1983, p. 4.
82. *NYT*, 24 August 1983, p. 1.
83. *FEER*, 1 November 1984, pp. 14–18.
84. *IHT*, 24 January 1985, pp. 15–17.
85. Munro, op. cit., pp. 183–184.
86. *FEER*, 6 December 1984, pp. 15–17.
87. For an interesting article concerning the Ver-Ramos relationship at the time Ver was appointed AFP Chief of Staff, see *FEER*, 7–13 August 1981, p. 12.
88. *IHT*, 7 November 1984, p. 2.
89. *FEER*, 29 November 1984, pp. 16–17 and *IHT*, 10 December 1984, p. 1.
90. *IHT*, 15 January 1985, p. 5 and *FEER*, 31 January 1985, pp. 30–31.

# 12

# The Vanguard Army: The *Tatmadaw* and Politics in Revolutionary Burma

*Jon A. Wiant*

### Introduction

On March 2, 1962, the Burma *Tatmadaw*[1] staged a bloodless coup, overthrowing the government of U Nu and ending Burma's fitful post-Independence experiment in parliamentary socialism. The coup, led by General Ne Win, *Tatmadaw* Chief of Staff, and some senior officers who called themselves the Revolutionary Council, initially promised little more than the preservation of the Union. There was nothing in the takeover to suggest momentous political, social, or economic change. After all, military takeovers were increasingly familiar facts of political life in countries emerging from the colonial experience. In 1960 Burma went through 18 months of military tutelage during the "Caretaker Period," and power was returned subsequently to civilians. Within a year it became apparent that this was no ordinary coup, no hiatus in parliamentary politics as the Caretaker Period had been. Rather, the coup brought to rule a group of officers who, once they consolidated their power within the Revolutionary Council, were committed to revolution in Burma. Marxist in inspiration, Leninist in application, this revolution had as its goal nothing less than an idealized Burmese state as indebted to Buddhist visions of the "just society" as to the radical socialist ideas which flavored its policy statements. Over twenty years, Ne Win led Burma along the "Burmese Way to Socialism," a tortured course of revolutionary change which plunged the country into near economic ruin but in its later years led to modest growth and a reasonably developed political system. Throughout, the *Tatmadaw* was the central pillar of the Revolution. Although its politicized leadership exchanged battledress for mufti in 1972, the *Tatmadaw* remains the seat of power and decisions involving Burma's future will involve the military centrally in plotting any new course.

## The Vanguard Army—A Legacy of Traditions

The Revolutionary Council, forged by peculiar and powerful forces is revolutionary in essence but wears the outward garb of a military council. This the Revolutionary Council deems undesirable (from *The Constitution of the Burma Socialist Programme Party,* 1962).

Dorothy Guyot described the Burman Independence Army, formed by the Japanese at the beginning of World War II as a "political movement in military garb."[2] Forty years later the characterization is critical to understanding political developments in contemporary Burma. The Burmese Revolution and the "Burmese Way to Socialism," the ideology that has guided the revolution are projects of the *Tatmadaw* and the "powerful and peculiar" circumstances which attended its birth and subsequent development, both as a national army and the vanguard of revolutionary change.

*Origins of the* Tatmadaw[3]

Two political and organizational traditions—one nationalist, the other colonial—came together in the post-World War II formation of the *Tatmadaw*. These antithetical traditions left their heavy impressions on both the structure and purpose of the *Tatmadaw*, whose development since Independence has been a product of the dialectic between the two.

*The Colonial Tradition.* The British colonial Burma Army was composed primarily of Indian soldiers, and troops recruited from Burma's many minorities. Ethnic Burmans were largely excluded from the force and in 1942 scarcely more than 10 percent of the Army was Burman.[4] Nationalists viewed the Burma Army as an expression of British policies which perpetuated disunity between Burmans and the minorities. The retreat of the army facing the Japanese discredited it both as a military force and as an organization fighting to liberate Burma from the Japanese or for Burmese nationalism. That it was to play a role at all in the formation of the modern *Tatmadaw* resulted from the restoration of British colonial rule at war's end. With the return of colonial authority came the return of the Burma Army.

*The Nationalist Tradition.* The "nationalist army" was a manifest expression of Burman, if not Burmese, nationalism. Its initial leadership was recruited by the Japanese from student nationalists at Rangoon University. Thirty nationalists, including Aung San and Ne Win, were spirited out of Rangoon by the Japanese in 1940–41 and given political-military training. Subsequently, as "The Thirty Comrades," they provided the Burman core around which the Japanese organized the Burman Independence Army (BIA). The BIA's role in Japan's invasion of Burma was not militarily significant but as an organization around which Burman nationalism could be mobilized it had no precedent.

After the British retreat, the Japanese demobilized the BIA but retained a 3,000 man Burman force, reorganized as the Burman National Army commanded by Aung San, under the effective control of Japanese "advisors." The Japanese instituted a military training program and opened a military academy at Mingaladon through which eventually passed nearly 800 Burman officers.[5] Perhaps 100–150 of these went to Japan for advanced military training. In 1943 Japan granted independence to Burma, Aung San became Minister of Defense and his junior colleague, Ne Win, was made commander of the "independent" *Bama Tatmadaw* (or Burma Army).

Relations with the Japanese were strained from the beginning of the BIA and the young nationalist officers suffered under Japanese tutelage. As early as 1942 Burmese communists were plotting against the Japanese but not until 1944 did Aung San and Ne Win consider active opposition. Japanese heavyhandedness fed these sentiments and the sham independence of 1943 convinced most nationalists that they had exchanged one colonial relationship for another. They were also concerned about their legitimacy, not only as nationalists but also in the eyes of the British who viewed them as fifth columnists and who by 1944 appeared poised to reconquer Burma. After sub-rosa negotiations with the British, facilitated by the Burmese Communist underground, Aung San led the *Tatmadaw* to the Patriotic Burmese Forces (PBF), the creation of the first Burmese army independent of either the British or the Japanese. As a military arm of the newly formed Anti-Fascist Peoples Freedom League, the PBF under Aung San and Ne Win symbolized a moment when the whole country was united in militant collaboration against a common enemy.

The war ended with the triumph of the PBF and the AFPFL. The Burmese nationalist army emerged cloaked in the mantle of legitimacy as both a political movement and a military force. Its leadership, inclined towards socialism since student days, moved to the left as a result of wartime collaboration with the Burmese Communists, many of whom were officers in the PBF.

*The Hybrid Army.* Between war's end and Burmese independence in January 1948, there were developments which had serious implications both for independent Burma and for the country's nascent armed forces. Three of these concern us.

First, was the reorganization of the Burma Army. Although many colonial authorities argued for the demobilization of the PBF, and some demanded the arrest of its leaders for betraying the British, Aung San fashioned an agreement with Lord Mountbatten providing for the merger of PBF forces with the colonial Burma Army. The hybrid from the union of these distinctly different traditions carried with it seeds of problems which would plague it. The PBF was reduced drastically in size, releasing many who had been mobilized during the PBF uprising. The demobilized veterans, with their own claim to chart Burma's future course, became a major political problem for the newly independent government.

In agreement with Lord Mountbatten, the army was organized on ethnic battalion lines. This resulted not only in perpetuating colonial communal and ethnic divisions but also divided the new army along lines of the two traditions. Battalions of Karens, Kachins, Chins, and Shans, were formed out of the colonial traditions. Battalions of Burma Rifles, however, were composed of veterans of the BIA/BDA/PBF tradition. The decision to organize along these lines compounded the cleavages within the army by reinforcing ethnicity with ideology.

Although the nationalists believed their struggle against the Japanese conferred upon them the right to lead the new army, under the Mountbatten agreement leadership remained with the British. Only about 200 officers from the PBF were absorbed into the new army. Ne Win, former commander of the PBF, was given command of one of the new Burman battalions but General Smith-Dunn, a Karen trained at Sandhurst, was the British choice for chief of the new army.[6]

This hybrid army was reorganized along conventional British lines primarily as an infantry force, with a small air force and navy unit. The PBF officers were trained by British advisors, uniformed in British dress, and armed with British materiel. The Burma Army was indistinguishable from other national armies emerging from the British colonial tradition but, under this surface, the structural problems introduced by the integration of the two traditions were severe.

These problems might have been managed, or at least minimized, had Aung San lived. His 1947 assassination seriously prejudiced the possibilities. He had fathered the nationalist force, negotiated its perpetuation with Mountbatten, and played an instrumental role in fashioning Burma's independence from Great Britain in January 1948. He was credited with the Panglong Agreement in February 1947 which provided the understandings on which the minorities would join with the Burmans in an independent Union, which the British considered a precondition for Independence. Although his role as the father of modern Burma became mythologized, he played a critical part in moderating post-war tensions among the colonials, Burmans, and the minorities. His death removed this unifying force.

## The Political Tradition

The leaders of the nationalist army came out of a political tradition rather than a military one. Ideas about politics and the future of Burma had been shaped during their student years and it was the war, first against the British, then against the Japanese fascists, which gave substance to these ideas. There was little ideological consensus among the nationalists as to the meaning of socialism or the appropriate roads to its realization. The wartime AFPFL, while presenting a common front against the Japanese, represented a breadth of [socialist] concerns running the gamut from "Comintern proletarian internationalism" to national socialism. The defeat of the Japanese destroyed the wartime unity of the AFPFL. Some Communists, including many who had been leaders in the PBF, rejected a negotiated independence from Great Britain and one group went underground in 1947, presaging problems ahead. Even within the core of the AFPFL there were disagreements over socialism and its goal. These unresolved ideological issues which animated the civilian politicians were closely tied to nationalist officers from the war years.[7]

While some officers accepted the idea of a military above politics—many did not.[8] This had two consequences, one immediate, and the other extended. First, when the Burmese Communists who remained in the AFPBL decided shortly after independence to go underground, some army officers followed them. Second, and structurally far more significant, a pattern of civil military relations emphasizing the separateness of the military from politics never really developed. Throughout the 1950s there were senior officers who maintained close links with civilian politicians and their parties and this porous wall between the military and political institutions meant the army was never far from the heart of politics. [Even Ne Win served as Deputy Prime Minister for a period in 1949–50.]

This tradition manifested itself in an ambivalent way. In 1958, when General Ne Win and the *Tatmadaw* formed the parliament-sanctioned "Caretaker Government" it was argued that the *Tatmadaw*'s separateness from politics enabled it to be the guardian of the state. When the *Tatmadaw* seized power in 1962 it appeared that it was the only legitimate inheritor of the socialist revolution begun by Aung San, a far more explicit characterization of its political role.

## National Unity and Corporate Solidarity

The third military tradition symbolizes the *Tatmadaw* as the protector of national unity and model of how unity may be achieved. The disunity of Burma at independence reflected both the historical problem of relations between Burmans and the minorities, and the extent to which questions central to the role of the state or its future were unresolved when Burma gained its freedom from Great Britain in 1948. Within weeks of independence, Burma was into both civil and communal war. The Burmese Communists broke with the AFPBL in March 1948 and went underground, their ranks swelled by demobilized veterans of the wartime nationalist army. Communist officers in the *Tatmadaw* mutinied, straining loyalties within the army. In 1949, the Karens started an insurgency which was joined by Karen units within the *Tatmadaw*. To compound problems for the Rangoon government—which at the height of the uprising controlled scarcely more than Rangoon—serious banditry in Burma's eastern Shan state was exacerbated by two nationalist Chinese divisions pushed out of Yunnan province by the Chinese Revolution.

By 1952–53, the *Tatmadaw* gained the upper hand in the insurgencies, and at least reasserted the primacy of the central government. The mutinies within it had demonstrated the fragility of its unity as an institution. Nevertheless, in the process of rebuilding and reextending the writ of Rangoon, the *Tatmadaw* became a homogenous institution. Defending the nation fashioned a new solidarity within the officers corps and Ne Win's reorganization of the *Tatmadaw*, particularly the replacement of ethnically based battalions with ethnically mixed units, made it a model of unity rooted in diversity.

*Self-Reliance and Nonalignment*

The Burmese government's post-independence adoption of nonalignment had profound implications for the development of the *Tatmadaw*. Although Burma accepted a British military mission and British materiel as part of the Independence agreement, this was terminated in 1953 as inconsistent with nonalignment. Similarly, a US aid package was rejected because it demanded recognition of possible US/Burmese security links. The British agreement provided both training and materiel assistance for the new army. After its termination, Burma was largely left to its own resources to train, develop and equip its military. As a result, the *Tatmadaw* developed as a force primarily suited for counterinsurgency, its principal security task. Cut off from the material abundance of a security assistance agreement with the US (or the Soviets or Chinese, for that matter) it remained precariously short of capital equipment. The army had a few light tanks, armored cars, and artillery pieces; the air force, a handful of fighters and transports; and the Navy a few frigates and river patrol boats. The *Tatmadaw* was, by and large, an infantry force with the battalion as the principal maneuver unit.

Nonalignment reinforced the stewardship of the *Tatmadaw*'s resources. New equipment was purchased from Burma's limited foreign exchange, so the appetites of military officers were held in check. Occasionally, there were accommodations with the principles of nonalignment, such as the $88 million concessional loan package from the US in 1958, but generally it learned self-reliance. This was important for both the state budget and for the image and effectiveness of the *Tatmadaw* as a national institution.

While the *Tatmadaw* developed a Spartan image, the demands of preserving the union against the insurgencies and widespread dacoity meant heavy pressure for defense spending. Defense expenditures annually claimed at least a fifth of the government's budget, most of this money in current expenditures accounts.

The anomaly in this pattern of self-reliance was the $US 88 million arms aid agreement negotiated with the United States in June 1958.[9] This was a credit-sales program under which the Burmese could purchase jet trainers, transport aircraft, and military vehicles. As a credit program it remained nominally consistent with the Burmese nonalignment policy of not accepting foreign military assistance. Official US description of the agreement as "multiyear token pay" suggests that the agreement was outright military assistance. For the Burmese, however, the semantic distinction was important and they felt that the agreement carried with it no security obligations to the US.

The *Tatmadaw* sent officers abroad for military training, primarily to Great Britain and the United States. The number of officers sent for training during the 1950s was probably less than 200–250, mainly junior field grade officers. Some went for command and staff training but many were sent for technical training not available in Burma.[10] Although foreign military training probably had some effect on Burmese military organization and tactics, it did not result in widespread adoption within the *Tatmadaw* of either US or English military doctrine. Unlike many contemporary Third World armies, it did not grow as a replica writ small of a Western military organization. The small unit tradition of the PBF exerted a more powerful influence.

*Expansion of Roles*

Several factors contributed to the *Tatmadaw* developing institutional roles within Burmese society which transcended strictly military functions. War and post-independence counterinsurgency and security operations thrust many officers into administrative activities, particularly at local levels. This was especially true in Burma's highland areas where civil administration was either weak or nonexistent. The *Tatmadaw* not only developed some experience in administration, in limited ways, but also accepted such responsibilities as a legitimate extension of its activities.

The creation of the Defense Service Institute (DSI) in 1950–51 led to a significant *Tatmadaw* penetration of the national economy, although such a role was not envisioned then. The DSI had its genesis in the need for assurance that at least the minimum material requirements of the military were met. It was first responsible for acquiring food and uniforms for the *Tatmadaw* and as a post exchange *cum* commissionary for the troops. The DSI was removed from Defense Ministry control in 1961 and reorganized as the Burma Economic Development Corporation. By then it controlled over 50 firms and extended into domestic trade, housing construction, international shipping and book publishing, while being the *Tatmadaw*'s logistical base. While few in the *Tatdamaw* were directly involved in the operation of the DSI and its subsidiaries, its development established the military's presence in the national economy and, more importantly, convinced some officers that they could be economic managers.[11]

*The Caretaker Tradition*

The *Tatmadaw* first intervened directly in politics when it seized state power from U Nu in September 1958. While this was a coup d'etat, it was orchestrated and publicly presented as a temporary transfer of political power to the military under the emergency provisions of the Burmese constitution. Ostensibly provoked by a serious split within the ruling AFPFL, the coup threatened to erupt into another civil war. According to their public explanations, the Prime Minister and parliament, unable to rule because of the factionalization of the AFPFL, invited the *Tatmadaw* to "caretake" the government while the civilian politicians placed their house in order.[12] The transfer of power was accomplished by an exchange of letters between Prime Minister U Nu and *Tatmadaw* commander General Ne Win, the latter pledging his support for parliamentary democracy and promising an early return of power to civilians when law and order were restored and elections held.[13]

Behind this semifiction of an orderly and temporary transfer of power were the disquieting unresolved political and ideological issues within the *Tatmadaw*. The political attitudes of its leaders were a reflection of the ideological debate within society at large, and the factionalism of the AFPFL had its corollary within the military. Some senior officers had close links to Nu's opponents within the AFPFL and the initial pressure for a coup came from these officers, who wanted to throw the *Tatmadaw*'s power behind that AFPFL faction and fashion a new civil-military coalition. Other officers supported Nu. Some were committed to socialism more radical than that advocated by either faction in the

AFPFL. General Ne Win's intervention temporarily suppressed this debate and his negotiations with Nu for the transfer of power preserved the unity of the *Tatmadaw* for the moment. A sense of common purpose was reaffirmed by the officers in their declaration of "the National Ideology and the Role of the Defense Services," a document executed on the eve of the takeover.[14] It stated that the *Tatmadaw*'s goals were, first, the restoration of law and order; second, the institution of democracy; and third, the establishment of social democracy.

This ideological affirmation and the acceptance of a "caretaker role" had a symbolic importance for the *Tatmadaw* for it both confirmed the legitimacy of their intervention in politics in the national interest and justified it in constitutional terms.

The caretaker government did what it said it would do, and made considerable progress in restoring order. The army was able to extend the government's power into areas long under insurgent control.[15] It also cleaned up the cities, displaced urban squatters and made the trains run on time, at least by Burmese standards.

The *Tatmadaw* also got a taste of managing the economy as its officers took over some state enterprises. The Defense Services Institute underwent great expansion as the military sought to bring some order to domestic trade. While forswearing involvement with the civilian political parties, the *Tatmadaw* built its own countrywide civic association which, though nominally apolitical, attempted to mobilize the population in support of the military government.[16] The army joined with the Buddhist *sangha* (monkhood) in a national anti-Communist campaign premised on the defense of Buddhism. Both the political organization and the "Buddhism-in-Danger" campaign were viewed as attempts by the *Tatmadaw* to undermine U Nu's support within the country, particularly since he had drawn much popular support through his exemplary Buddhist practices.[17] These fed fears that the military would not fulfill Ne Win's promises to hold elections, or at least would not allow Nu to return to power.

Many in the military were reluctant to return power to civilians but Ne Win held to his decision to hold elections. On February 6, 1960 U Nu and his reorganized Union party swept to power in a massive popular vote. The election results were a repudiation of the *Tatmadaw*, or at least its style of rule during the Caretaker period, and dashed the hopes of the faction within its leadership which wanted to form a coalition with Nu's opponents in the AFPFL.

After the election the *Tatmadaw* resumed its national security functions but, having tasted political power, there remained within its leadership sentiments that intervention was not only possible but could be legitimate. Within the year, Ne Win was again forced to come to terms with his senior officers who demanded that the *Tatmadaw* step in to preserve the Union and save it from Nu's policies. In February 1961 Ne Win ordered the immediate transfer to foreign attache positions of two officers who he believed were conspiring a coup, and ten colonels were summarily retired. Although Ne Win remained the faithful democrat, for the moment his own commitment to parliamentary socialism was wavering and the pressures to overthrow Nu were building despite the transfer or dismissal of some of the plotters.

## The *Tatmadaw* and Revolution

On March 2, 1962 Ne Win moved against U Nu in a coup supported by all the regional commanders. Moving quickly and bloodlessly the Revolutionary Council, as the *Tatmadaw* leadership called itself, arrested Nu and his ministers, sent parliament packing, and suspended the state constitution.

### *The Ambiguous Consensus*

The Revolutionary Council used national unity to justify its actions. The military had spent the 12 years since Independence fighting to preserve the Union and the *Tatmadaw* believed that Nu's promotion of Buddhism as a state religion and his plans to federate Burma threatened the very basis of Burmese unity. Many in the *Tatmadaw* also felt that Nu was undermining accomplishments of the Caretaker period and the corporate interests of the *Tatmadaw* as an institution.[18] While not opposed to the promotion of Buddhism, *Tatmadaw* officers felt that Nu's "vainglorious religiosity" transcended the leaders' traditional responsibilities for promoting Buddhism and compounded Rangoon's troublesome relations with the non-Buddhist minorities. Further, the officers were convinced that federation would reintroduce communal tensions with the *Tatmadaw*.

While concerns with national and *Tatmadaw* unity were widespread within the military, there was little other consensus within the Revolutionary Council on either the goals of the Revolution or the means to achieve them. Appeals to unity by the Revolutionary Council following the takeover masked ideological disagreement among the senior coup officers. The ideological ferment was a product of the political traditions of the officers, reinforced by alliances with AFPFL civilian politicians.

All subscribed to the goal of building a socialist state but there was little agreement on defining the meaning of socialism or the extent of its economic and political sweep. On April 30, 1962, the Revolutionary Council published its first ideological tract, *Myanma Hsoushilit Lanzin*

(The Burmese Way to Socialism) and all *Tatmadaw* commanders were required to attest their belief in the ideology.[19] While the vision of a socialist society it presented held the possibility of radical change, it was a platitudinous statement which left open the definition of the means to achieve this socialist vision.

## Consolidation to the Left

Despite the appearance of ideological unity, there was considerable political maneuvering within the Revolutionary Council.[20] Brigadier Aung Gyi, Ne Win's number two, saw the opportunity to fashion a coalition between the *Tatmadaw* and the stable faction of the AFPFL, and in Ne Win's four-month absence from Rangoon for medical treatment in London, Aung Gyi sought to turn the Revolution to this purpose. He was opposed by more radical officers who, in February 1963, forced the purge of Aung Gyi from the Revolutionary Council. This ideological shift within the Council, accompanied by the mobilization into the Revolutionary Government of more than 150 ex-Communists and left-wing socialists, marked the beginning of the Revolution's radical phase. Leftist officers within the Revolutionary Council attempted to forge a new socialist society based on an alliance of workers, peasants, and the *Tatmadaw*—a recreation of the wartime coalition for militant collaboration. Although the Revolutionary Council had announced the formation of a "revolutionary" Burma Socialist Program Party (BSPP) in July 1962, there was little effort given to party building or mobilization activities among workers and peasants until the summer of 1963, after the left wing on the Council had consolidated its power.

The "Burmese Way to Socialism" drew its intellectual inspirations both from traditional Burmese notions of state and authority and from the contemporary writings of Aung San, principally a small tract allegedly written by him in 1941 when the Independence Army was formed. Called "A Blueprint for a Free Burma"[21] it was a plan for national socialism in an organic worker-peasant community led by a single party state.

The ideas, briefly developed in the "Burmese Way," were expanded in a second ideological tract, *The System of Correlation of Man and His Environment,* written by U Chit Hlaing, a Marxist who joined the BSPP in 1962. Deeply indebted to Burmese political culture it borrowed heavily from Marxist economic explanation but implicitly rejected communism. Nevertheless, the "leftist" cast of the ideology and so many ex-Communists in the BSPP fed suspicions that communism was taking over the Revolutionary Council.[22] Puzzlement over the meaning of the "Burmese Way" led the BSPP to publish "The Specific Characteristics of the Burma Socialist Programme Party" (issued in 1964), a document that sorted out the ideological and organizational differences between the BSPP and the Burmese Communist Party on the one side, and parliamentary social democrats on the other. The "Burmese Way" was radical, but the radicalism was within a nationalist context, a kind of "fascism of the left" rather than a form of proletarian internationalism. The socialism of the *Tatmadaw* officer's student days jelled temporarily in a *Tatmadaw*-leftist civilian alliance which lasted for several years before its cost became so severe that neither Burma nor the *Tatmadaw* could bear them.

## Economic and Social Radicalism[23]

The "Burmese Way" called for the elimination of exploitation in society. With this justification the Revolutionary Council nationalized most manufacturing, financial, and trade activities. In rural areas, the Council introduced sweeping land reform measures designed to eliminate absentee land ownership and tenancy. The economic nationalization and land reform programs, executed with little planning and with only the guidance of army officers who had been seconded to administrative functions, wreaked havoc on the Burmese economy, nowhere more pronounced than in domestic trade. Mismanagement of trade in consumer goods and in domestic rice production and sales exacted a heavy price on the Burmese economy and on the legitimacy of the Revolutionary Government Socialist reconstruction policies. These problems were compounded by the decision to shut Burma off from the outside world, to bar foreign investment, and to reduce sharply any economic assistance received from foreign governments. While importation of goods necessary for development was not proscribed, curtailing foreign assistance meant that Burma had to finance imports from its foreign exchange earnings. These had shrunk precipitously as a result of the serious problems in trade and the inability of the government to acquire sufficient rice, the principal export crop, through the nationalized agricultural marketing board.

The Revolutionary Council committed itself to a range of socialist policies which were perhaps more successful in terms of the goals of the "Burmese Way" and the attempts to build a base among peasants and workers. The brunt of the nationalization programs was borne by Burma's small middle class and its larger alien commercial class, the latter primarily Indian and the object of considerable Burman animosity. The displacement of Indians from both the urban and rural economy—perhaps as many as 700,000 were expatriated during this period—affirmed the nationalism of the revolution while undermining the financial base of the middle class, and reduced sharply income disparities with the society. Development proceeded on the assumption that the more developed areas were to bear the burden of development for the least developed areas. Equity concerns were to be as important as raising the gross domestic product.

The Revolutionary Council, seeking to extend social benefits to the workers and peasants, embarked on an ambitious education program to extend primary education countrywide, restructure secondary and university education to stress socialist concerns, and achieve universal adult literacy. The government built rural health centers in each township and forced doctors from the urban areas to the countryside.

## The Tatmadaw Style

Poor performance in the economic sector hampered the government's efforts to achieve the desired social goals. Successful economic development, effective administration, and the mobilization of popular support for revolutionary goals demanded strong economic, bureaucratic, and political institutions. Having seized power in the name of the people, the *Tatmadaw* was reluctant to share power with them. Furthermore, it distrusted the bureaucracy and any organization outside itself. The practical implications of this attitude were threefold.

First, the *Tatmadaw* relied largely on its own personnel for staffing the government administration, organizing the bureaucracy, and managing the nationalized economy. Somewhere between 500 and a thousand officers were seconded to administrative and political positions. Although some of the more senior officers had acquired experience in military administration during the Caretaker Period, most of them had little background in the work their secondments demanded. In addition, the reservoir from which the *Tatmadaw* could draw its manpower was relatively small. Officers, particularly those assigned to central and local government management, had to perform numerous tasks, any one of which could have been full time. Most Revolutionary Council members held at least two ministerial portfolios—Colonel Kyaw Soe at one time held five—and continued down to township level. There a young major or captain was not infrequently chairman of the basic local government unit, chairman of the local party organization, the local peasant organization, and the local workers organization. He would also be chairman of the township land committee and, if economic enterprises had been nationalized in his township, he would be responsible for their supervision. Above the township, the regional military commander supervised all of these activities as well as commanding regular *Tatmadaw* units in the region.

Second, military organization, valued within the Tatmadaw, was used as the model for political and economic organization. This frustrated development and mobilization efforts in a number of ways:

- Standard operating procedure (SOP), the essence of military organization, does not translate well to political organization. Yet it was this organizational culture which the *Tatmadaw* officers brought to their work of political mobilization and economic management. The style may have been suitable for the exhortation of the masses, but it provided little flexibility and initiative for building institutions capable of adapting to novel developments or peculiar circumstances.
- Along with the relative inflexibility of SOP came chain-of-command, a concept equally antithetical to political participation. While centralized authority in Burmese history provided an antecedent for hierarchical organization, the "*Tatmadaw* commandism" frustrated efforts to develop participation and collective leadership called for in the ideology. While appeal was made to the idea of democratic centralism, emphasis continued on the latter at the expense of the former.
- The *Tatmadaw*, despite its professions of being of the people, remained a corporate entity apart from society. Its heavy presence in the BSPP severely limited the appeal of the party to peasants and workers. Its domination of the party meant that membership in the *Tatmadaw* was almost a prerequisite for advancing to senior party ranks.[24]

Finally, the centrality of the *Tatmadaw* in the Revolution, maintained to assure unity of purpose within the government, had the unintended effect of sowing disunity within it. The decision to rely primarily on the *Tatmadaw* for manpower in staffing government and party organizations introduced a structural problem that became increasingly troublesome the longer the military remained in power. As a consequence of administrative and political staffing, two separate *Tatmadaw* organizations developed, one generally military and engaged in endless counterinsurgency campaigns, the other political and bureaucratic and preoccupied with running the country.

As these two *Tatmadaw* developed, more or less independently, there was increasing competition between them that eroded the corporate solidarity of the whole *Tatmadaw*. Life in the two *Tatmadaws* was fundamentally different. The battalion commander assigned in the forward combat areas could expect to spend 300 days a year in the field on patrol or in combat in some of Burma's most inhospitable areas. Frequently living off the land, his life offered little opportunity to improve his lot. His nominal colleague assigned to township administrative duties had a reasonably comfortable life with numerous opportunities to supplement his salary. The growing separation also fueled controversy over which *Tatmadaw* symbolically embodied the revolution. It was within the party that this competition became most pronounced.

*Radicalism to Reformism.* Following the end of World War II Aung San reportedly feared that the *Tatmadaw* would take too large a role for itself and then only look after its own interests. He reportedly admonished his officers, "Countrymen, beware! Let not this fair land turn into a brothel land."[25] Ne Win expressed the sentiment more strongly when he chided *Tatmadaw* officers in 1969 for losing sight of their responsibilities to the people.

In the late 1960s, the Revolutionary Council concluded that the revolution was off track.[26] The economy was sour, the popular support envisioned had not materialized, and within the senior ranks of the *Tatmadaw* there was growing dissatisfaction with the radicalism of the Council's left wing. The spillover of China's Cultural Revolution into Burma in 1967 caused a new Communist insurgency in the northern Shan State, taxing further the *Tatmadaw*'s already extended resources.[27]

Two major policy initiatives had their geneses in the Revolutionary Council's gloomy assessment of the Revolution's twisted course:

First, in 1968 Ne Win convened an Internal Unity Advisory Board of old line nationalists and politicians of the parliamentary period to advise on a new constitutional system.[28] While rejecting ex-Prime Minister U Nu's recommendation for a return to parliamentary democracy, the Revolutionary Council endorsed a proposal to transfer power from the *Tatmadaw* to a new "socialist republic," led by the Burma Socialist Program Party and an elected national assembly. Subsequently a blueprint was drawn to the BSPP from a military dominated cadre organization to a mass party of workers and peasants. With a mass party, the government would reform the administrative structure of the state and open it more to popular participation. The major effort would then be directed towards drafting a new state constitution to replace the one suspended in 1962.

Second, to bridge the gap within the *Tatmadaw* and to broaden the security base, the Revolutionary Council introduced the concepts of "Peoples War" and the "Pyithu *Tatmadaw*" [Peoples Army]. The concept, presented at the 1968 Commanding Officer's Conference[29] had a number of interesting implications:

- The military part of the *Tatmadaw* was committed more directly to socialist construction. Its motto was "Fight While Producing, Produce While Fighting." Army troops provided labor in development projects and in agriculture. While units participated in some of these activities, in the future these were to be an essential feature of the *Pyithu Tatmadaw*. No construction project took place without the participation of the military. The *Tatmadaw* carved out jungle roads side-by-side with the people, built bridges, cleaned up towns and cities, repaired pagodas, dug irrigation canals, and joined workers in producing almost everything made in Burma. In the rice-growing areas, faced with chronic labor shortages at harvest time, the cultivators now found *Tatmadaw* volunteers coming into the fields to harvest the paddy and move it to government purchasing points. Symbolically, the action was portrayed as another manifestation of the "militant collaboration" between peasants and the *Tatmadaw*, but it also had its coercive side. The Tatmadaw presence at harvest time assured the government that its claim on the crop met the government's purchase goals.

- "The Peoples War concept also appealed to the idea of the "nation in arms." The *Tatmadaw* was to be enhanced by the mobilization of the people in defense of their country. Village militia were formed in unsecure or moderately troublesome areas and youth organizations, created under the party's leadership, were given military training.[30]
- In the areas most pressed by the Communist insurgency, the government deputized some marginally bandit groups, frequently remnants from old Chinese nationalist divisions which retreated into the Shan State in the 1950s to fight Communist insurgents. These so-called *Ka-Kwei-Yei* militias became another security irritant for the *Tatmadaw* and in 1971–73 the government outlawed them. By then the *KKY* were well established in the Shan State and a half dozen of them emerged in the mid-1970s as warlord armies deeply involved in narcotics and black-marketeering.[31]

The *Tatmadaw*'s security mission and other demands on the military kept it pressed. These pressures resulted in a heavy *Tatmadaw* burden on the state budget and, during the first ten years of the revolution, defense costs averaged more than 30 percent of total government expenditures.[32] Government autarchism precluded the *Tatmadaw* from subsidizing its expenses through foreign military assistance, and it was still required to purchase its material with precious foreign exchange earnings. This limited most purchases to ammunition and spare parts. There was some relief from this situation. The government negotiated a production licensing relationship with a German arms company to manufacture light infantry weapons in Burma. The Burmese government drew on the US foreign military sales credits remaining from the 10 year agreement signed in 1958 to replenish capital stocks, particularly wheeled vehicles, when the *Tatmadaw* was fully engaged with the Communist insurgents.[33] The *Tatmadaw* eventually overran the Communist base in the Pegu Yomah mountains and by early 1970–71, the BCP were all but eliminated in their historical base areas, but the communists remained strong along the Sino-Burmese border.

## The Institutionalization of Reform[34]

The reform measures discussed in the late 1960s were largely completed or their foundations laid by 1974 when a new state constitution, approved in a popular referendum, was promulgated. Conversion of the BSPP from a cadre party to a mass party was marked when the First Party Congress convened in July 1971. That Congress concentrated on the questions of economic reform and building new political institutions. The party elected its central committee and formed a politburo.

In 1972, the Revolutionary Council took a major step, albeit more symbolic than real, and announced that its members, excluding the Minister of Defense and *Tatmadaw* Vice Chiefs of Staff, were retiring, exchanging their battle dress for mufti. With little public recognition, perhaps another 150–200 field grade *Tatmadaw* officers, mainly those assigned to party or administrative functions, also retired. This had a number of implications:

- It confirmed the development of a group which had its origins in the *Tatmadaw* but had grown somewhat apart from it.
- The retirements contributed to the independence of local party and administrative organizations by divorcing them nominally from the *Tatmadaw*.
- Since most of the retiring officers were field grade the change enhanced promotion possibilities in the *Tatmadaw*.

The retirement of officers confirmed the Revolutionary Council's intentions to build the new socialist state on a base broader than the military; yet, the retirement did not create a civilian government but seems to have compounded tensions within the *Tatmadaw* between ex-soldiers, whose allegiance was to the party, and soldiers whose loyalties remained to the *Tatmadaw*.

While the *Tatmadaw* was retiring its officers, the Revolutionary Council was restructuring the administration preparing for the creation of Peoples Councils as replacements for the military Security and Administrative Committees. The Council also reorganized the country's judicial apparatus to make it consistent with the new socialist society.

From late 1971 through 1973, Burma was engaged in drafting a new constitution. The party was given the primary responsibility for mobilizing popular participation; nevertheless, party and government propaganda portrayed the *Tatmadaw* as centrally involved in the mobilization effort.

The political and administrative reform measures were accompanied by a major reinterpretation of "Burmese Way" economics. Earlier ideological formulations had concluded that because nothing was permanent there could be no fixed economic laws, as in Marxist doctrine; when circumstances change, the ideology must change to meet new problems. That time had arrived, and in 1972 the BSPP issued *Long Term and Short Term Economic Policies of the Burma Socialist Programme Party*.[35] This extraordinary document contained a penetrating critique of the past decade's experience in socialist economic construction and rejected the radical programs of the past. It called for less state presence, identified the need to put state corporations on a commercial basis and recommended better economic relations with foreign countries.

One of the most significant developments was the decision to seek capital from abroad under bilateral and multilateral agreements. Burma initiated agreements with the World Bank, the International Monetary Fund, the Asian Development Bank, and United Nations development agencies. It also greatly expanded its foreign borrowing and entered into new bilateral agreements with Western aid donors. By 1978/79, Rangoon had borrowed, under highly concessional terms, more than a billion dollars to finance economic construction in Burma and underwrite necessary imports.[36] Although Burma remained wary of foreign entanglements which might jeopardize its nonalignment, it removed many of the barriers developed during its autarchic 1960s.

The economic reform brought a major shift in domestic development priorities. During the radical period, economic advisors concentrated on development of the industrial sector for ideological reasons as much as for any compelling economic argument. Development priorities were shifted from industry to agriculture, Burma's principal source of foreign exchange. Changes were made in rice pricing policy and the government developed an infrastructure to promote high yield rice agriculture. Rice production increased sharply from 1977 and with improvements in purchasing by the state, Burma was again able to export significant quantities of rice and improve its foreign exchange holdings.

## Tatmadaw *and Political Mobilization*

The reform measures introduced a new dynamic in the *Tatmadaw*'s political activities, especially apparent in the growth of the BSPP and the new party-led Socialist Republic of the Union of Burma in 1974. The party today bears little resemblance to its embryo, when its small membership was coterminous with the Revolutionary Council.

The party has 113,409 cells organized in 17,940 primary party units, one in every village and several in each urban area.[37] Party headquarters, or organizing committees with full-time staff, exist in each of the 314 townships, and at the state and divisional level. At party headquarters in Rangoon, a permanent staff of over 400 superintends party interests on a daily basis.

The party claims a current membership of 1,500,900 with another 981,859 "friends of the party," a kind of probationary candidacy. Its statistics indicate that 4.2 percent of the peasants and 5.2 percent of the workers are party members. Over 6 percent of the youth joined the *Lanzin Youth* Organization and another 4 million younger children were mobilized in the Party supervised *Shesaung* and *Teza Youth*.

In addition to the youth organization the Party developed two major class organizations: the Peasants Association with over 12 million members and the Workers Association with about 5 million. Each has a central council and subordinate councils down to the township level.

While it made no distinction in political organization for the minorities, the Party runs the Academy for the Development of National Races in Ywathagyi, a training center for political cadre working with the minorities. Since its foundation in 1964 it has graduated 2,400.[38]

Mobilization activities have brought an infusion of new blood into the Party at all levels, even in leadership positions, but this may not mean greater popular participation. While 84 members of the original 200-man Control Committee remain on the 260-man Central Committee formed at the Fourth Party Congress, nearly half of the current Central Committee members are new to leadership. There is a consistent effort to bring new, younger party members into the leadership and similar changes take place at the subordinate state and division levels.

*Myanma Alin*[39] noted that after nineteen years the Party is established as the leading party of the State; that in the Burmese Way to Socialism it developed a program which reflects the true interests and welfare of the people; and that it is guided by an ideology unanimously accepted by party members. In short, *Myanma Alin* observed, "the Party and the State, the Party and the Mass and Class Organizations; the Party and all the people are indivisible and united as one."

The *Myanma Alin* editorial captures the positive side of party development and probably reflects the sentiments of the party visionaries. But other observations about the party must raise some question about this "indivisibility of the Party and the people," and whether, as Party doctrine declares, "the interests of the people are always kept to the forefront."

The Party meant to transform the military government, but the military has been reluctant to give up its ultimate hold on power even as it pledged itself to the value of the party institutions. The subordination of Army to Party and the triumph of Party interest seem true only to the extent to which the party and the Army remain indivisible. Here is the crux of the Party's problem. Despite the alleged broad development of the Party and its allied class and mass organizations, real control of the institutions remains rooted in the military. Statistics on party leadership reinforce the argument. Of the 84 party officials, on the Central Committee since its formation in 1971, 8 are active duty officers. However, 60 are retired officers, most having retired when Ne Win ordered the "demilitarization" of the Party. Only 17 civilians remained on the Central Committee, 10 of them representatives from the minorities.

Service in the military is almost synonymous with party membership. In 1981, the Party listed 143,747 members in the *Tatmadaw,* 85 percent of military personnel and nearly 10 percent of the Party's total membership. Active duty and retired officers make up most of the leadership at the divisional and state level, and it is only at the township level and in the primary party units where civilians appear to predominate. So rather than bridging the gap between the government and the people, the party may simply reinforce it by propagandizing the role of the people's participation while effectively excluding those outside the military from any substantive roles.

Access to power has been afforded by both the military and political wing of the *Tatmadaw.* This seems to have been a function of which wing stood in better favor with Ne Win and the old men of the revolution, and of its particular phase. In practice, the distinction between the two groups may be more analytic than real. The temptation to impose some order on Burmese politics, however, is compelling. The army and party remain largely impenetrable to the outside observer and judgments on politics within the institutions are highly speculative.

Disagreements between the two loose factions, however, seem less over the ideology of Burmese socialism than over which group plays the leading role in its implementation. The political faction faults the army for its reliance on "commandism" and the "conceit of its leadership role"; the Army criticizes the political types for their radicalism and inability to provide the leadership the revolution demands. Ne Win moderated these squabbles within the family and moved quickly to settle them if they threatened the revolution. Once Ne Win passes from the scene it is unknown who will be the moderator within the military.

## The Future of the *Tatmadaw* and the Revolution

As Burma's revolution enters its third decade, two questions preoccupy the country: Who will succeed Ne Win? What role(s) will the *Tatmadaw* play in post-Ne Win Burma? The questions are inextricably linked because during the Revolution's long course, Ne Win and the *Tatmadaw* have been linked. The *Tatmadaw* was the *ultima ratio* of his rule, the reservoir for his government's manpower, and the central pillar of the revolution. He trusted the *Tatmadaw* and, although on occasion he felt that trust might be misplaced, in times of difficulty he turned to it.

For the military's part, it too has been bound to Ne Win. He is responsible for the development of the *Tatmadaw* and the privileged position and legitimacy it enjoys. No military or party leader commands the same respect, the same *awza,* Burmese charismatic power, as Ne Win. He has been the unifying force, in the *Tatmadaw* and in the country. His successor cannot draw on the same historical traditions which underwrote his power. The bonds of corporate solidarity fashioned in forty years of shared experience are not easily remade. It is a mark of this solidarity that over a third of members of the Party's 15-man Central Executive Committee are former officers of the 4th Burma Rifles, the battalion Ne Win commanded in 1947 when the *Tatmadaw* was born from the union of the colonial and nationalist armies.

*Transition and Succession*

Ne Win's 20 year period of rule is waning. While he remains "Number 1", the transfer of power from him, and the other old men who made the revolution, to the next generation is already underway. Competition to succeed him has become a distinctive feature of *Tatmadaw*-BSPP politics and political maneuvering within the *Tatmadaw.*

During the Fourth Party Congress in August 1981, Ne Win made the surprise announcement that he would retire from the presidency in November after the election of a new *Pyithu Hluttaw* (National Assembly). He said he would retain, for the present, chairmanship of the party. On November 9, 1981 U San Yu, Ne Win's number two since 1970 and the General Secretary of the BSPP, was elected President. Although San Yu had long been considered Ne Win's heir apparent, his election to the Presidency diminished sharply any possibilities he might have to succeed Ne Win. According to the party, he resigned all his party positions to devote full time to the presidency. Ne Win held both the presidency and the party chairmanship; San Yu, stripped of his party base, is left with the largely ceremonial presidency, a sinecure for his retirement from active politics.

U Thaung Gyi, the BSPP Joint General Secretary since 1972 and a member of the 1962 coup group, was believed to have an edge on succeeding Ne Win. It was rumored that he would take over San Yu's vacated party positions. His untimely death on the eve of San Yu's election removed a figure who might have maintained unity between the party factions and the military.

Army Vice Chief of Staff, General Aye Ko, was named General Secretary of the Party and Secretary General of the State Council. Aye Ko spent the revolution as a military man with the military part of the *Tatmadaw*, and he has little support within the party. His appointment seems an attempt to postpone a decision on an ultimate successor for Ne Win.

Two figures initially dominated the discussion of succession in the early 1960s: General Kyaw Htin, *Tatmadaw* Chief of Staff, Minister of Defense, and Party Central Executive Committee Member; and Brigadier General Tin Oo, then Military Advisor to Ne Win, Joint General Secretary of the Party and former chief of the security services.

Kyaw Htin's strength was in the military, and his lineage the Fourth Burma Rifles. Tin Oo, junior in age and rank, had no tie to the great *Tatmadaw* but made his career in intelligence and security. He cultivated strength within the party and probably controlled the regional party structure. He had placed ex-military intelligence people in key national party positions and in the directorships of key state economic corporations. While outside the *Tatmadaw* chain of command, he had made alliances with some of the regional *Tatmadaw* commanders.

As of 1983, informed observers leaned slightly more towards Tin Oo both because of his relationship with Ne Win and the extent of his network within the party and administrative organizations. But in ways typical of the unfolding of Burmese politics, in May 1983 Tin Oo and his close confederate, Minister of Home Affairs ex-Colonel Bo Ni, were suddenly sacked, stripped of all responsibilities, tried, and sentenced to jail. Publicly, the charges involved minor abuses of their positions; privately, rumors were rife of wholesale corruption—including involvement in narcotics trafficking. Furthermore, some alleged that behind the scenes *Tatmadaw* officers had plotted to block Tin Oo's attempts to succeed Ne Win. Over the subsequent year, Tin Oo's proteges, real or imagined, were rooted out of their positions. The Military Intelligence Service, the foundation of Tin Oo's power, was all but dismantled.

Kyaw Htin and Aye Ko emerged from the struggle with their reputations enhanced but neither has sought to fill Tin Oo's shoes. At the same time, President San Yu appears to have rehabilitated his political career and has acted more and more in Ne Win's stead. All are in positions to replace Ne Win; none, however, can lay the same claims to greatness as Ne Win. Perhaps the elimination of the Tin Oo faction has moderated the tensions within the *Tatmadaw* and succession can take place without further rendering of *Tatmadaw* unity. Nevertheless, several questions about the future of the *Tatmadaw* remain unresolved and negotiation of these will place heavy burdens on a *Tatmadaw* leadership that is far from settled.

It is fruitless to push speculation too far in considering a successor to Ne Win, for there is no clear successor.[40] Succession presents the very real possibility of tearing at the *Tatmadaw*'s unity. It remains uncertain whether the institutions developed by the revolution are strong enough to contain the competition for rule once Ne Win passes from the scene.

## *The* Tatmadaw *Role*

The *Tatmadaw* may, as it did in 1962, go outside the system to reshape Burma's political authority. Other issues also loom large in determining the *Tatmadaw*'s role in the years ahead.

First, is the issue of military professionalism. The *Tatmadaw* has probably spent more time fighting in the field than any other Third World military force. The endless counterinsurgency has developed a lean and competent force structure but one that is undercapitalized and frequently undersupplied. The war will continue, although the apparent reduction in Chinese support for the Burmese Communists suggests it will be less severe than in the past, when *Tatmadaw* casualties were heavy. Karen insurgency and the endless campaigns in the eastern Shan State against warlord narcotics groups and insurgents will continue to place heavy demands on the *Tatmadaw*.

The reform movement of the 1970s opened mixed possibilities for the *Tatmadaw*. As a result of Burma's improved economic circumstances the *Tatmadaw*, particularly the Air Force, was able to purchase new aircraft. Since 1975 it acquired aircraft for both utility and air support roles and it received or has on order another 20 aircraft. Too, under terms of a 1974 narcotics cooperation agreement with the United States, Burma acquired 25 Bell 204 and 205 helicopters and five F-27 and F-227 transport aircraft. While generally committed to narcotics control activities, these aircraft have substantially enhanced the *Tatmadaw*'s air capability against insurgents.

After years without new material, the new acquisitions fed appetites for general modernization in the *Tatmadaw*. Unfulfilled, they could provoke restiveness but the government seeks to satisfy them. Then the pressures on the budget could become severe when general economic improvement raised hope for significant growth in nonsecurity sectors.

The alternative, seeking external military assistance, would mean a reorientation of the nonalignment policies which have guided the military. A modest military training agreement with the United States in 1980 seems a tentative step towards reorientation but such training, involving only a handful of officers, remains far removed from a military assistance agreement.

The second issue for the *Tatmadaw* is the extent to which it will remain directly engaged in running the country. The military controls the party apparatus at the top and any successor to Ne Win must rely on the party apparatus to run the country. But below the center, non-*Tatmadaw* people seem to be taking over the party. Most township party units are now controlled by civilians. In lower Burma, rice cultivation programs brought new wealth to the cultivators and gave them a vested interest in party activities. Pressure for their participation at higher levels seems to be building. Some time soon, the *Tatmadaw*, which made the revolution in the name of the people, and has been the revolution's vanguard, will have to share its power with the people or reverse the course of the revolution.

## Notes

1. The term *Tatmadaw* refers to the entire Burma Defense Services of which the Burma Army is the largest. In 1980 the International Institute for Strategic Studies in London estimated the *Tatmadaw* strength at 173,500. The Burma Army had 159,000 men organized in 4 light infantry divisions, 110 independent infantry battalions, 2 armored battalions, and 3 artillery battalions. The Navy had 7,000 men including 800 marines; Air Force strength was 7500 men organized in 2 air support squadrons and a transport squadron. IISS estimated that there were 38,000 in the paramilitary People's Police Force and 35,000 in the People's Militia. (IISS, *The Military Balance 1980-81*, London, 1980), pp. 66–67.

2. The characterization is from Dorothy Guyot, "The Burma Independence Army: A Political Movement in Military Garb," in Josef Silverstein (ed.) *Southeast Asia in World War II* (New Haven: Yale University Southeast Asia Program Monograph Series, 1967), p. 51.

3. This section draws on Guyot, *op. cit.*: Dhammika U Ba Than's *The Roots of the Revolution* (Rangoon: Defense Historical Research Institute, 1962) and from discussions with Professor Robert Taylor, School of Oriental and African Studies, based on his manuscript, "The Military in the Politics of Burma."

4. The term *Burman* refers to the dominant ethnic group in Burma which accounts for about 75 percent of the population. The remaining 25 percent is composed of a multitude of minority groups of which the Karen, Kachin, Shan, Kayah, and Chin are the largest groups. Burma also has a small Indian minority and an overseas Chinese community. The term *Burmese* is used for citizens of Burma or as an adjective for the country's institutions.

5. Data is from Robert Taylor's translation of Min Nyo, *Gyapan Hkit Sit Tekkatho* (The Japanese Era Military Academy) (Rangoon: Phan, 1969), p. 15 cited in *op. cit.*
6. For a revealing personal account of the trauma of military unification see General Smith Dunn, *Memoirs of the Four-Foot Colonel* (Ithaca, Cornell University Southeast Asia Program Data Papers, 1980).
7. Taylor, *op. cit.*
8. See Maung Maung, *Burma and General Ne Win* (Bombay: Asia Publishing House, 1969), and Maung Maung, *To a Soldier Son* (Rangoon: Sarpay Beikman Press, 1974), pp. 146-151.
9. Henry Kamm discussed the 1958 Agreement at length in *The New York Times*, July 25, 1970.
10. This training apparently ended in the 1960s although some aircraft maintenance and pilot training probably continued. *Forward*, 3:6 (November 1, 1964), p. 4.
11. Data is from "BEDC to be Nationalized," in *Forward*, 2.4 (September 22, 1963), p. 4.
12. At the conclusion of the Caretaker Period, the Ministry of Information published *Is Trust Vindicated?* (Rangoon, 1960). This document is the most complete compilation of activities during the first period of military rule.
13. See Appendix 3, *Ibid.*, pp. 543-544.
14. The "Ideology" is reprinted in Appendix 1, *Ibid.*, pp. 531-541.
15. *Ibid.*, pp. 19-58 provides a detailed breakdown of counterinsurgency activities during the Caretaker Period.
16. Called the *Kyant Khaing Yei Ahi phwei* (National Solidarity Association), it was ostensibly an apolitical movement. By 1960 it reportedly had 400,000 members organized down to village level.
17. The *Dhammantaraya* (Buddhism in Danger) Campaign is examined at length in E. Michael Mendelson, *Sangha and State in Burma* (John P. Ferguson, editor) (Ithaca: Cornell University Press, 1975) pp. 343-358 *passim* and in Donald E. Smith, *Religion and Politics in Burma* (Princeton: Princeton University Press, 1965), pp. 133-134, 241-242.
18. A number of U Nu's policies were viewed as a threat to the corporate interests of the *Tatmadaw*. Nu had blocked the creation of a National Defense University independent of the university system; until 1964 even the Defense Services Academy at Maymyo was under the state education system rather than the Ministry of Defense. Nu opposed the formation of a Central Intelligence Organization and the *Tatmadaw*'s proposed absorption of the paramilitary Union Military Police. He had also removed the Defense Services Institute from military control.
19. "*Myanma Hsoushilit Lanzin*" (The Burmese Way to Socialism) in *Lu Hnint Pat Wun Kyin Tou A'Nya Thaba T'Ya* (Rangoon: Burma Socialist Programme Party Headquarters, 1973). (Hereafter referred to as "The Burmese Way"). Ne Win presented it to the 10th annual *Tatmadaw* Commanding Officer's Conference. At the end of the conference the commanders signed a copy of the declaration pledging their full support. Ony then was the document publicly released.

20. This political maneuvering is examined in the author's *Lanzin: Ideology and Organization in Revolutionary Burma*, a Ph.D. dissertation Cornell University, 1983. See especially Chapter 2.

21. "The Blueprint" is reprinted in Josef Silverstein (ed.) *The Political Legacy of Aung San* (Ithaca: Cornell University, Southeast Asia Program Data Paper, 1972), pp. 13–15.

22. The charges were aired in the Burmese press in February 1963 and were repeated in such Western publications as *Life*, *Time* and *Newsweek*.

23. The period of economic radicalism is largely responsible for the images of perversity which characterized Burma in the Western press for much of the 1960s and early 1970s. David Steinberg's *Burma's Road Toward Development: Growth and Ideology Under Military Rule* (Boulder, Colorado: Westview Press, 1981) has a thoughtful discussion of economic radicalism and "the Economics of Political Inversion"; he, however, dates the end of the period in 1972. See pp. 27–28.

24. At the end of 1965, 16 of the 20 "Full Members" of the party were from the Tatmadaw and over a third of the candidate members (35,638 out of 99,638) were from the *Tatmadaw*. See *The Political Report of the Central Organizing Committee to the First Party Seminar* (Rangoon: BSPP Headquarters, 1966), pp. 130, 154.

25. Quoted in Ba Moe, "Our Independence," *The Guardian* (January 1968), p. 38.

26. The party seminars offered an annual opportunity to review the progress (or lack of it) in the past year in political, economic, and social activities. Seminar records offer unusually candid documentary on the travails of the Revolutionary Council and the fledgling BSPP.

27. An excellent study of the development and implications of the new Communist insurgency can be found in the recently sanitized and declassified *Intelligence Report—Peking and the Burmese Communist: The Perils and Profits of Insurgency* (Washington: Central Intelligence Agency Directorate of Intelligence, July 1971, released May 1980).

28. See the *Union of Burma's National Unity Advisory Board's Report to the Revolutionary Council of the Union of Burma* (Rangoon: Government Printing, June 1969).

29. See "Defense Services" *Forward*, 7:5 (October 15, 1968), p. 2 and "General Ne Win's Address to the 1968 Commanding Officer's Conference," *Ibid.*, pp. 4–11. Commodore Thaung Tin, Vice Chief of Staff (Navy) summarized the people's role in the concept of People's War at the 11th Passing Out at the Defense Service Academy at Maymyo, April 23, 1969:

> To protect our country we must not depend only on the standing army, but, we must bring together the people and bring into being "People's War." In the "People's War" all the people of the country must participate [. . .] Though an army may not have much weapons, if it has the active support of the people it can win the war against superior forces [. . .] In fighting a war, or building a country, our real strength may be found in our homeland. (Quoted in *Forward*, 7:19, May 15, 1969), pp. 6–7.

30. During this period, the press carried numerous articles on military training for youth. Moe Oo's "Training Air Minded Youth for the Future," *Forward* 8:4 (October 1, 1969) presented the government's objectives in the military programs.

31. Saw Shwe Boh recommended that "A determination to defend the nation and the people in the frontline, if necessary, should be constantly cultivated from early childhood. Such a will ought to be built up in the young even during study and playtime." (Quoted in "Youth in People's Militia Movement," *Forward*, 10"15 (March 15, 1972), p. 7.

32. Steinberg, *op. cit.*, pp. 165-166.

33. *The New York Times* (July 25, 1970).

34. See Chapter 5 in the author's *Lanzin: Ideology and Organization in Revolutionary Burma,* op. cit., and Steinberg, *op. cit.,* pp. 43-62.

35. Cited in Steinberg, *op. cit.*, pp. 44-47.

36. Ibid., p. 60.

37. Data on current party organization are from the *Political Report to the Fourth Party Congress* reprinted in *The Working People's Daily* (August 4, 1981) and from *Pati Yei-ya Saung* cited in *Botataung* (March 8, 1981).

38. Saw Shwe Boh, "Hand in Hand Forever" *Shaytho* (February 1980).

39. July 4, 1981.

40. For additional analysis of the prospects for transition, see Rodney Tasker, "Heir Not Apparent," *Far Eastern Economic Review* (29 November 1984) and Hugh MacDougall and Jon A. Wiant, "Burma in 1984: Political Stasis or Political Renewal," *Asian Survey,* XXV:2, (February 1985), pp. 242-243.

# PART THREE
# South Asia

# 13

# Civil-Military Relations in Post-Colonial India

*Glynn L. Wood*

Civil-military relations in post-colonial India have been a model for the Third World in that military capacity has been greatly increased without a major threat to civilian rule. Yet this achievement has not come easily. The 35 years of post-colonial history reveal considerable tension between civilian and military authority; and policy debates during the period reveal a variety of conflicting views on the appropriate role for the military in Indian life.

Initially, the Indian military was not a revolutionary army that had overthrown the colonial oppressor, but a military establishment created to sustain British rule. This establishment was passed to the independent nations of India and Pakistan as part of their colonial legacy.[1] Radical nationalists could argue that a more appropriate leadership for independent India might be the survivors of Subhas Chander Bose's Indian National Army, who fought the British in Southeast Asia as allies of the Japanese in World War II.[2] There were also naval mutineers who rebelled against the British during the last days of the Raj.[3] And, of course, Mahatma Gandhi and his followers argued even more radically that nonviolence precluded any need for a military establishment.[4]

However, the chaos of partition and the immediate confrontation with Pakistan over Kashmir confirmed the position of the colonial military organization. While Nehru took up the cause of the Indian National Army, and even made his final appearance as a lawyer defending three members of that Army who had been singled out for trial as traitors, no member of the Indian National Army ever rejoined the military.[5]

While the Nehru government accepted the military status quo and used the Indian Army during the early years of independence in relatively minor engagements in Kashmir, Hyderabad, and Goa, the military did not figure pominently in Nehru's foreign policy planning until the Indo-Chinese War of 1962. There was concern about Pakistan, and the Indian military participated in various United Nations peacekeeping missions around the world, but military concerns were secondary as Nehru launched his ambitious five year plans and put forward his anticolonial policy of nonalignment. Prior to 1962, military advice was seldom sought by the Prime Minister and in 1957 Nehru placed the Defense Ministry under the control of his closest friend, V. K. Krishna Menon.[6] Menon quickly antagonized top military leaders, with his violation of the seniority principle. Menon was at once the symbol of civilian control of the military during the early Nehru years and a symbol of political intrusion into the military's professional business.

The Indo-Chinese war was clearly the watershed for the Indian military. It effectively ended Nehru's nonalignment policy, escalated the Indian defense budget, and was the political end for Menon. Faced with severe criticism from his own party, Nehru removed Menon and set out on a program of military modernization with help from both the United States and the Soviet Union.[7] The major change in strategic views was the creation of an army prepared to fight on two fronts.[8] Historically, the British had looked to the Northwest for trouble, and Nehru followed their example until the Chinese crossed frontiers in the northeast.

More important was the changed evaluation of the importance of defense policy. From the humiliation of 1962 to the stalemate with Pakistan in 1965, to the Bangladesh campaign of 1971, the Indian military has been near center stage in Indian policy debates. No longer are there arguments about the usefulness of defense. Debates assume a strong defense, and move on to arguments over optimal means. And at least since Bangladesh, Indian foreign policy has aimed at maintaining regional hegemony and minimizing superpower influence in the region.[9] Some analysts argue that India's long-term goal is superpower status, and the evidence for that case is rather impressive.[10]

Viewed by the Indian military, events subsequent to 1962 have effected a major transition in status for them, and it is a success story that has generated a new set of arguments about the appropriate role of the Indian military.

## Strategic Rationale And Contemporary Disposition

While the Indian military inherited the pivotal position of the British Indian Army between Europe and the Far East, and a tradition of policing everything "East of Suez," the anticolonial rhetoric of Nehru and the Congress Party left little room for a global or regional policy of realpolitik. Neither did the limited means of the Indian military, which had lost a large proportion of its senior officer cadre and its European logistical base with independence and partition, foster such perspectives.[11]

While experts disagree on Nehru's long-term goals, his early years were clearly directed at economic rather than military development. That changed in 1962 and, while the Indian military has not recaptured the strategic position held by its colonial antecedent, it established clearcut dominance in South Asia and maintains a policy designed to expand that role over time.[12]

The Indian Army is the fourth largest in the world, behind only China and the Soviet Union.[13] It has some 860,000 men on active duty, including 115 infantry divisions and 10 mountain divisions, created in response to the Chinese incursion.[14] The army is deployed to deal with a two-front war, assuming hostile action from both Pakistan and China. Before 1971 this posture was somewhat complicated by east Pakistan, which played a minor role in defense planning until shortly before the civil war broke out in 1971.

In addition to its two major adversaries, the Indian Army has also been regularly engaged in counterinsurgency against Naga and Mizo rebels in the Northeast border lands above Assam. As many as 36,000 troops have been tied down in that campaign.[15]

The Indian Army has been eclectic in purchasing major equipment. Its inventory of equipment includes items purchased from the Soviet Union, the United States, Britain, France and Czechoslovakia.[16] The Soviet Union has been the major donor of military aid, although Britain and the United States have contributed.

With 100,000 men and some 1600 aircraft, the Indian Air Force is also a major element in Indian Defense.[17] The Air Force is deployed to support the army on both fronts, and has light bombers and fighter-bombers with the range to reach the major cities of Pakistan. The Air Force record was not strong during the early engagements with Pakistan, and the recent decision to upgrade its capacity with the MIG-29 was obviously made to gain an edge on the Pakistanis, who have purchased the F-16 from the United States.

The Army and Air Force appear to have an integrated plan for India's defense. Barring a military disaster, this integration should hold. However, it seems likely that the status quo can be maintained only by increasing the Air Force share of the defense budget, because prices for aircraft and related hardware are likely to inflate more rapidly than other military costs.

The Indian Navy has received the least attention in defense policy discussions and the least budgetary support. Currently, the Navy has some 46,000 men and approximately 100 ships and 150 aircraft.[18] Partly this is the result of the inheritance by the Indian Navy, for while the British Empire depended heavily on the British Indian Army, the Royal Navy needed no help in protecting the sea lanes of empire. The

TABLE 1
Indian Military Expenditures

| Year | Constant $ | % Increase |
|---|---|---|
| 1950 | 858,000,000 | - |
| 1955 | 996,000,000 | 16 |
| 1960 | 1,112,000,000 | 12 |
| 1965 | 2,595,000,000 | 133 |
| 1970 | 2,538,000,000 | -2 |
| 1975 | 2,980,000,000 | 15 |
| 1979 | 3,523,000,000 | 18[a] |

Note:
[a] The final increase is for a four-year period.
Source: This table is adapted from the SIPRI Yearbook, 1980 (London: Taylor & Francis Ltd., 1980), p. 21.

subordinate position was initially accepted by the Indian Navy, except for minor grumblings, until the Bangladesh War.[19] The action of the carrier USS Enterprise in the Bay of Bengal during that engagement, and subsequent superpower activity in the Indian Ocean, convinced at least some of India's defense planners that the traditional posture of the Navy is inadequate, given India's strategic position.

These arguments had an impact and capital investment in the Navy has accelerated. However, it is difficult in a tight economy to argue for full funding for a two-fleet Navy (one for the Bay of Bengal and another for the Indian Ocean) without cutting heavily into more established programs.[20] While the two-Navy argument is no longer considered radical, development in that direction is gradual at best.

When defense policy is reviewed over the past 35 years, two developments are conspicuous. First, radical changes were made in the size of defense expenditures (see Table 1). Indian reaction to the war with China moved the entire defense establishment to a higher level of activity during the 1960s, although growth during the 1970s operated within a rather narrow range. Second, India's strategic objectives and its interservice ratio for defense expenditures have been stable. The Indian Army's share of the defense budget varied from 70 to 75 percent during the 1970s.[21] In that sense, the Indian military has been an extremely stable institution, in the face of considerable external turbulence.

## Domestic Political System

In spite of a backward economy and a difficult international environment, the Indian political system has demonstrated extraordinary stability. India has survived the trauma of partition; displacement of millions of refugees; four wars; persistent insurgencies; and various forms of civil violence while functioning as a parliamentary democracy based on adult suffrage. This has been done with a society in which the annual per capita income is $140 and the literacy rate roughly 25 percent.

Much of India's political success can be attributed to Nehru's leadership of the Congress Party and the evolution of a second generation of Congress leaders (including Mrs. Gandhi) who are legatees to the Party tradition.[22] Congress and its opposition, many of whom are ex-Congress, have been committed to operating the system created by the Indian constitution. Except for the 19 months of Mrs. Gandhi's emergency, the parliamentary game has been played by all major political actors and when a government fails at the state or national level, rules of succession have been carefully followed.

The exception to this pattern was Mrs. Gandhi's decision to declare emergency rule in 1975.[23] At the time, Mrs. Gandhi had a majority in parliament large enough to clothe her actions in constitutionality, and when her bid for reelection failed in 1977, she quietly turned the government over to the Janata leadership. Returned to power in 1980, Mrs. Gandhi continued to have difficulties with state governments the courts and even her daughter-in-law until her assassination, but she attempted no major constitutional changes that would threaten civil liberties or parliamentary practice.[24] She was not pressed so hard as she had been in 1975 when the courts found her guilty of illegal campaign practices and when a major agitation directed against her by Jayaprakash Narayan succeeded in defeating her party in the State of Gujerat.[25] Mrs. Gandhi demonstrated that the parliamentary system could be derailed by a Prime Minister with a two-thirds majority in parliament, a majority she regained in 1980, and which her son, Rajiv, also attained in 1984. Therefore, any analysis of the political system must list that possibility against the greater likelihood that parliamentary democracy will be sustained.

## Civil-Military Relations

If the recent history of the Indian military has been a political success story, the political situation is not simply a matter of budgetary arm wrestling. Rather, proposals have been made to radically change the nature of the military establishment. The military has done well in maintaining a relatively stable pattern of growth and the more radical proposals have been eschewed.[26] Two functions in particular have been minimized despite pressure to the contrary: the handling of civil unrest and involvement in programs for economic development, although problems with Sikhs in 1984 temporarily reversed this policy.

The first is perhaps the most important. India's political leaders resisted the temptation to bring in troops to put down civil disturbances, and even during Mrs. Gandhi's period of authoritarian rule, civil disturbances were dealt with by police and by militias organized outside the Defense Ministry.[27] The only exceptions were those insurgencies in border areas like Nagaland, where troops have been required for prolonged periods.[28] Whether Rajiv Gandhi can return to this policy remained uncertain early in his tenure in office.[29]

The second function, economic development, has been suggested as appropriate for the military in peace time.[30] Advocates argue that the million trained men in uniform represent a tremendous waste of resources, unless otherwise employed. Proposals that this manpower be used in constructive economic activity are made regularly, so far with no success. The defense ministry is adamant that anything beyond emergency relief efforts would take away valuable training time and lower morale.

The treatment of both of these functions demonstrates the division of authority between civilians and the military in India. Politicians and bureaucrats appreciate the utility of a strong military in maintaining India's position in foreign affairs. Consequently, the military is treated rather well in perquisites, budgeting, and status. Since Menon, Defense Ministers generally have been responsible politicians with a reputation for getting the job done in a relatively nonpartisan manner, and they see little reason to antagonize a military establishment that has performed well since 1962.

### Intramilitary Political Dynamics

Within the military there is relatively little discord, perhaps because the dominance of the Army was so ingrained in the British colonial system and because the Army's status has been reinforced by India's strategic situation.[31] In any event, there has been consistency in budgetary allocations, with the Army, Air Force, and Navy holding close to the budgetary ratio of 70:20:10 over time.[32] There is an intrinsic tension in funding an Army which relies heavily upon manpower, cheap in India; and an Air Force and Navy that use more hardware, expensive in the world market. This theme runs through defense policy discussions, but there is little evidence of serious conflict between branches, and the budgets are consistent from year to year.[33]

## Economic Development

While no direct role has been assigned the military in India's elaborate plans for economic development, it is clear that an establishment consuming more than three percent of the GNP is a major player in the Indian economy.[34] Conventionally, armies have been seen as pyramids in economic development—enormous investments for which there is no return. Recently, this conventional wisdom has been challenged by theorists who argue that underdeveloped economies benefit from the manpower training that goes on in a modern army.[35] Attaturk's Turkey is often cited, wherein village lads learned skills ranging from literacy to mechanics before they returned to civilian life with attitudes and skills reshaped by a modern organization.

A second set of arguments has been put forward by Irving Louis Horowitz, whose investigation of national statistics led him to the conclusion that military regimes are more likely to invest in infrastructure than in consumerism.[36] Improvements in transportation, communication, power, and other basic systems are essential to the military and hence military governments are likely to give infrastructure investment a higher priority than would a more democratic regime. Certainly, military considerations after the Indian rebellion of 1857 led to crucial investments in rail and communications systems that accelerated economic growth in colonial India.[37]

Finally, there are the arguments that involve the transfer of technology which have been especially well received in India. Simply put, learning how to build ships, airplanes, and electronics for military uses also develops the skills required to handle high technology in more general industrial development.

There can be little doubt that the Indian military improved the manpower base, contributed to the communication and transportation infrastructure, and accelerated the transfer of technology to the subcontinent. However, there is little systematic data on how important these contributions have been to economic development.

## Decisionmaking Processes

The Indian military continues under the budgetary control of India's parliamentary system, in which the Prime Minister presides over a cabinet that, in principle, makes collective decisions.[38] That principle was not always observed, especially by Mrs. Gandhi's dictatorial rule under the emergency and by a Janata regime that often failed to achieve consensus. Most of the time, however, the Defense Minister has been a major figure in the cabinet, who had little difficulty protecting his turf, due to a lack of expertise in parliament (and elsewhere) to cope with this difficult subject matter and because much of defense policy is protected by security measures.[39] Except for a few journals of opinion and a rather prolific cadre of retired military officers, there are few authorities to contest issues of national defense. Other than an occasional scandal and the occasional war, the military managed its own affairs internally and raised few issues to the policy level. When that happens, the top military leadership could expect to have its case heard sympathetically and supported by the defense minister.

## Foreign Policy Objectives

Except for the brief interlude following the Indo-Chinese War, Indian foreign policy has been strikingly consistent in seeing Pakistan and China as its major potential enemies and in strongly resisting superpower influence in the region.[40] Other issues have come and gone but these are the core, although at times they seem to conflict. For example, India accepted military assistance from the United States during the Indo-Chinese War yet signed a friendship treaty with the Soviets in 1972 in response to the American "tilt toward Pakistan."[41] Mrs. Gandhi was also willing to establish a partnership with the Shah of Iran to police the area, despite the Shah's ties to the West.[42] All these run counter to basic nonalignment policy. But these steps were taken under duress, and more typical is India's opposition to the American use of Diego Garcia and the Russian occupation of Afghanistan.[43]

## Defense Policy Objectives

India's defense policy objectives are derived directly from its foreign policy objectives. The size of the Indian Army is related to the perception that India faces two potential fronts. Ten mountain divisions were raised after the Indo-Chinese War to maintain security along the PRC borders.[44] Until that expansion, former Army Chief of Staff, General K. S. Thimayya, wrote pessimistically, "We could never hope to match China in the foreseeable future. It must be left to the politicians and diplomats to ensure our security. . . ."[45]

Since General Thimayya wrote his article in 1962, India uses its diplomats much more carefully in dealing with China: and the army is certainly better prepared on the Eastern Frontier. India's decision to develop its own nuclear capability was made with the Chinese in mind, although it can be argued that the nuclear detonation in 1974 is hardly a major deterrent to Chinese aggression.[46]

If China is a formidable enemy for India, Pakistan is less so, particularly since the creation of Bangladesh, which reduced Pakistan to roughly one seventh the size of India.

The issue revolves around technology and leads to what India sees as unwarranted intrusions in the region by the West, particularly the U.S. While India would agree that the 1971 war eliminated any pretense that there was a balance of power in the region, the recent U.S. decision to upgrade and modernize the Pakistan military is seen as an attempt to reestablish the balance that led to the military stalemates of 1948 and 1965. India fears that Pakistan's acquisition of state-of-the-art weaponry on easy terms would leave India vulnerable while it pursues a more deliberate long-term defense policy.

In weapons acquisition and defense production India and Pakistan have followed contrasting policies for 30 years. Pakistan, until recently a close ally of the West, has not developed production capacity for military equipment beyond small arms.[47] On the other hand, India's military and economic development plans have been integrated, while experimenting with a variety of modes of weapons acquisition.[48] While some equipment has been purchased outright, the Indians preferred to arrange for joint production in country or to handle their own production domestically. The latter modes are both costly and slow, but are also relatively invulnerable to political interference from other countries. The arms embargo imposed during the 1965 Indo-Pakistani War demonstrated the wisdom in India's mixed strategy for production, because the embargo was much more damaging to Pakistan than to India.[49]

India's strategy does not work v.ell when Pakistan is able to obtain financing to purchase high performance weapons off the shelf, as in their recent F-16 deal with the United States. India then must balance the long-run goals of autonomy and self-sufficiency against the short-term threat of the F-16, and decide whether to make an expensive purchase off the shelf to counter the threat.

The other major goal, of reducing superpower influence in the region, is more difficult to tie directly to defense policies. Historically, the Indian Army was the major enforcer of colonial discipline in Asia and Africa.[50] Consequently, the Indians (and the Pakistanis) inherited Kipling's great game vis-a-vis the Russians. While the Indian Air Force was also a minor part of that game, the Navy was not. The Royal rather than the Indian Navy, controlled the sea-lanes before 1947, and thus it is not surprising that little was done prior to 1971 to build up Indian sea power. The American (and Soviet) presence in the area has been unwelcome to India, although the reaction to that presence has been largely rhetorical. However, the entry of the Enterprise battle group in 1972 set off a flurry of capital expenditures for the Navy, and more sophisticated arguments in favor of naval expansion are now being developed.[51]

### Cultural/Ethnic Patterns

The Indian Army is a model for multiethnic military forces whose history is ably documented in Stephen Cohen's book on the Indian Army.[52] The British assumed that certain groups were "martial races" and recruited accordingly. The myth of martial races became a self-fulfilling prophesy and the army system survived independence nearly intact. This communal system was not extended to the Navy or Air Force, where technical qualifications play a more substantial role in recruiting and personnel policies.[53]

### Conclusion

It would be hard to fault the Indian Military for its performance since 1947. Except for the disastrous war with China, the Indian military fought well when called on, and stayed in the cantonments while attending to their training schedules when they were not. The war with China was set off by political miscalculation, against the best advice of senior military officials.[54] The rebound of the military after that disaster has been both purposeful and well executed.

Indian troops have been used in a number of United Nations peacekeeping missions and have served well. Their most recent success in Bangladesh made them domestic heroes in both India and Bangladesh. Critics would point out that the Army is too large, given the threats, but it is not clear whether a reduction in force would effect major benefits for the Indian economy.[55]

It is not clear whether the present 70:20:10 budgetary ratio between branches of the military is optimal. While India has long land frontiers to protect, it is uncertain whether the ratio should be maintained in the face of inflated hardware prices for the Navy and Air Force. This is especially true if the responsibilities of a major regional power are taken seriously. Decisions to move into operational nuclear weapons or to create a two-ocean fleet that is credible (in both the Indian Ocean and the Bay of Bengal) would drastically change that budgetary ratio.

The external players most concerned with India's defense policy are Pakistan, China, the Soviet Union, and the United States. The major objective for Pakistan is to develop a deterrent (nuclear or otherwise) which would make an attack by India unprofitable. The present agreement with the United States to upgrade Pakistani military equipment is seen as a step in that direction, as has been Pakistan's decision to develop nuclear capability.[56] These steps will set off an arms race; one in which India will feel pressured to buy more weapons off the shelf as an emergency measure rather than continue their preferred policy of developing indigenous production at a slower pace through collaborative ventures.

China seems much less concerned with India's defense program. Neither land invasion of Tibet nor air or sea attacks by India seem credible, given present technology. India has cooled its rhetoric concerning the disputed border areas and seems less likely to provoke the Chinese than during the Nehru period. But it should be noted that no concessions on the borders have been made by either government.[57]

The Soviet Union still stands by its friendship treaty with India. Although India is clearly unhappy with the Soviet adventure in Afghanistan, there are many ties of trade and military assistance that place the Indian government on the Soviet side of most international issues. It is a useful ally for the Soviets, as they take positions opposing the Chinese and the United States, even though it seems that the Soviets receive less than they should like from the alliance.

United States interest in Indian defense policy is a by-product of the strategic calculation that Pakistan must be preserved and strengthened as a buffer between the Soviets and the oil fields of the Persian Gulf.[58] Our assistance to Pakistan is inevitably seen as hostile by Indian policy makers and thus raises the ante in the South Asian arms race. Of secondary importance is our use of Diego Garcia as a staging area to protect our interests in the Gulf.[59] This is interpreted as an extension of the western colonial order (and the U.S. did acquire use of the base from the British). Diego Garcia is likely to be used as a justification for a larger Indian Navy—a change which would definitely upset the budgetary ratio within the Indian Defense Ministry.

While the external problems listed could lead to drastic changes in the role of the Indian military, it is more likely that the most important challenges to the status quo will be domestic. The ability of any Indian regime to sustain civil order has been at risk in recent years. The most extreme political response was Mrs. Gandhi's declaration of an emergency for 19 months in 1975–76, which allowed her to rule India in authoritarian fashion.[60] Her decision was carried out without military involvement, although the emotion generated by this controversial move reverberated through the military. And Mrs. Gandhi's order to attack the radical Sikhs in the Golden Temple also had extremely adverse effects on military morale and eventually led to her assassination. The use of military force for a quick solution of domestic difficulties is tempting for political leaders with their backs to the wall. To the credit of Indian leaders, they have seldom taken that short cut in dealing with an increasingly unruly polity. Whether future political leaders can maintain that precedent is the major question concerning the role of the military in India.

## Notes

1. Stephen P. Cohen, *The Indian Army: Its Contribution to the Development of a Nation* (Berkeley: University of California Press, 1971).
2. Hugh Toye, *Subash Chandra Bose* (Bombay: Jaico, 1962).
3. Percival Spear, *The Oxford History of Modern India 1740-1947* (Oxford: Clarendon Press, 1965), p. 386.
4. J. Bandyopadhyaya, "Nehru and Non-Alignment," in B. R. Nanda, *Indian Foreign Policy* (Honolulu, U.S.: University of Hawaii Press, 1976), pp. 175-78.
5. Cohen, *op. cit.*, pp. 157-64.
6. Raju G. C. Thomas, "The Armed Services and the Indian Defense Budget," *Asian Survey*, March 1980, pp. 280-81.
7. Walter Andersen, "Domestic Influence on India's Foreign Policy" (mimeo: paper presented at the Western Association of Asian Studies Meeting, Santa Cruz, California, June 25, 1982) and Neville Maxwell, *India's China War* (New York: Pantheon, 1970), pp. 361-63.
8. Raju G. C. Thomas, "The Armed Services and the Indian Defense Budget," *op. cit.*, pp. 294-97.
9. Stephen P. Cohen and Richard L. Park, *India: Emergent Power?* (New York: Crane, Russak & Company, Inc., 1978), pp. 4-8.
10. Ibid., pp. 9-24, 43-53.
11. Manohar Malgonkar, *Distant Drum* (New York: John Day, 1966).
12. Cohen and Park, op. cit., pp. 25-40.
13. Trevor N. Dupuy, Grace P. Hayes and John C. Andrews, *The Almanac of World Military* Power (San Rafael, Calif.: Presidio Press, 1980), pp. 100, 174, 329 and 345.
14. Raju G. C. Thomas, "Security Relationships in Southern Asia," *Asian Survey*, July 1981, pp. 705-706.
15. Dupuy, Hayes, Andrews, op. cit., p. 175.
16. Ibid., p. 176.
17. Ibid., pp. 176-77, and Raju G. C. Thomas, "Aircraft for the Indian Air Force: The Context and Implications of the Jaguar Decision," *Orbis*, Spring 1980.
18. Dupuy, Hayes and Andrews *op. cit.*, p. 176.
19. Raju G. C. Thomas, "The Indian Navy in the Seventies," *Pacific Affairs*, Winter 1975-76, pp. 501-504.
20. Raju G. C. Thomas, "The Armed Services and the Indian Defense Budget," *Asian Survey*, March 1980, pp. 288-89.
21. Ibid., p. 284.

22. Stanley A Kochanek, *The Congress Party of India* (Princeton: Princeton University Press, 1968).
23. Myron Weiner, "The 1977 Parliamentary Elections in India," *Asian Survey*, July 1977.
24. "The Maneka Factor," *India Today*, New Delhi, April 30, 1982.
25. Marcus F. Franda, "India's Double Emergency Democracy: Part I, Transformations," *American University Field Services Report, Asia*, Vol. XIX, No. 17.
26. Raju G. C. Thomas, "The Armed Services and the Indian Defense Budget," *op. cit.*, pp. 289-94.
27. Stephen P. Cohen, "The Military," in Henry Hart, ed., *Indira Gandhi's India* (Boulder: Westview Press, 1976), pp. 207-32.
28. Dupuy, Hayes and Andrews, *op. cit.*, p. 175.
29. Jyotirindra Das Gupta, "India in 1980: Strong Center, Weak Authority," *Asian Survey*, February 1981, pp. 150-52.
30. Raju G. C. Thomas, "The Armed Services and the Indian Defense Budget," *op. cit.*, pp. 293-294.
31. Ibid., pp. 285-88.
32. *Ibid.*, pp. 283-84.
33. *Ibid.*, pp. 294-97.
34. Emile Benoit, *Defense and Economic Growth in Developing Countries* (Lexington, Mass.: Lexington Books, D. C. Heath & Co., 1973).
35. Lucien W. Pye, "Armies in the Process of Political Modernization," in John J. Johnson, ed., The Role of the Military in *Under-Developed Countries* (Princeton: Princeton University Press, 1962).
36. Irving Louis Horowitz, *Three Worlds of Development* (New York: Oxford University Press, 1966), pp. 254-71.
37. Percival Spear, *India* (Ann Arbor: The University of Michigan Press, 1961), pp. 282-84.
38. Raju G. C. Thomas, "The Armed Services and the Indian Defense Budget," op. cit., pp. 280-82.
39. Raju G. C. Thomas, "India," in Edward A Kolodziej and Robert E. Harkavy, *Security Policies of Developing Countries* (Lexington, Mass.: Lexington Books, 1982), pp. 132-36 and Cohen, *The Indian Army, op. cit.*, pp. 169-77.
40. Cohen and Park, *India: Emergent Power?, op. cit.*, pp. 25-42.
41. Marcus F. Franda, "India and the Soviets, 1975," *American University Field Service Reports*, Asia, Vol. XIX, No. 17.
42. Marcus F. Franda, "India and the Gulf," *American University Field Service Report, Asia*, 1978, No. 17, and Dieter Braun, "New Patterns of India's Relations with Indian Ocean Littoral States," in Larry W. Bowman and Ian Clark, eds., *The Indian Ocean in Global Politics* (Boulder: Westview Press, 1981), pp. 29-31.
43. Thomas W. Robinson, "The Soviet Union and Asia in 1980," *Asian Survey*, January 1982, pp. 25-27.
44. Raju G. C. Thomas, "Security Relationships in Southern Asia," *Asian Survey*, July 1981.

45. K. Subrahmanyam, "Nehru and the India-China Conflict of 1962," in B. R. Nanda, ed., *Indian Foreign Policy: The Nehru Years, op. cit.,* pp. 117–18.
46. Cohen and Park, *op. cit.,* pp. 43–53.
47. Stephen P. Cohen, "Pakistan," in Kolodziej and Harkavy, *op. cit.,* pp. 105–106 and Lawrence Ziring, *Pakistan: The Enigma of Political Development* (Boulder: Westview Press, 1980), pp. 226–35.
48. Cohen and Park, *op. cit.,* pp. 10–20.
49. Marcus F. Franda, "America and Pakistan: The View from India," *American University Field Service Report,* Vol. XIX, No. 2, p. 4.
50. Raju G. C. Thomas, "The Indian Navy in the Seventies," *Pacific Affairs,* Winter 1975–76, pp. 504–13.
51. *Ibid.,* pp. 500–504.
52. Stephen P. Cohen, *The Indian Army, op. cit.,* pp. 45–49.
53. Ibid., pp. 32–56.
54. Neville Maxwell, *India's China War, op. cit.,* pp. 65–256.
55. Emile Benoit, *Defense and Economic Growth in Developing Countries, op. cit.*
56. Stephen P. Cohen, "Pakistan," in Kolodziej and Harkavy, *op. cit.,* pp. 97–102.
57. Walter Andersen, "Domestic Influence on India's Foreign Policy," *op. cit.,* p. 10 and Thomas W. Robinson, "The Soviet Union and Asia," *Asian Survey,* January 1982, p. 26.
58. Stephen P. Cohen and Marvin G. Weinbaum, "Pakistan in 1981: Staying On," *Asian Survey,* February 1982, pp. 143–45, and Fred Greene, "The U.S. and Asia," *Asian Survey,* January 1982, pp. 8–10.
59. Joel Larus, "India's Nonalignment and Superpower Naval Rivalry," in Bowman and Clark, *op. cit.,* pp. 43–56.
60. Marcus F. Franda, *India in an Emergency: Introduction and Ten Essays* (Hanover, N.H.: AUFA Field Staff Collections, 1979), Part I.

# 14

# The Role of the Military in Contemporary Pakistan

*Stephen Philip Cohen*

### Introduction

There are armies which guard their nation's borders, there are armies which are concerned with protecting their own position in society, and there are armies which defend a cause or an idea. The Pakistan Army does all three.[1] From the day Pakistan was created it has helped to establish internal order and protect Pakistan's permeable and often ill-defined borders; it used its power and special position within Pakistan to ensure that it received adequate weapons, resources, and manpower. Finally, it always regarded itself as the special expression of the idea of Pakistan, and a few officers have argued for an activist role in reforming or correcting the society when it fell below the standard of excellence set by the military.

This chapter is divided into two major sections. The first examines the role of the Pakistan military within Pakistani society—particularly within the political system. The second examines the strategic aspect of the Pakistan military (and by military, we mean the army, which remains politically as well as strategically dominant).

### The Army and Politics: Organizational and Doctrinal Compulsions

The Pakistan Army is a hostage to its origins. It inherited much of the British view of civil-military relations, transmitted to each succeeding Pakistani generation at the Pakistan Military Academy, the Staff College, and in informal discussions in the messes. The British (in India) liked to envision the "proper" relationship between military and civilian as that between two "separate spheres" of military and civilian influence, while acknowledging that ultimate responsibility lay in the hands of duly appointed (or elected) civilians.[2] British India was seized and originally ruled by the sword, and was governed for many years by military proconsuls. But by the end of the Raj the role of the military had been limited and elaborate administrative and fiscal mechanisms were devised to control them. The military's sphere of influence was recruitment, training, discipline, and strategic planning; the actual use of the military, from the most minor "aid to the civil" operation up to the strategic deployment of the Indian Army in the Persian Gulf, South East Asia, and elsewhere was a political—and hence a civilian—decision.

A few of Pakistan's earliest political leaders were aware of the army's proconsul tradition, and made some effort to ensure that it would not reemerge in an independent Pakistan. On Pakistan's day of independence, August 14, 1947, Mohammad Ali Jinnah (who had just become Governor-General) scolded one young Pakistani officer. According to Asghar Khan (later an Air Marshal in the Pakistan Air Force) this officer complained that:

Instead of giving us the opportunity to serve our country in positions where our natural talents and native genius could be used to the greatest advantage, important posts are being entrusted, as had been done in the past, to foreigners. British officers have been appointed to head the three fighting services, and a number of other foreigners are in key senior appointments. This was not our understanding of how Pakistan would be run.[3]

Jinnah was deliberate in his answer. He warned the officer not to forget that the armed forces were the "servants of the people" and that "you do not make national policy, it is we, the civilians, who decide the issues and it is your duty to carry out those tasks with which you are entrusted." He stressed "moderation" in thought and action, not extremism. Jinnah repeated his warning in almost the same language ten months later during his only visit to the Staff College. He expressed alarm at the casual attitude of "one or two very high-ranking officers." After praising the defense forces as "the most vital of all Pakistani services," he warned the assembled students and instructors (largely British) that some of them were not aware of the implications of their oath to Pakistan, and promptly read it to them. Further, he added:

> I should like you to study the constitution which is in force in Pakistan at present and understand its true constitutional and legal implications when you say that you will be faithful to the constitutions of the dominion. I want you to remember, and if you have time enough, you should study the Government of India Act (of 1935), as adopted for use in Pakistan which is our present constitution, that the executive authority flows from the head of the Government of Pakistan, who is Governor-General, and, therefore, and command or orders that may come to you cannot come without the sanction of the executive head.

The constitution of Pakistan was to be suspended and altered by some of the very officers in his audience, including Yahya Khan, then the only Pakistani on the staff. They moved from the military "sphere" to the civilian in 1958, although Ayub had been asked on several earlier occasions to intervene.

The importance of legitimate and effective political leadership as a prerequisite for civilian control cannot be overemphasized. Relative power is not the decisive factor. Rather, the Pakistan military are concerned about incompetent civilian leadership hurting the quality and sometimes the very existence of the military as an organization and thus threatening what they believe to be the only real defense against India, and one of the main forces holding the state together. Continued intervention in politics has strengthened this feeling: if even one politician weakens the military (or establishes a paramilitary force such as the Federal Security force to balance or counter it), are they not letting down the state as a whole? Politicians come and go but the military is permanent; damaging it damages the survival of the state by weakening the army's capacity to step in and "set things right." Setting things right, of course, is the preferred model of intervention, and the generals would like to see their involvement in politics as a glorified "aid to the civil" operation.

They are less concerned about the initial intervention (which by definition is necessary when things have gotten completely out of hand) than hanging on to power too long. One of Ayub's close associates presented this argument, still widely shared:

> Some people would say that the army, to save itself, wanted to come in. I would say it's not the question of the army—nobody is going to destroy the army—these people were not going to destroy their own army. It was a question of saving the country, and sorting out the situation. Now, it is different *after* that. When General Ayub went on for 8 or 10 years, *that* is different—but when he took over, the intention was to clear the mess. It must be remembered that as far as the army is concerned, it is a professional army and an ordinary officer doesn't care about politics. People have relations in politics, but it doesn't make any difference— when I commanded the PMA, we used to stress these things from the beginning, "the army is completely aloof from politics," lots of stress on this.

There is a second, much neglected motive for intervention in Pakistan which derives from the separate spheres of responsibility. In addition to the practical question of civilian incompetence hurting soldier and state, there is a moral dimension to this issue. Professional soldiers take human life and destroy property in the name of the state; they are taught that the moral responsibility for killing lies with the government, and that decisions concerning life and death are morally neutral if politically legitimate. If the legitimacy deteriorates, the officer must reassess the morality of his actions. A government which lacks legitimacy can no longer be the arbiter of morality and the military and police rapidly find themselves in an untenable position. The Pakistani generals who have seized power were concerned about the legality of their initial action, and the legality of subsequent acts that they and their subordinates committed under martial law. This was an important issue for Ayub Khan, who ensured that legislation from the Assembly had it met after the 1970 elections, and he was found to be an usurper by the Pakistan Supreme Court in 1975.[4] President Zia and his advisors are no less concerned about the legitimacy of their actions, and have hesitated to abrogate the 1977 constitution of Pakistan. Even when Zia or another general decides that he wants to give up power, he will not do so until there is clear-cut settlement of the moral and legal responsibility for the violence of the past—including the hanging of Bhutto. The military are highly sensitive to their legal and moral status. Their training and indoctrination have emphasized the legitimacy of civilian, not military rule, and the generals therefore lack a clear-cut theory of military intervention which would permit them to undertake sweeping changes in Pakistani society; Islam now provides some guidance but extreme Islamic practices divide the officer corps as well as the broader population, and few officers would be inclined to pursue a revolutionary course of action.

In sum, the Pakistan Army is constrained by its past. This heritage tells them that intervention may be necessary but that it must be limited in scope and time; yet the diversity of Pakistani society and the slow emergence of responsible politicians make it difficult for them to relinquish power. And, once in power, the officer corps is tempted to tinker with the political system, and again one can trace this to the British. One subtradition of British India was a paternalist but activist Punjab school of administration. Pakistani officers sound like their British predecessors when they discuss the civil works they have constructed, the hospitals and medical services they provide for ex-servicemen and others, and the businesses and factories they run.[5] They are eager to prove that they are not a drain on the resources of the state and actively contribute to its modernization. Yet they are reluctant to assume responsibility for these larger tasks: they repeat that they will do so only within their proper sphere—welfare for ex-servicemen—and tasks (such as the construction of the Karakoram Highway) which civilian authorities cannot handle.

The army's involvement in waterworks and roads would be of only passing interest if it were not guided by essentially the same limited reformist approach when dealing with Pakistan's politicians. My 1964 analysis of this problem is essentially valid today:

> The difficulty in defining and establishing a suitable civil-military relationship is connected with the military's penchant for reshaping and reestablishing Pakistani politics. If civilian and military have their own spheres, there is as little justification for the military intervening in politics as for the politicians in military matters . . . The justification for breaking this rule in Pakistan is that the politicians first broke the "rules of the game" by meddling foolishly in military matters. Significantly, the official position is that the military is no longer in politics: the army is above politics and parties. The justification for [Ayub's] coup is that the army restored the balance between the military and the civil spheres by rebuilding the political structure (as one would rebuild an army after defeat or partition). But, of course, political problems are not the same as military problems.[6]

The present military leadership is aware that the efforts of Ayub, Yahya, and even Bhutto to reform Pakistani politics and create a stable balance between military and political spheres have failed, and are therefore discredited—hence their interest in religion and "Islamization" as a new strategy. After 1978 they pursued the rebuilding of Pakistan along "Islamic" lines with little enthusiasm; significant is the generals' loss of confidence in both their ability to find a working solution to balancing military and civilian interests, and in carrying it out.

*Civilian Control and Decisionmaking*

The recent situation in Pakistan is doubly serious because there was widespread belief within the upper ranks that a stable, orderly civil-military relationship is vital to the security of Pakistan. After he became Prime Minister, Bhutto received full military cooperation in a careful study of civil-military relations and decisionmaking, done largely by retired and acting officers. They concluded that the 1971 war with India revealed serious flaws in the military's performance and organization.[7] Bhutto was interested in discrediting his military predecessors and downgrading the reputation of serving officers but his reform of the decision-making structure was strongly supported by the military, and partially implemented under Zia. Bhutto's *White Paper* on Defense Organization was part of a concerted effort to ensure civilian control over Pakistan's defense process. The 1973 Constitution provided harsh punishment for challenging civilian rule, the *White Paper* provided the intellectual justification for it.[8]

According to one general who helped write the *White Paper*, there was agreement between Bhutto and the military on the principle of civilian control. The military saw this "civilian" as restricted to the political leadership:

> —that is, the chief executive along with the cabinet. But it does not mean that is the rule of the civilian servants in any way, the CSP (Civil Service of Pakistan), in other words. The CSP should not boss around the service chiefs as such. We distinguish between civilian supremacy and the dominance of the civil service officers over the service chiefs.

This is a critical and revealing point. It shows the limits that the Pakistan military were willing to go in submitting to "civilian" control even when they were demoralized and discredited.

The structure that emerged after several years of analysis and planning is similar to that found in many democratic countries.[9] It is in place now, but because there is no effective *civilian* leadership has not really been tested.

The system is now filled with anomalies since the Chief of Army Staff (and therefore subordinate to the Defense Minister and the Prime Minister) is also President. Serving soldiers are not technically members of the Cabinet (responsible for determining the size, role, and shape of the armed forces) yet a military man presides over it and appoints all of its members (who should be elected civilian officials, but are not, given the absence of national elections before February 1985). Below the DCC is the Defense Council. The military are members of this Council, which advises the DCC on military matters; it includes the External Affairs Minister, Finance Minister, and other cabinet members with a special interest in defense policy, and receives recommendations from a Joint Chiefs of Staff Committee, patterned after both the American and British systems. The JCSC gave Pakistan—for the first time—an integrated interservice mechanism for the higher direction of war, and it does function now, although for some time it lacked a chairman. Under the JCSC are a Director-General, Joint Staff, and then a complex bureaucracy of officers drawn from all three services (but dominated by the army). At the lower levels the system seems to be functioning but it is impossible for an outsider to judge its effectiveness.

For the first time in Pakistan an administrative structure exists above and beyond the army's own chain of command. In military terms, this is vital for several reasons. First, in 1965 and 1971, the three services of Pakistan went to different wars. There was no overall strategic plan and limited tactical cooperation. Pakistan's new security policymaking process will ensure that there will be at least a framework for decisionmaking. Second, it enables the military and the state to allocate resources better for weapons acquisition and the development of Pakistan's own defense production infrastructure. For the first time, there is central direction of the growing defense production system and a way to process and evaluate individual service requests for weapons. However, having a service chief as head of state distorts the entire process. Since officers can be retired or transferred by a decision of their superiors (and at the highest level that means Zia himself), they cannot perform their military duties without calculating political and personal consequences. Unless they seek early retirement, or unless Zia encourages dissent, debate, and discussion between himself and his immediate subordinates, it is likely that the decisionmaking process will become a series of yes-men, smiling their way to higher rank. This may keep peace within the military (a condition for Zia's continuation in power), but it hardly resembles the tough-minded and systematic decisionmaking process envisioned in the *White Paper*.

## The Zia System

In 1985 Mohammed Zia-ul-Haq completed his sixth year as President of Pakistan, his seventh year as Chief Martial Law Administrator, and his ninth year as Chief of the Army Staff.[10] He thus holds positions of authority within the military, the martial law system that governs Pakistan, and the government itself.

This is an astonishing accomplishment for someone once regarded outside the army as a temporary "front man" for the generals who deposed Zulfiqar Ali Bhutto. Except for a few officers who had linked their careers to his, Zia was not well known within the army, having been a junior lieutenant general when Bhutto reached down and promoted him to COAS in 1976. His military career was marked by competent service, and his demeanor inspires neither awe nor fear.[11]

Zia's rule has not been based upon wide popular support, and may be ended at very short notice, but it is important to note how he has functioned since 1977 and the steps he has taken to build a political structure to replace the one he destroyed. Zia's mode of operation and the structure is called "the Zia system."

Following the arrest of Bhutto in 1977, Zia received a congratulatory message from one of Pakistan's most respected generals who drew the analogy between 1977 and his own involvement in Ayub's coup of 1958; "the time came when we felt the army had to be protected, they were forming groups in the Army"; the Pakistan Army was and is highly professional, he explained in 1980.

This is an extreme view, even for those who support Zia. More representative of "the British generation," now almost all retired from public life, was the judgment of another of Ayub's associates. He was unsure as to whether the military could involve itself in national politics and still retain its professional outlook.

This cautious advice was widely regarded as prudent in 1977-78, even as late as 1980. It was not followed, according to Zia's supporters, because civilian politicians failed to come forward and accept the responsibility of governing Pakistan; the politicians, of course, argue that it would have been political suicide to associate with an unpopular military government. Finally, it was not clear until 1981 that Zia could transfer power: some generals regarded him as a lightweight and there were indications that several younger, pro-Bhutto officers had organized a conspiracy to assassinate Zia. Some of these have been convicted in 1985 for treason.

Zia and his close advisors moved in April, 1980 to retire, transfer, or reduce the responsibilities of a dozen senior officers, some of whom were suspected of disloyalty. This created opportunities for younger men whose promotion had been blocked. Zia and his associates also concluded that their own futures were better served by retaining power than by a quick devolution to the civilians, or by Zia's resignation and retirement. Contributing to this decision were concern for their own careers, reluctance of responsible politicians to come forward, fear of a Pakistan Peoples' Party revival, and the belief that a change in the senior leadership would erode the integrity of a demoralized army. They concluded that Pakistan could not be effectively governed without a drastic change in the 1973 Constitution, and moved to create an entirely new, "Islamic" system of political life.

The Pakistan Army officer corps is increasingly drawn from middle class, orthodox and religious families. Zia represents this class of officers. Zia and his advisors have launched Pakistan on a new political course, combining their religion and their military subtradition of order, discipline, and building organizational structures from below. There are strong similarities between their efforts to create Islamic advisory councils at the provincial and national level (the majlis-i-Shura) and Ayub Khan's earlier efforts at building "basic democracies." They differ from Ayub in their use of Islam and their systematic attempts to control, intimidate, or uproot all independent centers of political power (including the press, the judiciary, and Pakistan's weakened intellectual class).[12]

While practical considerations account for this military effort to "Islamicize" Pakistan (few officers are willing to challenge Zia and his colleagues as long as stability is maintained and the army does not have to deal extensively with civilian opposition), these steps do have a theoretical justification.

Men who hold such views of their role in society are unlikely to yield power quickly, or regard domestic opposition as anything but degeneracy. They share widely the view that the West is in moral decline, and criticism from that direction is evidence that they have chosen the correct—albeit difficult path. Not all in power in Pakistan would subscribe to these views, and there is evidence that Zia himself is not the fanatic he has been made out to be. He has freely added and dropped advisors, yielded to public opposition on several occasions (most notably after the protest of Shia's over the imposition of *Zakat*, a religious tax), and shown flexibility and creativity in strategic decisions. He may yet come to resemble a latter-day Ayub.

It appears that Zia and his advisors do have a vision beyond that of holding on to power, distracting the citizens of Pakistan with Islamic doctrine and a revolving political prisoner population that may number several thousand. However, their alternatives are not attractive. The military would be unwilling to yield power to any group which sought to raise the issue of Bhutto's death; given the wording of the Pakistan Constitution this might be fatal for Zia himself. Nor does the army have a clear vision of a radically different way of organizing Pakistani life.

They have been professional soldiers, and while most generals have learned to "play politics" within the military and in dealing with politicians and bureaucrats, they are notoriously lacking in speculative or conceptual skills, and the ability to articulate their ideas so that a mass public finds them intelligible. There is great concern that this generation of generals (and, one might add, their civilian counterparts in the bureaucracy and the entire intellectual class of Pakistan) are barren of imaginative plans for the future. The optimism of Ayub was replaced by the opportunism of Yahya and the hyperbole of Bhutto; they all failed and perhaps it will be Zia's contribution to lower expectations and merely survive until a trustworthy civilian leadership or a more ambitious group of generals emerge. Perhaps the first step in this emergence was the holding of a first national "referendum" in December, 1984, on the Islamic path for Pakistan; and then a more truly democratic national election in February, 1985. The referendum was passed nearly unanimously, and was taken by Zia to be a vote of approval of his own continuation in office as President, as well as on the Islamic path. The national elections, however, saw many genuine contests, even though formal political parties were banned and open campaigning was limited.

## Conclusion

In his brilliant study of the military and society, Stanislaw Andreski distinguishes between four kinds of "militarism."[13] There is idolization of the military, rule by the military, the peacetime militarization of society (even under civilian leadership), and the gearing up of a society for war. Pakistan has seen only the first two, and those on a sporadic basis. Military rule in Pakistan has been fitful, embarrasssed and apologetic. Zia's rule could deteriorate into violent and corrupt palace politics, ruining the military and destroying the state, but it also could be the first step towards legitimate and effective civilian rule.

It is futile to debate whether the military has been pulled into politics because of the incompetence of civilian leaders or pushed its way in to ensure that civilians did not pursue policies anathema to military interests. The army believes that it defends society from external enemies, and some officers will argue that the military has an important role in ensuring that Pakistan society is modernized and yet remains pure and truly Islamic. There is more than a little self-fulfilling prophecy in this argument since the military has intervened on occasions when they were dissatisfied with the performance of the bureaucracy or the political parties and they will not let the latter become effective national institutions.

If Pakistan is to recover from its intellectual and political exhaustion and break the cycle of intervention, reform, demoralization, and breakdown, many groups must be involved. Pakistanis of all regions must appreciate the military's sensitivity to domestic disorder, and they must be capable of demonstrating their own competence and authority to run Pakistan. The soldiers are not blameless, and must accept a decline in their relative status and influence as the price that must be paid to reduce intervention. A series of agreements, possibly with timetables and election schedules, must be worked out between civil and military for the sake of national survival, if not national unity.

This is clearly the core problem of Pakistani politics. The military is reluctant to withdraw from power because of doubts whether any civilian leaders are capable of running the state to their satisfaction. In view of Bhutto's fate, civilians are reluctant to come forward. There is no assurance that the military will not play a covert political role even if formal power should pass to a civilian government. But partial military rule is not accepted by most Pakistanis, even in the military, whose perspective has been strongly shaped by the British tradition of parliamentary democracy and civilian control. The discontinuities between civilian and military opinion on these basic questions are enormous.

The generals will not satisfy the politicians unless they allow completely free elections and restore a reasonable range of civil liberties. Those parties with grievances against the military will probably have to agree that they will not seek retribution. The military may have to be given a constitutional voice in the making of policies which most strongly concern them. A staged withdrawal from politics would reassure both the military and civilian politicians that both were keeping their promises, but it is unlikely to occur. With Bhutto's death it is not clear whether any party or individual can effectively run Pakistan even if the military remained neutral.

However, in addition to military and civilian groups Pakistan's friends and the states which border it contribute to the role that its army plays in politics.

As long as Indians associate military rule in Pakistan with a belligerent Pakistan it is difficult for the military to either withdraw from power or negotiate a settlement of bilateral disputes. There is little sympathy within India for helping Pakistan find both stability and security. India is burdened with its own problems and the generals are hardly candidates for sympathy, yet the Indian desire to have Pakistan a weak buffer is being reexamined in light of the 1978 Afghanistan coup and the subsequent invasion of that country by Soviet Forces.

Among Pakistan's friends, only the U.S. has the leverage and interest to hasten the restoration of representative government. The renewed American relationship with Pakistan has been harshly criticized by liberal Americans, who probably exaggerate the degree of influence that one state can have over another when it provides some economic aid and sells (at commercial terms) military equipment.

American and Indian encouragement of a return to a more open political system, even in phased steps, is an important but not sufficient condition. Pakistan's political future will be determined by the degree of trust between Pakistanis. Despite the bravado of the military and the potent symbolism of Pakistani nationalism, the absence of trust may yet tear the state apart; the military, above all, must understand their role in creating this state of affairs. Their suspicion of Pakistani politicians is leading some of them to speculate whether their future might not be brighter within a shattered Pakistan or even a larger India. This warning would be rhetorical in virtually any country other than Pakistan, whose bloodstained past provides the best precedent.

## Strategic Considerations

Pakistan has a most complex strategic threat calculus. To the north is China, to the east India, a state with vastly superior industrial resources and a much larger human base; to the west lie Iran and Afghanistan, never friendly but the latter now occupied by the Soviet

Union. At home there are important grievances which include dislike of military rule. Further, in three of Pakistan's provinces there are important populations with strong ethnic and tribal ties across the border in Afghanistan; while on the Indian frontier there is an unresolved dispute over the status of Jammu and Kashmir. Pakistani domestic politics remain intimately linked to political relations with Pakistan's neighbors; any analysis of threats to Pakistan's security must emphasize this overlap between internal and external problems. Many in the military question the loyalty of their intellectuals, poets, and professors to Islam and Pakistan. Some generals fear that such ideologically "impure" groups constitute a massive fifth column.

On the ground, specific conventional military threats have been identified. While civilian strategists tend to treat states as abstract statistical entities, army staffs are taught to look first to geography and terrain. The particular shape of Pakistan and the distribution of its population and lines of communication complicate defense problems.

Two major wars were fought over the Punjab-Sind-Rajasthan frontier; at its northern end there is a cease-fire line which delineates appropriate guerrilla territory. Parts of the cease-fire line are observed rather ineffectively by a token U.N. presence which serves no real peacekeeping function. Pakistan's only port, Karachi, can be attacked by land or air, and blockaded by any state with a moderate naval capability.

When military assistance to Pakistan was being discussed in the U.S. in early 1980 it was often asserted that such assistance was useless because Pakistan was helpless in the face of the Soviet threat. This is not the view of the Pakistan military. They analyze the threat from Afghan/Russian forces in the following way. 1) There is little incentive for the Soviets to undertake an invasion which leads them away from the strategic Persian Gulf. 2) A Soviet push through Baluchistan, towards the Arabian Sea or enroute to Iran, makes somewhat more strategic sense but might precipitate American intervention whether or not there was a Pakistan-U.S. agreement; Pakistan could do little to prevent the Soviets from achieving such an objective, but as in #1, it could at considerable risk resist with ground and air forces. 3) Far more containable, would be direct Soviet or Soviet-supported Afghan attacks on refugee camps in Pakistan—some of which could be struck by air or ground raids or by artillery from Afghanistan. While Pakistan could not prevent such attacks, it might inflict damage on the attackers and retaliate upon support facilities in Afghanistan. It could also increase the weapons flow to the Afghans, offer them training, and allow Pakistani "volunteers" to join them.

There is no evidence that Pakistan has done any of these things, but they could form part of a response to Soviet-Afghan pressure on Pakistan's highly permeable border. Finally, Soviet support for Baluchi and other tribal groups in their continuing struggle against the Government of Pakistan could probably be contained by the Pakistani government; if not, it might erode the integrity of the state, its economic base, and the loyalty of most of its citizens.

Even before the Soviet threat, Pakistan planners had to assume that a conflict with India could develop so quickly that there would not be time to raise new forces. Further, the length of the border denies a small, fast moving mobile force the ability to cover it. It is improbable that Pakistan could defeat an Indian force, then rapidly redeploy and strike elsewhere. It no longer has air superiority, cannot raise new forces in the course of a short war, and its army—a strain on Pakistan's resources—is still less than half the size of the Indian Army. It would be impossible to move large numbers of troops from north to south during a war without a considerable improvement in road and rail transport and the assurance of freedom of movement. The problem is insurmountable when one considers the possibility of simultaneous pressure on the Afghan frontier.

From the perspective of Pakistan's military staff a number of responses have been discussed. 1) Pakistan has acquired new conventional weapons, especially high performance aircraft and armor, and is trying to manufacture some of these itself, with limited success. 2) The idea of lightly armed militia to defend large areas at low cost has been revived. 3) Privately, some generals will discuss the possibility of rapprochement with one or more of Pakistan's more dangerous neighbors, even the Soviet Union, to reduce the threat of a two-front war. 4) Nuclear weapons are often talked about as substitutes for conventional defense forces.

The strategic choices open to Pakistan never were attractive, and are now increasingly risky and limited. It would be dangerous for Pakistan to provoke a confrontation with India today; even managing limited incursions from the Indian or Afghan frontier runs great risks of escalation; above all, there remains the possibility of active Indian-Soviet cooperation, which would place Pakistan in a hopeless strategic position.

## Force Levels and Disposition

The number and quality of weapons held by the Pakistan military is determined by factors largely beyond their control: the attitudes of weapons suppliers, of financial supporters, and the slow growth of the Pakistani arms industry. The actual *disposition* of forces was severely limited by geography even before the 1980 Soviet invasion of Afghanistan; that event complicates even the simplest defense task.

The Pakistan military today still carries out internal security, border patrol, and expeditionary tasks. The latter now involves thousands of officers and men serving as pilots, gunners, advisors, and training cadres in a number of foreign military establishments, notably the Middle East. It has given up the task of checking Russian/Soviet advances in exchange for a new role, that of preparing for conventional ground war against India. Most of the Pakistan Army's 400,000 soldiers and approximately 900 tanks are dedicated to the long border with India. There is a clear discontinuity between the self-image of the Pakistan military as the legatees of the British side in the "Great Game" of Central Asian politics, balancing the Russians, and the reality of Pakistani troop dispositions. There is also a substantive reason for the discontinuity. In 1947–48 Pakistan could not maintain a far-flung and costly series of forts, let alone challenge the Soviets in Afghanistan or elsewhere without the complete backing of a major power, and at the same time defend against India.

Thus, Pakistan's mainline forces, organized into approximately twenty divisions, grouped into six corps, largely face east, not west. One corps, based in Peshawar, has two infantry divisions; another, in Quetta, is forming but four major corps (containing most of Pakistan's armor) face the Indian Army.

Before 1980 the Pakistan Air Force, (PAF) was oriented towards India's border.[14] Most of Pakistan's major military airfields are well back from the Indian border which means that they are close to the Afghan frontier, and major Afghan military airports. The Soviet Union has introduced many aircraft and missiles into Afghanistan, supplementing aircraft already in the Afghan Air Force. Some of these aircraft are less than a minute's flying time from Pakistan, and the PAF is vulnerable to a surprise attack from the west. If there were to be a major Soviet or Afghan incursion into Pakistan, in hot pursuit of Afghan tribesmen or for purposes of harassment, PAF airfields would be under attack. This led to the PAF requirement for improved early warning and SAM systems, and many new high-performance aircraft to meet and counter regular intrusions by Soviet or Afghan MiG 21 and other aircraft. Much of the American arms sales program developed in 1981 is geared to meet this request.

*Weapons Acquisition*

Pakistan is a large country and possesses a substantial pool of educated, trained manpower, yet it cannot manufacture a crankshaft.[15] Pakistan became completely dependent upon the U.S. in the 1950s for arms and it was not until 1965, when American arms transfers were practically terminated, that Pakistanis considered building an indigenous arms industry. There has been considerable progress largely with Chinese and French help, but Pakistan is still dependent for new tanks, APCs, aircraft of all kinds, soft-skinned vehicles, artillery, electronics, radar, and fire control systems, and many other items. Pakistan does produce its light infantry weapons, most ammunition, shells, explosives, and mortars, and it recently acquired the capacity to rebuild and reconstruct its 700 Chinese supplied T-59 tanks and French Mirage III aircraft. It is able to rebuild the Chinese F-6 (MiG 19) aircraft and undertake major repair of most of its heavy armored vehicles.[16]

Pakistan belongs to the category of "intermediate" arms supplier. It must acquire the most advanced equipment from others yet it is capable of supplying simpler arms. Pakistan hopes to become the arsenal of the Islamic world. But this is a long-term project, fraught with difficulties and risks, and Pakistan cannot wait until it develops an indigenous capacity to manufacture high-performance weapons. For these it must turn to the international arms market or its friends.

Both have proven unreliable. The Chinese are regarded in Pakistan as reliable, tactful, and steadfast, although there is concern about the quality of equipment they supply and its future level. China is seeking defense technology from a number of Western states and Pakistan does not want to wait for this to "trickle down." India may insist that the French limit arms sales to Pakistan as one condition for its own purchases. The Soviet Union once provided a hundred T-55 tanks to Pakistan, but demanded a settlement of the Kashmir issue as the price of further assistance, and it is now an unlikely source of weapons. The U.S. in 1965 and 1979 cut off Pakistan from arms purchases and maintained a restrictive sales policy from 1967 onward; only the invasion of Afghanistan brought about a change in American policy but it was not until the Reagan Administration that a major program was developed.

The military component of the Reagan package had two parts. One provided for the sale of a $1.55 billion worth of armor and support equipment.[17] There was little public objection to this even from the Indian government. The latter concentrated its opposition on the separate sale of 40 F-16 Hornet aircraft and their spare parts and repair facilities. Critics argued that the F-16 was provocative since it has an excellent longrange ground attack capability as well as an air defense capability.[18]

While the capabilities of the F-16 are important, the larger problem is political. From the Indian perspective such a weapon symbolizes a broader American commitment to support Pakistan, and postpones the day when Pakistan will accept its status of relative inferiority. From the Pakistani perspective the F-16 and other American equipment barely restore their military credibility. They argue that genuine peace cannot exist between Pakistan and India unless Pakistan can defend itself against the larger Indian military machine; since Pakistan now has a live frontier with Afghanistan its military status has suffered, whatever new equipment it may receive.

These positions are not irreconcilable but because of the impending nuclearization of the South Asian region the stakes are higher now than they were in 1954, and America's store of goodwill in both India and Pakistan is nearly depleted. It is unclear whether the new mutual dependency between the U.S. and Pakistan as a result of this major program will enhance or weaken Pakistan's security.[19]

## The Nuclear Option[20]

The military in Pakistan do not like nuclear weapons. Generals have spoken and written opposing a Pakistani nuclear program; most have accepted the idea of nuclear weapons with varying degrees of enthusiasm. Pakistan did not rush into a nuclear weapons program without consideration of the relevance of such weapons to the security of the state. Zulfikar Ali Bhutto had advocated a Pakistani nuclear option, a civilian program which could be converted to military uses, but not until 1974 did the military seriously address the strategic implications of an Indian— and then a Pakistani—nuclear weapon. They were asked by Bhutto to staff the military implications of nuclear proliferation in 1974, although plans for a nuclear program began before then. Their analysis has these major points.

First, they assume Indian possession of several nuclear weapons, or the capacity to "go nuclear" instantaneously. Second, Pakistanis believe that Indian nuclear weapons are primarily directed against them, not China. They ridicule the idea of India catching up with the Chinese or that there are serious grounds for an India-China conflict. Third, if Pakistan is the target, then the Indian bomb must have a military as well as a political rationale, enabling Indian conventional forces to seize the rest of Kashmir from Pakistan or even to dismember all of Pakistan. Nuclear weapons held in reserve as a threat against Lahore, Karachi, Islamabad, and other vital targets would effectively paralyze Pakistan and make it unable to resist. Fourth, strategists conclude, a modest, "limited" Pakistani weapons programs is essential to deter India's nuclear forces. Pakistanis have observed that nuclear weapons have been actually used only when the enemy did *not* have them. Fifth, possession of nuclear weapons not only deters a nuclear attack, but (following the NATO example) is an effective deterrent against conventional attack.

A Pakistani bomb would provide the umbrella under which Pakistan could reopen the Kashmir issue. A Pakistani nuclear capability would paralyze not only the Indian nuclear decision but also Indian conventional forces, and a bold Pakistani strike to liberate Kashmir might go unchallenged if Indian leadership was indecisive. Such a nuclear force might enhance Pakistan's deterrent along the Durand Line. A major incursion into Pakistan could trigger a Pakistani nuclear response, directed against "purely military" targets in Afghanistan or the Soviet Union. The weight of these arguments has led Pakistan to pursue the acquisition of fissile material through both reprocessing and enrichment routes.

Pakistanis who have thought about nuclear proliferation generally believe that while the rapid spread of nuclear weapons was not necessarily in Pakistan's interests, it did not further threaten them since the states most likely to confront Pakistan already either had nuclear weapons or could acquire them. Pakistan's allies did little to challenge the obvious implications of this analysis: China had long refused to transfer nuclear technology and subscribed to a doctrine of self-reliance in nuclear matters; the U.S. at first ignored the Indian explosion, then turned upon both India and Pakistan for failing to sign the NPT. It was unwilling to provide sufficient conventional weapons to Pakistan to balance an Indian nuclear capacity.

The Pakistanis apparently reached the conclusion that a small nuclear program would enable them to punish an Indian attack so severely that it would be deterred to begin with. Such deterrence would work against a massive conventional attack as well. A Pakistani bomb might enable Pakistan to reopen the Kashmir issue by the threat of force: if nuclear weapons deter each other they may also inhibit direct military conflict between states that possess them; a Pakistani leadership that was bold enough could attack and seize Kashmir when India was in disarray. Pakistani analysts make the opposite case: an Indian government could do the same to a weak Pakistan.[21]

In sum, there are persuasive strategic reasons for Pakistan to go ahead with a military nuclear program, even if the political, diplomatic, and economic cost is substantial. Assuming that Pakistan will acquire a nuclear weapon, can we speculate on its strategic role? There has been interesting discussion of this in Pakistan and a few remarks can be offered.

Like India, Pakistani nuclear planners will have the choice of utilizing their nuclear force for tactical or strategic ends. Given the nature of both economies, there are also a range of targets which are ambivalent, including major power production centers, dams, and irrigation projects: none of these would directly cause much loss of life according to preliminary studies and would thus not be "provocative" like the destruction of urban areas would be; but such attacks might in the long run cause more loss of life.[22]

Open sources indicate that Pakistani strategists favor the most dramatic but realistically the most conservative use of nuclear weapons, which are "terror" weapons *par excellence.* There is no need to *use* them; mere possession is enough to frighten off the threat; the Quran and modern deterrence theory neatly dovetail. Such a strategy would simplify the command and control problem of Pakistan and require the minimum number of weapons. It would also simplify targeting and delivery since accuracy and timing are not crucial. Should proliferation come to the Subcontinent, India and Pakistan might adopt such deterrence-cum-terror strategies at first and then, when a stockpile of fissionable material is developed, consider diverting some of this stockpile to produce a few "tactical" nuclear weapons. This could well happen if Pakistan felt that it was falling behind in its arms imbalance with India, and that its stockpile of "strategic" weapons was not adequate to deter a conventional war.

This calculation is grim but does not justify the charge that Pakistan is a candidate for "crazy" status: that it would irresponsibly detonate nuclear weapons or that it would transfer them to areas of the world where they would likely be used. The Pakistan military *have* been self-destructive in the past, and it cannot be assumed that they will not be in the future. But I believe that the Pakistan Army has done much to rebuild its professional character; it is not likely to make such decisions any more irresponsibly than another state confronted with the same perplexing set of security constraints.

If a Pakistani bomb is relevant to the India threat what is its relation to Pakistan's hot frontier with Afghanistan, or to the turmoil of domestic politics? The same reasoning that applies to a hypothetical Indian attack may apply to a hypothetical Soviet-Afghan attack. Pakistan is no match for an all-out attack, nor would nuclear weapons be of much practical use, but they might contribute to the *deterrent* force at work. They could plausibly substitute for several new divisions; Pakistan would not be threatening the Soviet Union, but only a neighbor acting with clearly hostile intent.

If Pakistan were in such dire straits that it actually contemplated using a nuclear weapon, would it actually deliver such a weapon? Confronted by the Soviet Air Force (or even the Indian Air Force, let alone a combination of the two), would a handful of PAF nuclear-capable aircraft survive an initial attack or get through alerted and hostile air defense screens?[23] Pakistan might find its nuclear force both provocative and ineffective.

While a Pakistani nuclear weapon would be greeted with widespread support at home (it is practically the only issue on which Pakistanis agree), there is doubt that it will help any regime that does build, test, and deploy it. This is the "life insurance" facet of nuclear weapons; as the Indians discovered a number of years ago, and as other nuclear powers found out earlier, nonpossession creates some unease and public anxiety, but possession barely returns the needle to normal.

Pakistan's nuclear program is propelled by many motives. The most important are survival of regime and state, but considerations of national prestige, nuclear weapons as "bargaining chips," with friend and enemy alike, and the near-unanimous support for the nuclear program among Pakistanis of all political persuasions are additional factors. If any state wishes to influence the Pakistani decision to go nuclear it must understand that proliferation in South Asia is a complex affair. It is not an event as much as a process, which does not end with a test detonation, let alone the acquisition of special nuclear material; nor is more necessarily less. At certain force levels, should the region become nuclearized, relations between South Asian states and between the region and external powers may become more rather than less stable. The proliferation process is not casual. States seek nuclear weapons because of the pressures of technology, the presence of an action-reaction syndrome (an arms race), their relevance to status and symbolic gratification, and their utility as instruments of policy and strategic discourse. To enable the states of South Asia to deal with the more basic threats to their security and to deal effectively with the proliferation process requires more than quick fixes. The best strategy for dealing with nuclear proliferation may not be the best if it triggers a conventional war.

The irony is that the "best strategy" devised by nonregional states (especially the U.S.) to deal with the proliferation problem may also have increased the rate of proliferation. An effective antiproliferation strategy for South Asia must identify the minimum security requirements of both India and Pakistan and treat the nuclear issue as part of the security calculation of regional states, not try to eradicate it.

The most effective approach would be one which assists regional states in detaching South Asia (after the Soviet Union has finished its task in Afghanistan) from superpower conflict and simultaneously reconciling major regional disputes. If these can be dealt with at the negotiating table rather than on the battlefield then concern about the "threat" of Pakistan to India, of India to Pakistan, and of China to India, evaporates. The states can move towards their own regional peace agreement and devote their resources to their only permanent enemies: domestic disorder, poverty, and low growth rates. Pakistani arms could be at a level adequate to deter an unlikely direct Soviet or Indian attack but not so large as to enable Pakistan to successfully attack India. There is an upper limit beyond which Pakistan need not build, for it would be threatening to India; but there is an important lower limit. Below this mix of numbers, quality, and tactical disposition Pakistan cannot fall. India and Pakistan must jointly determine these upper and lower limits; the role of outsiders might be to help fill in those gaps and deficiencies so as to strengthen the security of both states. Pakistanis may have to reconcile themselves to second-rank regional status, but Indians cannot reasonably expect Pakistan to disarm and assume the status of a Sri Lanka or Bangladesh.

A regional settlement leading to a balanced imbalance of conventional arms must necessarily resolve the nuclear problem. Perhaps the states directly involved are willing to live with neighbors who can quickly cross the nuclear threshold; if this did not extend proliferation to other regions the U.S. and other powers could endorse such an agreement—and strengthen it with material inducements—including jointly controlled energy generating facilities.[24]

*Conclusion*

Pakistan is the only excolonial state to have been divided by war. The successors to the military regime of the time are aware that neither the international nor the domestic environments have much improved since 1971. Pakistan is now flanked by the Soviet Union, China, Iran, and India; more than 2.5 million Afghan refugees have crossed the Durand Line; Pakistan's friends do not always match their verbal encouragement with material support; in terms of equipment the military was in poorer shape in 1980 than it was in 1971; politically, it remains unpopular, and there appears to be no strong civilian leadership capable of assuming power. Finally, ethnic, regional, economic, professional, and class groups periodically express their unhappiness with continued military rule. It is widely perceived as incompetent and some in the military feel it to be damaging to the army.

Without underestimating the possibility that civil war, revolution, external invasion, or some other calamity may lead to another vivisection of Pakistan, there are factors which may enable Pakistan to survive and thrive. First, while it is not popular, the military leadership is not irrational and is aware of its predicament. Zia and other generals have encouraged debate, discussion, and criticism within the military, although they have not always allowed civilians to speak their mind. They are aware of the technical shortcomings of the military, of the regional dominance of India, of the ruthlessness of the Russians, and of the unreliability of their American ex-allies. Nor do they think the Islamic world will do much to help them, let alone the nonaligned movement. They hold the realistic view that they must rely upon their own resources and forge their own path in a world of peril. But this path is not apparent to anyone—Pakistani or nonPakistani.

If, as seems likely, the military continue in power in Pakistan, or retain a veto over security-related decisions, there is not likely to be a major change in the strategic style, for it represents a consensus with the military hierarchy. However, should the Pakistan Army withdraw from power and its dominant role in defense policymaking, it is conceivable (though unlikely) that a civilian government would reshape both structural and strategic components of security policy. They might pursue an expanded role for nuclear weapons or attempt to create a people's army. At present (1985), the military have gradually and successfully moved to increase civilian participation in government, through the electoral process. Pakistan does not have democracy, but it is more democratic than it was several years ago, and a new crop of civilian legislators will be able to claim the legitimacy of the ballot box.

This will not yet be able to challenge the legitimacy of the rifle, nor is there likely to be a serious conflict between newly elected civilian politicians and ministers, and a government dominated by President Zia. However, the process of evolution has begun, and certain basic policies may yet be challenged by civilians and unhappy soldiers alike.

Given the opportunity, many civilians, and some generals, would like to limit the size, role, and mission of the Pakistan military, although they would not go so far as to change its characteristic structure. There may also be attempts to modify Pakistan's foreign policy, especially if relations with the U.S. should change after the current arms agreement expires in 1987. Finally, there is the small but not incredible possibility that one of Pakistan's neighbors will seize upon its disorder and end the "Pakistan problem" once and for all. If the Pakistan Army were defeated and disarmed, Pakistan would fragment into separate, independent states, each virtually disarmed and under the protective influence of India or the Soviet Union. It is unlikely that India would want to reabsorb much of present Pakistan but it might conclude that an unstable, fragile, nuclear armed, and hostile Pakistan held greater risks than an immediate war.

Pakistan must thus search for a *via media* between concessions which would undo the state and a hard-line strategy that threatens total war as a form of defense—and might lead its neighbors to conclude that it is unredeemably irresponsible, especially in the case of India. Pakistan has no choice but to learn to live with its newly powerful neighbor and to accept its own *de facto* strategic inferiority. But such acceptance is in turn dependent on Indian statesmanship. If India insists that Pakistan has no legitimate defense needs, then Pakistan is in an impossible position. But if India has an interest in the continuing existence of a Pakistan capable of defending itself—even against India—because that capability is one, but not the only condition for the integrity of the state, then there may be reason to be optimistic.[25]

## Notes

1. This chapter is based upon Stephen Philip Cohen, *The Pakistan Army* (Berkeley: University of California Press, 1984).

2. Stephen P. Cohen, *The Indian Army* (Berkeley: University of California Press, 1971), pp. 29–30.

3. Air Marshal M. Asghar Khan (ret.), *Pakistan at the Crossroads* (Lahore: Ferozsons, 1969), reprinted in *Defense Journal*, IV, II, 1978, p. 9–10.

4. The best account of constitution building in the Ayub and Yahya years are in the three studies by Herbert Feldman: *Revolution in Pakistan* (London: Oxford University Press, 1967), *From Crisis to Crisis* (London: Oxford University Press, 1972), and *The End and the Beginning* (London: Oxford University Press, 1975); for copies of a number of documents pertaining to the 1977 martial law (and for important analyses of earlier spells of military rule) see various issues of the *Defense Journal* (Karachi); the charges against Bhutto are summarized in several *White Papers* issued by the government of Pakistan in 1978 and 1979.

5. One of the main activities is the Fauji Foundation. When India and Pakistan were partitioned, they shared in the welfare contributions donated by ORs during World War II; India distributed these to individual ex-soldiers, but Pakistan used the money to capitalize the Fauji Foundation which in turn used it to develop a chain of hospitals, light (and heavy) industries, and various service facilities, largely but not entirely for ex-servicemen. The foundation is headed by a retired general, and employs a number of retired officers. The Foundation is rumored to be one channel for the clandestine import of equipment used in the nuclear weapon program.

6. Cohen, "Arms and Politics in Pakistan," *India Quarterly*, (October-December, 1964), pp. 413–414.

7. A number of studies appeared after 1972, some of them clearly inspired by Bhutto. The most comprehensive was written by Fazal Muqeem Khan, a respected retired lieutenant-general. See *Pakistan's Crisis in Leadership* (Islamabad: National Book Foundation, 1973); also, the texts of a *White paper on Defense Organization* and a Staff study can be found in *Defense Journal*, II, 7–8 (July-August, 1976); this publication regularly included analyses of Pakistan's higher defense organization throughout the 1970s.

8. In the 1973 Constitution, any attempt to abrogate it by force or threat of force is treasonous (Sec. 6), the principle of civilian control is firmly laid down (Sec. 243–5), and an oath is specified for members of the Armed Forces, which states in part that "I will not engage myself in any political activities whatsoever. . . ." (Third Schedule).

9. The most comprehensive study of current Pakistani defense decisionmaking is in Shirin Tahir-Kehli, "Defense Planning in Pakistan," Stephanie Neuman, ed., *Defense Planning in Less Industrialized States* (Lexington: D. C. Heath, 1984).

10. For a survey of Zia's rule, almost five years after he came to power, see Stephen P. Cohen and Marvin G. Weinbaum, "Pakistan in 1981: Staying On," *Asian Survey*, XXII, 1 (February, 1982), pp. 36–146.

11. Zia's early anonymity was an advantage and a disadvantage. It worked to his benefit in that his opponents in and out of the military grossly underestimated both his ability and his tenacity; in this he resembles Indira Gandhi after she became Prime Minister in 1965, or her predecessor, Lal Bahadur Shastri. All three quietly undercut their political opponents, or set them against each other, while consolidating power. By 1985 Zia was no more charismatic than he was in 1977, but he was much more assured and confident; indeed, a sign of his success is that he is beginning to be taken for granted.

12. These arrests are most fully documented by Amnesty International in a major report, *Pakistan: Human Rights Violations and the Decline of the Rule of Law* (London: Amnesty International Publications, 1982); the Pakistan government has vehemently contested both particulars of the report and its general conclusions.

13. *Military Organization and Society* (2nd ed., Berkeley: University of California Press, 1968), pp. 84ff.

14. The most complete description of PAF history and operations is in John Fricker, *Battle for Pakistan: The Air War of 1965* (London: Ian Allen, 1979), which was written with the cooperation of senior PAF Officers.

15. According to Lieut-Gen. Abdul Hameed Khan (ret.), "Organization for Defense," *Nawai-Waqt*, Lahore, April 10–11, 1979. However, Pakistan has been able to manufacture a number of military items for several years, including the excellent 106 mm. recoilless rifle, an American design.

16. The F-6 and tank rebuild facilities are being provided by the PRC; the Mirage rebuild facility is French-supplied but paid for by Pakistan; the repair facilities of the Pakistan Army have been built up over the years, but with a major American contribution in the 1950s.

17. In addition to the 40 F16s, the U.S. has promised the following items: 100 M48 A5 tanks, 35 M88A1 recovery vehicles, 20 M109A2 self-propelled howitzers, 40 M110A2 8" self-propelled howitzers, 75 M198 towed howitzers, and 10 AH-1S attack helicopters. Pakistan did not seek the more modern M-60 tank because of its weight and because it already had a number of the M48 tanks in its inventory. In addition, it has received at least four destroyers, optimized for antisubmarine war. A separate economic agreement provided credits and loans at concessional interest rates for a five-year period; the military component of the package provides some credit but at commercial levels (about 14%), hardly a bargain. Both programs must receive annual congressional approval; their future is in doubt if Pakistan should detonate a nuclear device, as restrictive clauses have been written into the legislation.

18. James L. Buckley, then Under Secretary of State for Security Assistance, presented the outline of the agreement in testimony before the House Committee

on Foreign Affairs on September 16, 1981; critical and supportive witnesses appeared on September 22 and 23, 1981.

19. See Stephen P. Cohen, "Pakistan and America: The Security Dimension," *Defense Journal* (Karachi), VII, 8, 1981, pp. 7–11.

20. I have discussed this issue at greater length in *Perception, Influence and Weapons Proliferation in South Asia* (Washington: U.S. State Department, Bureau of Intelligence and Research, Contract No. 1722-920184), August, 1979. There are a number of perceptive articles on nuclear strategy and theory in various Pakistani military journals. For an indignant Indian view see Maj.-Gen. D. K. Palit (ret.) and P.K.S. Namboodiri, *Pakistan's Islamic Bomb* (New Delhi: Vikas, 1979). A more balanced approach is in Zalmay Khalilzad, "Pakistan and the Bomb," *Survival* (November/December, 1979), pp. 244–250.

21. Pakistani and Indian strategists are also aware of Western arguments that nuclear weapons have, indeed, prevented both a general war from breaking out between the U.S. and the Soviet Union, but that they have probably kept the Russians from invading Western Europe. If Bernard Brodie, McGeorge Bundy, and others can justify American possession of nuclear weapons in these terms, why—they ask—cannot a state in a far more vulnerable position acquire "just a few" nuclear weapons?

22. This is the conclusion of one study at the University of Illinois Program in Arms Control by Rashid Naim, "Asia's Day After."

23. This point is raised by Jeffrey Kemp in the context of an Israeli last-ditch nuclear retaliation in "A Nuclear Middle East," in John Kerry King, *International Political Effects of the Spread of Nuclear Weapons*. Some Western analysts who have studied the problem conclude that if a Pakistani nuclear force survived a conventional air attack it would be unstoppable, especially if it flew north or west through mountainous territory.

24. This was suggested by David E. Lilienthal just before his death in 1981.

25. Senior members of the Pakistani leadership were aware of this in 1980, and they stunned India by offering it a no-war pact on September 15, 1981. India itself had made such an offer as early as 1949 (and Pakistan had in turn routinely countered with a "joint defense" proposal). After two months' exchange of press releases and innuendos India formally responded positively to the offer on November 25th.

# 15

# The Armed Forces in Bangladesh Society

*Jeffrey Lunstead*

**Historical Development of Bangladesh's Armed Forces**

The development of Bangladesh's armed forces is intertwined with the tangled history of Bangladesh, which is unique in a number of ways. It is the only successful postwar armed secession and also one of the poorest countries in the world.

Bangladesh actually had two births, both traumatic. It was first born in 1947, as East Pakistan, with the partition of British India. Although Bengal did not undergo violence and transfers of population on the same scale as the Punjab in the West, there was considerable upheaval. The second birth occurred in 1971, when East Pakistan seceded from Pakistan to form the independent nation of Bangladesh. The secession followed 25 years of political and economic discrimination by Punjabi-dominated West Pakistan. Negotiations between East Pakistani leader Shiekh Mujib-ur-Rehman and the civil and military leadership of West Pakistan ended on March 25, 1971, when the Pakistani Army arrested Sheikh Mujib and tried to impose a military solution. Seven months of guerrilla warfare followed, with approximately 10 million refugees fleeing to India.

General war between India and Pakistan broke out on December 3, 1971 and Indian troops reached Dacca, capital of East Pakistan, in less than two weeks. Mujib was released from prison and returned to Dacca to head the new country.[1]

The Bangladesh government and its military forces thus started at a double disadvantage. First, unlike most newly independent countries, there had not been even the pretense of preparation for independence. Although the Pakistani government tried in the late 1960s to increase East Pakistani representation in the administration, little progress was made. Second, during the nine-month civil war preceding independence, a determined effort was made to destroy East Pakistani capabilities. East Pakistani soldiers and administrators in West Pakistan were interned, while those in East Pakistan were hunted down and murdered. Many of the intellectual elite of East Pakistan were wiped out as the Pakistan Army made the universities a special target. In addition, the physical destruction was enormous. Communications were severed due to the destruction of bridges, a vital link in the deltaic setting of Bangladesh.

The abrupt end of the civil war also left many weapons in civilian hands. While the core of the *mukti bahini* (liberation army) was formed of East Pakistani deserters, paramilitary and police, it was supplemented by civilians. When the fighting ceased, many of them were more interested in settling grudges and establishing their own power than in returning to civilian life. Calls to turn in their weapons went largely unheeded.

The Bangladesh military is a derivative of the British Indian military and the Pakistan military. The pre-1947 British Indian Army contained almost no Bengali's, as the British did not consider them one of the "martial races." At partition, in August 1947, military manpower and assets were divided between India and Pakistan. Pakistan found itself with an army composed almost entirely of personnel from its western wing. Structured along the British regimental system, there were no East Pakistan regiments. Pakistan therefore raised the first two battalions of an East Bengal regiment in 1948. Six more battalions were formed by 1970, and a ninth battalion was in training in 1971. Nonetheless, East Pakistanis made up approximately five percent of the total strength of the Pakistan Army in 1971. Only one general officer was from East Pakistan. The percentages of East Pakistanis in the Navy and Air Force were only slightly higher. One of the prime disqualifications for East Pakistanis attempting to join the Army was the height restriction. Only a few Bengalis could meet the minimum height of 5 feet 6 inches, later reduced to 5 feet 4 inches.[2]

Pakistan also formed a paramilitary force, the East Pakistan Rifles, essentially a border patrol force similar to forces maintained in West Pakistan—the well-known Frontier Scouts on the Afghan border, the Rangers on the Indian border.

When the Pakistan Army cracked down in March 1971, East Pakistani units stationed there rebelled and quickly deserted. A Bengali, Major Zia-ur-Rehman, declared independence on March 26 in Chittagong before slipping away to help found the nucleus of what became the *mukti bahini*. Army deserters were joined by those from the East Pakistan Rifles and the police. East Pakistani military estimated at 28,000 serving in West Pakistan were disarmed and interned.

The *mukti bahini* was theoretically a unified force, commanded by Col. M.A.G. Osmany. In reality it was an aggregation of numerous bands owing allegiance to particular leaders. Many of these leaders, former Pakistan Army majors, would later play important roles in

Bangladesh's political-military history. In addition to Zia-ur-Rehman, groups were led by Khalid Musharraf, M.A. Jalil, Kader (Tiger) Siddiquki and Abu Taher. Despite high enthusiasm, the poorly-armed and ill-trained *mukti bahini* had little success against the Pakistan Army, and independence was achieved only by the intervention of India.

Following the establishment of a Bangladesh government in January 1972, the three services were reformed as the armed forces in April. The Army had some 17,000 men, the Navy and Air Force perhaps 500 each. The East Pakistan Rifles were reconstituted as the East Bengal Rifles. General Osmany retired as Commander-in-Chief and chiefs were named for each of the three services. Colonel Zia-ur-Rehman became Deputy Chief of Army Staff. There was no combined staff.[3]

In the chaos following independence, armed force was not restricted to government institutions. Practically every political party and faction had its own armed wing—some larger and better armed than the Army. Mujib founded the *Jatiyo Rakhi Bahini* (JRB)—National People's Army—in 1972 as an armed force responsible only to him, with strength estimated at from 10,000 to 40,000. This force was used by Mujib to intimidate his opponents, and was greatly resented by the Army. The JRB was under the direct control of the President's Secretariat.[4]

In their early years the three military forces were grossly deficient in equipment. That captured by the Indian Army from the Pakistan Army was mostly returned to India rather than turned over to the Bangladeshis. Major foreign military aid was provided by the USSR. Following a military air agreement in 1972, Bangladesh received in 1973 10 MiG-21's, MI-8 helicopters and AN-26 transport planes. Yugoslavia in 1974 provided Bangladesh with small arms and naval patrol craft. Nonetheless, the Army and Navy remained seriously deficient in equipment. The army lacked heavy weapons and communications and transport. The Navy could not perform even the most routine patrol of the Bangladesh coastline.

Economic and political turmoil accelerated in the first three and one-half years of Bangladesh's existence, strongly affecting the armed forces. The government showed little ability to run newly nationalized industries, private paramilitary groups battled each other, and Mujib's rule became even more autocratic. By 1975 Mujib had modified the constitution and appointed himself president with dictatorial powers. All opposition to his policies was outlawed, and opposition parties banned.

Factionalism grew in the military just as it did in society at large. The most basic division was between the "freedom fighters"; those who were in East Pakistan in 1971 and joined the struggle against Pakistan, and the "returnees," interned in West Pakistan. The internees were not returned to Bangladesh until 1973 and 1974. They found that what they regarded as their rightful positions had been usurped by freedom fighters, who were granted two years additional seniority as a gesture of appreciation. The more numerous returnees, trapped in West Pakistan in 1971, resented this bitterly. Senior officers found they were not welcome in any position. The senior Bangladeshi officer, General Wasiuddin, was seconded to the Foreign Ministry and posted abroad.

Ideological differences also found their way into the Army. The Jatiyo Samajtantrik Dal (JSD)—National Socialist Party—was founded by leftwing critics of Mujib. Among the founders, who soon organized an armed wing, were Majors Jalil and Abu Taher, heroes of the independence struggle. The JSD called for the transformation of the Army into a "peoples' army," as in the PRC, and concentrated on infiltrating the enlisted ranks.[5]

The Army also suffered from personal disputes with Mujib. Smuggling became endemic along Bangladesh's border, and Mujib ordered the Army to stop it. When the Army moved against smugglers who supported Mujib, however, he tried to restrain it and cashiered several prominent officers.

Finally, the Army faced personal rivalries. Young officers had been promoted from major in the Pakistan Army to high command in the Bangladesh Army, stimulating their ambitions. The rivalry between Zia-ur-Rehman, now Deputy Chief of Army Staff, and Khalid Musharraf, Chief of General Staff, was particularly evident.

Direct military intervention in Bangladesh politics began in August 1975 when several hundred soldiers, led by young officers, principally majors, stormed Mujib's residence and murdered him, his family, and supporters. The majors installed a new president, Khondakar Mushtaque Ahmed, and moved Zia-ur-Rehman to Chief of Army Staff. Motivations for the coup seem to have been mixed. In large part they were personal; several of the most prominent majors had been cashiered by Mujib for their open resistance to his Awami League. Mixed with this was a feeling that Mujib had grown too close to India and the Soviet Union, and that the Army was being slighted at the expense of the JRB.

This event was termed a "putsch" rather than a coup by some observers because it was carried out solely by a group of midlevel officers using elements of one Army unit, the Bengal Lancers.[6] The senior officers seem to have been unaware of the plans. Following the coup the majors and their troops remained in the presidential palace, a power center competing with the military command. An uneasy truce prevailed while the parties negotiated the future of Bangladesh. In early November, however, four Awami League cabinet members in the Dacca Jail were found bayonetted and shot to death—presumably at the instigation, if not direct orders, of the majors. The pro-Mujib portion of the Army leadership then took action. On November 3, Brig. Musharraf assumed command, dismissing both the new president and General Zia, who was arrested. The majors were quickly sent out of the country.

Musharraf's countercoup did not have broad support, however, as he was perceived as "pro-Indian." The country had turned decisively against Sheikh Mujib and against India. In addition, Zia was a genuinely popular figure. A counter-countercoup took place on November 7. In a genuinely spontaneous movement, large numbers of enlisted men revolted, swept Musharraf out of office and reinstalled Zia. (Musharraf was killed.)

The great mystery of the November 7 events was the extent of JSD involvement. Trying to infiltrate the enlisted ranks for some time the JSD probably played some role, but the enlisted men's actions seem to militate against JSD control. In reinstating Zia the enlisted men restored a man to power who was widely perceived as conservative and pro-Western, with a strong Islamic orientation—hardly qualities one would seek in a leader of a class revolution dedicated to the formation of a "peoples' army."

It appears, therefore, that the events of August-November 1977 were motivated largely by personal grudges and rivalries, mixed with anti-Mujib, anti-Indian animus. There is no evidence that any organized group was in control, or that any foreign power played a hand.

The JSD claimed a role for itself, however, and attempted to buttress its position shortly after the coup, issuing demands which included the removal of distinctions between officers and enlisted men. The control of Zia, and indeed the entire officer corps, over the Army was fragile, and there were reports of attempted uprisings in various units. Zia regained control, however, and in late November arrested most of the JSD leadership. Following the reestablishment of basic discipline in the military, the JSD leaders were tried by a closed military tribunal in June 1976. Col. Abu Taher was sentenced to death and executed in July while other JSD leaders received jail sentences.

Having disarmed this challenge from the left, Zia next faced a challenge from the right. Four majors of the August coup had been given diplomatic postings abroad by Zia after he resumed power. In April 1976 several of the majors returned, apparently with the backing of Air Vice Marshall Tawab, chief of the Air Force, a noted rightwing, pro-Islamic figure. Negotiations between the majors and Zia on conditions for their return to the country broke down. Tawab was forced to resign and sent to London. One of the majors returned to his old regiment, the Bengal Lancers, and apparently attempted to start another coup. Zia arrested him, exiled him again, and disbanded the by-now infamous Lancers.[7]

Following the coups of 1975, National elections were promised and tentatively scheduled for February 1977. Following the November 7 coup, the country was nominally run by President and Chief Martial Law Administrator Abu Sayem, but the real power was exercised by Deputy Martial Law Administrator General Zia. Zia moved to consolidate his power and toward civilian status. On November 22, 1976, President Sayem postponed the elections, at Army urging, and on November 30 he handed over the post of Chief Martial Law Administrator to General Zia. In April 1977 Sayem resigned the presidency, Zia assumed it and a referendum in May 1977 gave Zia a favorable vote of 99 percent.

Zia's success was tempered, however, by continuing problems within the military. Factional disputes had not healed and a major crisis occurred in September-October 1977. On September 30, Army troops revolted in the division stationed at Bogra, but Zia brought the situation under control. On October 2, however, while the government was preoccupied with Japanese Red Army terrorists who had hijacked a Japan Airlines jet to Dacca, another mutiny broke out among Air Force personnel there. Air Force enlisted men shot a number of their own officers and stormed the control tower at Dacca airport where Air Force leaders were conducting the hijacking negotiations. The Army's ninth Division came to Zia's rescue and put down the rebellion. One of the key figures in suppressing the mutiny was Chief of General Staff, General Manzur.

The September-October 1977 mutiny is still a mystery. In both Bogra and Dacca the enlisted men revolted but were the events connected? It would seem so, but if they were, it was a remarkably disorganized attempt to overthrow a government. Was the JSD involved? Again it would appear likely, since this was clearly an enlisted versus officers revolt. But the enlisted men sought out some officers, leaving others alone, leading to suspicions that personal motives played an important part. The coup was probably a mixture of these two, as JSD activists within the armed forces seized upon existing discontent and attempted to foment a rebellion which they hoped to turn to their own ends.

The government was shaken by this coup attempt, and moved quickly to crush it. The JSD and two other radical parties were banned, their leaders arrested, and military tribunals set up to try personnel involved in the coup. The number of persons tried is not clear but is in the hundreds and at least 55 were executed. All of those tried appeared to be enlisted. Henceforth, vigilance was increased in the armed forces to discover and root out possible opponents of the government. Zia tried to win over the troops' loyalty by improving their pay and conditions.[8]

## Continued Civilization

The 1977 coup attempt did not stop Zia's progress towards a civilian government. A presidential election was held in June 1978 and Zia, a serving Army officer, was elected President. He founded a new political party, the Bangladesh Nationalist party (BNP), which won a majority of seats in the parliamentary election held in February 1979. Zia resigned from the Army, and his resignation was backdated, effective April 1978. As President, he now became Supreme Commander of the armed forces, and chose General Ershad as the new Chief of Army Staff.

All of Zia's energy and attention could not save him in the end, however, for on March 30, 1981, while visiting Chittagong, he was murdered during a coup attempt led by General Manzur, commanding general of the Chittagong division. The coup seems to have been motivated by a mixture of ideology and personal ambition. Manzur, like Zia, was one of the few surviving freedom fighters in the senior ranks of the armed forces. Manzur was resentful of the returnees, and Zia was determined to transfer him to command the Staff College, removing him from command of troops. This would have effectively removed Manzur both from power and from a chance for continued promotion. His poorly planned coup failed, however, as most of the armed forces rallied behind the civilian government. Manzur, after surrendering, was seized by enraged enlisted men and murdered.[9]

Zia's assassination may have been the last gasp of the freedom fighters. The coup participants were entirely from this group and the twelve officers hanged after closed military tribunals were freedom fighters. The two senior freedom fighters, an Army Lieutenant General and the commander of the Air Force, were retired in short order, and a number of midlevel freedom fighters were also forced out.

The Army not only suppressed the coup but also supported the civilian leadership and the succession process. The Acting President, former chief Justice Abdus Sattar, soon to be elected President in his own right, was a civilian. While Zia had relinquished his military rank, he maintained close links to the military, and this remained his ultimate power base. The military was still the most powerful institution in Bangladesh society although, like the other institutions, it was not particularly stable. Since the Zia assassination, the military as an institution was under a cloud. Zia had been a remarkably popular individual, perceived throughout society as untainted by corruption. In addition, he had made progress in moving Bangladesh toward food grain sufficiency, increased industrial production, and stable civilian political institutions. All this vanished in another burst of military indiscipline.

Still, the military had a role, and with a truly civilian president for the first time since 1975, this would have to be a new role. The military sought to define this role as the civilian political process ground towards the Presidential election, held in November 1981. There was intense infighting within the BNP, a deteriorating food and economic situation, and a deceleration of the development momentum, which Zia had personnally carried forward. Rumors of military intervention, to replace what was generally perceived as an inept administration, circulated widely as the election neared.

The military permitted the election to be held and Acting President Sattar was returned by a large majority. It was widely rumored that Sattar and Ershad had struck a deal before the election, but a newly confident President Sattar stated publicly that the military would not have any additional functions within the government, and that the only role of the armed forces was to defend the country's borders.[10]

Ershad responded two weeks later with a press interview which could be seen only as a direct challenge to Sattar. He warned that a recurrence of coups and killings could be prevented only if the military was granted its proper place, and that measures had to be worked out "to define clearly the role of the military in society."[11]

Sattar tried to hold off the military, but he could only delay, not stop, the accretion of power. In January the three service chiefs were named members of a new ten-man National Security Council, which was to "advise the government on all matters relating to national security as a whole." This minority representation did not satisfy the military, however, and in February the cabinet was dismissed at military insistence, and the NSC was reconstituted with the three service chiefs balanced by only three civilians.

Finally, on March 24, the military assumed complete control, as martial law was imposed and the government dismissed. General Ershad became Chief Martial Law Administrator and chief of the armed forces. In an address to the nation, Ershad stated that the armed forces moved "to save the country . . . from a social administrative and economic breakdown" and that "the government has failed totally because of the petty selfishness, unworthiness, nepotism, unbounded corruption and conflict of those in power." He promised general elections at an unspecified date.[12]

It quickly became obvious that the goal of the martial law regime was to change the nature of Bangladesh society. Grand plans for restructuring the administrative and judicial systems were announced, centering on moving offices and courts out of the cities and into the countryside. The practical obstacles were overlooked—courts were simply ordered to set up new divisions and have them in place by a certain date. In matters large and small, the regime demanded the military virtues—order, discipline, and efficiency.

In attempting to instill these qualities, the military plunged forward in most areas of national life, including some in which it had no expertise. The assumption presumably is that simply efficiency will bring about a change, even where resources or skills are lacking. The military leaders gave their attention to both large and small matters, those which involve substance and those largely show. Martial law administrative actions to reduce government ministries from 42 to 17, to decentralize the administrative and court systems, to denationalize industries and to bring "black money" into the open—all important measures—were matched by equal stress on less important issues such as the removal of shops built on sidewalks, enforcement of traffic laws, strict orders that utility bills be paid on time, and an elaborate dress code for government workers.

The new regime's main emphasis, however, was on the eradication of corruption. General Ershad indicated in numerous statements and interviews since his takeover that he views this as the most pressing problem for Bangladesh. A number of high-ranking civil servants and elected politicians have been arrested so far. Former Deputy Prime Minister Jamaluddin Ahmed was convicted on several counts of corrupt practices, given a lengthy jail term, a heavy fine, and had his immovable property confiscated. Other senior civil servants have been dismissed or transferred.[13]

The military maintains that it has taken on only a temporary role, but has been vague on the specifics for a return to civilian rule. General Ershad has spoken of holding general elections in two or three years, and stated that as long as he is a soldier, he will not become a politician. However, it seems likely that the current constitution will be modified, as it was essentially written for the late General Zia. It is also clear that the military seeks a new, and institutionalized, role for itself in whatever new order emerges. One of the prime factors motivating the coup was Sattar's refusal to grant the military such a role. Ershad stated that the military wishes to involve itself in "nation building" activities, and that it should be a part of the people, not cut off from them. Rumors abound that the military has been studying the Turkish and Indonesian models to devise a suitable system for permanent military involvement in the government of Bangladesh. In November 1982, Ershad announced that local elections would be held in August 1983, and that the constitution would be revived with certain amendments to ensure the future role of the military.

## Strategic Rationale For Bangladesh's Armed Forces

Bangladesh is surrounded on three sides by India, sharing only a short land border with Burma in the far southeast. The only feasible conventional threat could come from India. The two countries are linked by the 1972 Treaty of Friendship and Cooperation, which provides that "In case either party is attacked or threatened with attack, the parties shall immediately enter into mutual consultations in order to take appropriate effective measures to eliminate the threat." Since Bangladesh hardly can be expected to come to the defense of India, the treaty is in essence an Indian guarantee of Bangladesh's security. India's military strength is so overwhelming that Bangladesh could offer only token resistance to Indian military action.

In the event of hostilities with India, the Bangladesh forces would attempt to harass and delay the Indian forces long enough for international pressures to be brought into play. Such hostilities are unlikely, however. Although Bangladesh has several ongoing disputes with India, sharing Ganges River waters and ownership of a newly emerged island in the Bay of Bengal foremost among them, it lacks the strength for a military confrontation over them.

The Bangladesh military's main role lies in combatting insurgent movements. These could be indigenous or fomented by outside forces. There is at least one active insurgency in Bangladesh. The tribal people of the Chittagong Hill Tracts, bordering India and Burma have engaged in sporadic guerrilla warfare and several units of the Bangladesh Army are deployed there. The insurgents move back and forth across the borders of the three countries fairly easily in this remote and inaccessible region.

## Strength and Distribution of Bangladesh's Armed Forces

The Bangladesh armed forces currently total 75–77,000 men. Of these 70,000 are in the Army, 2–3,000 in the Air Forces, with approximately 75–100 pilots, and 3–4,000 in the Navy. In paramilitary forces, the Bangladesh Rifles number 30,000, and the Ansars, a little known group described as the "second line of defense" perhaps 15,000. All three forces have their headquarters at Dacca. The Navy's main base is at Chittagong, with a secondary base at Khulna. The Air Force maintains most, if not all, of its fighter aircraft at Dacca. The Army's five divisions are posted throughout the country, another indication that the main role of the Army is internal security.

Part of the reason for the chronic instability in the Bangladesh army stems from its pattern of growth. Emerging from the liberation war as a combination of guerrilla forces and surviving regulars from the Pakistani Army, the army took in new recruits at a furious pace, as reflected in the table below.

|      | '73    | '74    | '75    | '76    | '77    | '81    |
|------|--------|--------|--------|--------|--------|--------|
| ARMY | 17,000 | 25,000 | 30,000 | 59,000 | 65,000 | 70,000 |

The large jump between 1975 and 1976 reflects the induction of the disbanded Rakhi Bahini forces into the Army. Even a developed country would experience difficulties in expanding its army by 300 percent in 4 years. In Bangladesh, with a largely illiterate populace and a dearth of administrative talent, the problem was qualitatively greater.

Defense and security expenditures accounted for somewhat less than ten percent of the budget in recent years. All of the services are in need of upgraded equipment, but the country clearly cannot pay for large amounts of modern equipment. The Army is adequate in small arms, but lacks modern communications and transportation equipment, vital in Bangladesh's riverine territory. Of the ten MiG-21's received from the Soviet Union in 1972, it is unclear how many are flyable because of difficulties with maintenance and spare parts. The Air Force also flies Soviet helicopters and transport planes acquired in the early 1970's. These aircraft are presumably overhauled in the USSR. More recently the Air Force received approximately fifteen Chinese F-6's, equivalent to the MiG-19. The Navy, traditionally a coastal patrol force, has approximately ten Shanghai class patrol boats received from the PRC. The Navy acquired a blue water capability, however, with the recent acquisition of two fast frigates from the United Kingdom. The US provides no military equipment, but trains several Bangladesh officers each year in the US. It appears that Bangladesh is in the unique position of receiving some type of military assistance from the US, the USSR and the PRC.[14]

## The Impact of Bangladesh's Armed Forces in Society

It is clear that the Bangladesh military is the predominant institution in Bangladeshi society. What is not clear is precisely what role the military will play in that society. This is, in part, a reflection of the pervasive uncertainty in Bangladesh society as to what Bangladesh is, and what it should become. It is the difference between the nationalism of those who fought for independence from India in 1947 and those who fought for independence from Pakistan in 1971. The former emphasize Islam, stress the differences between Bangladesh's largely Muslim population and the Hindus of India's West Bengal, and wish closer ties with Pakistan. The latter emphasize the common cultural heritage of all Bengalis, downplay the importance of Islam—Mujib established Bangladesh as a secular republic—and are hostile to the link with Pakistan.[15] When freedom fighters and *Rakhi Bahini* were merged with the regular Army, it showed these same divisions. As most freedom fighters have been eliminated, the Army reflects much more the earlier nationalism.

It would be misleading, therefore, to speak simply of the impact of the Bangladesh military upon the political system. Rather, the two mirror each other. The Bangladesh military contains and reflects the divisions of Bangladeshi society. The military, however, has the power to enforce its will upon the political system or even to create the political system. The military ousted not only a ruler, but also the constitution and system of government which he had instituted. General Zia installed a new system personally tailored for himself. With his demise, it is unlikely this system will be retained intact, but the military will have the predominant role in deciding what the new system will be.

The military and the civil bureaucracy formed a de facto alliance under President Zia. This alliance largely unravelled during the first few months of Ershad's martial law. The military's contention that the takeover was necessitated by rampant corruption and a general failure of the government to work efficiently was directed in part against the bureaucracy. Martial law regime actions since, including the transfer and dismissal of senior civil servants and the trial on corruption charges of a few, have not instilled a sense of confidence in the bureaucracy.

Is this a temporary aberration? Will the military find that it needs the bureaucracy so that the state can function? The Bangladesh military officers corps, stretched thin even before the takeover, will be hard-pressed to take on the administration of the state. It seems likely, therefore, that the military and the civilian bureaucracy will reach an accommodation but it is not possible to predict how long this will take.

Among the civilian populace, there is resignation about the military's involvement in politics. There was almost no opposition expressed to Ershad's dismissal of President Sattar, despite his winning 66 percent of the vote just a few months previously. This does not indicate approval of the military actions but a recognition that there was nowhere else to turn. There seems to be considerable resentment among civilians against past indiscipline within the military and the costs this had imposed on Bangladesh, seen perhaps most clearly at the time of President Zia's assassination. Without credible opposition, however, the military is not likely to face a sustained civilian movement to force it back to the barracks.

One of the stated major reasons for the military takeover was that development had slowed down, if not stopped, in this underdeveloped country. The military promised that this would be reversed and it announced a number of immediate steps. Besides the need for greater government efficiency, they focussed on denationalizing the economy and on increasing the role of private enterprise, both domestic and foreign. These goals may conflict with the military's desire to bring "order into national affairs" and what appears to be a desire to turn Bangladesh into a "command" society. The problem is illustrated by the pharmaceuticals policy announced by the government in the early 1980s. When a new dedication to free enterprise and a new openness to foreign investment were being announced, the new drug policy cut substantially the number of drugs which the multinational pharmaceutical companies were allowed to manufacture, which they claim will substantially reduce their ability to make a profit. The military made some decisions which would have been difficult for a civilian government, as seen in the stringent fiscal budget announced in July 1982.[16]

The decisionmaking process at this time is unclear, and beset by the same uncertainties. If civil servants are to be left out of the process, who will provide the expertise to make formal decisions? The pharmaceuticals policy was apparently decided and announced without any consultations with the drug manufacturers. The military's desire to impose order is apparent, even when this flies in the face of reality.

It is also not clear how the military reaches its conclusions on matters affecting society. Although Ershad is clearly in charge, he depends on the goodwill of his fellow generals and, indeed, of the army in general. There is presumably some sort of consultative mechanism by which their views are ascertained. How far down does this mechanism reach? It probably reaches beyond the generals, at least to the midlevel officers who led the first coup of 1975, and perhaps to the senior enlisted ranks, which led the last 1973 coup and the abortive 1977 revolt. The system will almost certainly be modified as Bangladesh's leaders deal with the technical questions of running a modern nation-state.

Bangladesh's foreign policy is largely determined by external circumstances, and the military has little room for maneuver. India is the predominant focus of Bangladeshi foreign policy. Any government must deal with ongoing disputes with the Indians from a position of considerable inferiority. No government can afford to antagonize the Indians too directly. Within these limits, the military, with its increasingly "Bengali" posture, will move Bangladesh to increase ties with the Islamic states. Indeed, General Ershad's first visit after taking power was to Saudi Arabia. Ties with Pakistan will probably improve slightly, as will those with the US and the PRC.

It could be argued that the armed forces have enhanced Bangladesh's stability. In 1975 the country was turning toward an authoritarian one-party state and was slipping economically. To a lesser extent, the administration in 1982 was corrupt and unable to deal with the country's pressing problems, as a potentially disastrous food shortage threatened. But this is not the complete picture. While the military may have been justified in overthrowing an increasingly despotic Sheikh Mujib, it could not justify killing him and his family members, and several months later, several of his party colleagues. There can be no justification for the assassination of President Zia by a disgruntled general—or for the latter's murder by enraged enlisted men. The history of Bangladesh since 1975 is one of intermittent instability within the military, leading to general instability in the society. This severely hampers the ability of the government to deal with the nation's pressing problems. Even President Zia, with immense personal popularity, had to constantly look over his shoulder for possible rivals. In such an environment a government can hardly be expected to function well. Not only is the rational planning and decisionmaking process constantly interrupted, but each leader must live with the fear that he may be suddenly removed from office. This is hardly a recipe for domestic stability. Nor does it contribute favorably to Bangladesh's reputation in the international community. Already well known for its economic problems, Bangladesh is burdened with the image of a country whose government cannot provide continuity.

### Future Role of the Military and Government

It should be clear that the role of the military in Bangladesh is in many respects *sui generis*, and does not fit easily into any general typology. The classical third world "praetorian" coup, in which the military acts to replace an ineffectual civilian administration and focusses on development as an issue has been approached only by the latest military takeover. The earlier takeovers were more *ad hoc*, based often on personal grievances and ambitions. There was little of the defense of the "army as a corporate institution" which Perlmutter sees as typical of praetorian coups. Ershad's takeover showed some aspects of the praetorian model. He moved against an ineffective regime which was unable to guide the state towards modernization, and focussed after the takeover on the alleged corruption of the regime. The coup did not meet one of Perlmutter's conditions, however. While the Sattar regime was demonstrably ineffective, it was not weak. Sattar had just won a free election by a landslide margin, one of the chief paradoxes of Bangladesh.[17]

One can also see aspects of Perlmutter's "revolutionary" soldier in the Bangladesh military. The JSD, which had a strong influence in the military, fits this category. Anticorporate in mentality, opposed to exclusivity of the armed forces, it wished to bring about mass mobilization and the breakdown of class barriers. Ershad's takeover presents aspects of both these types. While strongly protective of the army as a corporate institution, Ershad emphasized that the army must work with the people and must become involved in "nation building" efforts. This is a difficult task, however. As in other South Asian countries, the Bangladesh military has a corporate identity which goes beyond that normally found in the military. It is based not simply on professionalism or a code of duty and behavior but also on privileges reserved for the military. Thus, the Bangladesh military has its own hospitals, its own farms which grow food for its men, and foundations to look after them when they are retired. In a resource-scarce country these are perquisites which will not be lightly given up. Accordingly, the transformation into a "peoples' military" will be difficult.

It is not clear to what extent the military has purged itself of dissension and become a unified force. The split between freedom fighters and returnees seems settled, as the freedom fighters now comprise, at least in the officer corps, only a small percentage. It is more difficult to assess the continuing influence of the radical JSD. It seems to have been reduced, yet this has not assured stability within the military. By taking over on the grounds of fighting corruption and increasing efficiency, General Ershad left himself open to criticism if he is unable to do so. Younger officers, impatient at the slow progress, may demand more stringent measures, more radical solutions. Given Bangladesh's almost intractable economic problems, progress will inevitably be slow. The potential for a future coup will continue, particularly as the post-1971 generations of officers comes into power. For these soldiers, the disputes between freedom fighters and returnees, the arguments of the JSD, etc., carry little appeal. They will presumably be loyal to the army as a corporate structure and impatient with inefficient government.

While the makeup of the military is uncertain, it is clear that it is now in politics to stay. Ershad has made it clear that the military will demand an institutionalized role in whatever form of government evolves in Bangladesh. In addition, since the Bangladesh military does not have a clear external role, it will be disposed in this direction. Some type of civilian government will almost certainly be installed, however. If for no other reason, Bangladesh is totally dependent on aid from the Western nations, particularly Japan and the US, which are likely to look with disfavor upon continued direct military rule.

## Notes

1. For a general description of the events leading up to Bangladesh's independence, see Robert LaPorte, Jr., "Pakistan in 1971: The Disintegration of a Nation," *Asian Survey* (February 1972) pp. 97–108.
2. See Subrata Roy Chowdhury, *The Genesis of Bangladesh* (New York: Asia Publishing House, 1972), p. 10, and *Area Handbook for Bangladesh* (US Government Printing Office, 1972), pp. 276–82.
3. P. B. Sinha, *Armed Forces of Bangladesh* (New Delhi: The Institute for Defense Studies and Analyses, 1979), pp. 2–6.
4. Sinha, p. 9.
5. Talukder Maniruzzaman, "Bangladesh: An Unfinished Revolution," *Journal of Asian Studies* (August 1975), pp. 891–911.
6. For instance, by Sinha.
7. The challenges to Zia from left and right and his response are detailed in Talukder Maniruzzaman, "Bangladesh in 1976: Struggle for Survival as an Independent State," *Asian Survey* (February 1977), pp. 194–97.
8. M. Rashiduzzaman, "Bangladesh in 1977: Dilemmas of the Military Rulers," *Asian Survey* (February 1978), pp. 130–31.
9. Zillur R. Khan, "Bangladesh in 1981: Change, Stability and Leadership," *Asian Survey* (February 1982), pp. 163–70.
10. As quoted in the Foreign Broadcast Information Service report of March 25, 1982.
11. *Bangladesh Observer*, December 9, 1981.
12. As quoted in the Foreign Broadcast Information Service report of March 25, 1982.
13. Reports on the martial law regime's reform measures may be found in the *Far Eastern Economic Review*, issues of April 2–8, p. 22; April 16–22, pp. 20–22; May 7–13, p. 35; July 2–8, p. 27.
14. Data on the strength of the Bangladesh armed forces may be found in the yearly issues of *The Military Balance* (London: International Institute of Strategic Studies), and in Sinha.
15. *New York Times*, March 11, 1982.
16. *Far Eastern Economic Review*, July 9–15, pp. 66–68.
17. Amos Perlmutter *The Military and Politics in Modern Times* (New Haven: Yale University Press, 1977).

# 16

## The Military and Politics in Afghanistan: Before and After the Revolution

*Ralph H. Magnus*

Both before and after the communist coup d'etat of April 1978 in Afghanistan the military formed a microcosm of Afghan society. It mirrored the faults and virtues of that society, whose study may provide us with valuable insights into the initial success of the communists in seizing power in Kabul, as well as their subsequent inability to consolidate that power nationwide. The disintegration of the Afghan military forces was so extensive that in less than two years communist political power could be sustained only by the massive intervention of the Soviet Union. Subsequently, despite Soviet and Afghan communist efforts, the lack of substantial progress in rebuilding the Afghan armed forces along communist lines as a basis of local political power remains perhaps the Achilles Heel vitiating military, political, and diplomatic efforts to sustain a communist regime without massive direct Soviet military support.

The first part of this study will examine the status and the tradition of the military in Afghan society and history. Our analysis will focus on the paradox of a highly warlike society almost totally lacking in organized military force, even to the limited extent that traditional Asian armies could be called organized forces.

The second section examines the creation of the modern Afghan military in the twenty-five years preceeding the coup of 1978. Here the paradoxes and ironies abound. Central, however, is the not uncommon pattern of military-political development of many Asian countries: through their endeavors to strengthen both internal stability and international status, ruling elites create modern military forces without simultaneously developing equally their social and political bases. The all-too-common result is that the ruling elite falls victim to its own creation. Of special interest is the irony that the creator and victim of this process in Afghanistan was Sardar (Prince) Mohammad Da'ud but even greater attention should be accorded the Soviet Union and the explanation of why the coup April 1978 was indeed a communist coup.

The final section seeks explanations for the rapid and almost total disintegration of the Afghan military under communist rule. This happened despite desperate Soviet efforts to reconstitute the Afghan military as an effective and loyal basis of communist political power, first through aid and advisers and later by the assumption of direct control and the burden of combatting the Afghan people's war of national liberation.

Finally, we examine both the theoretical and policy implications of the Afghan case. These implications, it will be shown, are interesting and important both in the Afghan context and for broader considerations relevant to the politics of the Third World and the security of the United States.

## The Afghan Military Tradition: A Dubious Legacy

The very name Pakhtun spells honour and glory,
Lacking that honour what is the Afghan story?
                                     Khushhal Khan Katak (1613–89)[1]

The Afghans are a people steeped in an heroic military tradition. Indeed, the martial valour of the Afghan warrior is proverbial in his own country and amongst his Asian neighbors. It was the Afghans who maintained their freedom against the armies of the Moghul Empire and ended the dynasty of the Safavids, the most glorious of all Iranian Islamic dynasties in 1722; and it was they who overthrew the victorious Hindu Mahrattas, conquerors of the Moghuls, at Panipat in 1761. The acme of Afghan military prowess, however, at least until their current struggle against the Soviet Union, was their relative success in three wars against the British at the height of their expansionist glory from 1838 to 1919. From these victories the Afghans felt they had gained the right to boast that they alone, of all Islamic nations, had never submitted to occupation or subservience to the European infidels.

Khushhal Khan Katak, the archtypical Afghan hero, warrior chief and national poet, knew full well the reverse of the Afghan warrior tradition, which he expressed again in his poetry:

No great deed will be wrought by the Pathans,
Heaven ordains that petty should be their achievement;
I seek to set them straight, they straighten not.
Crooked is the vision of the ill-intentioned.[2]

Overweening pride and independence made it virtually impossible for the Afghans to cooperate for long in any common military or political endeavour. The martial strength of the Afghan nation has thus been likened to a naturally tough and fearless tribal warrior who barely tolerates the leadership of his own elected tribal khans in a *lashkar* (tribal militia) to fight in some brief and furious offensive trust, or to carry out on his home ground superb mountain guerrilla warfare. Tribal wars "have been characterized by their blizkrieg nature, by their swift irresistable penetration and by the rapid, inevitable disintegration of the *lashkar*. Often the Pukhtun warrior will simply pack up and leave after a hard day's fighting without coordiantion with, or command from, the lashkar."[3]

As one might imagine, this martial tradition made most difficult the position of an Afghan ruler. From Ahmad Shad Durrani, founder of the Afghan Empire in 1747 to Barak Karmal today, the central authorities have had to rule one of the most turbulent and well-armed populations on earth, and yet their own regular army suffers from the traditional lack of discipline and from the divisiveness of many ethnic, linguistic, and religious minorities. From the mid-eighteenth century onward, two fundamental strategies were attempted. The first was to create at least the nucleus of a regular military force to provide royal control, often formed around a foreign contingent or a national minority. The Persian *Kizilbash,* backbone of the victorious Safavid armies, were imported by both Ahmad Shah and his son Timur Shah. As Persians and Shi'ites in a hostile environment, they could be relied on to be loyal to the throne.[4] But these forces, from 2,000 to 10,000 strong, were not sufficient for a major campaign. For a real war, the rulers had to rely on their own tribes and the *lashkars* of other tribes serving under their own leaders and kept in the field largely by the lure of loot and grants of lands in conquered territory. For internal security, the ruler had little choice but to rely on political skills of persuasion, conciliation, and the disunity of his potential opponents since he lacked both the authority and the financial means to create a standing army.

## Nineteenth Century Military Reforms

Amir Dost Mohammad (1826–38, 1842–63) was the first ruler to obtain military advice systematically from Europeans. He eagerly quizzed foreign visitors on conscription as well as technical matters. A colorful array of British, French, Persians, Indian Muslims and even American adventurers served in his forces and rose to high rank.[5]

These efforts were followed by even more ambitious attempts in the reign of his son, Amir Sher Ali (1869–79). European military manuals were translated into Pushtu and guns were reproduced in Kabul workshops. The first substantial foreign military aid was received from the

British in 1869, consisting of rifles, artillery pieces, and 1.2 million rupees. The regular army was increased to 37,000 infantry and 6,400 cavalry, or four times his father's forces.[6]

These regular forces, however, were not effective. There was not enough money in the treasury to meet the payroll; promotion and command depended on tribal and personal ties, and there was no system of military education for officers. It was the universal opinion of foreign officers that although good individual soldiers the Afghan military lacked the training, equipment, and leadership to be effective against a modern army. The real strength of the Afghans in war rested in the formidable terrain and in the masses of tribal warriors. Fighting on their own ground, Afghan tribesmen could overwhelm even the best of regular troops. The real problems of a European army fighting the Afghans began only after the "war" against the Afghan regulars was over, as was clearly demonstrated in both the First (1838–42) and Second (1878–80) Anglo-Afghan Wars. In each case, after defeating the Afghan armies, occupying the capital and deposing the amir, the British were forced by a nation-wide tribal uprising and the prospect of an endless guerrilla war to cut their losses and withdraw with the best political settlement they could obtain. In 1842 this restored the very amir they had deposed, and in 1880 they recognized the deposed amir's nephew, Abdur Rahman, who had spent the last decade in exile under Russian protection.[7]

These successes of the old Afghan tribal military tradition served as a powerful reinforcement for the morale of the traditional forces. The Afghan people had saved the nation and ousted the foreign invader after the regular military forces had collapsed and after some members of the royal family had been willing to accept the status of puppet ruler under the British.

Amir Abdur Rahman (1880–1901) was the creator of the modern Afghan state. He began, once again, by rebuilding the military base of his power. Although precise figures from the end of the reign are lacking when the forces were largest, the regular army came close to 100,000 in 1900.[8] The military forces was still mixed; a tribal militia was recruited by a conscription system enlisting one out of every eight males as a reserve; feudal cavalry units served as part of the regular army and in major campaigns tribal *lashkars* were called up to serve under their own *khans*, on a paid basis. Both the regulars and the reserves were entitled to 80% of the loot from a successful campaign.

Tribal divisions still weakened the army, but such was the justifiable fear of "The Iron Amir" that the army served as an effective force in supressing tribal independence and unifying the country under the rule of Kabul. The ruler made great efforts to develop Afghan nationalism on the basis that the Afghans were the last free Muslim nation, who had to defend their independence and honor against the unbelievers threatening them on every side. However, even as he wrote his own anti-infidel propaganda pamphlets, the Amir received a regular subsidy (100,000 rupees monthly from 1883 to 1893 and 150,000 from 1893 until his death) from the British government in India. Besides some special grants and gifts of supplies, the total cash payments over the twenty year reign amounted to 28.5 million rupees.[9]

Amir Abdur Rahman was careful to keep this aspect of his policy a secret from his own people. He adamantly refused to accept foreign military advisers, even though he had a number of foreigners including some Britons in his employ in other capacities. While receiving British subsidies and agreeing to be guided in his foreign relations by British advice, he refused to allow a British ambassador or agent to reside in Kabul. Instead, he accepted a single Muslim officer in the British service as an official representative whose movements were closely watched and restricted as if he were an enemy spy instead of an allied ambassador.[10]

The effects of Abdur Rahman's military reforms were mixed. By refusing to accept foreign training he severely limited the professional effectiveness of the army. Only a few officers had any formal military training or education, mostly in British India. It was not until 1904 that his son and successor, Amir Habibullah, established a Royal Military College, which in 1907 was put under a Turkish colonel. This established a tradition of Turkish military aid which continued down to the 1960s. The favoritism shown to the Durranis (the tribe of the ruler) in command positions and even in pay aroused the antagonism of other officers.[11] However, in the eyes of the ruler the army was probably effective enough for its major function, that of internal security. When Abdur Rahman's army was tested once again in battle against a modern foe (under his grandson, Amir Amanullah, in the Third Anglo-Afghan War (1919) it was once more shown to be effective more as a nucleus for a tribal army than as a regular military force.[12]

King Amanullah (1919-29) had been educated in the new military college and continued his grandfather's and father's military program. However, the military was not his highest priority, and as with many of his ambitious programs, his changes tended to be disruptive and inefficient. There was a major clash between the Afghan officers, led by Marshal Mohammad Nadir Khan, and the Turkish advisers, who wished to install a Turkish recruitment system, which resulted in Nadir's transfer to diplomatic exile in France. If the final test of an army can come only in battle, it is obvious that Amanullah's army failed miserably. When faced with a tribal rebellion inflamed by religious propaganda in 1928-29, the army and the entire apparatus of the centralized monarchy, created fifty years before by Abdur Rahman, collapsed; the troops deserted in droves and turned over their arms and forts to the enemy.[13]

## The Musahiban Monarchy to 1953

The sight of a Tajik bandit, Bacha-i-Saqao (who gave himself the title of Amir Habibullah Ghazi), on the throne of Kabul was more than any Pushtun could accept, including those who had rebelled against King Amanullah. When Nadir Khan returned from France and went to the border region, he was able to raise a large tribal *lashkar,* most of whom actually came from the Mahsud and Wazir tribes on the "British" side of the Durand Line. Following the reconquest of Kabul, he was forced to allow these tribesmen to loot the city, in lieu of monetary payments he could not provide. Within a few years the same tribes were back attacking the capital again, and it took the entire regular army to repel them.

Nadir Shah (1929–33), as an exiled young Afghan prince, had been educated in British military schools in India during Abdur Rahman's reign. With Habibullah's reign, he and his family, the Musahiban, returned to Afghanistan and served loyally in the armies of Habibullah and Amanullah, rising to the position of commander-in-chief and proving himself the ablest of the Afghan commanders in the Third Anglo-Afghan War. Following 1929, he and his four brothers worked tirelessly to rebuild the shattered Afghan army and state, which had been virtually destroyed in 1928–29. For a generation, however, they had to face the tribal forces which had deposed the Durrani monarchy and then had restored them to the throne. The tribal leaders never ceased to remind them of this.

Nadir accepted foreign loans and equipment offered by the British, Germans, and French. The Turkish mission was reestablished and a new military preparatory school was established for the children of tribal khans. The Musahiban family, ruling as a collective royal family from 1929 to 1953, felt that the only possible military policy was a slow and gradual buildup of the regular army to avoid giving offense to the khans and the conservative religious leaders who had opposed Amanullah's reforms. Thus, although military service was supposed to be universal, it was not enforced in the Pushtun tribal areas. Internationally, they strove to establish good relations with all their neighbors, especially with the Soviet Union and Great Britain. The *basmachis,* who were still fighting the Soviets in their Central Asian homelands from bases in Afghanistan, were removed south of the Hindu Kush. On the frontier with India the Afghan government gave no help or encouragement to anti-British movements, such as the old tribal uprisings or the new Pushtun nationalist movement of the *Khoda-i-Khidmatgara* (Servants of God), organized by Adbul Ghaffar Khan and associated with the Indian Congress.[14]

The foreign and domestic policies of Afghanistan remained unchanged until after World War II and the British withdrawal from the subcontinent. In the 1946-55 period, under the Musahiban rulers, there was a profound shift, amounting to domestic and foreign policy revolutions. Sardar Hashim Khan, prime minister and virtual dictator following the assassination of his brother Nadir Shah in 1933, resigned for reasons of health in 1946, and was replaced by his brother Shah Mahmud Khan Ghazi, former Minister of War. Shah Mahmud felt it was time to adopt a more liberal and relaxed position by allowing the political participation of the embryonic intellectual and educated middle class elements, who had been under suspicion for years as potential supporters of a restoration of Amanullah—in exile in Rome. Greater economic development was necessary and, due to the restrictions enforced by the war, Afghanistan had built up a considerable surplus of capital.

The most profound change was the British withdrawal since, in a larger sense, modern Afghanistan had been the product of a balance of power between the British and Russian empires. The establishment of Pakistan, including the frontier tribal areas of the Pushtuns, was considered by Afghans as a betrayal both of their interests and treaties with the British, as well as the new principles of self-determination. Lacking military force, Afghanistan confined its protests to the diplomatic front, especially in the United Nations. Even more important than the "Pushtunistan Question," however, was the need for a protector to replace Britain's balancing role against Soviet power. Shah Mahmud's policy was to court the United States for this honor, while endeavouring not to antagonize the Soviets. In this initial postwar phase the battle lines of the Cold War had yet to harden in Asia.

In virtually all areas the policies of Shah Mahmud were a failure, though certainly not entirely his fault. Afghan opposition to Pakistan succeeded only in antagonizing both Pakistan and the United States. On the other hand, the appeal for close political and economic relations with the United States only antagonized the Soviets and yielded little results. The Americans felt in any case that Afghanistan was too close to the Soviet Union and too far from American support to be included within the protective umbrella of the United States, and that any attempt to do so would only antagonize a more valuable ally, Pakistan.[15] Domestically, freely contested elections, a free press, and political expression by students backfired when the opposition leaders (including Babrak Karmal and Nur Mohammad Taraki) attacked the royal family and the traditional system of privileges for the wealthy, influential tribal, political, and economic leaders.

## Sardar Da'ud's New Model Army: 1953-78

In 1953 Sardar Mohammad Da'ud Khan, a professionally educated general and provincial governor, a contemporary of his cousin Zahir Shah (r. 1933-73), staged a bloodless palace coup to force the retirement of his uncle, Shah Mahmud. As prime minister from 1953 to 1963, and again as the first president of the republic from 1973 to 1978, Da'ud Khan was a strong autocrat, patriot, and modernizer. He felt that modernization could succeed only through a rapid shock treatment which would overcome both the fears of reactionaries and distractions of liberal competitive politics. As a military man he also knew that he needed a much stronger military base to accomplish his goal. This would form the basis for economic and social modernization, which in turn would allow for genuine political modernization, a not uncommon sequence for military modernizers in Afghanistan and elsewhere.

The boldness of Sardar Da'ud's program lay not in its conception but in its execution. He saw that the only way to modernize Afghanistan was to start with the army, but to do this effectively required massive foreign aid. This demanded a fundamental change in foreign policy.

He could have turned for this aid to Pakistan, a neighboring Muslim nation with an efficient modern army, reaching out for friends in the Muslim world. But this was politically impossible. There was a genuine feeling that the Afghans felt for their Pushtun brethren who, in their eyes, had been denied their right to self-determination in 1947. Certainly, the Afghan rulers feared as well a comparison of their backward development and traditional regime to the relative advancement and political freedom of Pakistan (this was before Pakistani military rule). Most important, however, was that Pakistan had to fulfill the function of the enemy against whom military modernization and the entry of foreign military missions was supposed to be directed. The Pushtun tribes had no interest in increasing the power of the rulers of Kabul, but they might be willing if they could be convinced that it was necessary to uphold the honor of the Pushtuns.

Turkey and Iran, as regional Muslim neighbors, might have been acceptable. Turkey, indeed, continued its traditional military connection of providing advisers and some training for Afghans in Turkey. But Turkey was far away, had just entered into a close alliance with the United States and, at American urging, had signed a defensive alliance with Pakistan in 1954. Emerging from the turmoil of the Mossadegh era, Iran was scarcely a viable choice, even if the Afghans could overcome their traditional hatred and contempt for the Iranians (a feeling fully reciprocated by the Iranians).

India was another intriguing possibility. But aside from the practical problems of getting substantial aid across Pakistan, there was the traditional antagonism between Hindus and Muslims. This had been exacerbated by the events of the Indian partition and the participation of Pushtun tribes in the fighting in Kashmir.[16] Any program which would employ only Indian Muslims as advisers would run into problems from the Indian side due to their secular constitution.

Sardar Da'ud first attempted to renew his uncle's approach to the Americans but he felt rebuffed and humiliated when it was revealed that the Americans had reported this fully to the Pakistanis.[17] Besides being rejected by the other side, an American connection would force Afghanistan into impossible concessions on the Pushtunistan question. Almost by a process of elimination, he was forced to turn to the Soviets.

Despite the obvious dangers of inviting a great power neighbor, dangers of which the Afghan royal family and elite were well aware, there were some advantages as well. It would aid in disarming the leftist, anti-Musahiban opposition, which had always exaggerated the ties of Amanullah to the Soviets and those of the Musahibans to the British. Soviet aid would be easy and rapid in its delivery and Pakistan could not interfere. There were many Soviet Central Asians who spoke languages understood in Afghanistan (though few spoke Pushtu). Despite their genuine sympathy for fellow Muslims who had lost their independence to Russian rule and their dislike of "Godless Communism," there was a certain grudging admiration for the economic and social progress achieved in Central Asia under Soviet rule. Internationally, Soviet political support might someday prove valuable in achieving Afghan objectives in Pushtunistan. Since the Americans had joined with Pakistan, only Soviet support could possibly counter American opposition. Finally, the dangers of Soviet subversion could be handled by the Afghan security services, aided by the popular distrust of foreigners and especially of Russian communists. On a more political plane, it was felt that the Soviet's own self-interest would restrain them from subversion. The post-Stalin Soviet leadership were obviously seeking a "demonstration project" to help them overcome the effects of Stalinism in the countries of the yet-to-be-named "third world." What better proof could the Soviets offer than disinterested aid to a poor, backward and autocratically ruled Muslim neighbor?

In the end Sardar Da'ud's personality was the decisive factor in Afghanistan's turn to the Soviets in the mid-1950s. He was supremely self-confident, and felt that he could outsmart the Russians on his own ground. The goal of a modern, unified and progressive Afghanistan was worth the risk. Using the Pushtunistan issue as the key, he persuaded the traditional forces of Afghanistan in a *Loya Jirgah,* the traditional great council of the kingdom called on special occasions by the monarch, of the wisdom of accepting Soviet military aid and advisers.[18]

Sardar Da'uds argument to the *Loya Jirgah* of November 1955 was that Pakistan's alliance with the United States had changed the balance of power in the region, and it was thus necessary for Afghanistan to redress the imbalance. It was obvious that this would mean an approach to the Soviet Union. A month later, Soviet Premier Nikolai A. Bulganin and Party Chairman Nikita S. Krushchev concluded their Asian tour with a visit to Kabul. There they announced an economic aid credit of $100 million, and support for the Afghan position on Pushtunistan.[19] In August 1956 the first military aid package was signed for $25 million.[20]

There is no doubt that the military aid increased the capabilities of the Afghan military, particularly the air force, armor, and artillery. Although their numbers varied, probably some 1,500 military advisers were present during the next two decades. Training in the USSR was provided for about a quarter of the officer corps. The practical value of this force was soon demonstrated when Sardar Da'ud announced in August 1959 that the government would no longer enforce the custom of veiling women. This, and the imposition of new taxes on the Durrani tribe in Kandahar, resulted in a violent uprising, which was suppressed in a few days by elite troops sent from Kabul.[21] Attempts to employ these forces in the Pushtunistan dispute were much less successful and, in fact, harmed Afghanistan and Sardar Da'ud's position as they resulted in the closure of the border to trade.

The military still exhibited some glaring weaknesses which were to become evident in the coups of 1973 and 1978, and especially in the post-1978 collapse of the military. Given the socioeconomic structure of Afghanistan, particularly its dismal educational level, the new model army could scarcely be called a modern force. There was a huge gap between the officer corps and the conscripts, serving a two year enlistment, who made up the bulk of the military. The latter were overwhelmingly illiterate and poorly trained, if trained at all. The conscripts were not representative of the entire population, as the Pushtuns continued to avoid conscription, which they considered a particularly onerous form of taxation. The majority of the ranks were thus Hazaras, Tajiks, Uzbeks and other nonPushtun minorities. Conversely, the majority of the officers were Pushtuns, reasonably well educated in the military schools and academies. Certain elite units, including the Guards Brigade, the armor, and the air force, were exceptions. During the liberal constitution period (1963–73), when Sardar Da'ud was in retirement and the king was attempting to create a constitutional monarchy, a serious effort was made to enforce conscription on the educated elite of Kabul, who had the same attitude towards military service as did the Pushtun tribesmen, and the same political influence to avoid it. This only served to spread the discontent of the Kabul elite to a wider audience in the military.[22]

It is not clear what the impact of discontent in the lower ranks played in the coups. In neither case was there much effort made to spread revolutionary propaganda to the ranks; units seemed to follow the orders they received from their officers, whether these were for the coup or against it. Numerous eyewitness reports of highly pleased soldiers on the streets after the coups of 1973 and 1978, however, might well have reflected a generalized popular discontent of the ordinary citizen with his treatment by society in general and the military in particular. Certainly, there did not seem to have been any groundswell of loyalty towards the king or the royal family.

The key to understanding the coups of 1973, which returned Sardar Da'ud to power as president of a republican government, and 1978, which installed a communist regime, is the officer corps. This was overwhelmingly Pushtun, but it was a basic fact of Afghan social structure that not all Pushtuns were equal, though in general they were the most privileged ethnic group. The informal social controls favoring the Durrani tribe and even the Mohammadzai subtribe of the royal family were the tightest. Thus, the rural, tribal young Pushtuns of nonelite status who entered a military career promising an honorable and ultimately elite status in the national leadership, eventually found their road to promotion and choice assignments blocked by the old inner elite of Pushtuns with close connections to the royal family.

Yet it was from just this group rural Pushtun junior officers that most candidates for training in the Soviet Union were selected. It was felt they were better suited to resist the temptations of communism than were officers from urban areas or from minority ethnic backgrounds.[23] Some, at least, of these returned as communist sympathizers and even as Soviet agents. They shared the general discontent of the younger generation of the educated Afghan elite to which they belonged. Their rural background and poor primary education did not qualify them for admission to Kabul University or for foreign study, which served as the major recruiting grounds for membership in the civilian political and economic elite. When they arrived in the capital, they sooner or later found that the choice positions had already been taken by those officers who had the right tribal or personal connections to the inner elite, just as did their civilian counterparts. It was from these young men, both military and civilians, that Hafizullah Amin, an educator and administrator from a rural Pushtun background and a nonelite tribe, the Kharot subtribe of the Ghilzai, could recruit for the communist *Khalq* (People's) party.

Even within the inner elites of the officer corps there were serious divisions hampering efficiency and loyalty. Factions were formed around members of the royal family, including Sardar Da'ud, Sardar Abdul Wali (the commander of Central Forces, Kabul), and their cousin, the King. Finally, during the constitutional liberal period from 1963 to 1973 in which both open and clandestine political activity was tolerated, when the King forced Sardar Da'ud into retirement, some factions grew to support various civilian politicians. These factions included that of former prime minister Mohammad Hashim Maiwandwal, as well as those of the two communist factions of the *Parcham* (Banner) and *Khalq* wings. Colonel Abdul Qader, the key officer in the coups of 1973 and 1978 had been a member of the *Khalq* party prior to its split and since then had generally been considered a *Parchami*.

## The Coups of 1973 and 1978

The coup of Sardar Da'ud in July 1973 was made in cooperation with the *Parchamis*. Such was the prestige of Sardar Da'ud and the hope that his decisive leadership could overcome the stagnation into which the constitutional experiment had fallen, that the coup was virtually unopposed. The modern educated elite, military and civilians alike, hoped that Afghanistan could return to the path of progressive national development. On the other hand, as a prominent member of the royal family, President Mohammad Da'ud reassured the conservatives that the new republic would not go too far towards communism. The *Parcham* was the communist faction most closely identified with the Kabul intellectuals, as well as with the Soviet Union.[24] The communist party, which had been founded by Nur Mohammed Taraki in 1965 as the *Khalq* (People's Democratic Party of Afghanistan), had split in 1967 with two factions—the *Khalq* and the *Parcham*. There were several other communist factions as well. The *Khalq* refused to support Sardar Da'ud's coup in 1973, feeling that this was not a genuine revolution and that Da'ud would betray his leftist allies. The *Parcham*, under Babrak Karmal, and their Soviet masters clearly felt that they were not strong enough to take over, but by backing the popular and not anti-Soviet, Sardar Da'ud, they would be his logical successor, either peacefully or by other means.[25]

Once in power, however, the wily Sardar Da'ud, now president of the republic, outmaneuvered his less experienced communist allies, both in the army and in the civilian bureaucracy, and proceeded to establish his personal rule. But by ousting his cousin, King Mohammad Zahir,

Da'ud had taken a fatal step. The Afghan military has always lacked a truly national focus or ideology, and it was only their personal loyalty to the monarch that had held together the diverse factions of the officer corps. Sardar Da'ud's action broke this bond and the unity of the Musahiban family—its greatest source of strength for half a century. Once he had betrayed his oath, every other officer would feel less bound to his oath to President Da'ud.[26]

The communists were soon eased out of major posts and pushed into the background by president Da'ud's domestic and foreign policies. Domestically, he reestablished tight political control, banning political parties and newspapers, and calling a *Loya Jirgah* to approve a new republican constitution with a strong presidential leadership and a single party system. He brought back into advisory positions the former leaders of the constitutional period, including Mohammad Musa Shafiq, who had been prime minister at the time of the 1973 coup and was particularly close to the exiled king. Even more significantly, he released and allowed to go into exile his own bitter personal rival in the royal family, General Sardar Abdul Wali, who joined the exiled king in Rome. In foreign policy, he moved away from dependence on the Soviet Union and towards a neutral position based on the support of the oil states of the Persian Gulf. As a necessary price in Gulf aid, he was willing to defuse relations with Pakistan over Pushtunistan. Thus, after thirty years, President Da'ud reversed the major foreign policy objective he had advocated. This added another element of discontent to the Pushtun officer corps, as well as to the heavily Pushtun *Khalq* party.

Needless to say, these moves were not received with equanimity by the Soviets; in the summer of 1977 they moved to reunite the *Khalq* and *Parcham* factions and to plan for a coup. In the words of Babrak Karmal:

> Da'ud had begun negotiations with the Shah of Iran. He had forged close links with Saudi Arabia. His relations with the imperialist powers had been growing. We got the impression that he wanted to become the Anwar Sadat of Afghanistan. Even in internal matters he had begun to indulge in horrible oppressive measures. Things began to go beyond limits within a matter of two years. It became difficult to carry on with him. So both groups of our party—Parcham and Khalq—launched a campaign for unity. We began to oppose Da'ud. Both groups became united. *Russia wanted that there should be a revolution here.*[27] (Emphasis added).

Hafizullah Amin, number two in the *Khalq* and the man best acquainted with the discontented leftist Pushtuns in the officer corps, was given the specific task of organizing the contacts of the party with the military.

Although the actual sequence of events in the coup of April 1978 may have been improvised and, in the words of the leading American scholar of Afghanistan, "accidental," it was hardly an accidental coup in the larger sense. The development of Afghan society and specifically of the military, especially under Sardar Da'ud, as well as the interests and planning of the Soviet Union over the previous two decades, had truly created the conditions in which the communist coup of April 1978 was surely an event waiting to happen. Sardar Mohammad Da'ud Khan, first president of Afghanistan, met his fate at the hands of his own creation—the modern Afghan army.

## After the Revolution: Military Disintegration and Popular Resistance

We are strong enough to keep all antidemocratic and international forces, who could turn against our revolution in the name of religion or because they are paid by a foreign power, under control. We shall defeat them. The people will follow us out of conviction or out of fear of punishment. [28]
(Nur Mohammad Taraki)

In the perspective of Afghan history, the events since the communist coup of April 1978 have followed a fully predictable pattern and logic of their own. It is the Soviet actions which require explanation and are subject to a variety of interpretations.

It was predictable that the newly united PDPA would once again split into its basic *Khalq* and *Parcham* factions, and that a bloody struggle for supremacy would ensue. The two factions represented two very different social groups, which had never gotten along before and were rent by ideological and personal conflicts. It was also logical that the *Khalq* faction should emerge victorious for it was the larger faction, particularly so in the officer corps, as well as the most ruthless. This was contingent, however, on Soviet nonintervention, which held in 1978 but not in 1979.

It was natural as well that the *Khalqis* in power could clash with the Soviet Union, particularly over what they felt was Soviet preference for the *Parchamis*. Within the military, increased Soviet aid was accompanied by an increase in the numbers and scope of activities of Soviet advisers. In one sense, this was welcomed and necessary, since the armed forces were engaged in a growing guerrilla war with "counter-revolutionary bandits." Through purges, desertions and the uncertain loyalties of those who remained, the number of qualified *Khalqi* officers was limited. But these *Khalqi* officers were precisely those who were strong Pushtun nationalists, and it was particularly humiliating for them to accept advice or orders in their own country from foreigners. When the Soviets wished to take over Afghan bases for their own strategic interests, these feelings were intensified. Amin's rejection of this request might have been the straw that broke the camel's back of Soviet patience with the *Khalqis*.[29]

Also predictable was that the *Khalqis*, once they had eliminated the *Parchamis* from power, would embark on a program of rapid and rash social and economic reforms, completely disregarding the sensitivities of the overwhelmingly traditional Afghan people and their well-known capacity for armed resistance. Paradoxically, the *Khalq*, socially closer to the masses of the Afghan people than the urban elite *Parcham*, had a more unrealistic view of their position in Afghan society than did their former allies. Perhaps influenced by Taraki's background as a poet and novelist the *Khalq* had an unrealistic romantic view of the revolutionary future of Afghanistan. They felt that all opposition elements were the remnants of tiny feudal elites, which would be swept into the dustbin of history.[30] The *Parcham*, perhaps because of its closer contacts with the Soviets but due largely to their higher social status as part of the traditional Kabuli elite, had a much more realistic understanding of the difficulties faced by any Afghan reformer, much less a communist reformer. Consequently, they wished to pursue a gradualist, national front of progressive forces, strategy. This only served to confirm the *Khalqi* suspicion that the *Parchamis* were still the "royal communist party" of pinkish Kabuli elites, who were interested only in collaboration with the old regime, just as they had collaborated with President Da'ud in 1973–75.

Within the military, it was predictable that there would be a split along two major fissures. The first would be the internal split of the communists into *Parchamis* and *Khalqis*. Second, there was the larger split between communists and noncommunists. Since the higher ranks of the military, with very few exceptions, were overwhelmingly Durrani Pushtuns they were naturally purged. But the majority of the officer corps was neither communist nor actively anticommunist. They were just trying to do their duty, draw their salary and look forward to a peaceful retirement.[31] A moderate political program, along the lines advocated by the *Parcham*, probably would have kept the support of this silent majority. But the internal logic of the communist factions dictated an opposite direction. The bulk of the officer corps was lost, physically by desertion or joining the anti-regime fighters, or morally as they attempted to hold onto their positions while doing as little as possible. The failure of the officer corps thus hastened, if it did not cause, the disintegration of the military as a whole.

As military organization and authority fell apart, and the army was under the great strain of fighting against its own people, the role of the Soviet advisers inevitably increased. They took an active role in combat operations and in some cases commanded Afghan troops. Ordinary soldiers deserted in droves, usually carrying their weapons as tokens to the *mujahidin* that they had given up their allegiance to the government. (This Arabic word means "strugglers for the Islamic faith." It has been adopted by the Afghan anticommunist and anti-Soviet national resistance.)

The fragile national consensus built on traditional loyalties to a ruling dynasty for over two centuries and reinforced over the past century by a concerted effort to create a feeling of modern nationalism, was shattered. In its place were the always powerful primordial loyalties of ethnic identity, tribe, village, family and religion. Within a year the army had been reduced to less than half of its nominal strength; it was rapidly losing its war against the Afghan people.[32]

*The Soviet Invasion and After*

There are many explanations for the Soviet invasion of December 1979, but most fundamental was that the Afghan military, and consequently the communist regime in Kabul, was approaching inevitable defeat. As the government lost control of the countryside, it lost its recruiting base. In the fall of 1978, before armed opposition became nationwide, the annual draft could be brought in without too much resistance. But in the fall of 1979 the regime had lost control of the countryside and there were no replacements available for those soldiers due to be mustered out. The Soviets believed that the massive invasion would overawe the *mujahidin*, reunite the communist party and establish under Babrak Karmal and the *Parcham* a more conciliatory policy acceptable both to the people and to noncommunist political leaders.[33] Within a few months it would be possible to withdraw the bulk of the Soviet troops, keeping only some specialist units and an augmented advisory mission. The key strategic airbases would remain under Soviet control.

Instead, the Soviet invasion had exactly the reverse effect. It removed the last pretense that the regime was a truly national one, revealing the truth that it was communist and a puppet of the Soviet Union. This transformed a civil war into a war of national liberation against the foreigner, something which was clearly understood by all Afghans from their own history. The Afghan people refused to be overawed. The PDPA refused to be reunited, except in the most formal sense enforced by the Soviets. In fact, elements within what remained of the military, including even *Khalqi* officers, became more disaffected and secret or open supporters of the *mujahidin*. Party meetings and congresses broke out in open fights between the factions.[34]

Since the Soviet invasion the military dropped to a quarter of its nominal strength. Even these numbers could be maintained only by lowering the draft age to 19, by forced reenlistments and by press gangs. Such discontented men thus dragooned into uniform were more dangerous to their masters than to the enemy. This has been amply demonstrated by the Soviet decision not to entrust Afghan units with key positions, especially defense of the capital. Weapons supplies are also restricted in the well founded belief that these weapons would find their way to the *mujahidin*. Isolated Afghan military garrisons do not really control the surrounding countryside; instead the most common arrangement is an informal understanding with the local *mujahidin* that neither will bother the other.

The burden of fighting against the increasingly better armed and more coordinated (on the purely military plane) *mujahidin* thus falls on the Soviets, however much they might wish to avoid the role. This has been amply demonstrated in the Soviet offensives of 1982, beginning in Kandahar and continuing through Parwan, Paktia, the Panjshir Valley and Paghman.[35] Desperate efforts have been made to recruit individuals and tribes to support the government. With very few exceptions these have failed.[36] The Soviets have no faith in the Afghan regular forces and none of these has significantly changed the basic fact that the Karmal regime is totally dependent upon the Soviet forces, and will remain so. The ultimate irony of the events since the communist coup is that, after over a century of effort by the government to unify the Afghan nation largely by military means, it is only with the disintegration of the military and the rise of a vast, popular and disorganized war of national liberation that a genuine Afghan nation may now be in gestation—but at an incalculable price.

## Conclusions

The major conclusion for Afghanistan ended the previous section. The Afghan military had served as the main supporter of the traditional state. It was relatively effective as a basis of modernization and national development, but only so long as the government adopted programs not too far in advance of social conditions. The strains which developed within the modern officer corps mirrored those of the entire educated modern elite. Officially organized and dedicated to a rational-legal order, the modern bureaucrat had to face the reality of the system of traditional privilege and official favoritism. This was perhaps the principal cause of the overthrow of the old regime. These strains, rather than communist ideology or even the covert activities of Soviet agents (these should not be entirely discounted), led a minority of the officer corps to collaboration with communist politicians and towards military coups.

The closest parallel, to my mind, lies in the present condition of Saudi Arabia. Many of these same strains are evident within Saudi society and the Saudi military. The pattern of a two-stage revolution, beginning with discontented members of the royal family in cooperation with military factions, political opposition, and Soviet agents, seems to be the most likely scenario for a possible Saudi revolution.

If this fear or hope, as viewed from the perspectives of Washington and Moscow, is a justified cause of concern, the lesson of Afghanistan might well give pause to Moscow. It is difficult to see what strategic military gains or political advantages obtained in Afghanistan can justify the costs experienced thus far, not to mention the costs yet to come. The United States should be encouraged by the Soviet blunder, which might make them reconsider before committing themselves to the military support of unpopular communist regimes in the third world. More importantly, the United States should be encouraged to take advantage of the fact that the forces of local nationalism are still stronger than those of communism—even when the latter are backed by the armed might of the Soviet Union. However, were we giving the Afghan people the kind of aid and support that their sacrifice, and an appreciation of the national interest of the United States, would dictate, we would certainly be in a better position to rejoice, and even to benefit from it regionally and in global perspective.

## Notes

1. Olaf Caroe, *The Pathans 550 B.C.-A.D. 1957* (London and New York: Macmillan & Co., 1965), p. 238.

2. Ibid., p. 242.

3. Akbar S. Ahmad, "Tribes and States in Central and South Asia," *Asian Affairs, Journal of the Royal Society for Asian Affairs* IX (1980), p. 155.

4. Vartan Gregorian, *The Emergence of Modern Afghanistan, Politics of Reform and Modernization 1880-1946* (Stanford: Stanford University Press, 1969), pp. 49-50.

5. Ibid., pp. 75-76.

6. Ibid., pp. 87-88.

7. There is an extensive literature on the Anglo-Afghan wars of the nineteenth century. The first of these, 1838-42, has attracted more historical reexamination in this century, see J. A. Norris, *The First Afghan War, 1838-42* (Cambridge: Cambridge University Press, 1967). There is no comparable modern history for

the 1878-80 war. Both the works of Dupree and Gregorian, mentioned above, have full and excellent basic treatments of this period.

8. Hasan Kawun Kakar, *Government and Society in Afghanistan, The Reign of Amir 'Abd al-Rahman Khan* (Austin: The University of Texas Press, 1979), p. 99.

9. Ibid., pp. 89-90.

10. Ludwig W. Adamec, *Afghanistan 1900-1923, A Diplomatic History* (Berkeley and Los Angeles: University of California Press, 1967), pp. 20-4.

11. Kakar, *op. cit.*, p. 113.

12. For the Third Anglo-Afghan War see Lieut.-General G. N. Molesworth, *Afghanistan 1919* (New York: Asia Publishing House, 1962). For General Molesworth's assessment of the relative values of Afghan regular versus tribal troops, see especially pp. 121-22 and 172.

13. Leon B. Poullada, *Reform and Rebellion in Afghanistan, 1919-1929* (Ithaca, N. Y.: Cornell University Press, 1973), Chapter VIII.

14. This was the assessment of the British Minister in Kabul, see: Admaec, *op. cit.*, p. 201.

15. Leon B. Poullada, "Afghanistan and the United States: The Crucial Years," *The Middle East Journal,* 35 (1981), p. 190.

16. Ahmad, *op. cit.*, p. 164.

17. Poullada, "Afghanistan and the United States," p. 187.

18. George Lenczowski, *The Middle East in World Affairs*, fourth edition (Ithaca, N.Y.: Cornell University Press, 1980), p. 245.

19. Ibid.

20. Dupree, *op. cit.*, p. 522.

21. Louis Dupree, "The Political Use of Religion: Afghanistan," in Kalman H. Silvert, ed., *Churches and States: The Religious Institution and Modernization* (New York: American Universities Field Staff, 1967), pp. 203-6.

22. Babrak Karmal underwent his compulsory military service in 1958. Ved Prataap Vaidik, "Interview With Barak Karmal, We Take Orders From None," *New Delhi* (April 27-May 10, 1981), p. 27.

23. Interview, Mir Mohammad Siddiq Farhang, former deputy minister of planning, member of the Wolesi Jirga and economic advisor to Babrak Karmal in 1980, Washington, D. C., 1981.

24. One of the best expositions of the origins of the *Khalq-Parcham* split and its social basis is that of Alexandre Dastarac and M. Levant, "What Went Wrong in Afghanistan," *Merip Reports* 89 (1980), pp. 3. See also Anthony Arnold, *Afghanistan's Two-Party Communism, Parcham and Khalq* (Stanford: Hoover Institution Press, 1983), pp. 37-51.

25. Louis Dupree, *The New Republic of Afghanistan: The First Twenty-One Months,* Special Paper, The Afghanistan Council of the Asia Society (New York: The Asia Society, June 1976), pp. 5-8, discusses the *Parcham*-Da'ud Khan cooperation and later split. The two-stage revolutionary theory of the *Parcham* and the Soviets, using Sardar Da'ud as an intermediate stage, is advanced by Mr. Farhang.

26. President Mohammad Da'ud's nickname among the frontier Pakhtuns was "Crazy Da'ud," stemming from the fact that his ambitions had led him

to split the family unity of the Musahiban, which had kept them on the throne of Kabul for two generations.

27. Vaidik, *op. cit.*, p. 28.

28. *Foreign Broadcast Information Service, Middle East and North Africa Report* (4 June 1978), p. S-5.

29. This, reportedly, is the opinion of Amin's mistress, who is quoted as having told Anthony Mascarenhas: "Amin told me he would never agree to giving the Russians a military base in Afghanistan because the people would not tolerate it. He was very angry with the Russians but he also knew they would not give up easily because of the Iranian situation." Anthony Mascarenhas, "How Russia Got Sucked Into Total Invasion," *The Sunday Times* (London), December 12, 1980. This is reprinted in *The Afghanistan Council Newsletter* VIX (January 1981), p. 19.

30. Farhang Interview. See also Dastarac and Levant, p. 4, as well as numerous statements of the *Khalqi* leaders when in power as reported in *The Kabul Times*.

31. This is an opinion based upon conversations and communications with a number of individuals, particularly a private letter from an Afghan officer who escaped in November, 1981.

32. Nancy Peabody Newell and Richard S. Newell, *The Struggle for Afghanistan* (Ithaca and London: Cornell University Press, 1981), p. 106.

33. Farhang Interview.

34. The persistance of hostility between the two factions is clear from numerous reports. According to an AFP report, the Interior Minister, Golabzoy, interrupted Babrak Karmal's speech to the PDPA Party Congress in March 1982, and was supported by the majority of the delegates. The conference, which was promoted by the Soviets to achieve party unity, was forced to adjourn a day early, see: "Golabzoy Interrupts Karmal at PDPA Congress," *Foreign Broadcast Information Service, South Asia Report*, 25 March 1982, p. C-1.

35. Some of the best accounts of the recent fighting comes from the eyewitness reporting of Edward Girardet in *The Christian Science Monitor*. See especially "A Brush With the Soviets in Panjshir" of July 19, 1982 and "Afghan Resistance: Familiar Pattern" of July 26, 1982.

36. The usual method of recruitment is the press gang, see the AFP report "Troops Round Up Males for Second Draft," *Foreign Broadcast Information Service, South Asia Report*, 21 January 1982, p. C-1.

# PART FOUR
# Cross-Regional Analysis

# 17

# Regional Threat Environments in Asia: Problems of Aggregation

*Sheldon W. Simon*

To search for a single Asian security paradigm is a fruitless enterprise. The region is too vast and variegated; and although there may be commonalities between the effects on their respective neighbors of a Soviet-occupied Afghanistan and the Russian garrison force in Etorofu, differences in these security environments far outnumber similarities. Instead of a single Asia, then, the security analyst must seek links among subregional situations. Equally important, the analyst should be sensitive to unique features of tension areas—those which cannot be ascribed to the interests and activities of more distant Asian members. Assessing Asian security, then, is more than an exercise in aggregation. Primary subregional military situations must be identified and assessed in local contexts and only then compared along such dimensions as the intrusion of outside actors and subregional linkages.

Asia is experiencing conflicting political tendencies. Third World elites strive for autonomy and control over foreign access. Yet economic globalism and competition for resources and markets inextricably link most Asian states to the international capitalist economy. Thus, one primary source of tension throughout the region is the stress induced by desire for political autonomy and national self-respect against the necessity to import capital for industrial states in order to grow. Parallel to this tension in political economy is a similar paradox in the security realm. The creation of effective military establishments for the protection of national integrity frequently requires the importation of weapons systems and technical assistance from industrial states, and sometimes entails formal security arrangements as well. Subregional conflicts may be compared, then, in terms of the mix of outsiders and regional members. Divisions across conflicts can also be compared to see whether the same outsiders are arrayed against each other and whether regional members are similarly aligned across subregions. Another way of phrasing this would be to ask if across subregions "friends of friends" maintain cordial relations and if "friends of enemies" are viewed with suspicion?

TABLE I
Asian Conflict Postures and Alignment Strategies

| A. | Regional | Global |
|---|---|---|
| | India - Pakistan | USSR - United States |
| | India - PRC | USSR - United States |
| | Pakistan - Afghanistan | United States + PRC - USSR |
| | PRC - Vietnam | United States - USSR |
| | ASEAN - Indochina | United States + PRC - USSR |
| | ROK - DPRK | United States + Japan - USSR + (PRC?) |

B. Asian Alignment Groups
    Group One: Pakistan, PRC, United States, ASEAN, Japan, ROK
    Group Two: Afghanistan, India, USSR, Vietnam, DPRK

Notes: The grouping of PRC with the ROK is an anomaly. It reflects, however, the probability that Beijing does not wish to see any alteration of the status quo on the Korean peninsula. Noteworthy, too, have been China's efforts since 1983 to negotiate a modus vivendi.

The author wishes to thank his graduate assistant, David Kravetz, for assistance in preparing the tables for this chapter.

Table I reveals that Asian regional adversaries are paired with extraregional great powers, resulting in the persistent juxtaposition of global enmities over local conflicts.[1] The reliability of outside mentors must be regularly assessed by regional political leaders as they weigh the benefits of external assistance against the costs of political and military dependency. Indeed, ASEAN's call for the creation of a ZOPFAN (Zone of Peace, Freedom, and Neutrality) in the mid-1970s can be attributed to America's perceived unreliability in the wake of the Second Indochina War. By associating with great powers Asian states run the risk of becoming extensions or proxies for the formers' conflicts.

At the other end of the continuum of great power-local power relations in Asia is a trend which may not occur until the end of the decade. Regional powers may obtain sophisticated weapons systems to enforce their policies regardless of large power preferences. For example, Indonesia and Malaysia through a combination of hydrofoils, mines and surveillance aircraft may be able to control their international straits should conflicts erupt between themselves and outside powers. The gradual development of indigenous military capabilities could also lead to demands for the withdrawal of great power overseas bases as they appear less necessary for regional security and more a symbol of regional subordination.

While regional powers are expanding their capabilities for external defense, most Asian armed forces are organized for internal security and administration.[2] Military preparations focus on ground forces to monitor domestic rivals and those elements of the population—frequently minority ethnic groups—who do not share political power and may collude with foreign interests to improve their position. Thus, internal security situations also provide opportunities for great power intervention, one aligning with the incumbent government and the other providing material and perhaps training for the insurgents.

Throughout the 1960s and into the 1970s, China backed insurgent groups in Southeast Asia. Its policy, however, changed when it no lonqer saw the countries of the region aligned with the United States against the PRC. Nevertheless, China assists at least one resistance movement—this time in Cambodia with the political backing of its former adversaries, the United States and ASEAN. Beijing's current targets are Vietnam and its Soviet mentor. The principle remains the same: to intervene in regional alignments seen as inimical to China. Only the names of the actors change.

## Roles of Intrusive Powers: The United States

U.S. security policy in Asia faces a credibility problem. It has appeared to vacillate widely since the Second Indochina War, puzzling ally and adversary alike. The thread of continuity has been the 16-year-old Nixon Doctrine, under which the United States inferred it would avoid ground action on behalf of allies in future conflicts by substituting military assistance. Asian fears of a U.S. withdrawal from East and Southeast Asia were exacerbated as the Carter administration began to reduce U.S. Army personnel in Korea (later rescinded) and drew down the Seventh Fleet. The abrogation of the U.S. defense pact with Taiwan and the enunciation of a "swing strategy," by which U.S. Asian assets would be shifted to Europe in the event of war there, all served to undermine Asian belief in the reliability of a U.S. commitment to a major security role in the region.

The Reagan administration has moved to improve these views of American reliability and capability by reemphasizing Asia's importance in U.S. security calculations and increasing Foreign Military Sales programs to the region, as well as upgrading U.S. naval and air forces in the Pacific. But, the new infusions of weaponry and armed forces may affect regional security situations in unintended ways unless the implications of Washington's increased involvement are systematically assessed.

Iran's revolution and the Soviet occupation of Afghanistan in the late 1970s undermined the underlying assumption of the Nixon Doctrine—that regional powers could protect western access to important areas. Moreover, the Soviets insist on an international managerial role equal to that of the United States. In effect, Soviet-American rivalries have been extended to all Asian conflict arenas. While the reality of Soviet and American alignments on opposing sides of these confrontations cannot be ignored, political traps exist. That is, each dispute grows from local contexts. If the local contexts are ignored, outside intervention may exacerbate tensions rather than allay them and prove counterproductive for global strategies. Military aid from a superpower, rather than enhancing stability, may trigger an arms race, providing opportunities for the other superpower to respond in kind—unless the local implications of armaments are carefully considered *before* aid decisions are made.[3] Thus, Indian concern about a multiyear $3.2 billion military/economic U.S. assistance program for Pakistan will be based on the capabilities of the weapons acquired as well as on Delhi's political assessment of the possibility that a militarily stronger Pakistan might become part of a U.S.-China alliance.[4]

Indeed, Washington's interest in a modernized Pakistan military establishment grows out of its global concern for the protection of energy sources in the Persian Gulf. U.S. plans for staging points and prepositioned supplies for a Rapid Deployment Force (RDF) depend on friendly states throughout the region, Islamabad included. Yet to grant the United States base rights would be to undermine a regime's nonaligned status and perhaps move adversaries toward an even greater countervailing Soviet presence. Moreover, U.S. bases in countries ruled by unpopular repressive juntas give an undesirable appearance of closeness to leaders whose days may be numbered. Officials in Delhi argue that the Soviet intervention in Afghanistan has provided the pretext for a substantial expansion of American capabilities in Southwest Asia and the Indian Ocean which can only exacerbate local tensions, while lacking the capability to force a Soviet withdrawal.[5]

Similarly, America's desire for a new security relationship with the PRC to counter growing Soviet Asian deployments is not greeted enthusiastically throughout Southeast Asia. Unsure of American reliability, ASEAN leaders welcome a China strong enough to deter Hanoi from considering expansion farther to the west, but they fear a China strong enough to threaten the region. The Soviet Union, by contrast, is seen as geographically remote and basically nonthreatening for the next several years. Moscow may even exert a restraining influence on both Hanoi and Beijing. While the United States is trying to inhibit a Soviet military presence in the region, then, some Southeast Asians may see a limited Soviet role as desirable.

### Roles of Intrusive Powers: The USSR

Strategically, the USSR is in a much less favorable position throughout Asia than is the United States, which possesses bases in Japan, South Korea, the Philippines, and Diego Garcia in the Indian Ocean. By contrast, Moscow has only its eastern Siberian ports and Kurile Islands north of Japan. These are frequently prey to bad weather and could be partially blockaded by mining straits from the Sea of Okhotsk into the Sea of Japan. Although Soviet vessels call at North Korea's Najin Port and operate in a limited fashion from Cam Ranh Bay and Danang in Vietnam, the Pacific Fleet lacks full use of base facilities in both countries.

Complacency is not warranted, however. Soviet military capabilities in Asia are large and growing, but are not multipurpose forces as are U.S. air, naval, and ground units in the region. Rather, the Soviets' primary targets are China, through ground deployments along the Sino-Soviet border, and U.S. strategic missile submarines. A secondary Soviet purpose is to protect its Pacific Fleet home waters off Sakhalin and around the Kuriles. Since 1982 the Russians have also upgraded their air and missile capabilities which threaten Japan and provide regular naval and air surveillance of southern China and Southeast Asia from Cam Ranh Bay.[6]

The Soviet surface fleet is not well equipped to attack U.S. carrier battle groups or blockade sea lanes, for they lack air cover. Air defense missiles and the Forger fighters aboard the *Minsk* and *Novossirisk* (Kiev-class VSTOL carriers) are designed for ship defense and ASW purposes, particularly to protect the Pacific Fleet's 22 SSBNs, a part of the strategic deterrent.[7] Defense of Soviet submarines is the prime reason for the posting of the VSTOLs to the Pacific Fleet. The Sea of Okhotsk is to be a Russian lake in which Soviet submarine-launched ICBMs can be safely maintained.

Soviet military superiority over China is much more evident. Tables II and III reveal the USSR's overwhelming naval superiority and the PRC's essentially coastal defense posture, with close to 90 percent of its antiship missiles deployed with coastal defense units.[8] While China's navy has 25 major surface combatants, it is unlikely they would steam far from shore in the event of war because of their lack of air defense. PRC naval strength, then, resides in its formidable numbers as a coastal defense force. A sea invader would pay a heavy price as it approached China's continental shelf.

The same overwhelming qualitative superiority applies to air force capabilities along the Sino-Soviet border. Soviet forces include 160 bombers, 850 fighters, and 500 interceptors east of Mongolia. While the PRC air force has some 5,000 aircraft, the number deployed along the Sino-Soviet border is unknown. But, the numbers mean little since Soviet forces surpass the Chinese in avionics, weapons performance, and aircraft capability.[9]

By 1981 the Soviets had deployed 51 divisions (460,000 troops) along the Sino-Soviet border—up from 46 in 1979. Two of these new divisions

TABLE II
Comparison of Soviet/Pacific and Chinese Naval Orders of Battle, 1983

|  | Soviet Union | China |
|---|---|---|
| **Submarines** | | |
| SSBN-ballistic missile nuclear subs | 28 | |
| "HAN" nuclear subs | | 2 |
| Other subs | 92 | 100 |
| **Major Surface Combatants** | | |
| Principal combatants | 89 (incl. 1 carrier) | |
| Destroyers | | 14 |
| Frigates | | 21 |
| **Other Surface Ships** | | |
| Minor combatants[a] | 225 | 1062 |
| Amphibious[b] | 20 | 510 |
| Auxiliary support ships | 80 | |
| **Aircraft** | | |
| Combat craft | 210 | 650 |
| Bombers | 120 | 150 |

[a] Includes fast attack craft, patrol crafts, mine sweepers and mine layers.

[b] Includes landing platforms, various landing craft, and hovercraft.

Source: International Institute for Strategic Studies, *The Military Balance, 1983-1984* (London: IISS, 1983), pp. 18, 85.

TABLE III
Soviet Deployment of Military Hardware Along Sino-Soviet Border, 1983

| Weapons | Quantity |
|---|---|
| Tanks | 7 divisions |
| Motorized rifle | 45 divisions |
| Artillery | 4 divisions |

Source: International Institute for Strategic Studies, *The Military Balance, 1983-1984* (London: IISS, 1983), p. 16.

were sent to Sakhalin and the Kurile Islands; and 150 additional aircraft were sent to the Soviet Far East in 1981. While the Soviets insist that this enhanced capability is not directed against Japan but rather toward China and possible U.S. aggression, Mig-23s operating from the Northern Islands engage in frequent missile exercises over the Sea of Japan.[10]

A major Carnegie Endowment study in 1981 concluded that on balance the West's advantages in seaborne air power, ASW capabilities, and geography are more significant for the outcome of maritime conflict in the Pacific than the Soviet advantage in gross tonnage over the Seventh Fleet (1.33 million to 575,000). The report predicted that the West could gain control of the sealanes by bottling up the Soviet Pacific Fleet in the Sea of Japan, by mining the Japanese straits, and conducting ASW operations against Soviet submarines deployed in the Pacific and Indian Oceans prior to hostilities. Richard Solomon of the Rand Corporation also foresees that the deployment of cruise missiles with the Seventh Fleet will counter the Soviet SS-20 missiles and Backfire-B bombers now in the Soviet Far East.[11]

The Soviets are undoubtedly aware of the political costs of their growing Asian military presence. This growth in Soviet military capabilities has heightened apprehensions in Japan and the ASEAN states. Moscow's efforts to exploit its military prowess are further eroded by the weakness of the Soviet economy, the low level of economic ties with noncommunist Asian states, and the financial drain from Soviet activities in Poland, Vietnam, Afghanistan and Cuba.

The Soviets may be searching, then, for a measure of detente in Asia. Brezhnev's Tashkent speech in March 1982 held open the possibility of a new relationship with China. Overtures from Moscow grew louder as Washington and Beijing openly differed over the provision of arms to Taiwan. China responded coolly, however, insisting that Soviet deeds rather than rhetoric are the proof of any policy change. It cites the continued Soviet military buildup in the north and consistent support for a Vietnamese controlled Indochina to the south as obstacles to reconciliation. For China, the Soviet threat is both a serious long-term security problem and a convenient device to solicit Western and Japanese credits for modernization.

China is careful not to engage in any crash military development program which would appear destabilizing to the USSR, or to seek massive infusions of state-of-the-art weapons systems from the West. By placing military modernization last in priority among the *Four Modernizations*, Beijing assures its citizens that the armed forces will not drain resources away from economic growth. As a corollary, this relatively low military profile reassures the USSR that China is not interested in challenging Soviet military superiority—at least in this generation.

Chinese efforts to form a united front with Japan and the United States constitute an alternative to rapid military modernization. American and Japanese capabilities deter the USSR because the former stand behind China's development in a yet-to-be-specified security relationship. Military technology is supplied along with satellite information on Soviet force dispositions to assist China in tying up 51 Soviet divisions, over 1000 aircraft, and perhaps one-fourth of Moscow's strategic missile force.

Beijing's long-term goal is to increase its maneuverability between the USSR and the United States through economic modernization, increased stability in Soviet relations short of rapprochement, and continued ties to the United States and Japan as sources of technology, investment, and security support.[12] While Beijing and Washington possess parallel security goals in containing Soviet military expansion in Asia, they do not share the combination of interests necessary for an alliance. Beijing will never again accept a junior partnership. America's security interest in China is equally expedient: to force the Soviet Union to maintain major military assets in East Asia, far from Europe and the Persian Gulf.

### Subregional Environments: Japan and Northeast Asia

Intrusive powers engage in military activities throughout Asia although their strengths vary from one subregion to another. Each subregion is characterized by a mix of local conflicts and friendships over which are juxtaposed the global postures of outsiders. Asia's most important "local" power is Japan—an anomaly in international politics because it is the second largest economy in the capitalist world but only a middle-ranked military power, with minimal force projection capability and a constitution which bars dispatching its forces to other countries.

Japan's defense policy is premised on America's commitment to deter and, if necessary, to defend the islands from both conventional and nuclear attack. Its military forces, then, complement U.S. deployments in and around the home islands. The only source of perceived threat to Japan, articulated in the annual Defense White Papers since 1980, is the Soviet Union; but the nature of the Soviet threat and how best to cope are issues of open debate.

The dominant LDP center view is that the Soviet Union is a potential threat in East Asia but is so bogged down in Europe, Afghanistan, parts of Africa, and along the Sino-Soviet border, that a significant threat to Japan is unlikely. A minority, more hawkish, view in the ruling party holds that the Soviet threat is increasing because of the deployment of 10,000 troops on the northern islands and the growing naval and air force buildup in the Soviet Far East.[13]

Both the Carter and Reagan administrations have pressured Japan to expand its air and naval power. Washington admonishes Tokyo that the United States spends between five and six percent of its GNP for defense, while Japan spends less than one percent. Per capita defense spending for the United States was $759 for FY 1981, while in Japan the same figure was $98.[14]

Some Japanese analysts contend that U.S. efforts to increase Japanese defense expenditures are misplaced since it has developed no overall strategy for the use of Japanese forces within the context of the country's

Peace Constitution. This riposte is somewhat disingenuous, however, since Washington has specified both the type of defense development it would prefer Japan to undertake and its underlying rationale. The United States has urged Japan to undertake the monitoring of Soviet naval activity in ocean areas up to 1000 miles from Japan, control the air and sea eastward to Guam and south to the Philippines. Additionally, Washington has asked Japan to develop the capacity to mine the northern straits leading to the Sea of Japan.[15]

While former Prime Minister Suzuki was reticent about acceding to these American requests, his successor, Prime Minister Nakasone, publicly committed Japan to developing these capabilities by the 1990s.[16] Any massive extension of Japan's maritime responsibilities along the lines urged by the United States would require significant changes in the strategic calculus of Japanese political leaders and the public, however. Many LDP Diet members believe that to enlarge the Japanese military role, as envisaged by the Reagan administration, would court electoral defeat. Supporting the Security Treaty is one thing, but challenging the antimilitary bias of the electorate is quite another.[17]

Skeptics denigrate Japan's potential contribution to East Asian defense by pointing out that even if Japan contributes additional ASW ships and aircraft, the JSDF cannot replace a redeployed U.S. carrier battle group. That is, Japanese surface forces in the Sea of Japan could not strike the Soviet coast. It has been argued that the entire concept of sea lane defense in the Indian Ocean-Pacific region is fallacious. No navy can protect the hundreds of ships transiting these waters at any given time, should a major war occur. Moreover, should Japan become involved in hostilities with the Soviet Union, its air bases would be among the priority targets for Soviet destruction. America's ability to defend Japan in a hypothetical major conventional confrontation is also constrained by the fact that U.S. assets might be committed to destroying Russian naval threats to the Persian Gulf rather than protecting Japan's home islands.[18]

## The Korean Peninsula: Fulcrum of Great Power Interests

Although the military balance on the Korean peninsula is currently seen to favor the North, relations among the contending outsiders augur for stability. In 1981 U.S. General John Wickham stated that North Korean forces possessed two-and-a-half times as many tanks, twice the APCs, artillery pieces and missiles, twice as many aircraft, and four times as many naval vessels as the South. The North Korean army also had nearly double the number of combat-ready ground forces, most of which are deployed near the DMZ or in a manner designed to protect major industrial and military facilities.[19]

Nevertheless, over the past five years U.S. military assistance to Seoul has narrowed the deficit. North Korean T-62 tanks can be knocked out by South Korean missiles and newly arrived U.S. A-10 tank-buster aircraft. The ROK air force is adding 36 F-16s, and the U.S. Air Force in Korea is increasing its complement of F-16s and A-lOs.

Politically, the outlook appears brighter. Persistence of the Sino-Soviet conflict and the development of a Sino-Japan-U.S. rapprochement in the 1970s shifted the bipolar system in northeast Asia to a looser, four power balance. Although the ROK-DPRK confrontation remains, the new strategic setting reduced the likelihood of either Soviet or Chinese support for a military solution to unification by Kim Il-Song. Moreover, the Russians have diversified their east Asian allies by adding Vietnam. Beijing has encouraged Pyongyang to make more contacts with Washington and Tokyo in hopes of associating the North in some way with the Sino-U.S.-Japan entente. Moreover, the PRC potentially benefits from the ROK's security relationship with the United States which increases the possibility of mining the Tsushima Strait against the Soviet Pacific Fleet in time of war. Conversely, a South Korea under communist control might provide the USSR with facilities comparable to those now available in Vietnam.

In private talks with Western visitors, Chinese leaders have approved the presence of U.S. troops in South Korea as contributing to the overall balance in east Asia. There were indications that Beijing may have been as concerned about possible U.S. troop withdrawal from the ROK during the Carter administration as were Japanese leaders.[20]

At bottom, Beijing wishes to avoid a situation in which the DPRK would call upon it for military assistance while attacking the South. Not to respond would forfeit China's influence to the USSR. On the other hand, to honor its security treaty with the North would destroy the PRC's incipient security ties to the United States and probably Japan.

As the United States upgrades its own forces in South Korea and provides additional military sales to the ROK, Pyongyang has escalated military tensions along the DMZ and even tried to shoot down an SR-71 reconnaissance aircraft. The North will undoubtedly urge the Soviet Union to provide Mig-23s to match the growing number of F-16s in the South. If U.S-Soviet relations remain acerbic, the probability of the Soviets agreeing to these requests will increase. These trends could draw the North Koreans closer to the Russians, their only supplier of sophisticated weapons to counter an enhanced ROK-U.S. combination.

TABLE IV
ASEAN Defense Spending and Military Manpower

| Country | Defense Spending[a] | | | Military Manpower[b] | | |
|---|---|---|---|---|---|---|
| | 1979 | 1981 | 1982 | 1979 | 1981 | 1982 |
| Indonesia | $1,470 | 2,692 | 9,926 | 236 | 269 | 281 |
| Malaysia | 693 | 1,447 | 2,077 | 64.5 | 99.1 | 99.7 |
| Philippines | 793 | 835 | 878 | 103 | 112.8 | 104.8 |
| Singapore | 410 | 718 | 852 | 36 | 42 | 55.5 |
| Thailand | 940 | 1,255 | 1,437 | 216 | 233.1 | 235.3 |

[a] In US million dollars
[b] In thousands
Source: International Institute for Strategic Studies, The Military Balance 1983-1984 (London: IISS, 1983), p. 127; The Military Balance 1981-1982 (London: IISS, 1981), pp. 80, 84, 86-88. Reprinted by permission.

## ASEAN's Growing Security Concerns

Following the Bali conference of 1976, the ASEAN states developed a diffuse security arrangement by which outside mentors (Great Britain and the ANZUS countries) provide military assistance and maintain local bases while the ASEAN five deal cooperatively with insurgencies and neighboring external threats to their members. ASEAN security techniques range from diplomatic coordination to bilateral military action in border regions. This coordination has stopped short of multilateral military efforts, joint planning and defense procurement. These types of military cooperation are eschewed as moving the Association too far toward a military pact. The five concur that such a metamorphosis could well be counterproductive for it would place ASEAN in a formal adversarial relationship to Vietnam and unnecessarily accelerate regional polarization.

The ASEAN states began to increase military outlays significantly in 1980. (See Table IV) As Robert Rau noted, they are investing in heavy-lift troop and material transport, sea patrol aircraft and light fighter-bombers—thus upgrading conventional force capabilities.[21] Indonesia and Malaysia are developing bases in areas where they believe future external threats could materialize. Kuala Lumpur plans an air training base on the Malaysian-Thai border at Gong Kedak which could support joint operations against communist enclaves. This base would also enable Malaysia to intercept intruders into its airspace. In Spring 1982, Kuala Lumpur decided to refurbish 40 A-4 Skyhawks and buy a squadron of F-5E interceptors, the backbone of Malaysia's air force into the 1990s. The new air power is premised on a shift in defense strategy to repulse an enemy invasion.[22] Jakarta is also upgrading naval and air facilities around the Natuna Islands, the east coast of Sumatra, and the west coast of Kalimantan against Vietnamese claims to waters around the Natunas.

Island disputes in the South China Sea encompass the Spratlys, Paracels, and Natunas. They are variously claimed by Vietnam, the Philippines, the PRC, Taiwan, and Indonesia for their strategic locations and undersea minerals potential. The 200-mile exclusive economic zone ocean regime, part of the 1982 Law of the Sea Treaty, requires negotiations among these states to sort out competing claims. Meanwhile, in addition to Indonesian forces on the Natunas, Vietnam has increased naval patrols in the area and the Philippines has posted small garrisons in the eastern Spratlys.

Thai military spending, while increasing annually since 1982, falls far short of what its military leaders deem necessary to defend against Vietnamese military forces operating in Cambodia.[23] The United States provided military credits of around $100 million in 1984 and 1985, which have permitted the Thais to upgrade their armor and acquire 155 millimeter howitzers with a range sufficient to force Vietnamese artillery to stay well back of the border. Thai Supreme Commander General Arthit has pressed the United States to sell F-16s as well, an aircraft that could significantly alter the regional air balance if acquired. As of early 1985, the United States had not acceded to the Thai request.

These developments suggest that the ASEAN states are moving to acquire regional military capabilities, as distinct from their current domestic counterinsurgency modes. These changes were undoubtedly triggered by Vietnam's occupation of Cambodia, its alliance with the USSR, and the latter's growing air and maritime presence in Southeast Asia. In the future, regional developments would also seem to justify ASEAN's military expansion as China acquires a blue water navy and modern weapons. A Chinese navy attempting to enforce maritime claims in competition with Soviet and Vietnamese forces could lead ASEAN to develop the military capabilities of enforcing its own exclusive economic zone against *all* outside powers.

Indeed, over the longer term the ASEAN states express greater apprehension over China's capabilities and intentions than those of the USSR and Vietnam.[24] Vietnam is seen as economically weak and militarily overextended and thus unlikely to challenge Thailand, especially if some form of compromise can neutralize the Khmer Rouge challenge to Hanoi's control of Cambodia. China, by contrast, though welcomed as Thailand's temporary protector and as a balancer against the USSR, is still feared "as a possible fountainhead of revolution, a threatening protector of Overseas Chinese, a territorial claimant to most of the South China Sea, . . . and as a potential source of large scale mass migrations."[25]

## Indochina: Threat or Stabilizer

There is a disturbing parallel between Vietnamese and Soviet foreign policies: their major successes have been achieved by the use of, or threat to use, force. Economic instruments of diplomacy are deemphasized except for Soviet subsidization of Cuba and eastern Europe through petroleum exports. When confronted with perceived threats to their major interests or opportunities to expand influence, both tend to rely upon the military.

In Hanoi's case, the last years of the 1970s found growing Chinese influence in Cambodia as part of an apparent effort to encircle Vietnam (just as the USSR appeared to be encircling China via its ties to the SRV). Vietnamese leaders saw these Chinese moves as the latest in a series of efforts (going back to the French and Americans) to utilize Laos and Cambodia to thwart Hanoi's rightful dominance in Indochina. Growing security cooperation between China and the United States, along with Thailand's success in working out a *modus vivendi* with the Khmer Rouge combined with the latter's deliberate border provocations led to a Vietnamese decision to remove the Pol Pot regime by force. Hanoi's military victory resulted, however, in a situation in which adversaries surround Indochina; and the noncommunist world has cut the three countries off from access to capital, markets, supplies and technology. Limited assistance from the Soviet bloc is a poor substitute. Knowledgeable observers in Vietnam describe its current economic condition as significantly worse than during the Second Indochina War.

Approximately 500,000 People's Army troops are deployed north of Hanoi, 160,000-180,000 in Cambodia and 40,000 in Laos. These deployments consume the bulk of the country's resources which had been devoted to economic reconstruction prior to Hanoi's invasion of Cambodia. Military manpower shortages have forced the army to draft a growing number of Vietnam's vocational and college students, thus diverting its future leadership away from developmental activities.[26]

The economic situation has also had an impact on military thinking. Some military analysts are openly arguing that Hanoi cannot afford to sustain a defense establishment with large numbers of regular troops equipped with sophisticated weapons on three fronts. Such a strategy will bankrupt the country.[27]

The USSR will probably try to keep VPA forces in their current fighting mode, however. Vietnamese dependence permits the Soviets to expand their use of the Danang and Cam Ranh Bay bases. Communication facilities have been developed at the latter to direct Pacific Fleet vessels in the South China Sea and longrange reconnaissance aircraft flying from Cam Ranh Bay as far as the Persian Gulf or over Australia.[28]

There is some friction between Moscow and Hanoi, however. Moscow delayed a decision on the aid it would provide for Vietnam's third five-year plan (1981-1985) and raised the price for POL products. The Soviets have been openly critical of Vietnamese administrative ineptitude; and although SRV leaders admitted their shortcomings, they bridled at Russian interference. Finally, the Vietnamese refused the Russians full base rights, keeping that decision as a bargaining chip in hopes of ultimately convincing the Americans (and perhaps China) to accept Vietnam's control of Indochina in exchange for a promise not to turn the bases over to the USSR.[29] Thus, while the Soviets have built electronic monitoring, air and naval communication, and berthing facilities in Cam Ranh and Danang, as well as a pier capable of docking nuclear submarines at the former, Soviet ships are not serviced dockside but by tenders in the harbor.[30]

ASEAN's most telling complaint against Hanoi is that by extending the Sino-Soviet conflict to Southeast Asia, Vietnam has brought Moscow into the region's politics on a permanent basis. But, so long as it is involved, some among the ASEAN five counsel that its presence is not entirely negative. By sustaining Vietnam's capacity to resist Beijing, Malaysian and Indonesian leaders conclude that the Soviet presence contributes to regional stability. Indonesian and Malaysian diplomacy would probably concede Vietnam a dominant role in Indochina with continued Russian aid if Vietnam's military occupation could be terminated and the provocative deployment of Soviet naval and air forces in the SRV significantly reduced.[31]

There is little reason to believe a negotiated solution will be found, however. Many thousands of Cambodians live in the Thai border area and fight for the Khmer Resistance, rely on intermittant sanctuary in Thailand, and are supplied with Chinese food and equipment. Moreover, the Khmer Rouge have no place to go. They are unacceptable to the Thais, third countries and, of course, the Cambodian regime. Vietnam must resolve this situation unless it is willing to risk widening the war by invading eastern Thailand to destroy Resistance sanctuaries and supply points. Because the Vietnamese are already overextended and because the Soviets would refuse to support further Vietnamese expansion into a region of secondary interest to Moscow, a VPA thrust into Thailand is improbable. Instead, festering guerrilla warfare is likely in Cambodia, in which the Vietnamese-backed Heng Samrin regime controls the population centers while the VPA forces guard road and rail links. Khmer Rouge guerrillas have rendered much of western Cambodia and the area around Tonle Sap insecure.

Nevertheless, a military stalemate has political benefits for Vietnam, for it justifies the VPA's occupation of Cambodia to protect and nurture the Khmer against the possible return of the hated Pol Pot forces. Even the creation of a tripartite political leadership for the Resistance in the Summer of 1982 which would provide a noncommunist facade has not seriously worried Hanoi. The Vietnamese know that despite traditional Cambodian enmity toward the Vietnamese they are still preferred over the barbarism that prevailed between 1975–1979. It will be many years before those memories fade.

### The South Asian Vortex

The Indian subcontinent and Afghanistan may constitute the potentially most volatile of Asia's subregions. On top of traditional Indo-Pakistani enmity and the unresolved Sino-Indian border disputes, the Soviet occupation of Afghanistan has added a new component to these local tensions. Islamabad perceives itself trapped between a threatening Soviet Union now on its northwestern border and India—a sometime Soviet ally—to its south.

American concern over Pakistan's security, because of its strategic location on the eastern flank of the Persian Gulf, led the Reagan administration to provide a multiyear $3.2 billion military and economic aid package, including some forty F-16 fighterbombers.

India, on the other hand, views itself as the rightfully dominant power on the subcontinent, particularly since the creation of Bangladesh in 1971. American efforts to rebuild Pakistan's military capacities are viewed with considerable misgiving. New Delhi rejects Washington's interpretation of the Soviet invasion of Afghanistan, claiming that Moscow's intentions are limited to shoring up the regime in Kabul and not the first step in a strategic design to move into the Persian Gulf or South Asia. Moreover, Indian officials argue, a confrontational approach to the USSR, will make the Russians even more adamant in their occupation of Afghanistan. Only a negotiated settlement by Pakistan with the Babrak Karmal regime offers any prospect of Soviet withdrawal if the *mujihadden* can be contained.[32]

Delhi argues that a militarily strengthened Pakistan could encourage Moscow to support Baluchi separatists in retaliation, thus having the paradoxical effect of destabilizing Zia's regime. Moreover, Indian officials insist that Pakistan will deploy any new military resources along the Kashmir-India frontier and not against Afghanistan, where they would not constitute a credible threat against the USSR in any case.[33] The Pakistanis retort that F-16s deployed along the Afghan frontier would deter the USSR from air attacks against refugee camps, thus serving to defend Pakistani military airfields near the Afghan border and its territory generally.[34]

Instability in the India-Pakistan confrontation stems from their three-front security problems. India must deploy against China in the Himalayas; Pakistan, near whose border 60 percent of its forces are located; and cope with internal disorders. Pakistan must deploy against India, where the bulk of its army is located; and Afghanistan, as well as control possible secession moves in, say, Baluchistan. Because each can claim to be arming against other threats (Pakistan-Afghanistan, India-China), an arms race can begin almost surreptitiously. This is precisely what Delhi believes to be inherent in the Reagan arms agreement with Islamabad.

Both the United States and the Soviet Union underwrote major competitive arms supply programs to the subcontinent in the 1980s. Moscow's began with a $1.6 billion arms package in May 1980. However, in April 1982, India announced a significant new arms agreement with France to purchase 40 Mirage 2000 fighters, with an option to acquire an additional 110 under licensed construction in India.[35] The French contract won against Soviet competition, demonstrating Delhi's desire to reduce its reliance on the USSR and may be interpreted as part of a new, more conciliatory, India outlook on security in the subcontinent. Suspicious of Soviet intentions toward South Asia in the wake of Afghanistan, the Gandhi government seems to be developing *modi vivendi* with both Pakistan and China. Negotiations are being held with the PRC over the 20-year border dispute. Talks with Pakistan aimed at some form of peace pact are also progressing—the most promising development being a permanent joint commission to deal with bilateral disputes. Indian officials have told their American counterparts that Pakistan's stability and integrity are important to India's security, particularly with Soviet forces at the Khyber pass.[36] Noteworthy, too, is a muting of Indian objections to American Indian Ocean deployments and the U.S. air and naval buildup on Diego Garcia. Although Delhi would prefer to see the superpowers leave the Indian Ocean, a strong U.S. presence to help persuade the Russians to withdraw from Afghanistan takes precedence. It could also serve as a bargaining chip at some point if the Soviets sought a negotiated reduction of tensions in Southwest Asia. Moreover, India's efforts to effect new relationships with the United States, China and Pakistan reduce the possibility of an entente among those states directed against Delhi's dominant position in the subcontinent.

In sum, India had been willing to rely almost exclusively on the USSR for diplomatic and military support as long as Moscow refrained from becoming directly involved in South Asia. The Soviet intervention in Afghanistan violated this dictum and has led to India's search for new relationships with old adversaries.

## Subregional Linkages and Asian Security

While a number of distinct threats exist in Asia, they are so connected that action in one area may have unintended ramifications in others. This concluding section will explore the linkages, related to great power efforts to exert influence in the region.

One of the most sensitive linkage issues in the 1980s is the evolution of U.S.-PRC strategic cooperation. This may entail both provocative effects on Soviet behavior—especially if tied to a growing Japanese defense capability—and cause apprehension in India and the ASEAN countries as China develops its military capacity. On the other hand, the PLA's gradual modernization could tie down large numbers of Soviet troops near the Sino-Soviet border without being seen as destabilizing by Soviet leaders. It is virtually impossible for China to catch up with the USSR technologically.[37]

Similar anxieties and opportunities are contained in the growing Japanese air and maritime capability. ASEAN leaders display ambivalence over a more formidable Japanese military establishment. From a positive perspective, a large JSDF could free Seventh Fleet assets to spend more time protecting Indian Ocean/Southeast Asian waters. Both Philippine President Marcos and Singapore Prime Minister Lee have publicly welcomed this possibility.[38] Mr. Lee has argued that it is preferable to have Japanese naval power in the region, with the United States, than to rely increasingly on China to balance the Soviet-Vietnamese alliance, for Beijing may still have ambitions of its own in Southeast Asia.[39] Moreover, Tokyo is seen as strategically supporting ASEAN. It stopped aid to Hanoi after its invasion of Cambodia, increased assistance to Thailand, and stated in its recent Defense White Papers that ASEAN's security is essential for Japan's security. ASEAN's keen interest in Japan's security role was demonstrated by plans in their June 1982 foreign ministers conference to query Tokyo about its intentions with respect to regional sea lane security.[40]

ROK officials are also contemplating political moves which could extend security concerns beyond the peninsula, including the possibility of joint efforts with Japan to block the Tsushima Strait in the event of war.[41] More realistically, the ROK has offered to sell nonsophisticated military equipment to ASEAN states with considerable early success. South Korean and ASEAN officers are also enrolled in each others' training programs.[42]

Linkages between Southeast and Northeast Asia go in the other direction as well, since Clark AFB and Subic Naval Base are justified in part for their role as U.S. air and naval staging points in the event of hostilities in Korea or around Japan. Clark and Subic are also links in the direction of the Indian Ocean/Persian Gulf as operating and supply bases for Diego Garcia.

Despite evidence of linkages among Asian threat environments, any plan to tie them together into a concerted anti-Soviet arrangement would be a gross error. Differences among friends and allies, and lack of mutual interest in the problems of other subregions, illustrate the absence of a strong basis for region-wide cooperation. At best, Asian security efforts might over time meet the criteria suggested by Robert O'Neill:

> the development of response capabilities [by] a series of local groupings for limited purposes . . . and to rely on a series of discrete deterrence relationships to prevent local crises from escalating . . . In this way individual states can both address their own particular security problems, be they regional or internal, and contribute to the stability of the global balance. Particular states can work within this framework with those they know and understand best and with whom they have the greatest degree of common interests.[43]

## Notes

1. This Table was adapted from Raju G. C. Thomas, "Security Relationships in Southern Asia: Differences in the Indian and American Perspective," *Asian Survey* (21,7) July 1981, p. 694.

2. See the discussion comparing LDC militaries across regions in Edward A. Kolodziej and Robert E. Harkavy, eds., *Security Policies of Developing Countries* (Lexington, Mass: D.C. Heath, 1982), pp. 331–361.

3. This warning is particularly well stated in the testimonies of Selig Harrison, Stephen Cohen, Ainslie Embree, and William Richter reported in the Committee on Foreign Affairs, *Security and Economic Assistance on Pakistan: Hearings and Markup* (Washington, D.C.: U.S. House of Representatives, April 27, September 16, 22, 23, November 17 and 19, 1981. U.S. Government Printing Office, 1982), pp. 95–219.

4. These ambiguities are presented in Walter K. Andersen, "U.S. Foreign Policy in the 1980s: South and Southwest Asia," in Ramon Myers, ed., *A U.S. Foreign Policy for Asia: The 1980s and Beyond* (Stanford: The Hoover Institution Press, 1982), pp. 17–37.

5. Cited in Leo Rose, "U.S. Policy in Asia: The India Factor," in Ramon Myers, ed., *A. U.S. Foreign Policy for Asia*, p. 53.

6. Information cited in William T. Tow and William R. Feeney, eds., *U.S. Foreign Policy and Asian-Pacific Security: A Transregional Approach* (Boulder: Westview Press, 1982), pp. 24, 57.

7. "Military Balance in Asia," *Far Eastern Economic Review, Asia Yearbook*, 1982, p. 23–24.

8. Tables II and III are taken from Donald C. Daniel, "Sino-Soviet Relations in Naval Perspective," *Orbis* (24,4) Winter 1981, pp. 790–791.

9. See footnote 7.

10. Hiroshi Kimura, "Recent Japan-Soviet Relations: From Clouded to 'Somewhat Crystal,'" *Journal of Northeast Asian Studies* (1,1) March 1982, pp. 17, 18.

11. The Carnegie Report is cited in Franklin Weinstein, "The U.S. Role in East and Southeast Asia," in Ramon Myers, ed., *A U.S. Foreign Policy For Asia*, p. 126. Solomon's statement was made to the Fifth U.S.-Japan Shimodo Conference and reported by *Kyodo*, September 12, 1981, as published in FBIS, *Daily Report Asia-Pacific*, September 8, 1981, C2-C3.

12. This assessment is made by Thomas Robinson, "Choice and Consequences in Sino-American Relations," *Orbis* (25,1) Spring 1981, pp. 29–52; and Gerald Segal, "China's Strategic Posture and the Great Power Triangle," *Pacific Affairs* (53,4), Winter 1980–81, pp. 682–697.

13. Lee Farnsworth, "Japan in 1981: Meeting the challenge," *Asian Survey* (22,1) January 1982, p. 58.

14. Cited in Stephen P. Gilbert, "Northeast Asia in American Security Policy," in William Tow and William Feeney, eds., *U.S. Foreign Policy and Asian-Pacifc Security*, p. 78.

15. See the statement by Assistant Secretary of State John Holdridge before the Subcommittee on Asian and Pacific Affairs of the House Committee of Foreign Affairs published as *Japan and the United States: A Cooperative Relationship* (State Department, Bureau of Public Affairs, Current Policy No. 374, March 1, 1982).

16. Reported in James Buck, "Japan's Defense Policy," *Armed Forces and Society* (8,1) Fall 1981, p. 96.

17. These views are discussed in Martin E. Weinstein, "Japan's Defense Policy and the May 1981 Summit," *Journal of Northeast Asian Studies* (1.1) March 1982, pp. 8, 24, 25, 27, 29 and 32.

18. See the article by former JSDF official Osamu Kaihara, "Japan's Defense Structure and Capability," *Asia Pacific Community* (12) Spring 1981. Especially pp. 58–60. Also see Taketsugu Tsurutani, "Japan's Security, Defense Responsibilities, and Capabilities," *Orbis* (25,1), Spring 1981.

19. Congressional testimony cited in Lee Young Ho, "Military Balance and Peace in the Korean Peninsula," *Asian Survey* (21,8), August 1981, p. 857.

20. Ahn Byung-joon, "South Korea and the Communist Countries," *Asian Survey* (21,11) November 1980, pp. 1101–1105.

21. Robert Rau, "Southeast Asian Security in the 1980s: An Intraregional Perspective," in Tow and Feeney, eds., *U.S. Foreign Policy and Asian-Pacific Security*, p. 108.

22. Ibid., and *The Asian Wall Street Journal Weekly*, March 8, 1982, p. 9.
23. U.S. Senate, Committee on Foreign Relations, *United States Relations With ASEAN, Hong Kong, and Laos: A Report* (Washington, D.C., U.S. Government Printing Office, March 1982), pp. 7-8.
24. *Ibid.*
25. Guy Pauker, *ASEAN Trends and Problems in the 1980s* (Santa Monica: The Rand Corporation, P6574, January 1981), p. 11.
26. William S. Turley "Vulnerabilities and Commitment in Vietnamese Domestic and Foreign Policies," *Viertel Jahres Berichte* (Bonn: The Fredrich Ebert Stiftung 1982).
27. Carlyle A. Thayer, "The Political Role of the Military in Vietnam, 1976-1981," a paper presented to the 1982 New Zealand Political Studies Association Conference at the University of Otago in Dunedin, p. 28.
28. Masashi Nishihara, "Indochina and the Security of Northeast Asia," in *Comprehensive Security: Japanese and U.S. Perspectives* (Stanford: Northeast Asian Forum, 1981), p. 82.
29. Thomas W. Robinson, "The Soviet Union and Asia in 1981," *Asian Survey* (22, 1), January 1982, p. 22.
30. Asia 1982 Yearbook, p. 30; and Nayan Chanda, "Snake in the Grass," *Far Eastern Economic Review*, May 7, 1982, p. 25.
31. Guy Pauker, *ASEAN Trends and Problems in the 1980s*, p. 12.
32. Walter K. Andersen, "U.S. Foreign Policy in the 1980s: South and Southwest Asia," in Myers, ed., *A U.S. Foreign Policy for Asia*, p. 26.
33. Leo E. Rose, "U.S. Policy in Asia: The India Factor," in *Ibid.*, pp. 54-55.
34. Stephen Phillip Cohen, "Pakistan," in *Security Policies of Developing Countries* (footnote 2), pp. 98-99, 104.
35. Paul Lewis, "India Buys New French Jets, Passing Over a Soviet Offer," *New York Times*, April 18, 1982.
36. Michael T. Kaufman, "Mrs. Gandhi Making the Most of Foreign Policy Openings," *New York Times*, June 6, 1982.
37. Robert L. Downen, "The Reagan Policy of Strategic Cooperation With China: Implications For Asian-Pacific Stability," *The Journal of East Asian Affairs* (2,1) Spring/Summer 1982, p. 61.
38. Cited in William T. Tow, "U.S. Alliance Policies and Asian-Pacific Security: A Transregional Approach," in Tow and Feeney, eds., *U.S. Foreign Policy and Asian-Pacific Security*, p. 32.
39. Lee Kwan Yew interview, Singapore Domestic Service, February 1, 1982, in FBIS, *Daily Report Asia Pacific*, February 10, 1982, 04-05.
40. Kyodo (Tokyo) May 24, 1982, in FBIS, *Daily Report Asia Pacific*, May 25, 1982, C1.
41. Yu-nam Kim, "U.S.-Korean Security Interdependence with Special Reference to Northeast Asia," a paper presented to the annual meeting of the International Studies Association, Cincinnati, March 25-27, 1982.
42. *ASEAN Briefings*, (36) July 1981, p. 2.
43. Robert O'Neill, "International Security Cooperation in the Asian-Pacific Region in the 1980s and 1990s," a paper presented at the Research School of Pacific Studies, The Australian National University, May 6, 1982, p. 38.

# About the Contributors

Lieutenant Colonel William E. Berry, Jr., is a career officer assigned to Asia, formerly a faculty member at the U.S. Air Force Academy.

James H. Buck is an emeritus faculty member, University of Georgia.

Stephen Philip Cohen is a faculty member, Department of Political Science, University of Illinois, Urbana-Champaign.

June Teufel Dreyer is a faculty member, Center for Advanced International Studies, University of Miami.

Stephen Jurika, Jr., is a faculty member, Department of National Security Affairs, Naval Postgraduate School, Monterey.

Jeffrey Lunstead is a career officer in the U.S. Department of State assigned to Asia.

Ralph H. Magnus is a faculty member and Coordinator of Middle East Studies, Department of National Security Affairs, Naval Postgraduate School, Monterey.

Patrick M. Mayerchak is a faculty member, Department of History and Political Science, Virginia Military Institute.

Lieutenant Colonel Harold W. Maynard is a career military officer assigned to a diplomatic mission in Asia.

David Morell is on the staff of the Environmental Protection Agency's San Francisco office.

Edward A. Olsen is a faculty member and Coordinator of Asian Studies, Department of National Security Affairs, Naval Postgraduate School, Monterey.

Douglas Pike is Director of the Indochina Archive, University of California, Berkeley.

Robert L. Rau is a faculty member, Department of Political Science, U.S. Naval Academy.

Edward W. Ross is the Assistant for China, Office of International Security Affairs, U.S. Department of Defense.

Sheldon W. Simon is Director of the Center for Asian Studies, Arizona State University.

Jon A. Wiant is a career officer in the Bureau of Intelligence and Research, U.S. Department of State.

Gregory F. T. Winn is a career officer at the United States Information Agency.

Glynn L. Wood is Academic Dean of the Monterey Institute of International Studies.

RAYMOND H. FOGLER LIBRARY
**DATE DUE**